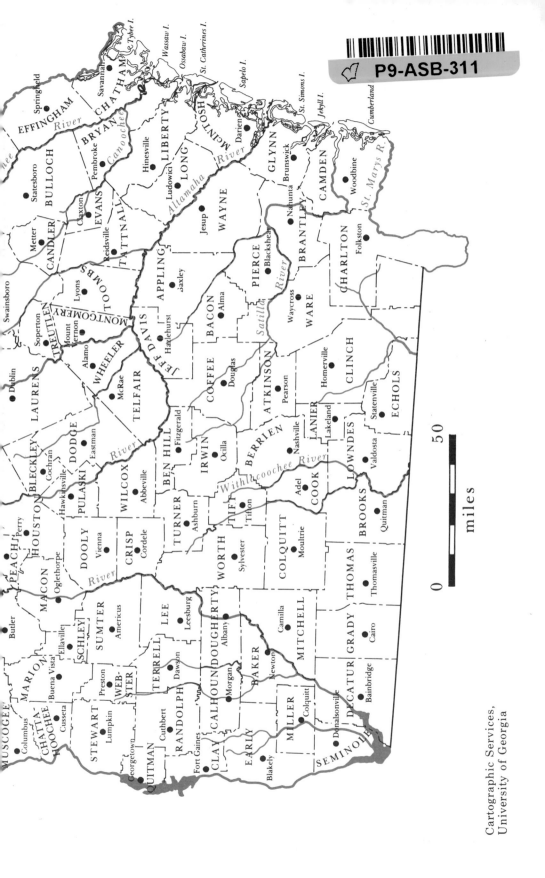

Cartographic Services,
University of Georgia

A HISTORY
OF
GEORGIA

A History of Georgia

KENNETH COLEMAN, GENERAL EDITOR
NUMAN V. BARTLEY • WILLIAM F. HOLMES
F. N. BONEY • PHINIZY SPALDING
CHARLES E. WYNES

THE UNIVERSITY OF GEORGIA PRESS
ATHENS

Copyright © 1977 by the University of Georgia Press
Athens, Georgia 30602

Printed in the United States of America
Set in 10 on 12 point Linotype Baskerville

The paper in this book meets the guidelines for
permanence and durability of the Committee on
Production Guidelines for Book Longevity of the
Council on Library Resources.

90 89 88 87 86   7 6 5 4 3

Library of Congress Cataloging in Publication Data

Main entry under title:
A History of Georgia.

  Bibliography: p.
  Includes index.

  1. Georgia—History.   I. Coleman, Kenneth.

F286.H58   975.8   77-7364

ISBN 0-8203-0427-1
ISBN 0-8203-0433-6 (text ed.)

to the

PEOPLE OF GEORGIA

this book is affectionately dedicated

Contents

Part Five: 1890–1940, by William F. Holmes

Part Six: 1940 to the Present, by Numan V. Bartley

Illustrations

Maps

Foreword

When I was Governor of Georgia, I commissioned the University of Georgia to prepare a new history of our state. That had not been done since the 1930s, and a tremendous amount had changed since then.

Now I am proud to write this Foreword to the fine work the historians have done. All of us who are from Georgia, or who share an interest in our state, will thank these six writers for presenting our history in such an accurate and readable way.

Georgia is unique in many ways. It was one of the original thirteen colonies. It is the biggest state east of the Mississippi River. It is still basically rural with beautiful, unspoiled land.

Like most Georgians, I am deeply attached to the land. I made my living as a farmer. The soil has always been an important part of my life and the lives of my family, friends, and neighbors. Through our love of the land, we share a common bond and become a community.

This family and community spirit was essential to Georgia's early settlers. This same spirit has withstood the test of time and circumstance. We were able to make it through the Revolutionary and Civil wars and still retain many of our original values and traditions.

This fine history explains the roots of these traditions. I congratulate the authors on their explanations of the cultural, social, political, and economic developments, past and present, that make Georgia the outstanding state it is today.

JIMMY CARTER

The White House
Washington, D.C.

Preface

Over the years Georgia has been well served by many able historians. Half a dozen general histories, several of genuine merit, have appeared over the past one hundred and sixty years. But just as times change and as people change, so does the way of looking at the past. New perspectives arise, new information comes to light, and each passing day becomes a part of history. Thus, with the passing of time, older general accounts of the past tend to lose much of the value they originally possessed. Hence every generation tends to rewrite history.

This general history of Georgia had its beginning in the spring of 1973 with a phone call to the general editor from then Governor, now President, Jimmy Carter; in the course of the conversation he asked, "How do we get a new history of Georgia written?" From this conversation there developed the plan for six members of the Department of History at the University of Georgia jointly to write this volume, with each covering the era in which he was most competent. It was early decided that this was to be a balanced book, with proportionate attention devoted to the recent period, including the bicentennial year of 1976.

While each author was solely responsible for writing his section of the book, the authors agreed that there would be similar coverage in all sections of economics, politics, education, life and society, and culture. Each author also read the entire manuscript and made suggestions for changes throughout. Each author prepared the bibliography for his part.

No one writes any history, especially a general one such as this, without the help of the works of earlier authors. The bibliography indicates the chief works relied upon, as well as those that should be most helpful to the reader who wants to know more than can be presented in a general history. Other people helped in many ways and deserve recognition. These include the staffs of the University Library, the Georgia Department of Archives and History, the Georgia Surveyor General Department, the Georgia Historical Society, the Atlanta Historical Society, the Historical Preservation Section of the Georgia Department of Natural Resources, and many colleagues and students of the authors. Advice on maps was secured from the Department of Geography at the university, and the maps were made by the university's Cartographic Laboratory. The dean of Arts and Sciences and the head of the History Department arranged released time for the authors to speed the completion of the book. The History Department secretaries typed and retyped the manuscript. The staff of the University of Georgia Press has been interested and helpful from the inception of this volume. To all of these and to others who have helped, we offer our sincere thanks in the hopes that their exertions have resulted in a better history of Georgia.

THE AUTHORS

A HISTORY
OF
GEORGIA

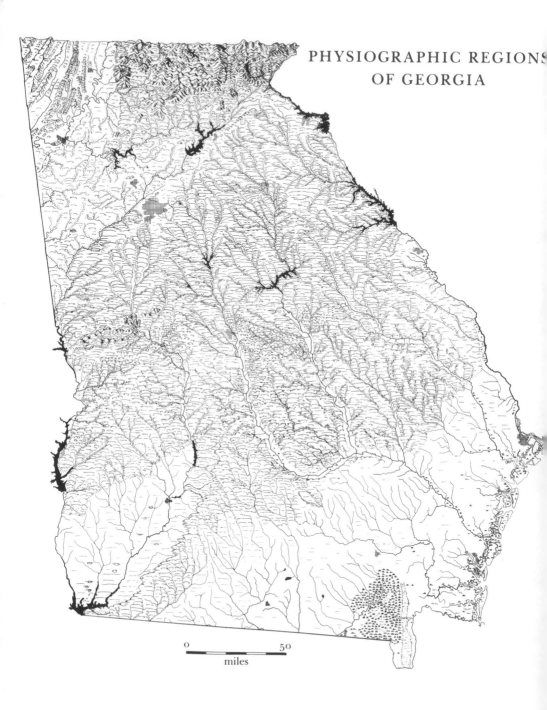

PHYSIOGRAPHIC REGIONS
OF GEORGIA

0   50
miles

Origins

If names on the land mean anything, then the rivers and mountains, lakes and towns of Georgia bespeak the state's varied and sometimes turbulent past. The names of the state's rivers reflect, in many instances, the Indians' former hold on the area. Rising in northeast Georgia cold and fresh from the mountains, the Chattahoochee cuts its way southwestwardly to a point near Columbus where it becomes Georgia's boundary with Alabama. The Flint, running a generally parallel course, joins the Chattahoochee in the southwestern corner of the state where Florida, Alabama, and Georgia converge. Across the ridges from the origins of the Chattahoochee, mountain streams run in a northerly direction and empty into the Tennessee River system and go on to the Mississippi. In northwestern Georgia, so loved by the Cherokees, the Oostanaula and Etowah form the Coosa, which then passes into Alabama.

All these rivers flow finally into the Gulf of Mexico, at one time a Spanish sea, but to the south and east of the Chattahoochee-Flint system there is a watershed dividing the streams that flow into the Atlantic from those that go to the Gulf. South of this point are the springs that form the Oconee and Ocmulgee, rivers that join to form the mighty Altamaha, which reaches the ocean near Darien. Here in the marshes at its mouth, as well as in other tidal swamps and lowlands on Georgia's coastline, the life of the rivers and the ocean is refreshed and renewed.

The dark and mysterious Ogeechee with its black water and its cypress swamps snakes its way to the Atlantic near Savannah. The St. Marys, which forms Georgia's border with Florida, has its exact origins lost in the primeval Okefenokee Swamp. Also in the Okefenokee the Suwannee rises, but it cuts southward across Florida and flows into the Gulf. Finally the Savannah, rising in north Georgia and South Carolina, passes the cities of Augusta and Savannah, two of Georgia's colonial settlements whose lives have always been tied to the river.

Between and around these waterways Georgia stretches in gradual physical change from tidewater through coastal plain, piedmont foothills, and eventually high hills and mountains. North and south, Georgia runs about three hundred and fifty miles; east and west, roughly two hundred and fifty. Georgia today is still blessed with unspoiled beaches and marshes as well as lush sea islands along the coast separated from the mainland by tidal creeks and sounds alive with fish, shrimp, and oysters. The sea islands were often the first land to appeal to the Europeans, but they were also loved and tenaciously held by the Indians. The marshes along the lowcountry river banks proved ideal for rice, the crop that made Georgia a prosperous colony in the eighteenth century.

Inland there is a wide band of slowly rising land. Here good soil is not so easily found, but the area is rich with wildlife. Deer, turkey, quail, and dove abound, but the trees are mainly pine and scrub oak. The early settlers disliked the pine, holding to the conviction expressed by William Stephens, the Trustees' secretary in Georgia, that it would suffer nothing of value to grow near it. This is ironic in light of the fact that pines later proved invaluable in the production of naval stores, in which Georgia has long specialized, and in the manufacture of paper. This long stretch of "piney woods," though, was settled late and has always been relatively sparsely populated.

The rivers show a series of rapids and the level of the streams drops at the fall line, the seacoast from ages past. Running through Augusta, Milledgeville, Macon, and Columbus, this line with its harnessed rapids of the Chattahoochee, Oconee, Ocmulgee, and Savannah provided the power that brought Georgia's first significant industrial development. These cities were all situated at the northernmost points of uninterrupted navigation on the rivers, and the towns developed their own river histories. Earlier the falls on the Chattahoochee and the Ocmulgee had been chosen by the Indians as important centers of tribal life and DeSoto's Cofitadhequi may have been close to the site of Augusta. At the fall line on the Savannah trading paths leading to the Creeks and the Cherokees converged. Goods were bartered, traded, or exchanged in Augusta and were loaded on boats for shipment to Charles Town or Savannah.

Above the fall line rise the red clay hills of Georgia, spotted with occasional granite outcroppings. Opened to settlement fairly late, this area, more than any other part of the state, was to look to commerce and industry, but at the same time this region contained the state's richest mid-nineteenth-century plantation belt. Also in this section the state university was established, crowning a movement spearheaded by New Englanders trained at Yale. In the slightly more elevated area west of Athens, Indian paths met on high ground near the Chattahoochee. Steel rails would one day meet here and create a city, Atlanta, which owed its first name, Terminus, and its very being to the changing patterns of the industrial revolution.

In the extreme northwest corner of Georgia is a small slice of the Cumberland plateau, with deposits of iron and coal. DeSoto and his party touched this section in the sixteenth century and saw as well the Appalachian valley-and-mountains region to the east. In that area the nineteenth-century Indians were ministered to by Moravians, spiritual descendants of the sect who first came to America when they arrived at Savannah in 1735. In the valleys of north Georgia the Cherokees made their stubborn last stand only to be thwarted by land-hungry whites and by sheer weight of numbers. Farther to the east, running along Georgia's border with Tennessee, North Carolina, and South Carolina, lies the Blue Ridge. In this section of rugged, rock-strewn peaks, the Appalachians have their southern terminus at a mountain named for Georgia's English founder. Oglethorpe never saw the full variety of his colony, but in his vision and sense of destiny he felt it.

PART ONE

COLONIAL
PERIOD

by

PHINIZY SPALDING

The Seal of the Trustees from 1733 to 1752

The Seal of the Royal Province of Georgia, 1754 to 1777

Spain and the Coming of the English

As far as is known, the first Europeans to look upon the soil that was to become Georgia were Spanish. Juan Ponce de León may have touched the coastal reaches in 1513, and when it was clear that there was a large land mass north of Florida the Spaniards dispatched exploratory expeditions to look for treasure and the northwest passage. Alonzo de Pineda in 1519 sailed along the Gulf Coast, and two years later Francisco de Gordillo appeared in the sea islands. He was followed by Lucas Vázques de Ayllón, whose ambitious colony in present-day South Carolina was defeated by its leader's death and an American winter. The survivors spread discouraging tales about the eastern seaboard as a location for Spanish settlement.

What Spain failed to do the French accomplished. First a colony was planted on Port Royal sound, and then a strongpoint named Fort Caroline was constructed near the mouth of the St. Johns River in Florida. Philip II sent Pedro Menéndez de Avilés to recapture the region for Spain. Menéndez, superb soldier, sailor, and a dedicated servant of the crown, destroyed the French settlement with dispatch. He also founded, in September 1565, the town of St. Augustine, the first permanent European settlement within the present limits of the United States.

Menéndez was one of the more effective Spanish colonial leaders in the sixteenth century. He followed up his colonization of St. Augustine with an inspection of the Georgia-Carolina coast where, in April 1566, on the island of Santa Catalina (St. Catherines) he met the Indian leader Guale, whose name gradually came to be used for the entire coastal area of Georgia. The chief, plied with presents, seemed pleased and swore his loyalty to Spain and Christianity. Impressed by the beauty of the islands and the possibilities for religious conversion, Menéndez left a garrison on San Pedro (Cumberland) and sent Juan Pardo and Hernando Boyano to probe the backcountry. Their reports —along with the pearls collected—encouraged the Spanish to persevere.

While he was in Spain during 1567, Menéndez was received by Philip II and was made captain general of the west. He and Francisco Borgia, head of the Jesuit order, agreed that missionary efforts in Guale must be pushed even though earlier efforts had been disheartening and had resulted in martyrdom for Fray Pedro Martínez. Martínez became "the first Christian martyr on Georgia's soil," though hardly the last. The Franciscans succeeded the Jesuits in Guale in 1573 and proved to be far better missionaries.

In Spanish imperial planning two basic institutions evolved: the presidio and the mission. The presidio was usually a compact frontier fort defended by Spanish troops and Indian allies. The presidios were spaced so they would be helpful to the friars at the missions; both the presidio and the mission were used to good effect in Guale. Of the two, the mission was the more important. It was the task of the soldier to impose and keep order, but it was the responsibility of the lonely missionary to convert and educate the Indian to the point that he would be a fruitful subject for the king. Ideally each mission had two friars to perform the various demands and responsibilities placed upon their shoulders, but in Georgia there was usually only one. Two soldiers from the nearest presidio were generally assigned to a mission, but often the troops on such a remote frontier were troublemakers or "jailbirds," who caused almost as many problems as they solved. Unlike the British system, which was generally spread into the backcountry by Indian traders who were then followed by farmers, the Spanish system was highly organized and had as its central focus the Indian himself. It was hoped that in the mission workshop, fields, and chapel the Indian could be brought to embrace the Spanish system. This was the dream of Menéndez: to deliver safely into the hands of Philip II the coastal areas of Guale, Orista, Chicora, and the inland region of Tama. For it was in the latter—what is now central and lower Georgia—where the fine soils to lure the farmers of the Caribbean or Old Spain were reported to be abundant. Beyond Tama lay, perhaps, the fabled riches reported by the natives.

Menéndez left America for the last time in the summer of 1572, secure in the knowledge that he had laid a firm foundation. He designated his able nephew, Pedro Menéndez Marqués, his successor. It was Marqués who saw to charting and mapping the coast and who expelled intruders, mainly French, from Guale. He made Spain's claim to the area secure, at least until Francis Drake's destructive raid at St. Augustine in 1586. Spain then pulled back from Port Royal, but such a move had the effect of emphasizing the significance of Guale. It also tended to make the missions all the more attractive to pirates and freebooters, but Spain and the Franciscans held onto this area for another century.

The mission system fixed itself upon the coast in the 1580s and 1590s. The friars, dedicated to lives of poverty and hard work, labored long and selflessly to bring the civilization of the white man to the natives. Many became fluent in the Indian dialects, and communication and transportation between missions, utilizing the inland passage and Indian-designed boats, were perfected. Calm and order reigned.

In 1597 Juanillo led a bloody Indian uprising that nearly destroyed Guale. But the Indians, who resented Spanish meddling in tribal affairs, were finally defeated at San Pedro. Punitive expeditions had the Indians begging for a return of the missionaries, and the decision was made to rebuild and restaff. (It is an interesting sidelight of the Juanillo revolt that some of the captured Gualeans had been enslaved by the Spaniards. When word of this reached the Spanish king, he ordered that the Indians be immediately released and freed.)

So complete was the restoration of the missions by 1603 that Governor Gonzalo Méndez Canzo, who went to Guale on a personal inspection, could point with pride to the region's achievements. Guale was important not only because of its location, but also as "a bountiful granary" that provided food for Florida. In addition to foodstuffs, Guale was the source of Indian labor used on roads, in the fields, or on the military works of St. Augustine.

The Guale mission buildings were not the impressive structures associated with the later California, New Mexico, or even Texas missions. Georgia's older outposts were usually little more than palm-thatched huts built in the wattle-and-daub technique often used in Indian houses. The community was located around a sort of common plaza where much of the life of the associated Indian village took place. Georgia's most important mission, on San Pedro, was rebuilt with wood, iron nails, and shingles after the revolt in 1597, but other missions were not so well constructed. The tabby ruins on the sea islands and nearby mainland, once thought to have been Spanish in origin, are actually nineteenth-century survivals of sugar houses and other abandoned outbuildings.

In 1606 Juan de la Cabezas de Altamirano, bishop of Cuba (Santiago), made an episcopal visitation to the Guale missions. He stopped at San Pedro both going into and departing from Guale, and on this favored island he confirmed some three hundred Indians before moving on to Talaxe, on the south bank of the Altamaha. Over two hundred and fifty were confirmed there. And so it went up the coast to Santa Catalina. In his report the bishop could, with justification, say "that Guale had been fully restored" to the Spanish crown after the Juanillo revolt.

The fifty years following Cabezas Altamirano's visit are looked upon as the golden era of Spanish Georgia. They were quiet years, when the soldier and missionary held sway. The Spaniards actively probed the backcountry during the 1620s, and the first missions were put in the western Apalache region in 1633. This area became the center of a prosperous agricultural section that produced grains and skins and acted as a forward base for Spanish advances inland to the falls of the Chattahoochee.

But Guale's quiet days were numbered, for to the north, in 1607, only one year after the visitation of the bishop of Cuba, the English established a tenuous settlement at Jamestown. The Spaniards resented the presence of the Virginia colony on land they claimed but did nothing to expel the British. The Virginia grant followed by others pushed England's claims southward to the thirty-first parallel. Charles II then awarded a vast area called Carolina to eight of his loyal backers in 1663 and extended the grant southward to the twenty-ninth parallel so that the Carolina grant included even St. Augustine itself.

Protests from Madrid did no good, and although the two countries decided, in a treaty of 1670, that actual possession would determine ownership, there was never any doubt England would get as much as she could—treaty or no. Prophetically, in that same year, the English jumped all the way from the settlements on Albemarle Sound to Charles Town. A Spanish expedition against Charles Town was thwarted by high seas and with this reprieve the new Carolina colony grew rapidly.

In 1670 there began a deadly struggle for the coastal and inland areas to the south and west of Charles Town. The Carolina Indian traders, with the able Dr. Henry Woodward in the vanguard, began to lure the natives from their Spanish habits. The traders weakened the mission system by offering cheap goods and by purchasing prisoners of war from their Indian allies—prisoners sold into slavery by the Carolinians. Reflecting Spain's concern, a new inspector, Antonio de Arguelles, was sent to reconnoiter the situation of 1677. Spanish control of the Guale missions was intact, he reported, and the presidio on Santa Catalina still held the line as the northernmost outpost, but the garrison there could never withstand a serious attempt to capture it.

Spain had no intention of simply handing territory over to her enemies, but her punitive expeditions sent up the Chattahoochee River in 1689 had the effect of forcing the Creeks eastward to the Ocmulgee where they fell under strong English influence. Nor did Spain's settlement at Pensacola in 1698 improve that nation's position in respect to the Anglo-Spanish conflict. The French, moving eastward from the Mississippi, established an outpost at Biloxi in 1699 and then checked further Spanish expansion westward with a fort on Mobile Bay in 1702. Though conflicts between France and Spain were minimized after the Bourbons came to the Spanish throne in 1713, the frontier competition between these two powers helped build international tensions in the general area of Georgia during the eighteenth century.

Spanish strength gradually ebbed. In 1680, Santa Catalina was attacked by a large force of English allied Indians, and though the assault was unsuccessful, most of the inhabitants were frightened and soon abandoned the mission. The Spaniards fell back to Sapelo and the final retreat from Guale had begun.

The siphoning off of Spanish support among the natives and the increasing piratical activities along the shores of Guale finally put an end to the missions in Georgia. Following the destructive raids in 1683–85 and incursions into Florida by Chief Altamaha and his Guale followers, now called Yamasees, Governor Juan Marqués Cabrera ordered the remaining missionaries and neophytes south of the St. Marys River in 1686. The era of the Spanish missions in Georgia had ended. It left no tangible remains beyond an occasional ruined garden or a few fruit trees, but the friars and soldiers of the Spanish king had been on Georgia's coast for over one hundred years. Their examples of courage, fortitude, and missionary work make up an integral part of the whole fabric of Georgia history.

After 1686 Georgia continued to be a battleground between the Spanish, French, and English. All vied for allegiance of the Creek and Cherokee Indians, and to the west the Chickasaws and Choctaws were plied with gifts as well. At first it appeared as though the Carolinians would have their way, particularly during Queen Anne's war, 1702–13, when all Florida seemed on the verge of falling to the British. The prosperous Apalache missions were laid waste; the town of St. Augustine was taken—only the fort held out. Spain, however, was still determined to hold Florida for strategic purposes. A counterthrust against Charles Town failed, but she regrouped after 1713 under Philip V.

For the British, major trouble began to come from the west and south and took the form of renewed activity on the part of the Yamasees. Grievances against the English mounted until the Indians struck the Carolina frontier in 1715. Caught off guard, the colony reeled; refugees poured into Charles Town with tales of death and devastation. France and Spain took heart.

As the Yamasees and their allies spread chaos, the French moved deep into Alabama country and constructed Fort Toulouse; the Spanish reappeared in the Georgia backcountry when the Creek Indians returned to the Chattahoochee. Although the Carolinians rallied to defeat the Yamasees, Carolina's frontiers were left exposed when that tribe fled to the Spanish in Florida. So Carolina initiated a campaign in England to point out the danger to the British position along America's southern borders and to encourage settlement there.

A whimsical view of eighteenth-century migration to Georgia

University of Georgia Libraries

In fact the Carolina proprietors, for different reasons, had been trying for some time to do precisely that. It was a period of impractical colonial schemes, but the writings inspired by Sir Robert Montgomery's project for the Margravate of Azilia beggar description in their over-statement. In 1717, Montgomery received the approval of the Carolina proprietors to settle between the Savannah and Altamaha. A resident margrave would preside over the affairs of a kind of feudal colony to be called Azilia. Emphasis would be placed upon the growing of silk, coffee, tea, almonds, olives, and other exotic items, but the scheme vanished in a few years. The Carolina proprietors were overthrown by 1720, so the area of Georgia remained one claimed by many but possessed by none.

For years the strategic value of the Altamaha River had been known, so to protect their frontiers the Carolinians set up Fort King George at the mouth of that river in 1721. John Barnwell and others saw this as part of the move to offset Spanish and French gains along the Chat-tahoochee, but the fort did not prosper. The site was unhealthy, the Spaniards were incensed, the troops stationed there were quarrelsome, the cost of upkeep was exorbitant. It was abandoned in 1727. Carolina seemed powerless. Indian raids were on the increase again, the Creeks were in a nasty mood, and the Spanish and French seemed more active than ever. At this point, after 1727, the impetus passed to British shores where philanthropy, religion, and imperialism joined together and resulted in the creation of the English colony of Georgia.

II

Oglethorpe and the Founding
of Georgia

The first half of the eighteenth century was not a period of reform in British history. Still, able and good men such as Thomas Bray founded societies to spread the Anglican gospel and to establish libraries in colonial America; James Oglethorpe advocated sailors' rights; Bishop George Berkeley, with experience in America, called for a colony where English unfortunates might go. Men of public spirit such as John Lord Viscount Percival, who in 1732 was created the first Earl of Egmont, cooperated in these ventures.

James Edward Oglethorpe, one of this group, came from a respected and well-to-do family. He was elected to Parliament in 1722 as representative from Haslemere, Surrey, which position his father and two elder brothers had held previously. By 1728 Oglethorpe was getting to be known for his untiring work, and in 1729 he became chairman of a parliamentary committee to look into the status of English jails. What he and his committee uncovered was shocking. Out of this investigation Oglethorpe emerged a national figure. Though his work failed to bring dramatic improvement, a number of prisoners were released, but what could be done with these people? It was concluded that they might compose the nucleus of a new colony in America, and if put south of Carolina they would protect that colony's frontier and settle land coveted by Spain and France. The province could produce items needed in England, be beneficial to the balance of trade, and the Indians in the general area offered unlimited possibilities for missionary work. The Georgia scheme seemed to bring together many loose threads of moderate English reform, and by 1730 the motives for founding the new colony—philanthropic, economic, imperial, mercantilistic, and religious—had coalesced in the Georgia movement.

Twenty-one prominent men requested a royal charter for the proposed new colony in 1730, a request that was granted in the summer of 1732 when the "Trustees for Establishing the Colony of Georgia in America" were incorporated. Georgia was defined by the charter as the land between the Savannah and Altamaha rivers, inland to their headwaters, and thence "westward to the South Seas." By 1732 plans for actual settlement were well underway.

Georgia was not created simply to be another Maryland or South Carolina. Georgia must be something new and refreshing—a kind of Holy Experiment. Like Pennsylvania, Georgia was to be a refuge for European Protestants who suffered injustices at the hand of their overlords. The charter of Georgia also anticipated that the colony would help relieve the problem of unemployment at home by providing unfortunates with "a comfortable subsistence" in America. The Trustees were given broad powers, and even the customary consent of the colonists to laws passed for them was waived. The king's assent to acts of the Trustees was stipulated, however, and he was also granted a veto over any governor who might be appointed. Suspicious of their prerogatives, the Trustees never named a governor and passed only three laws during their corporate existence. They preferred to rule by decree or ordinance, neither of which was susceptible to direct royal review. It was expected that the governmental business of Georgia would be carried on by a sort of executive committee of the Trustees called the Common Council, but often this group lacked a quorum. As it turned out, a mere handful of the seventy or so men named as Trustees during the corporation's twenty-year existence did the work and shaped policy. Of these men, the most prominent were Oglethorpe, Percival, and James Vernon.

Control of the colony was given to the Trustees for only twenty-one years. After that Georgia was to revert to the crown. Other restrictions were that no Trustees could hold office in the colony or own land there, and grants to individual settlers were not to exceed five hundred acres. This would prevent Georgia from developing into a colony of large plantations and would fit the design of the province as a frontier outpost capable of defending itself.

When the Board of Trustees was constituted in July 1732, a campaign was begun to raise money and put the colony into the public consciousness. The philanthropies it represented commended themselves so strongly to merchant and minister, visionary and imperialist, middle class and nobility, that the Trustees were flooded with contributions. They even found it necessary to set up a screening committee to interview prospective settlers, and in the process of weighing the merits of would-be Georgians, any released debtors who might have applied were eliminated. The Trustees picked carefully not only because of the number to choose from, but also because their settlers would receive from the Georgia Board free passage to America, supplies and foodstuffs for one year, seeds and agricultural tools, and land upon which to farm. It proved to be the most selective winnowing process of any British colony in America. The first transport to Georgia was made up primarily of small businessmen, tradesmen, and unemployed laborers drawn mainly from the London area. Perhaps fewer than a dozen released debtors came to Georgia during the entire Trusteeship period—a figure probably not as large as the count for other British colonies in North America during the same period.

In the summer of 1732 Oglethorpe, anxious to see the colony settled, became impatient. Percival counseled caution, but Oglethorpe persuaded his other colleagues to move ahead. Some months before sailing, Oglethorpe's domineering mother died, so he offered to accompany the first colonists to Georgia himself. In the enthusiasm of the moment the Trust was in no position to balk at Oglethorpe's demand that the first boatload leave as soon as possible.

On 17 November 1732 the ship *Ann* sailed from Gravesend with Oglethorpe, a store of good beer, and approximately one hundred and twenty settlers. The colonists, their leaders, their minister Henry Herbert, their doctor William Cox, and Captain John Thomas of the *Ann* all adjusted themselves to the routine of shipboard life. Oglethorpe was everywhere, encouraging the fainthearted, nursing the sick, instructing on the proper mode of colonizing. He had read widely in the colonial literature of the times and thought a new colony, especially on an exposed frontier, needed a strong and compassionate leader. Oglethorpe was determined to be just that. Aboard ship he visited below decks to hear complaints and imposed a rigid but reasonable discipline. He even acted as godfather at the baptism of a child born at sea—a boy appropriately dubbed Georgius Marinus Warren.

The *Ann* arrived off Charles Town on 13 January 1733, after a swift crossing. Oglethorpe hurried ashore and was met by Governor Robert Johnson, his council, and other prominent Carolinians. Johnson had been told by London to do all he could to smooth the way for Georgia, so he helped secure farm animals, tools, rice, provincial troops, money, and boats to expedite the settlement of the colony. The Georgia settlers stayed on the *Ann* at Charles Town, but finally were allowed ashore at Beaufort–Port Royal on 15 January. While the settlers adjusted to their new surroundings Oglethorpe, with the help of the Carolinians, looked for a suitable place to plant the colony. The Altamaha, suggested by Johnson, was simply too close to the Spanish and too far from the Carolinians. The site ultimately chosen by Oglethorpe was a fairly obvious one. After he saw Yamacraw Bluff he made up his mind. It was high ground, possessed a source of fresh water, was defensible, afforded an overlook of the inland waterway and the outlying islands, was immediately accessible to South Carolina, and had nearby a small tribe of Indians. Oglethorpe visited the bluff and conferred with Tomochichi, chief of the Yamacraw Indians, who lived there. Probably owing to the intercession of Indian trader John Musgrove and his mixed-breed wife Mary, Tomochichi gave his approval for the location of a settlement there. Oglethorpe then returned to Carolina.

On 1 February 1733 (12 February, New Style) in mid-afternoon, Oglethorpe and his little flotilla approached Yamacraw Bluff. Captain Francis Scott and a small group of armed men, left there earlier to make arrangements for the colonists, fired a welcoming salute. The salute was returned and the settlers climbed the steps Scott had built up the 40-foot bank upon which Savannah was to be located. Soon Oglethorpe was approached by Tomochichi and his followers. The two leaders talked, John Musgrove acting as interpreter. Apparently Oglethorpe and the dignified Tomochichi established a basis for mutual trust from the start and laid the groundwork for the May 1733 treaty with the Creek Indians. Tomochichi and his escorts returned to their village just upriver from Savannah and the colonists were left in sole possession of the site. That night the settlers slept in four large tents erected for them, but Oglethorpe spent the night in the open, by the watch fire atop the bluff. British Georgia had been founded.

The weeks following the founding of Savannah were incredibly busy. The colonists, working together, began to clear the townsite of pines, using the lumber for the first houses. Provisions were made for defense, and with the help of Tomochichi, Oglethorpe made friends with the Creeks, who signed a treaty recognizing the right of the English to settle on their land. The long history of Indian land cessions to Georgia had begun.

Oglethorpe also planned Savannah along the distinctive lines still apparent today. By establishing the urban pattern modeled on wards built around squares, he enabled each neighborhood to form its own feeling of community. He envisioned Georgia's first settlement as a town centering on the original four squares, which he laid out before his return to England in 1734. A square was surrounded by forty lots, all 60 by 90 feet. There were twenty lots north and twenty lots south of each square with the four ten-lot groupings, into which each ward was divided, called tithings. To the east and west lay four larger Trust lots, to be reserved for public use. Each square was expected to become the center of the neighborhood's social, economic, and religious life.

Peter Gordon's view of the river, bluff, and new settlement of Savannah, 1734

Settlers also received an additional 5-acre garden plot at the edge of town, and a 45-acre farm plot in the country.

Oglethorpe thought of more than a social or economic orientation when setting up Savannah. His system of tithings and wards, with a male head of household envisioned for each lot, was the basis of the military organization considered necessary for protection. A constable was in charge of each ward, and every man took his turn standing watch.

As for government, Georgia's rulers were mysteriously vague. Because the charter forbade Trustees to hold office or own land there, Oglethorpe could be given no title nor the usual prerogatives of a governor. He was vested with only the general powers to administer oaths, parcel out land, and issue licenses to those who wished to leave the province. He was not given full authority to run Georgia, but the Trustees must have understood that Oglethorpe would assume power once he reached America, and this he did.

Designated officials were few in number and almost powerless from the start. Before the settlers left England, the Common Council named three bailiffs, two constables, two tithingmen, eight conservators of the peace, and one recorder for Georgia; but there was no chief executive with specific powers to control these officials. Presumably Oglethorpe was to give them instructions and lay down the guidelines the colony was to follow, but he lacked time for such a task.

From the first, Oglethorpe's letters complained that there were not enough hours in the day to accomplish all that he had to do. Everywhere he turned there were decisions to be made, Indians to negotiate with, complaints to hear, Carolinians to ingratiate, Spaniards to mollify. He had too much to do, but he seemed incapable of delegating authority. The upshot was that everyone depended on him; the other officials were looked upon as ciphers. Not until July 1733 did Oglethorpe convene the first court, composed of the three bailiffs and the recorder, and inform the inhabitants of the names chosen for the first four wards, the squares, and the streets. At that time, too, the grants of land were confirmed. Up to that point the government of the colony had been all Oglethorpe, and a precious chance for the officials to grow in experience along with the town had been lost.

Savannah seemed to prosper in spite of its lack of guidelines, but sickness struck in late spring and robbed the town of its physician, William Cox, and of many other useful citizens. Oglethorpe believed that the rum being brought into Georgia from South Carolina was the main cause of the fever, and he determined that such traffic must be stopped. Rum also had a debilitating effect on the Indians, so trade in it in the backcountry was ordered to cease.

Soon after the first court met in Savannah, a ship came into port with a number of Jewish families on board. Georgia's charter specifically excluded only those of the Roman Catholic faith from the colony, but the Jews lacked the permission of the Trustees to go to Georgia. They appealed to Oglethorpe and he gave his consent. The Trustees in London objected to his action, but once settled in Savannah the Jews contributed significantly to the town.

To secure Georgia's defenses, Oglethorpe not only fortified the site of Savannah but also secured the inland passage, the Ogeechee River, and the Altamaha. Fort Argyle on the Ogeechee protected the southern overland approach; Thunderbolt, on Augustine Creek, guarded the eastern flank; and various small hamlets to the south and northwest of Savannah were settled, beginning in 1733, all primarily for defense purposes. Owing to barren soil and isolated locations, many of these satellite settlements were abandoned by 1739 when war broke out with Spain. By that time Fort Frederica had taken over the main defense responsibilities for the southern frontier.

Oglethorpe wanted to befriend as many Carolinians as he could, but the more he saw of Carolina the more reservations he had. He was struck by what he felt was the decadence of life in Charles Town and by the nature of settlement between there and Savannah. Slavery, large landholdings, and rice seemed to Oglethorpe to dominate everything in Carolina. The whites were too few and could only with difficulty defend the area in time of invasion and insurrection. Because the colony was oriented to a staple crop economy, the white yeoman farmer was unable to compete. Oglethorpe was determined that Georgia would not become another Carolina; the province had not been created to make a few rich. Rather, Georgia was to hold out hopes to many for a reasonable livelihood.

Georgia was, however, to be more than an agrarian province. It was part of the rhetoric surrounding Georgia that it was expected to produce enough silk, potash, wines, and similar products to help relieve Britain of her reliance upon others for such items. High hopes were held particularly for the production of silk, even though similar hopes had failed earlier in other southern colonies. So important was this item thought to be that the Trustees put silkworms on their common seal, and it was part of the Trustees' regulations that one hundred white mulberry trees must be planted for each ten acres of land cleared in their province. It was known that mulberry trees prospered in Georgia; the Trustees did not realize that it was the wrong variety that did best. Italians were brought to Georgia to instruct in silk culture and it was a testament to the determination of the Trust that Georgia actually became an exporter of silk. But production was artificially supported and could not survive without subsidies.

Schemes to make Georgia a major producer of wines, potash, pearl-ash, and olives were similarly doomed. The colony simply lacked the experience, the proper climate, or the capital base required for these products. That the Trust was serious is attested by the time and money spent on the Trustees' garden in Savannah, where plants and cuttings from Italy, France, the West Indies, and elsewhere were cultivated. This garden, actually more of a nursery, proved difficult and expensive to maintain and was finally abandoned.

After a year it was time for Oglethorpe to return to England and consult with the other Trustees. Before he could depart, however, he received word that the first contingent of Salzburg Lutherans, leaving their Austrian homeland to escape religious persecution, had arrived in Charles Town. He delayed his own departure in order to escort these new arrivals to Georgia and help them with their settlement, named Ebenezer. With their pastors Israel Christian Gronau and John Martin Bolzius establishing policy, the Salzburgers ultimately proved to be the most prosperous element in Trusteeship Georgia. Though the original site of Ebenezer proved undesirable, the location of the new town—at Red Bluff on the Savannah River about twenty-five miles above Savannah—was satisfactory.

It was not until mid-June 1734 that Oglethorpe arrived back in England. He was greeted as a hero. Oglethorpe brought with him the venerable Tomochichi, his wife and queen, Senauki, his great-nephew and heir, Toonahowi, and five Yamacraw warriors. Aware that complaints as well as adulation awaited his return, Oglethorpe was able to blunt the attacks of his critics by using the popularity of the Indians as a foil. They were received by the Trustees, George II and Queen Caroline, and even the archbishop of Canterbury, and although the Yamacraws were clothed in little more than their innate dignity, the imperial officers seemed more nervous than these native Georgians. Oglethorpe used the Indians to demonstrate the importance of Georgia to British officials and the public.

But the real accomplishments of Oglethorpe's visit lay in his ability to secure from Parliament a large grant to Georgia for bolstering England's defenses on the frontier and his success in imposing on the other

Trustees his ideas of what the colony should become. He secured passage of the three Georgia laws that he hoped would make the colony economically and institutionally different. Oglethorpe impressed his fellow Trustees with the need to control Georgia's southern borders, and he got approval to create a new settlement near the southern extremity of the Georgia grant. Oglethorpe reached the zenith of his colonial career during this visit to England. The country fairly bristled with excitement over Georgia, and new and youthful colonists anxious for experiences in America applied to return to the New World with Oglethorpe.

However, reports of dissension in Savannah began to filter across the Atlantic, so having satisfied his critics in the mother country, Oglethorpe became anxious to return to Georgia. Therefore the long delay in sailing to America with almost three hundred settlers, including a new contingent of Salzburgers, a group of Moravians, and the young ministers John and Charles Wesley, seemed especially annoying. Oglethorpe, with his reputation higher than it had ever been, was received with shouts of joy and thanksgiving when he appeared at Savannah on 6 February 1736. He was armed with what he felt to be a mandate to do what was necessary to make Georgia a novel province that would act as a future guidepost for colonial America.

III

The Vision of Georgia and the Challenge of Spain

Upon his return to Georgia in 1736, Oglethorpe had to put into effect the Trustees' laws and he had also to lead his new settlers to the recently authorized strongpoint in the south. Other problems demanded his attention. The first group of Salzburgers was dissatisfied with the original site of Ebenezer, and their recently arrived compatriots made it clear that they wanted to join the other Salzburgers rather than go to the new town, Frederica, to be set up in the south. To add to his woes, Oglethorpe found Savannah alive with factions. There were bitter complaints against Thomas Causton, the keeper of the Trustees' store, and Noble Jones, the surveyor. The Spanish were assuming a more threatening posture and rumors of warlike expeditions were commonplace. Some of the new arrivals became impatient, and the Carolinians, once so enthusiastic over the Georgia project, were becoming disenchanted. (Governor Johnson's death robbed Georgia of its most influential friend. He was succeeded by the contentious Thomas Broughton, who lacked Johnson's belief in the two colonies' interdependence.)

The three acts of the Trustees, which Oglethorpe now introduced, were interrelated and had a direct bearing upon the kind of colony he, Egmont, and the others wanted. It was consistent with their ideas of Georgia as a frontier buffer area that the Trustees forbade the introduction of Negro slavery or of blacks into their province. Such a prohibition was in line with the desire that Georgia grow into a colony dominated by white yeoman farmers.

In similar fashion, the act to regulate the Indian trade was not only in line with good defense policy but also reflected the Trust's efforts to build an economic base, independent of a staple crop, that would give Georgia entrée to the backcountry. This act created a Georgia Indian commissioner and required annual licensing, with payment of a fee and posting of a bond, for anyone who wished to trade with Georgia Indians. To the Carolinians this act demonstrated that the Georgia authorities were trying to divert the Indian trade to Savannah. Appeals from South Carolina through various channels in England finally resulted in the emasculation of the Trustees' act, and the trade itself, which flirted briefly with Savannah, remained Charles Town's.

The final act brought over by Oglethorpe tied in neatly with the other two pieces of legislation. "No Rum or Brandys nor any other kind of Spirits or Strong Waters by whatsoever Name they are or may be distinguished" were to be allowed in Georgia. The Trustees had been requested to pass such legislation by Indian chiefs, who had complained that overuse of rum in the Indian trade had a pernicious effect on the natives. Oglethorpe agreed and also felt that rum had brought the fatal fevers to Savannah in 1733. To restrict Georgia to wholesome wines and English ale and beer would build up the colony's strength, improve relations with the Indians, and teach the colonists lessons in frugality and virtue.

Intent upon creation of a province peopled by those of a middling sort who led useful lives on small farms, the Trust ruled that its grants could not be alienated or leased. Furthermore lands could be passed on to the next generation only through a male heir. Each farm, ideally, would have its owner in residence and because the vast majority of grants were for fifty acres, there would be a large concentration of able-bodied men to defend the province. Thus Georgia would not only teach its colonists a new life, it would also provide a solid buffer against Spain and France.

Besides his other responsibilities, Oglethorpe oversaw the planting of the new settlement on St. Simons Island. He picked the site of Frederica carefully and located it on the inland passage where it cut deeply into the island before turning back once again into the salt marshes. By mid-March 1736, over one hundred men, women, and children were settled there, each family living in its "bower of palmetto leaves" and in possession of its own town lot. Oglethorpe visited the Highland Scots who had earlier set up the town of Darien on the Altamaha, just a few miles by water from Frederica. There the doughty representatives of the Mackay, McIntosh, Dunbar, Cuthbert, and other families presented a stern and warlike appearance. The southern extremities of Georgia were manned by loyal British interests.

To make sure the province's defense was adequate, Oglethorpe, Tomochichi, and Hugh Mackay from Darien, accompanied by Indian and Scottish allies, probed southward toward Florida. A frontier fort to be named St. Andrew was designed for the northern end of Cumberland Island, and on the southern tip Fort William was to guard the mouth of the St. Marys. Oglethorpe then moved farther south to the island of Amelia, and then on to the mouth of the St. Johns, projecting a fort there grandly named for that English slayer of dragons, St. George.

In England, the Trust complained of lack of information. Mounting annoyance with Oglethorpe as a poor correspondent and the general desire to have someone in Georgia to provide detailed and reliable data led to the appointment of William Stephens as secretary for the colony. Stephens, a graduate of King's College, Cambridge, and a member of Parliament for twenty years, had come upon evil days. Colonel Samuel Horsey employed Stephens to oversee a survey of properties in Carolina, and when Egmont read Stephens's 1736 report from America he knew that the Trustees had found a resident secretary. Stephens was delighted to take the position, and the faithful record that he kept daily is not only one of the finest of all American colonial journals, it is filled with wit, perception, and tales of the lusty life of frontier Georgia. Sent to England in regular installments, Stephens's journal became required reading for the most active Trustees. The secretary soon discovered, after being reprimanded for expressing himself too bluntly, that the Georgia Board did not really want an objective assessment of events in the colony, so he trimmed his sails to suit the wind.

When Georgia was divided administratively into two counties in 1741, Stephens was named to head the northern district, centered in Savannah, while Oglethorpe held titular control of the southern county from Frederica. Two years later, Stephens became president of the entire province and remained in that office until he resigned in 1751 at the age of eighty. He retired to "Bewlie," his plantation on the Vernon River, near Savannah, where he died in 1753.

Oglethorpe and Stephens did not always see eye to eye. Oglethorpe was jealous of the growing esteem in which Stephens was held by the Trustees, and this may also account for Oglethorpe's growing alienation from Savannah, which became Stephens's stronghold. After 1737 Oglethorpe visited there less and less frequently and even failed to make a courtesy call at Savannah in 1743 as he left Georgia for the last time. He maintained that Frederica was healthier and that the Trustees' laws were more closely followed there. Savannah, on the other hand, was a hotbed of malcontents.

In 1736, however, the Spanish posed a greater danger to Georgia than did the anti-Trustee faction. The establishment of Fort St. George at the mouth of the St. Johns was hardly less dangerous to Spain than the French settlement of Fort Caroline in the sixteenth century. In

1565 Spain had acted quickly, but in 1736 she decided on more diplomatic means. The Spanish minister in London tried to force the British government to deny the extreme claims made by Oglethorpe and at the same time Spain reasserted her claim to the entire Georgia coast. Prime Minister Walpole was annoyed with Oglethorpe for stirring up old problems and the Trustees, in constant fear that war would break out, bombarded him with admonitions of caution and letters disassociating themselves from his forts in the south. Oglethorpe insisted that the St. Johns was the proper boundary between Georgia and Florida.

Finally Oglethorpe and Antonio de Arredondo, diplomat and soldier as well as author of the best account of the validity of the Spanish claims, met on St. Simons Island in August 1736. After much discussion Oglethorpe promised to abandon Fort St. George with the final boundaries to be determined by their home governments. Oglethorpe considered that he had won a concession as his posture on Cumberland and Jekyll did not seem to be seriously questioned.

Although he thought he had calmed international tensions, Oglethorpe had simply put off the ultimate confrontation. He and Egmont even feared that Walpole might sacrifice Georgia to the Spaniards to keep peace. To forestall such a disaster Oglethorpe left the colony late in 1736; he wanted assurances from Walpole himself that Georgia would be supported and he also was determined to secure a regiment to take back with him to America. Probably against his better judgment, Walpole granted both requests, and in addition Oglethorpe was made "General and Commander in Chief of the Forces of South Carolina and Georgia." By May 1738 some of the soldiers assigned to Oglethorpe's regiment were already in Georgia, but Oglethorpe and his contingent did not arrive at Frederica until 19 September. The entire command numbered just over 625 soldiers. Their presence alarmed the Spanish and upset the military balance along the Georgia-Florida frontier.

Upon his return to Georgia Oglethorpe learned that the friendly neutrality of the Creek Nation was being sorely taxed by the French. It was suggested that he attend a conference to be held in August 1739 in Creek country. This was just the sort of dramatic stroke that appealed to Oglethorpe and, in spite of a touch of fever, he went to Coweta and Kashita on the banks of the Chattahoochee. There he talked, drank, and smoked peace pipes with the Creek leaders for over two weeks. Though he was not able to wring from the Indians a promise to fight with Britain in any upcoming English-Spanish confrontation he was assured that they would not join the Spanish.

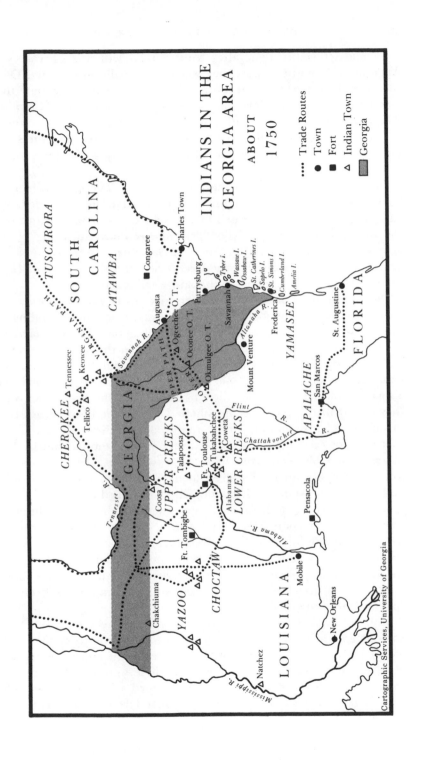

INDICANS IN THE
GEORGIA AREA

ABOUT
1750

···· Trade Routes
● Town
■ Fort
△ Indian Town
▨ Georgia

Cartographic Services, University of Georgia

In mid-September 1739, after fruitful talks with the Cherokees at Augusta and amidst rumors that war had actually broken out, Oglethorpe and his party set out down the Savannah River. En route they learned of a slave uprising—the Stono Rebellion—in South Carolina. The province, face-to-face with armed insurrection, was on the verge of hysteria. It was feared that the Spanish had been the fomenters. To Oglethorpe, the rebellion was proof that the Georgia plan for a colony was superior to Carolina's.

Oglethorpe faced distressing news in Savannah. The ancient chieftain Tomochichi, ally to the English and personal friend to Oglethorpe since 1733, had died. He paused to act as a pallbearer in the funeral of the dignified old Indian, who "desired his Body might be buried amongst the English in the Town of Savannah." Shortly after the funeral Oglethorpe convened the freeholders of the town and officially informed them that England and Spain were at war.

Oglethorpe had for some time been anxious to invade Florida. He envisioned an army of about thirty-five hundred men, not including his own regiment and those who could be raised among the Georgians. He hoped two thousand Indians would take part in the campaign, but he had to be content with only a fraction of that number. Carolina was expected to raise the lion's share of men and money. Though the Yamasees, old adversaries of the English, got in the first blows when they raided British positions on Amelia Island, Oglethorpe struck back in January of 1740 and captured two outposts on the St. Johns.

It was not easy to raise a sizable army on the frontier, but by May of 1740, after his rendezvous with the Carolinians, Oglethorpe had a force of roughly fifteen hundred men. To oppose him the Spanish under Governor Manuel Montiano, who had pulled in his garrisons to concentrate his strength at St. Augustine, had about eight hundred men. When he reconnoitered the Spanish stronghold, Oglethorpe discovered that the fort had been strengthened and that six half-galleys anchored in St. Augustine harbor commanded its narrow and tortuous entrance. Their presence threw into disarray Oglethorpe's plan for a joint land-sea attack against the town, so he attempted to starve the Spaniards into submission.

Montiano was determined to try anything before surrender. On 15 June at Fort Mosa he surprised a supposedly mobile party that Oglethorpe had stationed north of St. Augustine. Of the approximately one hundred and forty men at the fort sixty-three were killed, more than twenty captured, and the rest barely escaped with their lives. This debacle gave a needed boost to the Spanish and demoralized the British.

Tomochichi, Mico of the Yamacraws, and his nephew Toonahowi
University of Georgia Libraries

When Oglethorpe heard that Spanish reinforcements were arriving and that the Royal Navy would soon depart Florida waters, he knew he had been beaten. He ordered a retreat commencing 4 July and fell back slowly to St. Simons, assuming a defensive position.

Throughout 1741 the Spanish built up their strength. Montiano ultimately commanded an invasion force that numbered slightly less than two thousand men, though British accounts made it several times that size. The armada in which it sailed consisted of sloops, half-galleys, galleys, Indian piraguas, and men-of-war, altogether numbering fifty-two ships. The main body of the Spanish force appeared off St. Simons on 28 June 1742. A week later the expedition passed Fort St. Simons, on the southern tip of the island, and anchored behind it in Jekyll Sound. Oglethorpe ordered the fort's evacuation and the Spanish occupied the site. On 7 July Montiano sent several contingents of troops up the military road that connected Fort St. Simons with Frederica. When word reached Oglethorpe of the Spaniards' approach he presumed Montiano's full army was preparing an attack on Frederica. Oglethorpe himself led a charge into the astonished Spanish, who were maneuvering to assume a defensive posture. The force of the charge was irresistible and broke the Spanish ranks. Oglethorpe pursued the demoralized enemy down the military trail and stationed troops along the way to block any new advance of Montiano's army. He then returned to Frederica for reinforcements.

In the meantime, Montiano ordered men up the military road to protect survivors of the first fight. The British opened fire on these troops from behind trees to the Spaniards' north; the Spanish returned the fire. British regulars fled but were met by Oglethorpe who was hurrying to the front. By the time he reached the scene the Spanish had retreated in good order. The invaders lost only a handful of men at this second encounter, frequently referred to as the Battle of Bloody Marsh, but the fact that their best troops had been unable to dislodge the British proved disheartening.

The next few days were spent in abortive expeditions, some effective British ambushes, and "psychological warfare" on the part of Oglethorpe. Montiano's numerically superior forces seemed paralyzed; he was worried about Oglethorpe and the possibility of hurricanes, but when British ships appeared on the horizon he ordered a hasty retreat.

There were other minor encounters as the Spanish felt their way back to St. Augustine, but the important fighting had taken place on 7 July 1742 and was decisive in frustrating Spain's plans for Guale. Her ships and troops continued to operate along the eastern seaboard, but the expedition against Georgia was Spain's last full-scale effort to dislodge the English on the southern frontier.

Faced with charges brought by an officer of his regiment and depressed by the fact that his friend Egmont, in ill health, had resigned from the Trustees, Oglethorpe turned his thoughts toward home. After another unsuccessful foray into Florida he sailed for England in 1743.

As a military leader Oglethorpe was no strategist. During the Florida campaign his premature invasion alarmed the enemy and tired his own men. His plan for the capture of St. Augustine and its fort had merit, but when the half-galleys rendered the original idea questionable he seemed unable to develop alternative plans. Nor did he take advice well. On the other hand, Oglethorpe was an exceedingly vigorous leader who possessed unlimited personal courage. He never asked his troops to do anything he himself would not do, and in spite of sporadic discipline problems in his regiment, he was respected by his men.

Oglethorpe appeared at his best on St. Simons Island in the summer of 1742. Such challenges seemed to inspire him, and during the Spanish invasion he was daring and decisive. By his victory on St. Simons he turned back the challenge of the Spanish. That he was not so successful in defeating the domestic opposition is the story of another chapter.

IV

Life in Georgia under the Trustees

After Oglethorpe's second departure from Georgia in 1736, dissatisfaction with the Trustees' control increased. Charles Town merchant Samuel Eveleigh, an astute observer and friend of Georgia, had said all along that Negro labor and fee-simple landholding would be essential for Georgia to succeed, and he also pointed out the futility of prohibiting rum. Complaints began to pour in to the Trustees on other points too. Land either had not been surveyed, had been found to be underwater at high tide, had proved to be barren, or was too far from Savannah. Some said the peculiar arrangement of having a 60′ × 90′ town lot, a garden plot just outside Savannah, and a 45-acre tract elsewhere was highly inconvenient. Furthermore, to use hired white servants to clear and cultivate land in Georgia proved exorbitant.

From the start restrictions on female inheritance of land caused objections, and the stipulation that land could not be leased, mortgaged, or alienated was viewed as unreasonable. Other regulations relating to the soil specified planting mulberry trees and clearing and fencing land upon a set schedule. On paper these restrictions, called the "Rules of 1735," were harsh. In fact they were leniently enforced. Requests from widows or daughters of landholders with no male heir were usually allowed, but Oglethorpe proved especially reluctant to approve transfer or removal of settlers from their original grants. Still, numerous transfers were ultimately made in spite of his opposition.

Gradually all land restrictions fell by the wayside. Female inheritance was permitted if accomplished by will or deed, and maximum landholding was increased to 2,000 acres in 1740. Short-term leases were permitted and other obnoxious requirements were reduced or eliminated. The Trustees decided to give land in fee simple to those who paid their own way to Georgia, and finally, in 1750, full fee-simple tenure to all settlers was permitted. The collapse of the land policy of the Trustees, coming at about the same time as the legal introduction of blacks, signaled the demise of the concept of Georgia as a colony of yeoman farmers and encouraged the rise of small plantations.

Of all the Trust's legislation for Georgia, the Rum Act was the most unrealistic; given the time and the situation the act was unenforceable. Public houses in Savannah always had rum ready for sale, and Oglethorpe was enraged by the rum-drinking proclivities of the workmen at Tybee Light—only a short boat trip from "wet" South Carolina. Owing to its distance from Carolina there probably was less rum in Frederica, as Oglethorpe claimed, but it is difficult to conceive of soldiers and rum being separated for long, and after 1738, when Oglethorpe returned with his regiment, it is likely that other liquors were available there too. The Rum Act was also unwise economically as rum was a popular item in the Indian trade. Its prohibition made it harder for Georgia to develop strong economic ties with the natives. By 1742 the Rum Act, openly violated, was ignored by all.

The act prohibiting Negroes in the colony, however, was the one about which people felt most strongly. Because this prohibition was closely related to the land restrictions, it might be thought that as the land regulations changed so would those relating to blacks, but such was not the case. Basically this was because Oglethorpe and the Trust considered the act essential for the defense of Georgia and central to their overall concept of what the province should be. Unlike the circumstances surrounding the land rules, there were also vocal and influential supporters of the Negro ban.

Although slaves from South Carolina had been used at Savannah in Georgia's infancy, Oglethorpe was determined that Negroes be excluded from the colony. Slaves would be useless for frontier defense, and the kinds of crops the Trustees wanted grown were not those traditionally cultivated by slave labor. Slavery bred indolence in the owners and encouraged the feeling that hard labor could not be performed by whites. If the land grants were kept small and if the owners worked their own fields, black slavery would be a luxury neither desirable nor desired. White servants could do the job just as well, or so reasoned the Trustees.

From these issues of land, rum, and blacks there developed in Georgia an articulate opposition to Trustee policy. This group grew bolder whenever Oglethorpe was away, and during his absence in 1737–38, the dissenters were outspoken. In 1733 Thomas Causton had noted the presence of some "Grumbletonians" before Savannah was even settled, but in March 1738, "the Club" or "the Malcontents," as William Stephens called the disaffected, met publicly at a Savannah tavern and invited interested parties to take part. (These people were, Stephens noted with disapproval, mostly Lowland Scots.) Patrick Tailfer, David Douglass, and Hugh Anderson were among the most active. To Stephens's mortification, his son Thomas became one of the leaders of the dissenters.

In December 1738 a memorial to the Trustees was issued from Savannah containing the signatures of 117 of the colony's settlers, including two of Savannah's magistrates. This document called for fee-simple landholding and the right to own slaves. Until cheap labor became available any "Misfortunes and Calamities" that beset Georgia must be laid at the Trustees' door. To counter the effect of this memorial the Highland Scots at Darien submitted their own petition to the Trust. In addition to citing the inadvisability of slavery on such an exposed frontier, the Scots spoke out sternly against the institution as a *"Scene of Horror"* shocking to people of sensibilities. From Ebenezer, Pastors Bolzius and Gronau rallied their people to the side of the Trustees in another address. The effect of these two documents was to lessen the impression the Savannah petition made in London.

After 1739, a number of the opposition, unable to move the Trustees, left Georgia to live in Charles Town where they composed a regular colony of émigrés. Anderson, Tailfer, and Douglass were among this group of "mean pittifull Wretches," in the words of one of the Trust's friends in Savannah.

Throughout 1739 and 1740 there was a sharp public exchange between the friends and the opponents of the Trustees, but in June 1741 the Charles Town refugees published *A True and Historical Narrative of the Colony of Georgia.* The book is a searing condemnation of Trustee policy and contains a mock dedication to Oglethorpe. To literary historian Moses Coit Tyler, this work "as a polemic . . . is one of the most expert pieces of writing to be met with in our early literature." This literature of controversy, which broadened to include Oglethorpe's role in the St. Augustine expedition of 1740, is one of the first meaningful intercolonial literary exchanges about issues surrounding a southern colony and its way of life.

In spite of all they could do the Trustees saw their strength declining, and when Bolzius, James Habersham, and George Whitefield asked that Negroes be introduced, they gave their approval in 1750. By 1752, when the charter was surrendered to the king, Georgians had the right to import slaves without restrictions; the colony was free to develop economically as it so desired. There were a few blacks in the colony even prior to 1750, but the abandonment of the prohibition on slavery caused the number of Negroes in Georgia to increase dramatically. Tied to the consideration that restrictions on the size of land grants had also been overthrown, the effect of these changes meant a marked upturn in trade, population, and affluence for the colony. It was now feasible to introduce rice culture on a large scale to the coastal areas, and the prosperity that came with such culture meant the establishment of the plantation system along Georgia's tidal rivers and the nearby mainland. As the years went by the number of blacks in the colony began to approximate the number of whites, but in the coastal parishes devoted to rice growing the slaves soon outnumbered the whites by wide margins.

Agitation or no, day-to-day life in Georgia went on much as usual. The settlers adjusted to the new environment and its challenges by following the crafts and trades they brought with them or by adopting different specializations that seemed more appropriate for the New World. The settlements at Savannah, Frederica, and Ebenezer developed busy village lives, but the active presence of the Trustees' store appeared to interrupt the natural growth of the economy. With its control of supplies and credit the store and its keeper, Thomas Causton, exerted a powerful influence over the economy until the operation was closed by Trustee order in 1739.

In Ebenezer the patterns of community life were largely dictated by the ministers, whose influence was all-pervasive. With the importance the Salzburgers placed upon Christian works and charity, it was no surprise that Ebenezer established the colony's first orphanage. George Whitefield visited the Salzburgers and was deeply touched and resolved, apparently, to establish an orphanage himself. The result was the Bethesda Orphan House, an institution that became as well known as its founder. Whitefield preached throughout America and England to collect money to support Bethesda, and although the orphanage was controversial, he was able to fend off its critics. Bethesda gradually became more of a school than an orphanage and a number of Georgia's colonial leaders owed their reading, writing, and mechanical skills to it.

Elsewhere in the field of education, the Trustees supported what few secular teachers there were during the colony's first twenty years, and although educational opportunities at the primary level were scarce in Georgia, so were they in the other British colonies. Among the most successful early teachers in Savannah were Charles Delamotte and James Habersham. Delamotte proved to be Georgia's most dedicated and productive instructor, and his departure from Savannah was all but a time of mourning. Fortunately he was succeeded by a fine teacher in the person of Habersham, who handled the educational aspects of Bethesda with dedication. John Dobell taught in Savannah too, helped with a small allowance from the Trustees. In 1743 he reported proudly that he had about twenty-five children in his school and that ten of them could already write. The pastors or catechists sent from Germany instructed the youth at Ebenezer.

Feeble efforts were made to educate the natives. The Moravians at Irene, upriver from Savannah, established a school for Indians and ran it until they left Georgia in 1740. Thomas Bray's charitable corporation, the Society for the Promotion of Christian Knowledge, had as one of its aims education of the American Indians, but it did little in Georgia.

As for the overall picture, it should be recalled that Georgia was a frontier province in constant danger of invasion. Though such stalwarts as John Wesley wished to see a suitable school in Savannah, the dangers under which Georgia labored for the first fifteen years of its existence dictated the strengthening of fortifications rather than the building of schools.

From the start, Georgia had a varied religious experience. The charter of the colony specifically prohibited only Roman Catholics, and it has already been noted that the first boatload of Jewish emigrants was admitted in July 1733. Although virtually all Christian religions were tolerated, the Anglican church was given preferential treatment. Another of Bray's organizations, the Society for the Propagation of the Gospel in Foreign Parts, cooperated with the Trust to provide Georgia with ministers. The first Anglican minister to Georgia, Henry Herbert, who came on the *Ann*, became ill after being in America only a brief time and died on the return voyage to England. His successor, Samuel Quincy, was unsatisfactory and was replaced by John Wesley. Wesley really wanted to be a missionary to the Indians, but his commission from the Trustees made no reference to that wish. He came to America with Oglethorpe in February 1736 and with the zeal and energy of youth he entered into the pastoral duties assigned him in Savannah.

Wesley performed all his tasks diligently and plunged into the life of the colony at once. Initial reaction to Wesley was good, but some of his congregation wondered about his unbending formality on ritual and dogma. These problems probably could have been overcome had Wesley not run afoul in a matter of the heart. He became interested in a young girl named Sophia Hopkey, niece to the wife of Thomas Causton, and when Sophia married another, Wesley was most unhappy. After he excluded Sophia from communion a suit was brought against him for defaming her character. Though he denied the jurisdiction of the Georgia magistrates, claiming it was an ecclesiastical question, he was informed that he must appear in court to answer charges. As chief magistrate, Causton charged the grand jury on the matter. The jury returned ten true bills against Wesley, and though he subsequently demanded trial, his case was never heard.

Feeling that he could accomplish nothing more in Georgia, Wesley gave notice that he was leaving the colony; there was no serious effort to prevent his departure. By the end of 1737 he was gone from Savannah. Though this early chapter in Wesley's ministerial career ended unhappily, the young man himself had learned much, and he had contributed a high sense of duty and moral purpose to Georgia. Wesley was succeeded by George Whitefield who, though a conscientious minister at first, tended to spend less and less time in Georgia. There was a succession of other ministers until Bartholomew Zouberbuhler, fluent in French and German as well as English, was appointed to the Savannah vacancy in 1745, a position he held until his death in 1766. He was a prodigious worker and was widely respected. On 7 July 1750 dedication ceremonies were held for the long-delayed Anglican church building in Savannah. Being also the anniversary date of the victory over the Spanish in 1742 and the initiation of civil government in 1733, it was a joyous occasion.

In general, however, organized religion in Trusteeship Georgia, with the possible exception of the Salzburgers, did not fare well. The Scottish Presbyterians at Darien had a minister only briefly and had little effect on the mainstream of Georgia's religious development. Furthermore, permanent church buildings were late to come to Georgia. In the vicinity of Ebenezer the Salzburgers put up three houses of worship, but even those thrifty folk required the aid of the Lutherans in Germany to construct Jerusalem Church. Even the established Church of England did not complete its first structure in Savannah until years after Georgia's founding. Occupied with the day-to-day problems of staying alive, Georgians had little time to erect fine buildings to house their government, much less their churches.

The people of Georgia had ample opportunities for diversion. Frequently pleasure was linked to practicality, and hunting provided not only recreation but food for the table. Deer, bear, and birds of all kinds were plentiful, and there are accounts of the skies being black with pigeons. Turkeys, geese, ducks, and other birds were readily available. Besides hunting, there were fishing and swimming in the low country streams that teemed with shad, flounder, and trout. The Indians particularly enjoyed oysters and clams and introduced Georgians to American shellfish.

Time was set aside too for general recreation. Secretary Stephens sometimes furnished wine or beer at Trustee expense on such days, and Oglethorpe was generous with his own or the Trust's provisions. Commemoration of George II's birthday and accession to the throne were usually marked with raising the flag, firing salutes, drinking the king's health, and possibly even a special church service. Oglethorpe's birthday and the anniversary of the landing of the first colonists at Savannah were also times of general revelry and rejoicing. In 1737, after the formalities of toasts and the discharge of guns, the crowd of Savannah dignitaries sponsored a cold buffet and dancing at a local tavern. St. George's day in April and St. Andrew's day in November brought out the English and the Scots respectively. The Scots seemed to be particularly raucous, often to the disapproval of William Stephens. Cricket in a Savannah square was one thing; holding horse races from the Trustees' Garden to Johnson Square was quite another!

Medical practice in Trusteeship Georgia was as basic as it was in other British colonies. There were many quacks and few doctors, and even among the latter the treatment was often worse than the disease. Fortunately for Georgia, Oglethorpe chose his sites for settlements well and both Savannah and Frederica were spared in their early years the disastrous yellow fever epidemics that struck Charles Town periodically. Malaria, imperfectly understood, was a serious problem, as were various other agues and "fluxes" that contributed to Georgia's high death rate. Infant mortality was high too, and although the settlers tried as many home remedies and Indian herbal concoctions as they could, the scarcity of qualified doctors and the ignorance of correct diagnosis and treatment meant that many died and few were cured.

In the economic field, Trusteeship Georgia showed many of the halting characteristics that other American colonies demonstrated in their first years. The colony had inadequate docking facilities, lacked credit, had no merchants of established reputation, and possessed no clearinghouses. Augusta, at the head of navigation on the Savannah and strategically located on several of the most important Indian trails, prospered after its founding in 1736. Augusta traders were usually representatives of Charles Town merchants, so its prosperity had little impact on the rest of Georgia; the boats from Augusta, bound for Charles Town, glided silently by Savannah. The early merchants in Savannah handled Indian goods, but in no way was their business comparable to that of Charles Town. Harris and Habersham, a trading establishment founded in 1744, dealt in skins and pelts, but other items

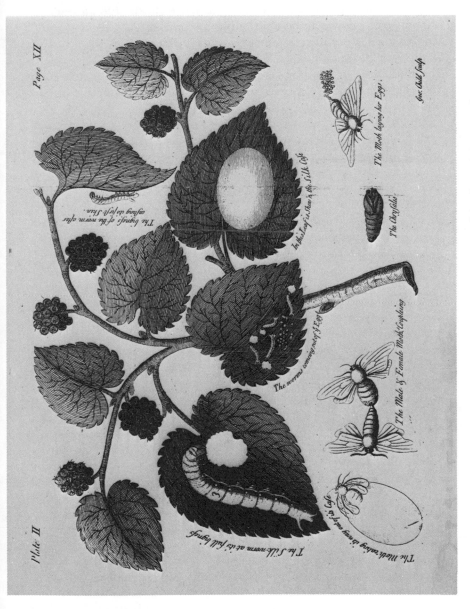

were more important. Georgia, in the final analysis, simply lacked the economic backing that was necessary for entrée to the Indian trade.

Lumbering gradually became important to Georgia's economy, and has remained so to this day. Barrels, staves, shingles, and planks of all kinds were in constant demand in the West Indies and provided a ready commodity to exchange for sugar, molasses, or some desirable item from the islands. Cattle, too, proved profitable and soon distinctive brands were used to identify the animals of different owners.

The high hopes of the Trustees where certain crops were concerned were soon felled. Olives were early abandoned, and the experiment with grapes and wine was a failure too. Some potash and pearlash were produced, but never on a large scale; the same held true for naval stores. But silk was the major disappointment. Though some was produced, it was always under more or less artificial conditions and the effort expended hardly made it worth the time spent. The crop of 1750 was a good one and the Trustees were encouraged to support erection of a filature in Savannah, but production never reached expectations.

One omission of the Trustees in their economic planning had been a concern for food production. Yet the colonists, most of whom were not farmers, needed encouragement in this area. Oglethorpe understood this and instituted bounties to boost production of crops such as grains and Indian corn. By 1740 Georgia was usually self-sufficient in foodstuffs. There were all kinds of vegetables: peas, greens, squash, pumpkins, and beans, in addition to Indian corn, the basic staple. Rice, sometimes homegrown but often brought in from Carolina, was important in the diet. Wheat and flour were usually imported, and Savannah was liberally supplied with bakers, just as she was with tavernkeepers. Shoemakers, tallow chandlers, bricklayers, carpenters, farmers, woodcutters, cordwainers, and midwives were found in the early days at Frederica. The variety of trades indicates that a broad cross-section of the English middle class came to Georgia.

In general, the economic picture of Trusteeship Georgia was not as bleak as some have made it out to be. The colony could never be described as a startling economic success, but Georgians in the 1740s were not on the point of starvation. The picture that emerges is of a province of small landowners who were, to a large degree, self-sufficient. There were complaints and objections aplenty, and some of the people agitated for more voice in their government, but that was a healthy sign. Georgians had learned what it took to get along economically, and that in itself was a considerable accomplishment for any colony's first twenty years.

One of the last crises of the Trusteeship period occurred in 1749 when erstwhile friend and interpreter, Mary Musgrove, marched on Savannah with a following of Creek Indians. She felt that she had not been given her due by the Trustees and, having fallen under the influence of her third husband, the renegade Anglican priest Thomas Bosomworth, she threatened to bring down the wrath of the natives on Georgia. Bosomworth cajoled the Indians into ceding their claims to Sapelo, Ossabaw, and St. Catherines islands to Mary; in addition, she was designated "Queen of the Creeks." Armed with her title, her land cession from the Creeks, and a large store of nerve, Mary and her entourage approached Savannah with demands that her right to the islands be recognized and that a salary promised to her as interpreter by Oglethorpe be paid at once. Reacting as soon as he heard of their approach, Noble Jones called out the local militia, and the Bosomworths discovered that their position was an unpopular one in Savannah. Failing to intimidate the officials, Mary then had recourse to the courts and appeals to London. In 1760 she received legal title to St. Catherines and also got a cash settlement in excess of £2,000.

After the return of peace to Europe and America in 1748, fewer Trustees showed interest in Georgia than ever before. No new plans were proposed and land grants by 1750 seemed more a reward for old friends than anything else. At approximately this same time a slow economic upturn in Georgia began. This upturn has often been attributed to royal government, but it actually started during the Trustees' regime.

Toward the end of their tenure in Georgia the Trustees called for the meeting of a Georgia assembly. Its members were popularly elected and they convened at Savannah in January 1751 and chose merchant Francis Harris as speaker. The assembly had no power to appropriate money or to legislate, but it reported opinion in the colony and recommended courses of action. The strongest sentiment expressed by the group was the fear that once the Trustees had surrendered their charter the Carolinians would take over the colony. The Trust was asked to make certain that the king would retain Georgia as a separate province after governmental authority passed to the crown.

In 1751, the Trustees' usual request for money from Parliament was rejected. Discouraged, they decided to surrender the charter a year before it reverted automatically to the king. Even so, the Trustees' de facto government continued under Henry Parker and then Patrick Graham who, in 1754, had the honor of passing an intact colony to the first royal governor.

The domestic phase of the Trusteeship period has generally been considered a failure. The crops that were to be grown were never produced successfully and Georgia did not become the Eden that many had expected. The Trustees passed only three laws during their corporate existence; by 1752 all of these had been negated or abandoned. The hope that Georgia might become a self-reliant province of soldier-farmers had not succeeded, and even the early debtor-haven dream had not come to pass.

And yet there were positive accomplishments. The Trustees had overseen the settlement in Georgia of over fifty-five hundred colonists of whom almost thirty-five hundred had come at their own expense. Though many of these colonists were dead or had abandoned Georgia by 1752, still there were about three thousand people in the colony at the time of the charter's surrender. Granted that perhaps as many as eight hundred of that total were Negroes, most of them brought into the colony after 1750, still the number of permanent white settlers established on the southern frontier is significant.

Georgia had also played its role of buffer against Spain to perfection and had borne the full brunt of the Yamasee-Spanish assaults during the War of Jenkins' Ear. By settling on the disputed land, England took the initiative against both Spain and France. Finally, Georgia acted as successful host to persecuted European Protestants. She provided the Moravians as well as the Salzburgers with a refuge, and though the former group left for Pennsylvania after five years the latter proved to be a permanent addition to Georgia.

V

Georgia as a Royal Province

The decade following the end of Trustee rule in Georgia was one of significant growth. During these years Georgia began to expand slowly but solidly after the peace treaty of 1748 ended fear of Spanish invasion. The next war, 1756–63, with the French and later the Spanish, never really touched Georgia, and when the Treaty of Paris decided this contest, the colony grew more spectacularly than in the previous decade.

The passing of Trustee authority brought no startling change. Most Georgians bore their old rulers no particular ill will, and there were few surprises at the new form of government they received. Royal rule as instituted by Captain John Reynolds, a navy man designated as Georgia's first governor, was looked upon as something of a reform. It would be comforting to have a well-organized system with a strong governor to establish policy and make decisions. Along with his executive powers, the governor brought instructions to provide Georgians with a full-fledged legislature and a complete set of courts, neither of which the colony had enjoyed before, so Reynolds was greeted with cheers when he arrived at Savannah in October 1754.

The original Commons House of Assembly, the elected house of the legislature, was composed of nineteen members, each of whom had to own 500 acres of land to qualify for a seat in that body. The Commons House could initiate money bills and other forms of legislation and had to approve all bills before they became law. The House elected its own speaker subject to the approval of the governor. To vote, Georgians had to own 50 acres of land, a qualification easily met by most free white men. The Upper House of the Assembly could initiate any sort of legislation except that involving money and also had to give its consent before a bill became law. There were twelve men in the Upper House, all appointed by the king.

The members of the Upper House composed the Governor's Council. The governor sat with this body to grant lands, make appointments, and hear appeals from lower courts. Acting in such a capacity, the council performed enormously important duties for Georgia. Sitting as a judicial body, for instance, the council formed the supreme court for the colony. The council, made up of leaders in the colony, was expected to be invaluable to the governor and was envisioned as a bulwark against too much democracy in the elected Commons House.

The lowest courts, the ones with which ordinary people would have the most contact, were the courts of conscience, presided over by the local justices of the peace. Above these was the General Court, headed by a chief justice and two assistant judges, none of whom, originally, were trained in the law. Appeals from the General Court were to the Governor in Council, and in some cases to the Privy Council in England. But appeals were costly and time-consuming and were seldom made. There was also an admiralty court to try cases arising on the high seas and those concerning customs violations.

The only political subdivisions within the colony were the parishes, eight created in 1758 and four more in 1765. Parishes were electoral, taxation, and ecclesiastical units and were responsible for the upkeep of roads and relief of the poor. Parish officials, consisting of vestrymen and church wardens, were named by the voters in elections that seldom incited much interest.

The cornerstone of royal rule was the governor, more powerful in Georgia than in most other royal colonies. He was paid from England rather than by the local assembly and was vested with wide executive powers. He could convene, dissolve, or adjourn the assembly; he was the prime granter of land in the province; he acted as chief judge when the council was sitting in its judicial capacity; and he commanded the militia and conducted Indian negotiations. In the exercise of these functions the governor was to consult with the council, and like his counterparts elsewhere, he had to take political reality into consideration.

The first assembly to meet in royal Georgia convened in Savannah in January 1755. It dealt with such basic issues as the passage of a slave code, the construction and repair of roads, and the reorganization of the militia. The militia was of particular importance to such an exposed colony, as Georgia had only a few regular troops stationed in it since the departure of Oglethorpe's regiment. Reynolds, touring Frederica in 1754, was horrified to note the town "in ruins," with "houses falling down" and dismounted, rusted cannon lying about.

Reynolds's military plans for Georgia's defense proved impractical and too expensive, and he ran into political trouble. It would seem logical for a new governor to rely at first upon longtime and respected residents, and the council was anxious to be of assistance. But Reynolds was unable to take advice, even when he needed it desperately.

Any effort to correct him made him only the more determined to do as whim dictated. The upshot was that he fell out with both houses of the assembly and even interfered in the judicial process. He soon put forward his private secretary, William Little, as his personal favorite, and between the two of them they tried to monopolize political power in the province. The result was an empty treasury, inflamed public opinion, and the alienation of most of the important political leaders. Jonathan Bryan, a member of the council and a well-to-do planter, headed a move to secure the governor's recall. After an investigation the Board of Trade removed Reynolds and he returned to shipboard command. The experiment with a military man had been a sad failure, for with his arbitrary methods and his meddling, Reynolds had reduced Georgia to a group of quarrelsome factions.

Lieutenant Governor Henry Ellis, a different type of man entirely, arrived in Georgia in February 1757. Ellis, a wealthy man of thirty-six, had seen much of the world including the polar areas, Africa, and the Hudson Bay region. He dabbled in science and natural history and was a fellow of the Royal Society, to which Oglethorpe also belonged. The sight of this wry man walking Savannah's sandy streets in 1758 checking the summer heats with his thermometer and taking notes became a familiar one. He enjoyed figures, calculation, compilation; he was a man of the Enlightenment, and reason was his guide. In addition, he was adept at taking advice and leaned heavily upon Governor William Lyttelton of South Carolina. Ellis was well received in Savannah and on the evening of his arrival observed the burning of an effigy of William Little. The lesson was not lost on Ellis; he acted with caution until he had familiarized himself with Georgia.

When Ellis's policies were announced they showed that he had profited from Reynolds's mistakes. He mastered the lower house by defeating the Little candidate for speaker; he secured the appointment of his own men to the General Court; he ingratiated the council by consulting with it and following its suggestions. In less than six months Ellis had taken a difficult situation and imposed order and peace on the colony. Although he remained in the province only three years, Ellis left in 1760 with the affection and gratitude of the inhabitants.

Ellis was succeeded by James Wright, whose tenure as governor stretched for two decades, with an interruption during the early years of the American Revolution. Wright, who was as astute and honest as Ellis though lacking his tact and flair, followed essentially the policies of his predecessor. There is no question but that he was the best-qualified royal governor of Georgia and one of the most able chief executives ever to hold that position in Georgia's long history. Wright knew South Carolina well, having served as the colony's attorney general, and had invaluable contacts from his time in London as Carolina's colonial agent. He brought with him to the job administrative skill, devotion to duty and the British crown, and ambition for himself and his colony.

Ellis and Wright saw Georgia's problems as threefold and interrelated: lack of wealth, lack of people, and lack of defenses. They devoted major portions of their Georgia careers to correcting these flaws. Wright arrived in Georgia at a propitious time. The Cherokee War, a small part of the French and Indian War, was bypassing his colony, and there was never a serious threat that a major French or Spanish expedition would invade Georgia. Wright found his province calm and mildly prosperous. With efficient government guaranteed by the king and with fertile soils drawing many new people to the colony, the population by 1763 approached ten thousand. Furthermore, Ellis had been an excellent Indian diplomat and had secured from the Creeks in 1757 the islands of Ossabaw, St. Catherines, and Sapelo as well as the area above Savannah where Tomochichi's village once stood. Finally, the industrious Congregationalists who moved en masse from Dorchester in South Carolina to the Midway district in 1752 were having a good effect on the economy. By 1760 they were producing considerable amounts of rice and other products for export. Their growing village of Sunbury was recognized in 1762 as an official port of entry for the colony.

Wright's first concern was for defense. He was faced by a situation that was well-nigh insoluble, given the resources at his command. Georgia was spread out thinly down the Atlantic coast as far as Darien and Frederica, but there was no active fort or fleet to protect the settlements. Wright inherited one lone gunboat from Ellis, and even it could not be adequately manned; the militia was ragged and too few, and there was no real rallying point for the colonists as there had been in 1742 when the Spanish invaded St. Simons Island.

The same held true for the vague and indefinite backcountry boundary with the Indians. It was possible for a war party to arrive at the outskirts of Savannah without an alarm being sounded. It would have taken an incurable optimist, which Wright was not, to maintain that Georgia had even minimal protection against her enemies. French privateers hovered off the coast in the early 1760s, and when Spain entered the war in 1762 the worst was expected. These fears, though, were groundless and only a year later Georgians were relieved when news arrived that hostilities had ceased. The Treaty of Paris of 1763 seemed almost designed for weak, little Georgia. Under its terms Spain ceded Florida to England. France, menacing Georgia in the backcountry Alabama area, gave up all her land east of the Mississippi River to victorious England, except for the lower reaches of the river, which she ceded to her ally, Spain. Georgia's boundary to the south was soon pushed to the St. Marys. The time was ripe for the colony, absorbed since its founding by Spanish and French threats, to concentrate on population growth.

Following upon the heels of the British victory, Wright was able to reaffirm Georgia's old agreements with the natives and also get significant land cessions from the Creeks in 1763 at the Treaty of Augusta. Attended by four southern colonial governors and Indian Superintendent John Stuart, this Augusta conference provided the first clear-cut line between Georgia and the Creeks. Following trails, streams, and rivers, the boundary was extended up the Ogeechee and beyond, west and northwest of Augusta. It was not until 1768 that the new boundary was actually surveyed, although land grants were made in the region before that date.

The last important pre-Revolutionary Indian land cessions came in 1773. The natives had run up large debts with the Georgia traders and pressure was being put on Wright by would-be settlers and speculators for more land. Northwest of Augusta settlers from Virginia and the Carolinas had been spilling into the Broad River valley. So once again Wright and Stuart met the Cherokee and Creek representatives at Augusta, where two large cessions of land amounting to over two million acres were made. In return, the Indian debts were assumed by the government. The land ceded north of Augusta was the larger of the two parcels and would later become Wilkes County. To the south, the Creek boundary between the Ogeechee and Altamaha rivers was pushed deeper into the backcountry.

Wright was successful in his relations with the natives because his policies were fair, realistic, and consistent. When Wright arrived in 1760, Georgia comprised roughly one million settled acres. He added over six million additional acres legally, openly, and without warfare. Few colonial governors could match such an achievement.

In other areas, too, Wright proved his effectiveness. A political struggle developed with William Grover, chief justice of the colony, whom Wright believed to be derelict in his duties. A nasty bit of verse impugning the virtue of the governor and both houses of the legislature, which many attributed to Grover, was posted publicly in Savannah

Georgia five-shilling note, 1762
University of Georgia Libraries

in late 1762. Out of this came an alliance between Wright and the assembly based upon harmony and mutual respect that was to last until the Stamp Act furor.

Another question upon which governor and legislature agreed was the one of conflicting claims to lands south of the Altamaha, land highly desirable after 1763 when Florida became British. Governor Thomas Boone of South Carolina saw an opportunity for his colony to bypass Georgia and make grants to speculators and friends in Charles Town. In April 1763 Boone announced that he would receive applications for lands south of the Altamaha, and in less than a month he had given his approval to more than four hundred warrants for over five hundred thousand acres.

Wright and the Georgia legislature were exceedingly alarmed. Playing down Carolina's charter rights, Wright stressed to the Board of Trade that Georgia's growth would be stunted if the South Carolina grants were permitted. The board gave assurance that the southern region would be added to Georgia, as it soon was. However, Boone's warrants were never voided, and it was left to the two colonies to work out the problem for themselves. Few grants were ever actually issued to the Carolinians, so a possibly explosive situation was averted.

In all ways Georgia showed the effects of efficient government, expansion, and prosperity. Savannah, which in 1754 was a town of fewer than two hundred frame houses, began to reflect the good times. A few gabled homes were built by 1760, and more and more two-story structures made their appearance thereafter. Tabby and brick became more common, especially for use on the ground floor. Artisans and small merchants often carried on business on the ground floor and lived above in the English style.

Georgia looked more to overseas trade to market her produce in the late 1760s. Although only fifty-two ships cleared Savannah in 1755, more than three times that many put to sea in 1772. In addition, there were fifty-six sailings from Sunbury in the latter year, and at least thirty-six seagoing vessels called Georgia home. Numerous small craft confined themselves to the inland passage and the navigable streams of the province. The crops and goods these vessels carried from Georgia reflected the variety and abundance of her agriculture, Indian trade, and primary industries.

The firm of Harris and Habersham had constructed the first wharf in Savannah able to handle seagoing vessels. Thomas Rasberry, another of the early merchants on the bluff, explained in his letter book a good deal about the tastes and economic potential of his customers. The firm of Cowper and Telfair set up business in 1767, also reflective of the wave of prosperity that had come to the colony, and only two years later thirty-two merchants advertised in the Gazette. Waterfront lots came to be prized, and by the mid-1760s there were over a dozen merchants' warehouses located there. Apparently the wharfage and warehouse area was already beginning to take on some of the characteristics it still retains and was referred to at times as "commerce row."

Although there were merchants in the towns of Sunbury, Ebenezer, Darien, and Augusta, the lack of surviving records renders a re-creation of their commercial lives next to impossible. It seems clear that these towns varied widely in their commercial makeup just as they did in other ways. Ebenezer, sober and industrious, contrasted markedly with Augusta some one hundred and twenty-five miles up the Savannah River. The latter town, the entrepôt for the Indian trade and a growing market town as the backcountry attracted settlers, was more like the stereotypical idea of frontier communities. Here the rugged and individualistic traders loaded their horses with goods and set out for the Indian country, returning with deerskins and pelts that were sent downriver for overseas disposition. It was a brawling, bustling, lively settlement, "the metropolis of the upcountry." In contrast, the more sedate port and town of Sunbury was dominated by coastal rice planters and their needs. The Midway-Sunbury area became so influential that St. John's Parish could claim both Lyman Hall and Button Gwinnett, signers of the Declaration of Independence, among its inhabitants.

Throughout the countryside and up and down the tidal rivers, marshes were drained and prepared for rice culture. The availability of credit, slaves, and large grants of land had all stimulated Georgia's economy. By 1775, slavery had begun to establish itself as the most important social and economic institution in the province and rice, which was most successfully tended and harvested within a plantation context, became Georgia's most important money crop. The plantation system and slavery were given an added boost when it became clear that indigo could be profitably grown by this same black labor force.

The institution of slavery affected the outlook of the owners and the organization of coastal society, and influenced the religious and cultural patterns of the province. The labor of the blacks on the new rice plantations altered Georgia's economic outlook just as the rich customs and speech habits of the slaves mingled with those of the English and helped produce a coastal society that was far different from that found on the Georgia frontier or in the backcountry.

In Georgia's woods and open pastures cattle and hogs grazed, grew fat, and were slaughtered. The meat was eaten locally or was pickled or salted for export to the West Indies. Lumber was cut and put to use in dozens of ways, much of it being also shipped to the West Indies. In return, rum, sugar, or molasses were imported. Georgia rice found its way to the Mediterranean and wines were brought in from Portugal and Madeira. Most manufactured goods were sent from England, but there was a lively intercolonial trade too. The value of Georgia's exports rose in 1770 to almost £100,000; three years later that figure reached £121,000. The province was taking advantage of her stable government and good lands.

To industrious Ebenezer should go the title Silk Capital of Georgia. The filature set up there in 1759 made the handling of silk easier and more convenient. In 1760 over one thousand pounds was exported, and in 1767 the high point in silk export was reached when almost a ton left Georgia for Great Britain. Though production never reached the proportions the Trustees or the royal governors hoped for, it clearly could be produced in Georgia. The Salzburgers grew a little cotton, and the first commercial shipment was made in 1764 when eight bagsful were sent to Liverpool. Throughout the remainder of the royal period

Georgia sent between two hundred and three hundred pounds yearly to England. The Ebenezer Lutherans produced a bit of upland rice for their own consumption, processed beef and pork for shipment overseas, grew quantities of corn and other grains, and engaged in general farming.

Georgia's settlement pattern was overwhelmingly rural, but the plantation system did not dominate the economy by the time of the Revolution. There were, of course, large landholders and landholdings. Governor Wright owned eleven plantations and 523 slaves; Lieutenant Governor John Graham owned 25,000 acres; James Habersham owned in excess of 10,000 acres and 198 slaves. But these men were the exceptions. Wright reported in 1773 that the colony contained 1,400 plantations with 120,000 acres in cultivation, an average of about 850 acres per plantation. But if Graham, Wright, and Habersham were excluded, these plantation figures would shrink markedly. In fact, moderate-sized farms interspersed with some smaller plantations were the general rule in the lands of the 1763 cession between Ebenezer and Augusta, while the farms in the 1773 cession were of the subsistence, frontier sort. Wheat, not grown to any extent in the lowcountry, was common in the upcountry, and it was hoped the colony would soon be growing enough grain to make it independent of the northern colonies for flour. Livestock was successfully raised in the backcountry, being grazed on ungranted or unoccupied lands. Range cattle had been a factor in the economy since Trusteeship days—and were to remain so for many years thereafter. Some tobacco was grown in the backcountry primarily owing to the influx of Carolinians and Virginians after 1763.

It was rice, however, that was the chief money crop for Georgia. With the opening of new lands, improved credit, and better shipping facilities, the amount of rice exported from Georgia rose to more than twenty thousand barrels on the eve of the Revolution. This crop composed about one-third the value of all of Georgia's exports in the royal period. Rice culture was creating a monied and landed aristocracy by the time of the American Revolution. Indigo was also grown to some extent in the lowcountry.

The small, independent farmer and not the great rice planter was characteristic of Georgia in 1776. Although the farmers left few records, there is no doubt that this element was increasingly making itself heard, hence the lowcountry references to the influx of "Crackers" into the upcountry from the Carolinas and Virginia. In the recently ceded Indian lands these new Georgians dug in determinedly, engaged in general farming, and developed religious and political attitudes that differentiated them from the Anglican-oriented rice and mercantile society on the coast.

Georgia's population, as well as trade, grew rapidly in the royal period. In 1753, the province was estimated to have almost thirty-five hundred people, more than two-thirds of them white. In 1755, Reynolds counted forty-five hundred white inhabitants. The careful and diligent Wright said that Georgia was at the ten thousand level in 1761, with over six thousand whites in that number. There were ten thousand whites alone in Georgia by 1766, and Wright reported in 1773 that there were thirty-three thousand people in Georgia, fifteen thousand of them Negro slaves. By 1776, Georgia had forty thousand people, with a few more whites than blacks.

Most of the slaves were found on the lowcountry plantations between the Savannah and Altamaha rivers. Inland the population fell off, particularly the number of blacks, but by the time of the Revolution the majority of white Georgians lived above Ebenezer in the 1763 and 1773 cessions. So rapidly did frontiersmen move into this land that in a year's time they ran into conflict with the Indians. Violence broke out and Governor Wright was called upon to restore peace.

Increased population brought more recreational activities, best seen in the records surviving for Savannah. Clubs and fraternal organizations were popular there from the start. The Freemasons had a loyal following, numbering among their membership some of the most prominent residents of the city. The St. Andrew's Society, an early social club for Scots, opened its membership to any who might care to join. This club had a charitable purpose as well as a social one, as did the Union Society, founded in 1750. The Union Society met quarterly and was at first oriented toward craftsmen, but it broadened its base to include professional men and others. Its main interest other than social was to help educate needy and worthy children.

There is evidence that there was more book buying and reading in colonial Georgia than might be expected in so new an area. Engineer William Gerard De Brahm commented upon the high quality of conversation he found as well as upon the number of booksellers. Savannah had a subscription library dating back to the early 1760s, and the Savannah Library Society, its successor, was formed in 1774. There were five libraries in Georgia worthy of note by the 1760s—three in Savannah and one each in Ebenezer and Augusta. Although the holdings leaned heavily toward religion, there was considerable variety available. James

Johnston had the best bookshop in the colony, and prints, maps, and the like were available in other settlements as early as 1765 as well.

A sure sign of advancing maturity was the establishment in Savannah of the colony's first newspaper, the *Georgia Gazette,* in 1763. James Johnston, its editor, was a hardworking and respected young Scotsman who arrived in Savannah in 1761. At Johnston's printing office Georgians could purchase ink and stationery, books, legal forms, and associated items. He was also the official printer for Georgia. It is to the pages of his distinguished newspaper that the researcher must go to look into the everyday lives of the colonists.

Though there was no school of Georgia painters, Thomas Bembridge did a number of canvases of pre-Revolutionary Georgians, and James Habersham commissioned no fewer than seven paintings from Jeremiah Theus, prominent Charles Town artist. Much of the music apparently departed Georgia with the Moravians, but the Lutherans at Ebenezer kept alive some of the German musical traditions. St. Paul's Church, Augusta, owned the first pipe organ in the colony, but even the availability of an organ could not attract a really satisfactory minister for the parish. Although most music of which there is a record was religious, secular music was enthusiastically performed and enjoyed in taverns and private homes.

The Church of England, the established church in Georgia, found itself in the sorry plight by 1775 of having few church buildings and even fewer ministers. Bartholomew Zouberbuhler, Anglican priest at Christ Church, John J. Zubly at the Independent Presbyterian Meeting House in Savannah, John M. Bolzius at Ebenezer, and John Osgood of the Congregationalist Church at Midway were the four best-qualified and hardest-working clerics in royal Georgia. Of these men only Zouberbuhler was Anglican and by the time of the Revolution both he and Bolzius were dead. John Osgood's parish, embracing the entire Midway district, was made up of about three hundred and fifty whites and fifteen hundred Negroes by the early 1770s. Although Sunbury was the thriving town of the area, Midway was more central and was the location of the main church. The faith and prosperity of the Lutherans at Ebenezer was illustrated by the brick church they built there in the late 1760s, the oldest church building standing in Georgia today.

The educational opportunities available to Georgians by the time of the Revolution were fairly primitive, but considerably improved over what was available in the early days of the colony. Although Bethesda had failed to secure college status, through formal education and also in teaching trades it remained the best school in the colony. Schools were available in the towns and sometimes on plantations, but their quality depended entirely on the teacher. Royal Georgia was not so fortunate in this respect as Trusteeship Georgia had been. The pay from teaching was simply too meager, and though the Salzburgers kept a school to train their youth, one of their teachers, John Adam Treutlen, is a perfect example of a teacher who abandoned the profession in order to make a successful living. Alexander Findlay and James Seymour set up a school in Savannah in 1768 and were praised by the local officials, but low pay caused both men to abandon teaching by 1771. Augusta, Sunbury, and other settlements had similar experiences. There were opportunities in Savannah to study languages, bookkeeping, sewing and needlework, dancing, swordsmanship, and the like, but again the instruction lacked continuity. And Bethesda, the leading school in the province, burned in 1773 and was revived only at a considerably later date.

It should be pointed out that, with the exception of the interpreter-entrepreneur Mary Musgrove, the role of women in pre-Revolutionary Georgia was largely confined to domestic duties associated with raising children and maintaining a household. Unmarried women—like unmarried men—were looked upon with suspicion. The pressures in society to conform to the expected were too difficult to overcome, particularly in a weak, young, and vulnerable colony such as Georgia. Generally speaking, what education Georgia women had was either of the needlework-and-tatting variety or was as a result of pragmatic experiences in the school of hard knocks. Death in childbirth was a commonplace, and the colony's chronic shortage of qualified doctors and midwives tended to depress rather dramatically the average age expectancy of mothers as well as infants.

In the two decades of royal government in Georgia most people were primarily concerned with their own and the colony's development. Rapid growth in population and wealth brought a spirit of self-confidence to Georgians, perhaps more than was deserved in so young and weak a frontier colony. Georgians were sure they could take care of themselves until there was real danger—from the Spanish or the Indians before 1775, and then from the British. Ironically the very success for which Governor Wright worked so hard was one of the main things that allowed many Georgians to rebel in 1775.

VI

A Decade of Problems
1763–1775

In 1763 England emerged from the Great War for Empire as the strongest nation of the day; France and Spain lay humbled. But it was a victory with inherent problems. During the war the British trade laws had been openly violated in America, and the continental colonies seemed reluctant to bear a share of the financial burden for their own defense. Sentiment developed in England that it was time to overhaul the rusty imperial machinery. It seemed only fair that the American colonists, who the British thought had gained most by this signal victory, should now be expected to foot some of the bills incurred for their protection and benefit. The heart of the matter was Britain's effort to secure a steady and dependable revenue from the colonies to help defray increased imperial expenses. This "New Colonial Policy" set off, to the astonishment of the mother country, a movement that became the American Revolution.

No one in Georgia would have dreamed of revolution in 1763. The colony was riding a wave of prosperity and had just signed a treaty with the Indians that opened a vast new area for settlement; her boundary was extended to the St. Marys River by the Proclamation of 1763; and Governor James Wright worked well with the legislature and was widely admired as an administrator. Georgia was on the threshold of a decade of remarkable growth, but she was also on the threshold of a period of political and constitutional turmoil. In this ten-year span Georgians found new leaders to follow and new principles to expound. Where, in 1763, the people of the province considered themselves loyal subjects of the crown, by 1775 they thought themselves Americans who only voluntarily rendered their allegiance to George III. Soon even that fragile cord would break as the colonies declared their independence.

The decade of troubles started innocently enough in 1764 with Parliament's passage of the Sugar Act, the first piece of legislation that was intended to raise revenue in America. Though there were protests from New England, where the act was denounced as a tax, the Sugar Act caused little excitement in Georgia. William Knox, Georgia's agent in England, was instructed to join in the protests of the other colonies, but the merchants were more concerned that the Sugar Act might endanger Georgia's lumber trade with the Caribbean islands than with abstract theories of taxation and representation.

At first it appeared that even the Stamp Act of 1765 might be accepted in Georgia with a minimum of grumbling. When the invitation to attend the Stamp Act Congress in New York arrived, the legislature was not in session, so the colony was not represented at that gathering. On the last day of October, the day before the Stamp Act was to go into effect, an effigy of a stamp master was hanged and burned in Savannah. This event marked the first appearance in Georgia—though hardly the last—of the Savannah mob. Governor Wright and James Habersham, president of the council, looked upon such developments with foreboding and hoped to prevent further disorders in the streets, but only a few days later a sailor, impersonating a stamp master, was "hanged" in front of a delighted throng at Machenry's tavern. At the same tavern on the next day, the Sons of Liberty met and resolved to let any stamp master who might enter Georgia know that he was not welcome. This date, 6 November 1765, marked the first appearance in Georgia of the Sons of Liberty, an organization that had originated elsewhere to oppose the Stamp Act and force the resignations of the stamp masters.

Governor Wright was in a quandary. After 1 November, if he followed the letter of the law, most forms of business could not be carried on without use of stamped paper, but in Georgia there was neither master nor stamps. Should transactions requiring stamps be allowed to continue in spite of the Stamp Act? Wright was a stickler for the law, but he had no intention of letting affairs stagnate, thereby affording his opponents a chance to assume power. Ships were permitted to clear with certificates attesting that no stamps were available. Finally on 5 December the stamps arrived, but still no master; half-filled boats began to clog the harbor. The year's rice crop was being brought to town and the longer the delay the more concerned the merchants and planters became. Fearing that Wright would appoint a temporary stamp master, the Liberty Boys marched to the governor's house. He approached them, musket in hand, and asked what such effrontery meant. They said they wanted assurances that Wright would appoint no interim master; he replied that he would do what he had to do. The next day, 3 January 1766, George Angus, the stamp master, arrived in Savannah.

With support from mercantile and planter interests, and bolstered by rangers he had called into town from outlying areas, Wright re-

The fort on Cockspur Island at the mouth of the Savannah River, 1764

opened the port and cleared approximately sixty ships with stamped paper. This is the only known instance of stamps' being sold in any of the thirteen colonies that later rebelled. But after clearing the ships it appears that Wright, the royal officials, the merchants, and the Sons of Liberty tacitly agreed that no more stamps would be used pending the outcome of moves in Parliament to repeal the act. Threats to destroy the stamps led Wright to send them to Fort George on Cockspur Island for safekeeping.

Wright's troubles were not over. South Carolina expressed her dismay at the sale of stamps in Georgia and roundly denounced the colony. There were hints of invasion on the part of the Carolinians who wished to give Savannah a demonstration of how to safeguard American rights. These "Incendiaries from Charles Town" were successful in rousing considerable support in the backcountry and at the end of January Wright awaited the coming of what he called a rabble army estimated at as many as seven hundred men.

Wright had safeguarded the stamps, a symbol of royal authority, but by so doing he left Savannah open for attack. The timely arrival of HMS *Speedwell*, where Wright sent the stamps on 2 February 1766, released the troops on Cockspur for duty in town. After considerable hesitation, the "army" of Carolinians and Georgians entered Savannah on 4 February, but they came as an already beaten group. Wright had secured the stamps and had armed soldiers and sailors to back up his authority. The dissidents, obviously lacking a leader, began to quarrel and dispersed after a few hours.

Wright, Habersham, and their friends were relieved. The crisis was over, but nothing in Georgia was ever quite the same after the Stamp Act. Even its repeal in the spring of 1766 could not erase the memories of attempted intimidation and Liberty Boys in the streets. In Georgia, the Liberty Boys were not successful, but they had given Governor Wright a scare from which he was never fully to recover. Only by adroit handling of the situation had he averted a breakdown of royal authority.

After a calm and peaceful year, confusion and protest broke out again in 1767 upon passage of the Townshend Acts. These acts included efforts to raise an American revenue through import duties on a list of commodities including tea. Massachusetts took the lead in objecting to these measures and sent out a circular letter suggesting united opposition on the question of Parliament's right to tax Americans. Wright told the Commons House that if it considered the circular he would have no choice but to dissolve it. Little daunted, the house did exactly that and was dismissed in late December 1768.

It was not until well into September 1769 that organized opposition to the Townshend Acts, with Savannah merchants in the lead, began to jell in Georgia. Two mass meetings suggested boycotts of British goods and declared the legislation unconstitutional, but there was no further action. Once again, the suspicions of the more radical Carolinians were aroused, and Charles Town voted to boycott Georgia because of its continued trade with Great Britain. By the time the assembly met again, in October 1770, all the duties, save the one on tea, had been repealed.

One sign of increasing unrest in the colony was the frequent contention between the Commons House and Wright. Where in years past the two had seen eye-to-eye, the Stamp Act and later events soured the relationship. After 1765 the Upper House fell out with the Commons House on the question of Georgia's colonial agent, William Knox, who published a pamphlet in favor of Parliament's right to tax the colonies. He was dismissed, but the two houses could not agree on a successor until 1768 when Benjamin Franklin was chosen.

The Commons House in 1769 demanded that Wright allow representation to the new parishes south of the Altamaha. This he said he could not do without permission from London, which he had requested. The house disputed his claim and exempted the new parishes from the year's tax bill. The argument continued in 1770 but was resolved when the home government gave permission to grant the new parishes representation. Though the incident was closed, the result was more strained relations between Wright and the legislators.

It was the issue of Wright's veto of the house's choice for speaker, though, that caused the bitterest recriminations between the executive and legislative branches. In April 1771 the Commons House elected Noble Wimberley Jones speaker, but he was rejected by Wright, undoubtedly because Jones had become one of the colony's radical leaders. The Commons House then selected Archibald Bulloch but made it clear that the veto exercised in the case of Jones was not to be considered a precedent. Wright, who indignantly cited his instructions from the king, dissolved the assembly.

While the governor was in England for eighteen months between 1771 and 1773, James Habersham, president of the council and friend and associate of Wright, was designated acting governor. Twice in the spring of 1772 Habersham rejected Jones for speaker, but at his third election Jones declined the honor. At that point the house once again chose Bulloch but refused to expunge the record of Jones's election from its minutes, whereupon Habersham dissolved the assembly. The issue had become a question of some constitutional significance, and

James Oglethorpe

James Habersham

Sir James Wright, Royal Governor

Noble W. Jones

Reverend John J. Zubly issued a pamphlet attacking the veto power. In December 1772 William Young was elected speaker, and though the confrontation appeared to be resolved as a victory for the executive, the cumulative effect was more animosity.

England and the colonies teetered on the brink of an abyss in 1773, though neither seemed aware of it. The preceding several years had been relatively calm, and it seemed far-fetched to think that mother country and colonies could not get along indefinitely. Georgians of all political hues could welcome Wright home and take pride in the fact that his distinguished service had been recognized by the baronetcy that had been granted him. The governor himself, tempered by the problems of empire, seemed to sense danger. He was aware that there were injustices in the system and he constantly urged London to correct them. But to Wright a law or a proclamation, no matter how ill-considered, must be obeyed. Though he probably questioned the wisdom of the Stamp Act, he felt that proper channels should be used to secure its repeal. Wright was not indifferent to the American position, but he subordinated it to his instructions from the king. As the revolutionary movement developed it became increasingly difficult to reconcile the English and American viewpoints. Wright, who certainly considered himself an "American," just as Thomas Hutchinson did in Massachusetts, knew that Britain would have to reach some sort of lasting constitutional agreement with the colonists before amicable relations could be restored.

The last scene in the colonial drama began with the Tea Act of 1773 followed by a whole series of "tea parties" up and down the coast, the most famous of which was Boston's. Charles Town had its party too, but Savannah had no tea assigned to it, hence it had no opportunity to demonstrate its feelings so clearly. England's harsh reaction to the affair in Boston—legislation usually called in America the Intolerable Acts—caused outrage in Georgia as it did elsewhere.

An August 1774 meeting in Savannah, where all parishes were represented, produced a series of statements and positions that put Georgia more in focus in relation to the other American colonies. Still, the resolutions adopted were far from radical or extreme, concentrating as they did upon the constitutional relationship between mother country and colonies. The meeting scored the efforts to subvert the old privileges and rights of Englishmen and called for redress, but then rejected the idea of sending delegates to the first Continental Congress in Philadelphia. The Congregationalists from the Midway district showed their disgust at this failure; a meeting in Midway designated Lyman Hall to represent St. John's Parish at Philadelphia, but Hall did not attend so Georgia was not heard from at the first Congress.

In an effort to reverse this drift toward radicalism, Wright and his allies encouraged counterpetitions to the Savannah meeting. The governor had little success; the situation was getting out of hand. The committee of the August meeting recommended a provincial congress to convene in January 1775, concurrently with the assembly. A St. John's Parish gathering of December 1774 adopted the Continental Association (a boycott of British trade recommended by the Continental Congress). Other parishes should do likewise, St. John's suggested, before going to the provincial congress in January. Early in the new year, a meeting in Darien enthusiastically adopted the Association. These fiery Scots also denounced quitrents, England's disallowance of colonial laws, and slavery, all of which they pledged to work against.

The Georgia assembly convened in Savannah on 17 January 1775 and the provincial congress the following day. There was a disappointing showing at the congress, with only five of the twelve parishes sending representatives. (St. John's refused to participate because several parishes represented had not adopted the Continental Association.) The congress proved to be moderate in tone but was badly divided from the start. Christ Church (Savannah) appears to have dominated the proceedings. When the congress named representatives to attend the second Continental Congress, all three were from that parish: Archibald Bulloch, Noble W. Jones, and John Houstoun. The Continental Association was adopted with reservations. Since the congress could not speak for all of Georgia, there seemed little more to do so it adjourned hoping that the Commons House would approve what it had done.

Apparently at least six members of the congress were also representatives in the Commons House. Wright's opening address was a model of decorum and reason. In it can be seen Wright's personal beliefs and his agony at the throes Georgia was going through. The speech was an eloquent appeal for clear thought and moderation and showed Wright searching for a middle ground upon which all Georgians, hence all Americans, could stand. He cautioned the Commons House to consider "the terrible consequences" of adopting measures that might fly in the face of England and warned that the rule of law was indispensable to the enjoyment of liberty.

Believe me, when I tell you I am at this time actuated by further motives than a show only of discharging my duty as the King's governor. I have lived amongst and presided over you upwards of fourteen years, and have other feelings. I have a real and affectionate regard for the people, and it grieves me that a Province that I have been so long in, and which I have seen nurtured by the Crown, . . . and grew up from mere infancy . . . should, by the imprudence and rashness of some inconsiderate people, be plunged into a state of distress and ruin.

Wright was not sure that he had the strength to block ratification by the Commons House of what the provincial congress had done. Although the Upper House still supported the governor and he had a following in the Commons House, Wright adjourned the assembly on 10 February before it could act.

St. John's Parish was disgusted with both groups. Believing that the congress was weak-kneed and that the assembly was worse, St. John's opened negotiations for annexation by South Carolina. The Charles Town leaders made it clear that annexation was impractical. So the parish again named Lyman Hall its representative, this time to the second Continental Congress. Hall attended and took along with him over one hundred and fifty barrels of rice and £50 for the relief of the poor in Massachusetts. Though he was received and admitted by Congress in May 1775, he did not vote because he did not represent the entire colony.

Throughout the spring of 1775 the power of the royal officials was slowly drained away. Wright discovered that his dispatches were being opened in Charles Town with forgeries being sent on in his name. In effect he was being isolated from England and the support of other loyal officials in the empire. In May the Commons House ignored Wright's call to meet in Savannah. His authority, once unquestioned, was now openly flouted.

It may well be that the news of Lexington and Concord, which reached Savannah on 10 May, marked the turning point toward the complete collapse of royal authority. Savannah was much agitated by the news, and on 11 May a meeting was held at Noble W. Jones's house to discuss Georgia's position. The upshot was that Jones, Joseph Habersham (both of whose fathers were on the council and were warm friends of Wright), and others broke into the royal magazine and made off with about six hundred pounds of powder. A reward offered by the council for information as to the identity of the culprits had no takers. Habersham, Jones, and their friends had challenged the royal government and had succeeded.

An additional insult to royal authority came just a few weeks later, on 2 June, when the guns at the Savannah battery were spiked so they would be unable to salute the king's official birthday two days later. The determined Wright, however, put some of the cannon back in working order so that they were fired and toasts were drunk to George III as had been the custom in the past.

The following night, 5 June, saw Savannah divided into hostile camps as Wright gave a banquet in honor of the monarch. At the same time, Joseph Habersham and others collected a mob that went from Peter Tondee's tavern to inspect some "tories" who had recently come to town. Wielding clubs and guns the crowd paraded through the streets making a great clatter. A liberty pole—Georgia's first—was erected in the public square near the courthouse so that Wright's guests could see as well as hear what was transpiring.

This incident was revealing. Royal government still existed in Savannah, but it was powerless to impose its will on Georgia's citizens. Already Wright had begun to turn his thoughts to England; there seemed nothing he could do in Georgia. The use of the mob to terrorize the king's friends made it apparent to Wright that his usefulness was at an end.

This fact was brought home to him at the end of June when the public storehouse was broken into and shot and guns were taken by the same group of radicals. It was all done openly and as though there were no longer a governor. In Sunbury, too, royal authority was ignored. When a ship bearing illegal cargo was seized by the customs officials a group of local people convened at the liberty pole, intimidated the king's officers, and freed the vessel. There were examples in other parishes of the courts' being interfered with and royal officials overawed. The whole colony was dividing into warring camps.

Throughout June there were meetings of the various factions in Savannah, some attempting to compromise differences of opinions between the revolutionists and others aiming to push the course of revolution still further. Committees were set up to maintain law and order and to assume control of the situation now that royal government was a cipher. Gradually a group of prominent radicals emerged from the confusion and called for a new provincial congress.

On 22 June Savannah delegates were named for this congress, to meet on 4 July 1775. A Council for Safety was created to oversee the enforcement of boycotts and seek possible solutions for the crisis between Georgia and Britain. William Ewen was chosen president of the council with Seth John Cuthbert as secretary. Other members included Joseph Habersham and his first cousin, Joseph Clay, Edward Telfair, George Walton, John Glen, Francis H. Harris, John Morel, William

LeConte, George Houstoun, William Young, John Smith, Samuel Elbert, and Basil Cowper.

Though reconciliation between mother country and Georgia was
still a possibility, it became more remote as the province drifted into
the radical camp in June and July. The Council for Safety, in the
absence of an effective legislature and executive, assumed powers and
prerogatives that only the governor and the assembly dared exercise
in earlier days. The Liberty Boy mobs were being transformed into
protectors of the rights of Georgians as well as military defenders of
Georgia. Leadership was now coming primarily from Savannah and
included many members of the mercantile class. Joseph Habersham
was perhaps the single most prominent figure at this time. Certainly he
was instrumental in fitting out a Georgia schooner which, acting with
a Carolina boat, waylaid the *Philippa,* laden with gunpowder, at the
mouth of the Savannah River. The *Philippa* noted a red-bordered
white flag with the words "American Liberty" written thereon flying
from the schooner's mast. The ship was taken to Cockspur Island
where Habersham and his party removed six tons of gunpowder and
seven hundred pounds of bullets. Wright had gloomily predicted this
would happen; there was no way he could prevent it.

For many reasons Georgia had lagged behind the rest of the rebel-
lious American colonies. She was younger and poorer than the other
provinces, was more in need of protection from England because of
her exposed frontiers, and had as chief executive an exceedingly able
man who knew his province intimately and had been in his post for
fifteen years. Georgia had reached a degree of maturity by mid-1775
largely because of the wise handling of provincial affairs by Governor
Wright. It was also because of Wright's far-sighted policies that it was
feasible for the colony's second provincial congress to gather on 4 July
1775. This group would consider constitutional and political issues of
the first magnitude—issues that would determine the course Georgia
would follow in the future. From Wright's point of view he had done
his job too well, for his policies had helped prepare Georgia for revolution. And for himself, there was only exile.

PART TWO

1775–1820

by

KENNETH COLEMAN

The Great Seal of the State, 1777 to 1798

The Great Seal from 1799 to 1863

VII

Georgia in the American Revolution
1775–1782

The more radical American rights group, now beginning to be called Whigs, moved throughout the first half of 1775 to increase opposition to Britain. By June Governor Wright was sure that he could no longer control happenings in Georgia.

A second provincial congress, representing all of Georgia's twelve parishes except two small ones south of the Altamaha, met in Savannah on 4 July. This body was the first to take positive political action rather than only to enunciate political principles and colonial rights. Christ Church and St. John's parishes largely dominated this Whiggish body. After organization, the congress heard the Reverend John J. Zubly, one of its members, preach a special sermon entitled "The Law of Liberty" in which he clearly applied the ideas of Locke to religion, as many clergymen were then doing in America. Zubly urged Americans not to lose sight of their glorious connection with Britain; American rights within the empire was Zubly's solution to the current problems.

Zubly drew up and the congress adopted a petition to the king phrased in much bolder language than had been used previously in Georgia. The petition urged George III to recall his armies and fleets and to insure justice to Americans if he wished to command their fortunes and loyalty. On 10 July the congress expressed its ideas about the unhappy state of affairs in America in a set of nineteen resolutions that declared the colonies subject to the king but not to Parliament and set forth the same ideas about American rights within the empire promulgated in many documents already adopted in the other colonies.

The congress created a council of safety and gave it full power to act during the recesses of the congress. Additionally, the congress fixed the size and election of future congresses and declared all who paid toward the general tax eligible to vote. It provided for the raising of £10,000 for necessary expenses. The Continental Congress was informed that the colony was now fully incorporated with its sister colonies and would bear its proportionate share of the expenses of defending American rights. This congress took Georgia into rebellion and became her first revolutionary government.

After the adoption of the Continental Association by the provincial congress, there was an all-out attempt to get it signed by individuals and enforced. Local parochial committees differed in their interpretations and actions. Many Georgians favored the export of the colony's products. Because it was hard to police a sparsely inhabited coastline like Georgia's, much agricultural produce must have been exported.

Throughout the last half of 1775 the Whig revolutionary government took over more powers from the royal government. Governor Wright and his council could do little but object to Whig actions. By September Wright said that the power of his government was gone. The assembly did not meet, and the general court held no session as the assistant judges refused to act. Meetings of justice of the peace courts depended upon the local situation. Some militia units replaced Tory officers with Whigs. Revolutionary government operated through the provincial congress, the council of safety, and the various parochial committees, with no clear line of demarcation between their powers. These bodies did what they thought needed to be done and could be accomplished, with no real check on their powers except public opinion.

Georgia Whigs, like those elsewhere, often used strong methods of persuasion to convince people doubtful of British tyranny. There were several cases of tarring and feathering, and threats of more. The two most famous cases were John Hopkins, a mariner, in Savannah on 24 July 1775, for loose talk against American liberty, and Thomas Brown in Augusta. Brown would take ample revenge later. By such rabid Whig action, some neutrals were undoubtedly made Tories.

Another Georgia problem was the Creek Indians on the frontier. Indian Superintendent John Stuart, an able official trusted by the Creeks, was suspected by Georgia and South Carolina Whigs because of his loyalty to the crown. There was great fear that Stuart would influence the Creeks to attack the Whigs. Stuart defended himself against such accusations before he left for the safety of St. Augustine. He opposed Indian raids upon the frontier, regardless of orders from London. One way to maintain Indian peace was to see that the Indians received their accustomed amount of munitions and other trade goods. Whigs were hard put to find the necessities for the Indian trade. In July and September Georgia and South Carolina Whigs captured ships bringing gunpower for the Indians, but gave them only a part of the powder. Whigs tried to deal with the Creeks through Augusta Indian traders, but a shortage of presents and trade goods and Stuart's reputation among the Creeks worked against the Whigs.

Actual combat began in Georgia in early 1776. In mid-January the British navy, hoping to purchase provisions, sent vessels to the mouth of the Savannah River. Governor Wright urged the Whigs to cooperate; instead the council of safety arrested Wright and other royal officials. In February additional vessels and two hundred troops arrived, and Wright and several of his councilors broke their paroles and boarded HMS *Scarborough* at Cockspur Island.

The British wished to obtain several vessels loaded with rice anchored above Savannah. Two to five hundred Georgia militia and perhaps a hundred South Carolinians gathered to defend the town and harbor. On the night of 2 March British troops landed on Hutchinson's Island, opposite Savannah, and boarded the rice vessels anchored above the island. The next day Whigs sent to unrig the vessels were surprised and detained by the British on the vessels. Whig forces on the bluff in Savannah, finding the vessels out of artillery range, sent down a fire ship that burned three or four of the rice vessels. The rest, containing some sixteen hundred barrels of rice, sailed down the back river, on the South Carolina side of Hutchinson's Island, a channel the Savannah Whigs had thought too shallow to be used. Prisoners were released by both sides, and the British sailed away with Wright and most of the royal officials still loyal to the crown. Royal government thus ended in Georgia.

The departure of Governor Wright and the collapse of royal government put Georgia fully into the rebel camp. In retrospect, Georgia's participation in the revolt seems almost inevitable. Georgians were Americans and had become more conscious of this as the differences with Britain widened. Initially the leaders of the revolt came from the younger and not so wealthy Savannahians, from St. John's Parish, and from the Scots in St. Andrew's Parish. Leading opponents of rebellion, the original Tories, tended to be officeholders and Anglican clergymen, wealthy and leading Savannahians, most of the Indian traders, recent immigrants from Britain, and a number of Germans from Ebenezer and Quakers from Wrightsborough. Many Georgians, like the Germans and Quakers, did not want to take sides and thereby gave the impression of being more loyal to Britain than they were. In the end, events forced most people to take sides. While Georgia had a number of Tories, there were always more Whigs and neutrals.

The collapse of royal government also speeded the regularization of the new revolutionary government. On 15 April 1776 the provincial congress issued Georgia's first temporary constitution, the Rules and Regulations of 1776, which created a government of the usual three departments. The provincial congress, a one-house legislature, dominated the government and elected the plural executive consisting of a president and a council of safety. The court structure remained essentially that of the colonial period. All current laws continued in effect unless they conflicted with actions of the Continental or provincial congresses. The Rules and Regulations was a simple document of thirteen brief paragraphs containing only the broadest outline of the government. It voiced standard Whig doctrine by stating that governmental power originated with the people and that governments existed for their benefits. Completing the separation from England, the provincial congress stated on 12 June that henceforth governmental authority rested in the province instead of the king, and on 2 July 1776 the Continental Congress declared independence.

When the Rules and Regulations became operational on 1 May 1776, the provincial congress selected Archibald Bulloch, an early leader of the revolutionary movement in Georgia, as the president and commander-in-chief. A capable executive, he served until his mysterious death late in February 1777. His successor, Button Gwinnett, served until a new state constitution went into effect in May. There was no clear delineation of powers between the provincial congress and the president and council of safety under the Rules and Regulations, although the provincial congress dominated when it was in session.

Although Georgians joined the movement for independence belatedly, most of them worked for independence by the spring of 1776. In April the provincial congress instructed its Continental delegates to work for the welfare of all the colonies. Georgia's three delegates—Button Gwinnett, George Walton, and Lyman Hall—voted for independence when the decision was made in July. On 8 August President Bulloch read the Declaration of Independence to the council of safety. Two days later in Savannah there were several public readings, a public dinner with toasts to the "United, Free, and Independent States of America," and a mock funeral procession and the "interment" of George III before the courthouse. Similar but unrecorded celebrations probably occurred elsewhere in Georgia.

In the late summer of 1776 efforts to create a more permanent state government began. These culminated when the provincial congress adopted a new constitution on 5 February 1777. This document declared the legislative, executive, and judicial departments separate and distinct but gave most power to the legislative. Representation was fairly proportional, and all white males twenty-one years of age who owned property worth £10 or who followed a mechanic trade were eligible to vote. People qualified who did not vote were subject to a fine of not over £5, but there is no evidence that this provision was ever enforced. Legislative power resided in the unicameral House of Assembly, which annually elected the governor, his council, and other state officials. The governor and council, acting together, called the executive, carried on ordinary executive duties, but could not grant pardons, remit fines, or veto legislation. The governor could hold office but one year out of three. A superior court, the ordinary trial court, was created for each county and consisted of the chief justice, who presided over all superior court sessions in rotation, and three or more assistant justices, who resided in the county. Justice of the peace courts continued as before. Juries, being the judge of both fact and law, possessed more than ordinary powers.

Eight counties—Wilkes, Richmond, Burke, Effingham, Chatham, Liberty, Glynn, and Camden—replaced the old parishes and gave the voters more direct control of local government. The assembly elected those county officials—sheriffs, tax collectors, justices of the peace, etc.—who performed state functions. The constitution required that state-supported schools be created in each county. Various safeguards for individual and political rights indicated economic and social gains of a democratic nature. The constitution prohibited the entail of estates and provided for a more equal division of property among heirs. Provisions for the free exercise of religion and the prohibition against forcing anyone to support a religious denomination except his own disestablished the Church of England as the state religion. Further the constitution guaranteed freedom of the press, trial by jury, and the principles of the habeas corpus act, and forbade excessive fines or bail.

A hallmark of this constitution was simplicity of style, brevity, and restriction to fundamentals. Most of it could be understood easily by a layman. The political philosophy behind the document was that of the eighteenth-century Whigs—natural rights, separation of powers, government by the consent of the governed, and guarantees of citizens against arbitrary government. When this constitution was written, Georgia's conservatives had been effectively silenced. Thus the document was more radical than those of some other states where conservatives were still powerful. The old order had been overthrown, and the common man became more influential in government than ever before.

This was the great revolutionary victory of the more radical Whigs, who were ready to profit from it.

Conservatives were soon complaining about this constitution and of the type of people in control of Georgia's government, which one said "is so very Democratical & has thrown power into such Hands as must ruin the Country if not timely prevented by some alteration of it." Yet, the change in political leadership was more apparent than real. The old upper-class leaders were only partially replaced and some would reassert themselves during and after the war.

From the summer of 1776 through 1778, Whigs controlled Georgia's government. Many loyalists moved to Florida where they harrassed Georgia as members of a partisan military unit known as the Florida Rangers, commanded by Thomas Brown. When the new constitution went into effect in May 1777, it made little difference in the operation of Georgia's government. Agitation for the control and expulsion of the loyalists usually lessened as soon as the immediate incident passed, and Georgia was one of the last states to enact legislation against loyalists. In the fall of 1777 many were expelled; and in March 1778 a confiscation and banishment act declared 177 loyalists guilty of high treason, banished them from the state, and confiscated their property. The hopes of immediately securing considerable state income from the sale of confiscated property were largely unfulfilled.

In reality, during this period Whigs spent more time fighting other Whigs than they did Tories. Once the loyalists had left or been silenced, the Whigs soon fell to fighting among themselves. The two major groups came to be the country or radical faction, and the town or more conservative faction. Perhaps the division began with the election of the officers of the Georgia Continental Battalion in January 1776, but it was not obvious that early. Lachlan McIntosh, a Darien Scot and a leader of the conservatives, became colonel and later brigadier general. Radical Button Gwinnett had hoped for this position, and he and McIntosh never got along well thereafter. Gwinnett became president under the Rules and Regulations in February 1777, and this put him in a strategic position to oppose McIntosh.

About mid-March 1777 McIntosh's brother, George, accused of cooperating with British sympathizers and roughly treated by the Gwinnett government, added to the McIntosh-Gwinnett animosity. The unsuccessful 1777 expedition against East Florida increased this bitterness. When the assembly approved Gwinnett's actions in the campaign, McIntosh called Gwinnett "A Scoundrell & lying Rascal" before the assembly. Gwinnett challenged McIntosh to a duel, in which both men were wounded. Gwinnett died three days later. Feelings ran high, and after considerable delay McIntosh was tried and acquitted. However, he soon left the state for reassignment by General Washington.

Another cause of excitement in early 1777 was the suggestion that Georgia and South Carolina unite. William Henry Drayton presented this proposal to the Georgia assembly in January and tried to convince Georgians of how much better off they would be as a part of South Carolina. Few Georgians agreed, so nothing came of the proposal except intemperate letters by Drayton and an offer by Governor John Adam Treutlen in July of a £100 reward for the arrest of Drayton.

On 4 November 1775 the Continental Congress authorized Georgia's first revolutionary troops. The Georgia provincial congress elected Lachlan McIntosh, colonel; Samuel Elbert, lieutenant colonel; and Joseph Habersham, major. These troops might be enlisted in Georgia, the Carolinas, and Virginia. Georgia had possibly twenty-five hundred to four thousand men available for military duty, but if more than half of them were taken at once, there was danger that the economy would deteriorate badly. In February 1776 the Continental Congress created the Continental Southern Military Department—Georgia, the Carolinas, and Virginia—commanded initially by Major General Charles Lee. Neither Lee, the Continental Congress, nor Georgia could provide the men and supplies needed for the frontier state, and Georgia's defenses languished. In the summer of 1776 the Continental Congress authorized Georgia to raise two more battalions of foot, a regiment of rangers, two companies of artillery, and four row galleys for coastal defense. In the fall another battalion was authorized. Recruiting for all these could take place as far north as Pennsylvania. Actual enlistments came from all these states and included a very few blacks. The acquisition of arms and munitions, food, and other military supplies was difficult. Some munitions came from the West Indies, apparently from British and Dutch islands. Thomas Young secured clothing for Georgia troops in the West Indies and food for the British West Indian islands in Georgia. By the fall of 1776 the state collected foodstuffs in south Georgia and removed cattle from the sea islands to keep them out of British hands.

As early as the fall of 1775 talk began of capturing St. Augustine with its British garrison of about one hundred and fifty men and Tory refugees from the southern colonies. East Florida needed more food with the increasing number of refugees, and the Florida Rangers stole much of this food from south Georgia. On 1 January 1776 the Continental Congress recommended to the Carolinas and Georgia that they capture St. Augustine, by then reinforced with additional British troops. By August General Lee planned an expedition to destroy the settlements along the St. Johns River, and General McIntosh and Georgia Continental troops broke up these settlements. Lee thought this was all that could be accomplished, but Georgians insisted on a serious attempt to capture St. Augustine. In September some American troops got as far as the St. Johns, but most never got out of Georgia. Once the expedition ended, cattle-stealing raids from Florida resumed.

Almost as soon as the 1776 expedition was over, planning for the 1777 one began. General Robert Howe, the new Continental commander, conferred with President Gwinnett and the council of safety in March. Georgia had only four hundred troops available but her leaders insisted that Howe should furnish enough to capture St. Augustine, something that Howe was sure he could not do. Gwinnett planned his campaign without consulting either McIntosh or Howe. Militia and Continental troops reached Sunbury by mid-April where the council of safety prevailed upon Gwinnett and McIntosh, who could agree on nothing, to return to Savannah and leave active command to Colonel Samuel Elbert. The militia arrived at the St. Johns before the Continentals and fought British regulars and Florida Rangers before returning northward. The Continentals found that their boats could not get through Amelia Narrows, just below the St. Marys River, hence on 26 May Elbert decided to abandon the expedition. Raids from East Florida resumed at once.

The new year had hardly arrived when Georgians began planning another St. Augustine expedition. Howe and Georgia officials differed over the possibilities of capturing St. Augustine, and the Georgia governor and council offered 500 acres of East Florida land to anyone who could operate between the St. Marys and St. Johns rivers for three months. By the end of April about two thousand Whig troops were ready: Continentals under Howe, Georgia militia under Governor John Houstoun, South Carolina militia under Colonel Andrew Williamson, and the Georgia navy under Commodore Oliver Bowen. Howe and Houstoun immediately differed over which should command, and Bowen refused to take orders from either since it was not clear if this navy was Continental or state. When the expedition reached the St. Marys at the end of June, the Florida Rangers retreated. Howe now decided that no more could be accomplished and started north. Houstoun and Williamson wanted to continue operations but decided they could not do so alone.

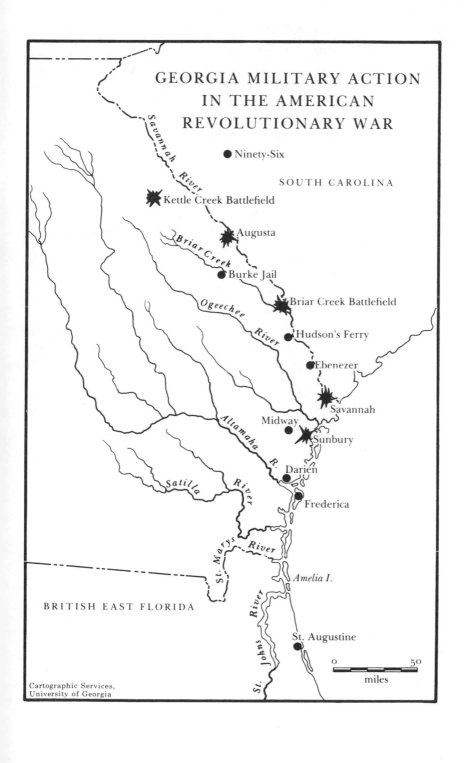

GEORGIA MILITARY ACTION
IN THE AMERICAN
REVOLUTIONARY WAR

● Ninety-Six

SOUTH CAROLINA

Savannah River

✷ Kettle Creek Battlefield

✷ Augusta

Briar Creek

● Burke Jail

Ogeechee River

✷ Briar Creek Battlefield

● Hudson's Ferry

● Ebenezer

✷ Savannah

Midway ●

✷ Sunbury

Altamaha R.

● Darien

Satilla River

● Frederica

St. Marys River

Amelia I.

St. Johns River

BRITISH EAST FLORIDA

St. Augustine ●

0   50
━━━━━━━━━━
miles

Cartographic Services,
University of Georgia

Thus ended the third and last attempt to capture St. Augustine. This last expedition was the largest and had the best chance of the three for success. In each expedition, hot weather, inadequate transportation and supplies, sickness, and Indian troubles on the Georgia frontier were blamed for failure. But the greatest problem was the inability of the commanders to cooperate with each other. These expeditions were Georgia's major military effort in the first three years of the war, and they accomplished nothing. Both British and Whig military leaders opposed any actions, and it was always the civilian officials who insisted upon the expeditions. Perhaps Governor Patrick Tonyn's Florida Rangers were the key to British success. This unit was composed of Tories who knew well what they were fighting for and who fought or raided whenever there was any chance of success.

Besides the attempts to capture St. Augustine, Georgia's greatest military problem was the Creek Indians. Initially the British had the advantage, but they had no troops in Georgia with whom the Creeks would cooperate. George Galphin, an important Indian trader, became a Continental Indian commissioner and was always able to find Whig adherents among the Creeks. In fact, the Creeks returned to their earlier policy of playing one group of whites against the other to their own advantage.

Soon both Indians and whites would find it easier to choose between the British and the Whigs in Georgia. Immediately after their return to Britain, Governor Wright and Governor Lord William Campbell of South Carolina began insisting on the recapture of their colonies. After the British failure at Saratoga in the fall of 1777, the ministry instructed the new commander-in-chief in America, Sir Henry Clinton, to consider the recapture of South Carolina and Georgia. Clinton decided to proceed against Savannah in the winter of 1778, hoping to get loyalist and Indian reinforcements from the backcountry before he tried to capture Charles Town. An expedition of twenty-five to thirty-five hundred troops was organized in New York under the command of Lieutenant Colonel Archibald Campbell, and General Augustine Prevost in St. Augustine was directed to cooperate with Campbell. The British planned to reinstate civilian government in Georgia and leave any punishment of rebels to this government. The recapture of Georgia and the reinstitution of civilian government there, it was hoped, would encourage similar action in other colonies, which the British also hoped to recapture.

In late November 1778 Prevost sent two expeditions into Georgia to cooperate with Campbell, who did not arrive on schedule. Hence these expeditions returned to Florida having achieved nothing. After repeated delays the New York expedition arrived off Tybee Island on 23 December 1778. With a local guide, the troops marched into Savannah unopposed on 29 December and captured the city before most Whigs realized what was happening. General Robert Howe, Governor John Houstoun, and Colonel George Walton of the Georgia militia did not coordinate their defenses, and each tried to blame the other once the town had fallen. Had the British been delayed a few days, troops from South Carolina might have reached Savannah in time to effect a different outcome. The Whigs suffered 450 captured and 100 killed or drowned in the swamps trying to escape. British losses were reported at 7 killed and 19 wounded.

On 14 January 1779 the British invited Georgians to take an oath of loyalty to the king and receive full pardon for past disloyalty. General Prevost returned to Georgia, and Campbell proceeded to Augusta to be the first British officer "to take a stripe and star from the rebel flag of Congress," as he phrased it. He arrived on 31 January and scoured the countryside for sixty miles around to make his presence known. About fourteen hundred men submitted, took the oath of loyalty to the king, and allowed themselves to be formed into royal militia units.

Once the shock of the capture of Savannah wore off, Whigs considered what they could do to counteract it. Many collected at the Burke County jail and in backcountry Wilkes County, and by mid-February it was obvious that all of upcountry Georgia had not submitted. The anticipated help from loyalists and Indians did not materialize when Campbell arrived in Augusta. Governors Wright and Campbell had overestimated the number of backcountry loyalists, and Superintendent Stuart had not been informed of the invasion in time to raise Indians to cooperate. Soon after Campbell reached Augusta, General John Ashe arrived opposite the town with twelve hundred North Carolina Whig troops, and Campbell discovered that his newly formed militia was of extremely doubtful loyalty. Hence on 14 February he abandoned Augusta and took station at Hudson's Ferry, about twenty-four miles above Ebenezer. The same day Whig militia under Colonels Andrew Pickens, John Dooly, and Elijah Clarke surprised about seven hundred Tories under Colonel John Boyd at Kettle Creek, in Wilkes County. Boyd and many of his followers were killed, and this ended the effort to raise Tories in the upcountry. Throughout February, General Benjamin Lincoln, the new Continental commander in the South, pushed the collection of troops to oppose the British.

On 3 March General Ashe was surprised and defeated by Lieutenant Colonel James Mark Prevost at the confluence of Briar Creek with the Savannah River. This ended Lincoln's action against the British for the time being.

On the same day that Prevost defeated Ashe at Briar Creek he was made lieutenant governor of Georgia in the reinstituted colonial government. Governor Wright, Lieutenant Governor John Graham, and Chief Justice Anthony Stokes returned to Savannah in July and resumed their old duties. Wright delayed calling an assembly because he correctly believed that many who had taken the oath to the king did so from expediency. Wright thought more troops were necessary to insure the loyalty of many Georgians, but these troops he never got.

The capture of Savannah prevented the newly elected state assembly from meeting. An attempt to convene it at Augusta in early January 1779 brought only representatives from Wilkes, Richmond, and Burke counties—inadequate for a quorum. This meeting elected an executive council to keep a government in operation. It had to abandon Augusta when Campbell arrived later in January, but it returned in February.

Whig attempts to regularize further their state government resulted in the meeting in Augusta on 24 July of a body calling itself "the Representatives of the Counties of Wilkes, Richmond, Burke, Effingham, Chatham, Liberty, Glynn, and Camden and other free men of the State." This meeting never claimed any legal authority for itself but created a Supreme Executive Council to which it gave full executive powers, subject to the approval of the people, in an effort to keep the government as close as possible to the constitution. John Wereat became the president of this council and the chief executive of the state government, which operated in Wilkes and Richmond counties.

Thus in the spring and summer of 1779 Georgia was divided between Whigs and Tories. Tories controlled the area of twenty-five to forty miles around Savannah, while the Whigs held the upcountry and part of the lower coast. Neither side had enough strength to mount a serious offensive, but each raided the area of the other. In the upcountry, South Carolina and Georgia Whigs cooperated fully. By the end of April, General Lincoln felt strong enough to attack the British in Savannah, but in his maneuver to get there he left Charles Town unprotected, and General Prevost crossed into South Carolina and marched against that city. Hence Lincoln rushed back to protect Charles Town, and nothing came of his maneuver.

There was little hope for the recapture of Savannah without more Whig troops. Unexpectedly in early September 1779 the French naval commander Count Charles Henri d'Estaing arrived at Savannah with four thousand troops and twenty-two ships of the line, intending to capture the city from the British. General Lincoln collected what Whig troops he could, and General Prevost and Governor Wright worked feverously on the defenses of Savannah. On 16 September d'Estaing demanded the surrender of Savannah but granted Prevost's request for a twenty-four-hour delay. Prevost used this time to get eight hundred more troops into the city from Beaufort and to strengthen its defenses with four to five hundred slave laborers. Then d'Estaing's demand was refused. Lincoln had by now joined d'Estaing with some fifteen hundred troops. The allies outnumbered the British about two to one but were never able to cooperate effectively. After a bombardment did considerable damage to the town, on 9 October d'Estaing led an unsuccessful attack upon the British lines. After this failure, the French sailed away and the Whigs recrossed into South Carolina. Had the French stormed Savannah upon landing, they might well have taken it, but they took no action until it was too late.

Despite the failure to liberate Savannah, the Whigs still controlled the upcountry. Late in December 1779 a group calling itself an assembly, but apparently short of a quorum, met in Augusta. It elected George Walton as governor and an executive council with delegates from five counties, four of them upcountry. Neither the Supreme Executive Council nor the Walton government would recognize the authority of the other. Thus Georgia Whigs split into two factions, both claiming to be the state government but neither having the strength to govern effectively. An assembly, elected at the call of the Supreme Executive Council but dominated by the Walton faction, met in Augusta in January 1780 and created a unified and constitutional state government. It elected Richard Howley governor and a full slate of state officials and declared the acts of the Supreme Executive Council illegal. This assembly, the first in Georgia's history not dominated by the coast, concerned itself with the development of the piedmont as the key to Georgia's future. Augusta became the capital, and a new town was ordered laid out adjacent to the Wilkes County courthouse to be named Washington. To attract much-needed settlers, each new head of a family could receive a 200-acre headright.

But upcountry Georgia was not to be free of the British for long. Once the siege of Savannah had failed, Sir Henry Clinton in New York pushed his plans to capture Charles Town and South Carolina. Clinton and his expedition arrived at Tybee Island in January 1780 and on 12 May captured Charles Town together with General Lincoln and the entire Whig army. Both Clinton and Lincoln had stripped Georgia of troops for use at Charles Town, and most of these troops never returned. Soon after the fall of Charles Town, Tory troops under Colonels Thomas Brown and James Grierson occupied Augusta, leaving only the 1773 Indian cession (Wilkes County) to the Whigs. Just before the fall of Charles Town, Wright had called for the election of the first colonial assembly since his return in 1779. This assembly met from early May until 10 July and worked hard to restore Georgia to her pre-Revolutionary status. It declared illegal all the acts of the state government and disqualified politically 151 prominent rebels. Throughout the summer the colonial government extended its power throughout Georgia, but many still refused to submit to it. One of the most noteworthy actions of the royal government was the provision made in the summer of 1781 for the growing upcountry. The assembly created two new parishes, St. Peter and St. Mark, from the 1773 Indian cession and the western part of St. Paul's Parish and a western circuit court for these three northernmost parishes. However, it is doubtful that either the court or the new parishes ever actually operated.

The financial support of the restored colonial government came from parliamentary grants, so that taxation was never necessary. In 1781 the assembly did enact a 2.5 percent duty on exports of the colony to be granted to the king in lieu of parliamentary taxation. Because the two houses of the assembly could never agree, they enacted no confiscation and banishment bill against rebels in time to take effect before the British left Georgia. Governor Wright continued to lead the restored government as he had before 1776; he always had the backing of the council and had no real fights with the Commons House. His biggest trouble was with the British army, which would never send enough troops to Georgia to control it all and make it the model restored colony that would, it was hoped, entice other Americans to resume their colonial status.

If the colonial government was inadequately supported, the condition of the state government was much worse. On 5 February 1780, after Georgia was stripped of troops for Charles Town, Governor Howley called upon Georgians to stand firm. After Charles Town fell to the British there was immediate danger that upcountry Georgia would be overrun and on 25 May Howley decided to go to the Continental Congress to which he was a delegate. Stephen Heard, the president of the council, became the state's chief executive. With Augusta again under British control, all that was left to the Whigs was Wilkes County and the upper part of Richmond. In July Wright reported that all Georgians except eight hundred to nine hundred men in the upcountry had submitted, but this was probably too optimistic. Many Whigs abandoned the state, but others stayed and fought. From the end of May 1780 until July 1781 the whereabouts or existence of a state government is uncertain. With Augusta in British hands, tradition has it that the government moved about in backcountry Wilkes County and even into South Carolina, and it may have done so. If there was a government, it was too weak to accomplish anything.

From mid-1780 to mid-1781 savage guerrilla warfare raged in the Georgia-Carolina backcountry. Tories reportedly murdered Whig Colonel John Dooly in his bed in the summer of 1780, and Nancy Hart had the pleasure of revenge upon the murderers, if legends about Nancy can be believed. Whig partisan leaders—Elijah Clarke, John Twiggs, Benjamin and William Few, James Jackson, and John Dooly—matched the exploits of Tories James and Daniel McGirth, Thomas Brown, and James Grierson. Partisan groups assembled when there appeared to be any chance of success against the enemy and then dispersed to their homes. Elijah Clarke made an attack upon the Tories in Augusta in mid-September, but when Colonel John H. Cruger reinforced Thomas Brown and his garrison the Whigs retreated, leaving some of their wounded whom they could not transport. According to tradition, it was from these wounded that Colonel Brown selected thirteen to be hanged from the staircase of the Indian trading house, the White House, and watched their death agonies from the bed to which he was confined by his wounds. After this action at Augusta, the Tories made a determined effort to subdue all of upcountry Georgia, but they did not succeed. Wright's pleas for a few more troops to bring all Georgia under his control went unheeded.

By April 1781 General Nathanael Greene, the Continental commander in the South, had begun an offensive against the British. The few troops at Greene's disposal made this offensive difficult, but Greene persisted. Georgia and Carolina militia under Colonel Elijah Clarke and General Andrew Williamson began a siege of Augusta in April and were joined by General Andrew Pickens and some Continental troops in May. The town fell on 5 June, and upcountry Georgia was free of the British.

Now General Greene sent Joseph Clay, his paymaster general, to Augusta to try and form a state government where apparently there was none. Dr. Nathan Brownson, head of Continental hospitals in the South, came to unite the Georgia militia. An assembly met in Augusta on 17 August with representatives from every county except Camden.

It elected Brownson governor together with a full slate of state officials, county officers for most counties, and congressional delegates. Expired or expiring state laws were renewed. This assembly also began trying to reclaim citizens who had taken the oath of loyalty to the king and to induce those who had fled the state to return. By the time a new assembly met on 1 January 1782, most of Georgia was in Whig hands, and representatives from every county attended. Finances were the main concern of this short session. Salaries were reduced and assembly-men agreed to serve gratis. Settling the state's wartime accounts was begun. No tax bill was considered, however, probably because the confused conditions in the state made it impossible to collect taxes.

After the capture of Augusta, the Whig military situation was still critical, but it improved slowly. Troops were very difficult to obtain. In 1779 the Georgia Continental line had been reduced from five battalions to two, with scarcely enough troops to fill them. In 1780 the Continental Congress considered raising a battalion of Negroes in Georgia, but nothing was done. The weak state government could not help raise troops until the summer of 1781 when the upcountry was free of the British. Henceforth a few state units, especially the Georgia State Legion under Lieutenant Colonel James Jackson, were raised. These were usually filled with people who wanted to establish their loyalty to the United States. In January 1782 Brigadier General Anthony Wayne arrived in Georgia as Continental commander, bringing a few troops with him. Though outnumbered about two to one by the British, Wayne immediately took the offensive and drove the dispirited enemy forces into the Savannah area. More ex-Tories now joined the Whigs as the ultimate Whig victory became clearer. Neither side was in a position to launch an offensive against the other, but each feared that the other was. Through the first half of 1782 there was no great change in conditions in Georgia.

The British evacuated Savannah on 10 and 11 July 1782 because they needed the troops elsewhere, and Lieutenant Colonel James Jackson received the surrender of the city. Several hundred ex-Tories joined Whig troops at the time of the evacuation because they wanted to remain in Georgia. Most civilians who left went to East Florida or the West Indies. There has been considerable dispute about how many people left Georgia at this evacuation; it could hardly have been more than three thousand to thirty-five hundred whites and thirty-five hundred to five thousand blacks. About five thousand of these went to East Florida, and it is impossible to know how many returned to Georgia in the next two years before East Florida was returned to Spain. Tradition has undoubtedly exaggerated the number of Georgians who left permanently.

The evacuation of Savannah by the British ended the war so far as Georgians were concerned. Some results of independence and separation from Britain were obvious by then and over the next few years. Politically, Georgians had more control over their own destiny with British authority gone. An increasingly democratic government was obvious in the broader suffrage base, the weakened executive, and the stronger legislature. Certainly the ordinary Georgian was in a better position to make himself heard than he had been in 1775. The return of the British to Savannah in 1778 and their control of that area until 1782 resulted in a new importance for the upcountry. By the time the British left, upcountry leaders had emerged and taken control of the state. The apportionment of the legislature was fairer to the upcountry than it was in many of the older states, and the coast lost its political dominance.

Typical leaders before and after the war help to indicate changes. Colonial leaders are well illustrated by Governor Wright, James Habersham, and Noble Jones. Wright was a professionally trained lawyer with good connections who climbed the ladder of colonial officeholding in South Carolina and London before his appointment as governor of Georgia. In Georgia he became one of the largest and wealthiest planters. Habersham and Jones had good but not wealthy English backgrounds. They had prospered economically and politically in Georgia and by the time of their death in 1775 were leaders in every sense of the word.

During and after the Revolution, Elijah Clarke and George Walton became typical leaders in many respects. Clarke was a North Carolina Regulator and illiterate frontiersman who came to Georgia in the 1770s with no material goods but with the ability to succeed in the rough-and-tumble frontier society. He became a leader in the guerrilla fighting in the backcountry and an Indian fighter after the war. In the 1780s he was a member of the assembly, a member of the council, and a militia brigadier general.

Walton was a Virginia orphan who came to Georgia at about the age of twenty. He read law and became a militia colonel during the war. He was governor, chief justice, member of the Continental Congress, member of the Constitutional Convention, and a United States Senator. His aggressive leadership especially appealed to frontiersmen. Walton undoubtedly would have risen in colonial society, but it is impossible to conceive of Clarke's accomplishing what he did without the disruption of the war years. These men and many others profited from the war.

The most obvious economic change of the postwar years was rapid growth of population, production, and wealth. Much of this would have come without the war, but it seems safe to assume that it was speeded by the war and independence. In social affairs perhaps the most obvious change was the disestablishment of the Church of England and increased religious freedom. In education the creation of what amounted on paper at least to a statewide public school system, topped by the university, was an advance that could not have come in the colonial period. True, the system was not fully implemented for a century, but the dream was always there to be championed by its advocates. Certainly the war had ended the growth of "tone" to society for which Governor Wright and other colonial leaders so ardently hoped. Now there was more equality between free men than ever before in Georgia, and the common man could exert himself more. Education was more readily available to him than previously, and his support of religion was now voluntary. Certainly the revolt against England had been aimed by Americans at control of their own affairs, and generally Georgians succeeded.

VIII

Political Development in a
Frontier State
1782–1820

With the fighting ended, Georgia's state government returned to Savannah to resume, it was hoped, much that had been interrupted by the British capture of that city three and a half years before. But 1778 was gone and could never return to Savannah and Georgia. The British had left for good, and independence was a reality. Yet conditions in the state were bad in almost all ways. A brief session of the legislature attacked the problems of loyalists, government finance, and relief for people in need. The exit of Continental troops worried Georgians, still afraid of what the British in East Florida or Charles Town might do.

The peace treaty signed in Paris in 1783 provided for the return of the Floridas to Spain. The imminent evacuation of East Florida by the British created problems for Georgians: first, there was the desire to regain stolen or escaped slaves and horses, and second, the desire for the return of some of the Tories from East Florida. Few slaves or horses were secured, but many of the Tories wanted to return to Georgia, where they felt at home, rather than begin life anew elsewhere. At least several hundred, and probably more, returned. By this time the Georgia Assembly had begun to mitigate the rigors of the confiscation and banishment acts. In 1782 the assembly allowed ninety-three Tories to reclaim their Georgia citizenship by paying a part of their property to the state or by serving as Continental troops. Over the next quarter of a century the assembly passed special acts to remove penalties for individuals or to restore all or part of their confiscated property. Of course many Tories, especially those most obnoxious to Georgia Whigs, never returned. The sale of confiscated property went forward rapidly once the war was over, but payment was something that many Georgians found difficult, and there were continual delays in collections. The amount the state finally realized from the confiscations was considerably less than originally expected.

Besides punishing Tories, the government also rewarded Whigs. All who served in the armed forces were entitled to land bounties, and many leaders were given large amounts of land. General Nathanael Greene, General Anthony Wayne, Count d'Estaing, Colonel Elijah Clarke, Lieutenant Colonel James Jackson, officers in the Continental line, and children of dead officers and heroes received the largest grants. Permanently maimed veterans received pensions as high as £30 a year, and widows up to £10. At least three slaves were emancipated for their war services, and one of them, Austin Dabney, was given a pension for his injuries.

Throughout the Confederation period (1781–1789) government in Georgia followed the pattern developed during the war itself—a weak plural executive and a dominant assembly. The major attempt at executive leadership was made in July 1783, when Governor Lyman Hall gave the assembly a complete picture of conditions in the state and suggested several important actions. Only a few of these were taken immediately, but others were implemented later. Hall pointed out the need for increased population and wealth, Indian land cessions and peace, revision of the state's land laws, consideration of the state's financial condition, and action on military defense. Gradually the government became less concerned with problems of individuals and began to enact mainly laws of general application. In the 1780s Georgia passed laws on citizenship, naturalization, tariffs, patents, copyrights, and other subjects which have belonged to the central government since 1789.

Several people elected to the assembly or to the council refused to serve. William O'Bryan refused to serve as president of the executive council, and in 1788 James Jackson, the thirty-year-old hero of the Revolution, refused to serve as governor on the grounds that he was too young and inexperienced.

The courts met more regularly as peace and tranquility returned. A high point of the superior court session in all counties was the charge of the chief justice to the grand jury and the jury's presentments. Chief Justices George Walton and Henry Osborne used their charges to bring up matters of national and state importance as well as local items. If the majority of the county grand juries presented the same item, the governor and council or the assembly usually acted on it. The chief justice, who presided over all superior courts, was the one unifying influence in the courts and could exert considerable influence.

County self-government really began only after the confusion of the war years had abated. Henceforth counties gradually acquired more powers over their own affairs with control of roads, poor relief, and election of more local officials. The first county governmental agency was the superior court. Local functions were divided between these courts and commissions created by the assembly for specific functions. By the 1790s, special commissions declined in number, and more and more local functions were assigned to the inferior court, which then became the major organ of county government. Local self-government began in towns and cities also with Savannah, Sunbury, Augusta, and Brunswick being given special commissioners, and with Savannah's incorporation in 1787.

The location of the state's capital gives some indication of sectional importance. While Savannah again became the capital in 1782, the increased importance of Augusta and the upcountry led the executive (governor and council) to reside there part time and the assembly to alternate its sessions between the two cities. In 1786, the assembly directed that a new town, to be called Louisville, be located within twenty miles of Galphin's Old Town on the Ogeechee as the capital and seat of the university. Augusta was to be the capital until Louisville was ready for occupancy, which was not until 1795. Offices moved to Augusta slowly, and the Chatham County justices and Chief Justice John Houstoun, from Savannah, claimed a portion of the records of the secretary's office as the records of Chatham County and kept them. The executive suspended these officials, and the records were soon in Augusta.

Georgia's finances were at a low ebb when the British left in 1782. There had been no state tax during the years of British occupation, and the state government had supported itself from loans, paper money, and goods bought on credit or impressed. Georgia had issued certificates or printed paper money to the amount of about $4 million during the war, but much of this was greatly devalued by a 1783 law and soon disappeared. Expenses, including considerable outlay for Indian treaties and defense, were between $100,000 and $150,000 a year during the 1780s, considerably more than income. There was almost no specie, and state treasury certificates were the main type of state income and the only way the state could pay her obligations. In 1786, the first year there was a general accounting, Georgia was owed from $1 million to $1.5 million mainly in personal bonds for the purchase of confiscated estates. The public debt that year was listed at about $1 million.

In the 1790s, with the Indian problem transferred to the United States, state expenditures averaged from $25,000 to $35,000 a year and almost evenly balanced income. In the first decade of the nineteenth century, the budget was balanced at about $70,000 a year, and some debt payments were made. In the second decade both income and expenditures increased to slightly over $300,000 a year. By 1820 the state debt had been reduced to $151,546.

In the 1780s and 1790s the state's tax structure and rates stabilized and thereafter changed little until the 1850s. Taxes were levied upon agricultural land and upon urban real estate and merchandise. A poll tax (on slaves under sixty, free white males, and free persons of color) and various miscellaneous levies (on professional licenses, pleasure vehicles, billiard tables, gambling devices, and legal suits) completed the state tax base.

One of the most important concerns of the state government was relations with the Creek Indians. Once the war had ended and whites came into Georgia in increasing numbers, there were insistent demands for more Indian land west and north of the 1763 and 1773 cessions. The lands most desired were between the Ogeechee and Oconee rivers. Georgia-Creek relations in the 1780s were complicated by several factors. First and foremost was the mixed-breed Alexander McGillivray, an able chieftain among the Upper Creeks who opposed almost anything that white Georgians wanted. McGillivray was a master at playing Georgia and the United States against the British and the Spanish, he hoped to the benefit of the Creeks. When the British gave up the Floridas to the Spanish, the British Indian trading firm of Panton, Leslie and Company remained and exerted considerable influence as one of the main Creek suppliers of European goods. The Spanish were willing to give the Creeks sufficient munitions to raid the Georgia frontier but never enough to carry on a real war that many Creeks and McGillivray wanted. Georgia was not strong enough to fight the Creeks alone, and she could never get adequate help from the United States or South Carolina. Neither the United States nor the Spanish ever knew what the other had promised the Creeks, so both were at a disadvantage in their Creek relations. But the Creeks, as always, remained divided in their feelings and allegiance. The Lower Creeks, who lived on the Chattahoochee and Flint rivers nearest to Georgia, were usually more friendly and less under the influence of McGillivray than were the Upper Creeks. It was the lands of the Lower Creeks that Georgians desired, and some Lower Creeks were usually willing to sign treaties of cession, treaties that McGillivray always repudiated as illegal.

Georgia's first postwar Indian dealings were with the Cherokees, who at Long Swamp in October 1782 ceded the land south and west of the Savannah and Tugaloo rivers. A few Lower Creeks confirmed this cession at Augusta in 1783, when they ceded Creek lands east of the Oconee. Georgia immediately created the counties of Washington and Franklin out of this cession, which McGillivray and his followers continued to deny the legality of until 1790. Georgia's claims to this land several times almost led to war with the Creeks and did produce several more treaties. Treaties were secured at Galphinton in 1785 and at Shoulderbone in 1786, and negotiations but no treaty at Rock Landing on the Oconee in 1789. Attempted United States negotiations, at Galphinton and at Rock Landing, came to naught because McGillivray would not cooperate. McGillivray even suggested in 1787 that if a separate Indian state were created south of the Altamaha, the Indians would then give up the Oconee lands so ardently desired by Georgia, but nothing came of the proposal. Finally in 1790 President Washington convinced McGillivray to come to New York, where he signed a treaty of cession for the Oconee lands.

Frequently when the Creeks caused trouble, Georgians asked for help from the central government but never got any effective aid. Georgia was a frontier state that had been badly devastated by the war, and many Georgians felt that the state had little time, effort, or money to contribute to the central government. Hence her relations with the Continental Congress were based more upon pragmatic needs than upon political theories about a strong or a weak central government. Georgia's delay in granting to Congress the requested power to levy import duties and control foreign trade seems to have been more from neglect than from serious objection to the award of these powers. Finally in 1786 Georgia approved Congress's request for a 5-percent impost and amendments to the Articles of Confederation. The state passed several acts to pay her part of requisitions by Congress, but there is no record that she ever paid anything. Probably the hoped-for income did not materialize, and the assembly provided no alternate sources. Yet when the final settlement between the states and the United States was made in 1793 a balance of $19,988 was found to be due Georgia by the United States for supplies furnished during the war.

During the Confederation period, Georgia and South Carolina argued over the boundaries between the two states. The attempt to settle this argument began in 1783 but did not succeed until 1787, when commissioners from the two states met in Beaufort, South Carolina, and agreed that the boundary in the upper reaches of the Savannah was the Tugaloo-Chattooga or western branch of the Savannah. South Carolina's claim to the land west of the Altamaha–St. Marys headwaters was given up.

Georgia's hope of securing something from her vast western domain, mainly inhabited by Indians, is illustrated by the unsuccessful attempts at the creation of two counties far to the west of the line of settlement. In 1784 land speculators petitioned for a new county, Houstoun, to be located at the Muscle Shoals area of the Tennessee River. In 1787 this was the area in which land was to be granted to men from the State of Franklin—men who it was hoped would join Georgia in her anticipated war against the Creeks. But the war did not materialize, the land grants were never made, and the county was never created. The attempted founding of Bourbon County in the Natchez district on the Mississippi seems more fantastic. This county, which was actually created in 1785, was backed by land speculators in the area. But the Spanish, in control of this territory, made it clear that they wanted no new Georgia county or settlers; so ended Bourbon County.

Georgia could have saved herself this trouble had she ceded her western land to Congress as requested in 1780. In response to a later request, Georgia in 1788 ceded all her western lands between the thirty-first and thirty-third parallels, only the southern half of her western land. This land was also claimed by Spain and was cut off from the rest of the United States by Georgia on its north and east. In return, Georgia asked that $171,428 be repaid to her as expenses to quiet the Indians in this territory and also that the rest of the state's territory be guaranteed to her. Congress refused the cession upon these terms and asked again that Georgia cede all her western land, something she refused to do at that time.

Georgia's interest in the central government and her hopes for benefits from it led to her participation in the writing of the new constitution in 1787. The assembly elected William Few, Abraham Baldwin, William Pierce, George Walton, William Houstoun, and Nathaniel Pendleton as her delegates to the Constitutional Convention that met in Philadelphia in May. Few was present for the opening of the convention and remained throughout, except for the month of July when he was attending Congress in New York. Baldwin arrived on 1 June and remained throughout the rest of the convention. Pierce attended during June, and Houstoun attended in June and July. Baldwin was Georgia's outstanding delegate, and Pierce wrote some interesting sketches of the members of the convention. Georgia's delegates favored a stronger central government and generally voted with the large-state delegates. When the convention was badly split over the matter of representation in the upper house, Baldwin was given credit by some for creating a tie vote and putting off a decision that might have split the convention permanently. Out of this argument came the famous Connecticut Compromise on representation and the origin of money bills. Georgians, interested in the foreign slave trade, helped to secure the provision that allowed it to continue until 1808. Few and Baldwin signed the completed Constitution on 17 September. Had Houstoun and Pierce been present, they undoubtedly would have signed as well.

Pierce arrived in Savannah on 10 October and brought the first known copy of the Constitution to Georgia. Three days later it was published in the *Georgia State Gazette*. Within a week the assembly, in special session to consider Indian troubles, called for the meeting of a ratifying convention in the winter. The convention opened on 28 December with delegates from ten of the eleven counties, including Governor George Mathews, and other political leaders. The document was debated on 29 December and unanimously ratified on 31 December. Both Georgia's quick action and unanimous vote in favor of the Constitution can be attributed to her relations with the Creek Indians. Her greatest problem in 1787 was a threatened Creek war, and Georgia needed help if she was to defeat the Indians. As she had not been able to secure the desired aid from the old confederation or from other states, many Georgians hoped that the new and stronger central government would be helpful. The upcountry could hope for protection, while Savannah and the coast desired better trade regulations. Thus the entire state united in favor of the new Constitution.

When the government under the Constitution went into effect in 1789, Georgia's electors voted unanimously for George Washington as president but scattered their second votes and gave none to John Adams, who was elected vice president. William Few and James Gunn were elected as United States Senators, and George Mathews, Abraham Baldwin, and James Jackson to the House of Representatives.

Once Georgia had ratified the new Constitution, there was interest in remodeling the state's government as well. The 1788 assembly provided for a state constitutional convention, with its members elected by the assembly itself, to meet after nine states had ratified the federal Constitution. The convention met in Augusta in November 1788 and wrote a new document modeled somewhat on the federal Constitution. A ratifying convention in January 1789, instead of ratifying, proposed eleven amendments. Early in May a new ratifying convention approved the constitution, which went into effect in October 1789.

This new state constitution provided for a two-house legislature consisting of a senate and a house of representatives, with members elected for three-year and one-year terms respectively. Each county was to have one senator and two to five representatives, roughly proportional to population but with the coast somewhat overrepresented. For the first time in her history, Georgia now had a single executive without an executive council. The governor was given a legislative veto and he could grant reprieves and pardons in most cases. This constitution made no basic change in the court structure provided in the constitution of 1777, except to abolish the chief justiceship. While the governor and assemblymen had to meet property qualifications, the only qualifications for voting were age, residence, and payment of a tax the preceding year. The governor and other state officials were elected by the assembly, and the constitution contained about the same individual guarantees as that of 1777. This constitution is generally considered to have been more conservative than the one of 1777, but, except for the increased governor's power and a two-house legislature, there are few specific points that prove this. It was more a rearrangement of the document than a basic change.

As provided for in the constitution of 1789, an amending convention met in 1795 and considered apportionment in the House of Representatives. Total membership for the house was set at fifty-one and the representation of each county was specified in the constitution. Chatham and Liberty counties were given four representatives each, seven counties three each, and the remainder two each. Senate representation remained at one senator per county. This apportionment, for the twenty counties then existing, gave the upcountry the advantage in both houses. Louisville was designated as the seat of government, and the governor and principal officers were directed to locate their offices there.

The year 1795 also saw the most exciting political event in Georgia's early national history, the Yazoo land fraud. In 1789 the South Carolina Yazoo Company, the Virginia Yazoo Company, and the Tennessee Company had purchased from the assembly 15.5 million acres of land for which they promised to pay $207,000. This sale fell through because the three companies tried to pay for the land in depreciated Revolutionary currency, which the state refused to accept. Land speculation in Georgia reached its peak in 1794 and 1795, when four new Yazoo companies—the Georgia Company, the Georgia-Mississippi Company, the Upper Mississippi Company, and the Tennessee Company— aided by liberal bribes, succeeded in getting through the assembly a bill that sold them between 35 million and 50 million acres of Georgia's western territory for about $500,000. Governor Mathews signed the

Yazoo law early in January 1795. Many legislators were given stock in the Yazoo companies, and Senator James Gunn was one of the principal stockholders in the Georgia Company.

Once the law and the method of its passing became known, a great outcry arose against it. Grand juries, newspapers, and many citizens condemned it. United States Senator James Jackson resigned his senate seat to run for the legislature and oppose the Yazoo act, and the 1795 election saw a wholesale turnover of legislators. The 1796 act of repeal declared the original law contrary to both the United States and the state constitutions, against the public interest, and fraudulent. All records connected with Yazoo were collected and a public burning was held by the assembly "with fire brought down from heaven" to consume the iniquitous records. But it was not so easy to erase Yazoo from the memories of Georgians.

The state provided for the refund of money paid into the treasury in purchase of Yazoo lands, but some of the land had been sold by the companies to third parties who refused to take the refunds and insisted that they were entitled to the land. The state rejected this view, and the matter dragged on in the courts. In 1798 Congress made another effort to negotiate the cession of Georgia's western lands and set up a territory that included all Georgia's western claims. Finally in 1802, Georgia and the United States agreed to terms of cession. The Yazoo claims were now transferred to the United States government. John Randolph led a group in Congress who opposed any settlement with the Yazoo claimants. In the case of *Fletcher* v. *Peck*, decided in 1810, the Supreme Court declared that the Georgia repeal act of 1796 was an unconstitutional infringement of a valid contract. Finally in 1814 Congress provided financial settlement with the Yazoo claimants, and the matter passed into history.

A constitutional amending convention met in 1798 with Governor James Jackson, who was very popular because of his fight for the repeal of the Yazoo act, as one of its major leaders. This convention wrote a new constitution that followed the outline of the one of 1789 but was about twice as long. The House of Representatives was to consist of from one to four members per county, according to population, using the federal ratio of counting three-fifths of the slaves. Each county retained one senator. There were still property qualifications for office-holding. To vote one must be a twenty-one-year-old male citizen, have paid his required taxes, and have lived in his county for six months. The Yazoo sale was declared void, and it was provided that no public

Lachlan McIntosh

Elijah Clarke

James Jackson

William H. Crawford

lands could be sold until the land was laid off into counties and the Indian rights extinguished. Otherwise the assembly was given broad powers to legislate as it deemed necessary.

The governor and other executive officials, university trustees, state boards, higher militia officers, and judges continued to be elected by the assembly. The governor was given the usual executive powers. Superior and inferior courts continued as formerly. Probate matters were vested in the inferior courts, which were to acquire more county executive functions over the next half a century. With only twenty-three formal amendments, this constitution served Georgia until 1861. It was the first state constitution written when the state was relatively tranquil and no major change in government was taking place. General tendencies gradually effected throughout the nineteenth century were the popular election of more officials, the transfer of more duties from the assembly to executive officers or judges, and the transfer of duties from the state government to county governments. Before the supreme court was created in 1845 laws were occasionally ruled unconstitutional by individual superior court judges and by the conference of superior court judges held annually.

In addition to constitutional change, actual political operations and party divisions were significant. When the war ended in 1783, there was no great political division in Georgia nor did the adoption of the United States Constitution in 1789 divide Georgians. At this stage they were Federalists, but this did not mean that they would accept without question whatever the central government did. Two early United States Supreme Court cases decided against Georgia brought out considerable opposition within the state. In *Georgia* v. *Brailsford* (1794) and in *Chisholm* v. *Georgia* (1793), both involving Georgia's Revolutionary confiscation laws, the decisions were unfavorable to the state. In *Chisholm* v. *Georgia* a South Carolina resident sued the state, and when the decision went against Georgia by default, she refused to honor it. This case led to the adoption of the Eleventh Amendment to the United States Constitution, which prohibits the use of United States courts for suits against a state by citizens of another state or of a foreign nation. Yet in 1799 when the assembly called for the repeal of the Alien and Sedition Acts it expressed the hope that it would not need to pass any "violent resolutions against them" as the Virginia and Kentucky legislatures had done.

One thing the United States government did which all Georgians approved was its efforts to move the Indians west of the Mississippi. After the cession of Georgia's western territory to the United States in

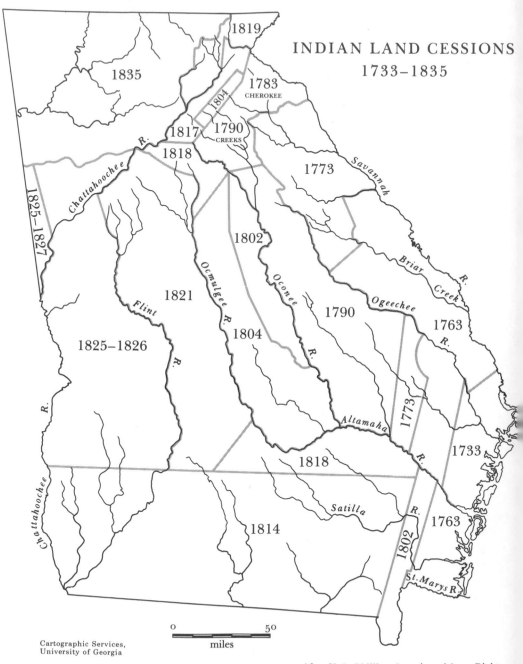

INDIAN LAND CESSIONS
1733–1835

1819

1835

1783
CHEROKEE

1804

1817

1790
CREEKS

1818

1773

Savannah

1825–1827

Chattahoochee R.

1802

Ocmulgee R.

Oconee R.

Briar Creek R.

1821

Flint

1790

Ogeechee

1763
R.

1825–1826

1804

R.

R.

1773

1818

Altamaha R.

1733

Chattahoochee R.

1763

1814

Satilla R.

1802

St. Marys R.

0   50
miles

Cartographic Services,
University of Georgia

After U. B. Phillips, *Georgia and State Rights*

1802 and her promise to remove the Indians from Georgia, the federal government secured from the Creeks the greatly desired lands between the Oconee and Ocmulgee rivers in 1802 and 1804. In 1803 President Jefferson suggested the removal of all southern Indians to lands in the new Louisiana Purchase, for what Jefferson undoubtedly believed would be the benefit of both whites and Indians. In 1805 there were further negotiations with the Creeks in Washington but no land cession. While many Cherokees favored removal in 1809, after a delegation visited the western territory, nothing was done.

Unanimous ratification of the Constitution did not mean that Georgians favored the Hamiltonian system that many equated with the Federalist party by the end of Washington's presidency. Instead, most Georgians favored the more democratic orientation of Thomas Jefferson and his followers toward the small farmer. Georgians voted for Jefferson in three presidential elections (1796, 1800, and 1804) and for his followers in every election through 1824. The Federalist party was not helped by the fact that most of the Yazoo leaders were Federalists, but Federalism could hardly flourish in an agrarian frontier area like Georgia. While there were Federalists in Georgia until about 1810, they steadily declined in numbers and influence after 1796. James Jackson, although a leader of coastal aristocrats, became the dominant political leader in Georgia and allied himself with the more democratic Jeffersonians in national politics.

Jackson's opposition to the Yazoo Act enhanced his political importance and secured for him the governorship in 1798, leadership in the constitutional convention of that year, and a seat in the United States Senate in 1801. Jackson appealed to both aristocrats and the common folk through his bombastic personality and his leadership abilities. Through his strong leadership, he had formed a personal party following in state affairs by the time of his death in 1806. Two of Jackson's ablest political lieutenants were William H. Crawford and George M. Troup. Crawford, a Virginian by birth, lived in the upcountry and became the leader there, but he soon devoted himself more to national than state politics. Troup was more popular in the older sections of the state and became the coastal leader of the emerging party. Since Troup remained in Georgia and sought office there, the old Jackson party soon came to be called the Troup party.

The nineteenth century began with the Jackson-Crawford-Troup followers in control of Georgia politics, but opposition soon surfaced. The Jackson followers in the upcountry were the Virginia faction, and they were opposed by the North Carolina faction led by John and

Elijah Clark, the sons of the Revolutionary Elijah Clarke who had died in 1799. Troup defeated Elijah Clark in the statewide congressional elections of 1806 and 1810. Even so, strongly partisan state politics did not develop this early in Georgia.

There were almost universal objections in the state to the British actions that led to the War of 1812. While Georgians objected to the maritime and trade actions of the British, they were more directly concerned with the British and Spanish influence over the Creek Indians exercised from Florida. After raids on the Georgia frontier, the Indians usually escaped into Spanish Florida. There was always the fear of war, but after 1800 the Indians became less belligerent. Many Georgians joined the widespread alarm after the British *Leopard* stopped the USS *Chesapeake* in 1807. Georgians supported the Jeffersonian embargo and Madisonian nonintercourse acts, despite their adverse effect upon cotton, the state's major export. By 1810 many Georgians were demanding war against Britain. Georgia with her undefended coast and common border with Spanish Florida was in as vulnerable a position as any state.

In January 1811 President Madison commissioned Georgia's ex-Governor George Mathews to secure East Florida if possible. When Mathews stirred up a revolution led by ex-United States citizens in East Florida, the revolutionists, with United States gunboats, took the town of Fernandino on Amelia Island in March 1812, but their attempt to take St. Augustine failed. Mathews was now abandoned by Madison and his actions disallowed. Mathews, reportedly on his way to Washington to horsewhip Madison, died in Augusta on 1 September, and Governor David Mitchell replaced him as agent to secure Florida. Mitchell had already mobilized some militia and sixty-day state troops to invade Florida, but Congress refused to authorize such action. Savannah militia and volunteers marched to St. Augustine in July 1812 but failed to capture it. After this force returned, central Georgia militia arrived at St. Marys but accomplished nothing. The summer of 1813 saw considerable talk and some work to improve Georgia's coastal defenses. At Savannah an attempt was made to build defenses with slaves furnished voluntarily by planters. A fort was built at Sunbury, and Thomas Spalding got munitions from the state to arm his slaves on Sapelo Island. The United States sent one thousand small arms for the Georgia militia. But as with so many other things during the War of 1812, Georgia's defense efforts tended to be more talk than reality.

Tecumseh, the great Indian leader, had come into the Creek country in the summer of 1811 to arouse the Indians against the United States, at which he had some success, mainly among the Upper Creeks or "Red Sticks." The British sent the belligerent Indians arms through Pensacola. The massacre of whites at Fort Mims in Alabama in August 1813 aroused Georgians, and many volunteers set out for the Indian country. General John Floyd collected a militia force near Fort Hawkins, on the Ocmulgee, and built Fort Lawrence, on the Flint. But the most important fighting was Andrew Jackson's overwhelming defeat of the Creeks at Horseshoe Bend in Alabama in March 1814. In the peace settlement, the Creeks were made to give up the entire southern part of Georgia in order to cut them off from easy contact with Florida. This land was Georgia's greatest immediate gain from the war.

In May 1814 a British fleet under Admiral Alexander Cockrane appeared off St. Marys and raided the nearby islands and up the rivers. Banks and individuals sent their valuables to the interior, and some people fled, but the British soon sailed away. The next January another expedition under Admiral George Cockburn landed on both Cumberland Island and at St. Marys and went up the river as far as Coleraine before news of the peace treaty arrived and the British withdrew. Georgia's hopes that the United States would secure Florida were dashed by the Treaty of Ghent, which ended the war, but only five years later by the Adams-Onis Treaty the United States acquired Florida.

Another matter helped by the War of 1812 and completed later was the removal of the Creek Indians. The defeat at Horseshoe Bend in 1814 broke the spirit of many Creeks. In 1818 it was possible for the United States to secure some one and a half million acres from them around the headwaters of the Ocmulgee, and land lying between the Altamaha-Ocmulgee and the 1814 cession. Georgians wanted all Creek lands, or as a minimum the land to the Flint, and were very dissatisfied at the relatively small size of this cession. In 1820 President Monroe requested funds to extinguish all Indian claims in Georgia, and further negotiations with the Creeks went forward.

Georgia also moved to secure Cherokee lands. In 1817 many Cherokees in Georgia favored removal, while those in Tennessee opposed it. Yet the Georgia cession of that year was a relatively small one. In the next two years there was a major removal of Cherokees to the west, but by 1819 few Georgia Cherokees favored removal. In that year there was a further cession of Georgia land about the same size as the 1817 cession, but thereafter Cherokee cessions would be more difficult to secure.

During the War of 1812 there had been little bitter political infighting in Georgia, as there was general agreement to fight the British first. There was depression before and during the war and hatred of Britain; together they occupied the attention of Georgians. Once the war ended, the price of cotton climbed steadily so that by 1818 it averaged thirty-four cents a pound. Such prosperity brought content-ment, but the price of that fleecy staple began to decline thereafter and that fact was undoubtedly one of the major causes for the increased political bitterness that arose between the Troup and Clark parties.

In 1819 John Clark, the leader of the Clark party, announced that he personally would run for governor. George Troup resigned his seat in the United States Senate to oppose Clark. Thus ended the decade of relative quiet in state politics and began the decade of bitter Troup-Clark factionalism that was to arouse most Georgians and amaze people who tried to explain Georgia politics. This was probably the most exciting election the state had experienced to date. As the governor was still elected by the assembly, assembly elections often were influ-enced by whom legislative candidates favored for governor. When the assembly met and cast its ballots in November, Clark was the victor by only thirteen votes.

A new political era began in 1819–20. Politics in Georgia since inde-pendence had been mainly concerned with state affairs rather than national. Political divisions tended to be oriented toward personalities of state leaders rather than toward party organizations, and national party divisions were important only in presidential election years. Only at time of foreign war or threats of war and in her efforts to get rid of Indians did Georgia feel the need of help from the central government. Georgia was still a frontier state in which there was general agreement that the Indians should be removed but much less agreement as to how land freed from Indians should be distributed. Most Georgians were convinced that they could take care of themselves and seldom needed the intervention of either the state or central government.

IX

The Expanding Frontier Economy
1782–1820

Land was the basis of wealth of the great majority of Georgians in the colonial period, and it continued to be in the early national period— land for cultivation, for timber and naval stores, and for collecting deerskins. At the end of the Revolutionary War land-granting regulations were the most important single item in the state's economic policy. Farms and plantations had generally been small or medium-sized in the colonial period, and there had been no large land speculation in Georgia. The size of farming units did not change in the early national period, but Georgia saw her greatest land speculation ever, and land-granting policies sparked many hard-fought political battles.

Georgia claimed some one hundred million acres of public and ungranted land in 1782, a little over one-third of which was within the present-day boundaries of the state. About nine and a half million acres were available for settlement while the rest was still held by the Indians. Much of the ungranted land in the older part of the state was considered of little or no economic value and was not desired by settlers. With the rapid immigration into Georgia which began as soon as peace returned, the demands for land increased greatly. There were two viewpoints on how land should be granted. Coastal planters wanted it distributed gradually at a high enough price to bring substantial income to the state and to maintain the value of coastal lands. The other position was that land should be given or sold at a very cheap price to actual settlers in order to increase population and economic production. The second view appealed to small farmers in the upcountry and people in other states who wanted to move to Georgia. This view was a continuation of Georgia's traditional land-granting policy and would help to get rid of the unwanted Indians sooner. These viewpoints were a part of the coastal-upcountry differences that were obvious until after 1800.

Until 1803 Georgia distributed land through a headright system similar to the one that had been used in the colonial period. This system was supposed to insure that land was given to people who would use it and not in large blocks that would be held for speculation. In 1782 the head of a family in Georgia was entitled by headright to 200 acres for himself and 50 acres for each other member of his family up to 1,000 acres.

The end of the war was the signal for land speculation to begin in Georgia with a vengeance. This resulted in part from the sale of bounty grants by veterans who did not want to take up personally the lands to which they were entitled. But this speculation was also the result of a new spirit, perhaps resulting from a feeling of invincibility that came with independence. In the late 1780s and early 1790s several governors (George Walton, George Mathews, George Handley, Edward Telfair, and Jared Irwin are the best examples) signed grants for much larger amounts than the 1,000 acres that the law allowed. With the constitution of 1789 land granting, except for the formal grant signed by the governor, came to be controlled by county officials—a procedure that made dishonest administration of the law much easier than when there was central control by the governor and council.

Veterans' bounties were a matter of lively concern in the 1780s and 1790s. Soldiers who had served in Continental or state units, in the militia, or in the Indian wars in the 1780s were all entitled to bounties. Revolutionary bounties ranged from 2,200 acres for a major general to 200 for a private. Indian war bounties of the 1780s were larger for soldiers with little or no actual service. The distribution of Revolutionary bounty lands did not begin until 1784, when the new counties of Franklin and Washington were created and a special land court was created to handle grants. As best as can be determined, probably about two thousand veterans were granted about 750,000 acres in Georgia. Some veterans from other states who moved to Georgia took up their Continental bounties there as the state was glad to make such grants. Veterans just moving to Georgia were entitled to headright grants as well.

The first spectacular land fraud was the pine barrens scandal during the early 1790s. In newly created Montgomery County there were numerous entirely fictitious "surveys" of land. Pine barrens were described as oak and hickory land with nonexistent streams and other natural boundaries. These descriptions of good agricultural land were made only to be sold to out-of-state speculators. Governor George Mathews in 1794–95 signed grants for several hundred thousand acres per grantee. One person received one and a half million acres out of thirteen million acres so granted. There were similar grants in at least six other counties, so that by 1796 three times as much land had been "granted" as there was in the existing counties. There is no record of how much of this land was later sold, but it was a part of the speculative fever then gripping the country. These scandals and the more famous Yazoo fraud of 1795–96, described in the previous chapter, did nothing to bring more settlers into the state, but they illustrate a new economic morality and greater imagination than had been seen in Georgia land dealings previously.

The Yazoo fraud did more to reform land-granting procedure than anything else could have done. Once the Yazoo law was repealed and James Jackson became governor in 1798, he immediately opened negotiations to cede to the United States the state's land west of the Chattahoochee. Jackson and many others felt that the land east of the river was sufficient for the state and would allow for much better planning of land policy, use, and internal improvements. All other states had given up their western lands by then. An agreement, negotiated in 1802, ceded the western lands to the United States for $1.25 million and a promise to extinguish Indian claims to the remaining land in Georgia as soon as this could be done upon reasonable terms.

The followers of James Jackson changed the method of land granting so as to reduce speculation. When Governor John Milledge called a special legislative session in May 1803 to deal with land policy, he emphasized the desirability of ending speculation. The new land-granting system enacted in 1803 provided for the complete surveying of land in any Indian cession and laying it out in lots of 202½ or 490 acres, depending upon its value. The land was then distributed by a lottery in which all citizens were eligible to participate. Every free white male citizen of the United States who was a Georgia resident for the past twelve months was allowed one chance in the lottery, as was every family of orphans under twenty-one years of age. Every man with a wife and minor child and every widow with minor children secured two chances. The land given in the lottery was free except for fees of $4.00 per hundred acres. The state sold fractional lots, fraudulently secured land, and reverted lots. Three new counties—Baldwin, Wilkinson, and Wayne—were created, with provision for the laying out of town sites with the sale of lots and the construction of public works. A new town on the south bank of the Oconee near the head of navigation was ordered laid out for the new capital, to be named Milledgeville in honor of the governor.

This new land distribution system, under which nearly three-fourths of the land in the state was granted, remained virtually unchanged until the last public lands were distributed. It gave equality of opportunity for land acquisition to all Georgians, but by producing little income it defeated the chances for internal improvements and educational and other social services that may have been more important than free land in the long run. Such a system, fundamental to the state's development, could be expected in a frontier state.

As new lands were granted and settled, the legislature usually provided commissioners to lay out county seats, reserve land for public buildings, sell town lots, and create a county academy with the money derived from lot sales. This system secured better-planned towns and cities and established important public services at once; delayed services would have prevailed if town planning had been left to the settlers. Georgia probably received less than ten cents an acre for land distributed under the lottery system, compared with the minimum price of $1.25 an acre received by the federal government for its public lands.

As more land was ceded by the Indians and opened to white settlement, transportation within new areas became important. Without facilities to take in people and goods and to bring out agricultural products, these areas would contribute little to the state's advancement. Initially internal improvements were built and maintained as they had been in the colonial period, with little or no public expenditure. Road maintenance was to be performed by all adult males, free and slave, giving several days of labor a year. In 1791 supervision of this duty was assigned to the county inferior court, and road construction and maintenance became almost totally local. Attempts at maintaining standards and seeing that the work was actually done were limited to little-enforced state laws, and roads were often in dreadful condition. In 1799 Judge George Walton commented to the grand juries upon the absence of roads in Glynn and Camden counties. At this time the road connecting Augusta and Savannah was good enough for a stage to make the trip in two to four days. In 1803 the legislature created a toll road, specifying that a causeway be built, for twenty miles north of Savannah, but this system of construction was not generally used in Georgia. Ferries and major bridges were usually built with private funds and operated as toll facilities. Smaller bridges were built as a part of the road by the county governments. Although the state did little beyond instituting this road labor system, the federal government built a few roads in Georgia. The first, between Georgia and Tennessee in northwest Georgia (Cherokee territory), began as a federal project, but in the end the state spent approximately $5,000 in 1804 and 1805 to build the road. In 1811, the federal government built a road from Milledgeville westward beyond the Chattahoochee and eventually to

Fort Stoddert, near Mobile in Alabama. In 1815 there was another federal road from Athens northwestward to the Tennessee River (present-day Chattanooga). Once these roads were built, they became a part of the state system with the usual county maintenance and might soon deteriorate.

Inadequate road construction and maintenance made river transportation very important, and this had a great deal to do with settlement and agricultural development. An attempt soon after the Revolutionary War to use the same method of river improvement as was used for road maintenance was generally unsuccessful. In 1796, a $4,000 lottery was authorized for work on the Savannah River above Augusta. That year a system was authorized for the Ogeechee River and Briar Creek in which the state appropriated funds and authorized a lottery and subscriptions by private individuals and the involved counties. All these methods were used by stream improvement companies, which charged tolls for the use of the stream they improved with private funds. In 1798 a canal was authorized between the Altamaha at Darien and the Brunswick harbor to the south, but it was not constructed. All in all, none of these methods of stream improvement worked very satisfactorily, so that Georgia's internal transportation was still woefully inadequate by 1815.

The War of 1812 more than anything else to date convinced many Georgians of the inadequacy of their internal transportation and that improvements were essential. The prosperity and increased state income of the immediate postwar years encouraged the state to finance road building and stream improvement, with the major emphasis upon the latter. David B. Mitchell, who returned to the governorship in 1815, urged improved transportation facilities, and George M. Troup used the idea as a part of his winning political program. By 1817 the state had a surplus of over $500,000, and more was anticipated. In 1815 the legislature appropriated $10,000 each for improvements of the Savannah and Oconee rivers and in 1817 adopted the first comprehensive statewide internal improvements system. A total of $66,000 was appropriated for improvement of nine specific streams as far west as the Ocmulgee, and a permanent internal improvement fund of $250,000 was set up to be invested in bank or other profitable stock, the income from which was to be used for future internal improvements. Additional specific appropriations were made later, and the permanent fund was increased to $500,000 in 1821. Clearly, rivers were the key to the state's thinking about internal transportation, and roads were generally considered adjuncts or feeders to rivers.

For actual transportation of freight on the rivers, pole boats were the main method used before 1816; they were slow and costly upstream but generally satisfactory downstream. Steam navigation of Georgia's rivers began in April 1816 on the Savannah River. The next year the legislature granted Samuel Howard, the organizer of the Steam Boat Company of Georgia, a twenty-year monopoly of steam navigation upon all Georgia rivers that he desired to use. Despite its monopoly, the Steam Boat Company of Georgia was insolvent by 1821, and the United States Supreme Court (*Gibbons* v. *Ogden*, 1824) declared such monopolies illegal. In 1820 a teamboat (propelled by twenty-four horses walking upon an endless belt) arrived at Augusta from Savannah, but this form of propulsion did not last. By 1820, steam navigation on Georgia's rivers was just beginning and its importance for the next several decades brought more concern for river improvement.

Transportation improvements were aimed mainly at aiding agriculture, the recovery of which during the 1780s concerned the coastal area with its rice and indigo plantations. Both of these crops had been hurt during the war years. Indigo's decline was tied to the ending of the British bounty and the rise of cotton, and it soon lost all economic importance. Rice production was damaged by the departure of large numbers of slaves and the neglect and destruction of the irrigation systems. The coastal area recovered slowly because of the capital needed and the greater interest of new settlers in the upcountry. By 1800 rice production had attained its prewar level and continued to increase. But rice cultivation could not expand beyond fresh water coastal swamps, which it required. Rice planters were frequently the best and most scientific farmers of this era, and rice was raised commercially only upon plantations with a slave labor force. During and after the War of 1812, Thomas Spalding and some other coastal planters perfected sugar production. Though the cane grew well, sugar never became a major crop in Georgia.

Relatively few settlers came into the southern part of the area between the Ogeechee and Oconee, since it consisted largely of pine barrens that were poorly suited for agriculture. In the 1780s and 1790s the upcountry north and west of Augusta was the coming agricultural area in Georgia, and most of the new settlers took up land there. These settlers, mainly from the Carolinas and Virginia with a few from elsewhere, were mostly small farmers who worked their own land and owned few if any slaves. Tobacco, which grew well, became the chief money crop of the upcountry, with warehouses for its inspection set up

Eighteenth-century log cabin with stick and mud chimney
University of Georgia Libraries

at Augusta and in other towns. Upcountry farmers grew some wheat and more corn. Cattle, hogs, sheep, and poultry flourished for local use.

Cotton soon became the most spectacular money crop and replaced tobacco in the upcountry. Some experiments in growing cotton had been conducted in the colonial period with the West Indian perennial variety, but not enough was grown to be of commercial value. In the 1780s sea island cotton began to be grown on the coast islands. While this cotton was a very valuable commodity, it could be grown only on the coast. The upland, short staple, cotton produced the great revolution in southern agriculture and life. Quantity production of this cotton could not come until after Eli Whitney developed the cotton gin in 1793 at Mulberry Grove, Nathanael Greene's plantation, near Savannah. Whitney and his partner, Phineas Miller, originally tried to manufacture and own all the gins and then lease them to users. As gins were so simple mechanically they could be easily copied and this resulted in innumerable patent infringement suits and little profit to Whitney and Miller.

Cotton could be grown on large plantations with slave labor, on smaller farms, or even in small patches for home use. Its production cycle was relatively simple and easily learned. While upland cotton could be grown in most of the state, it grew best in the piedmont area that was just being settled when Whitney improved the cotton gin. Hence by 1820 cotton production was beginning to change the agricultural pattern of the piedmont, dominated until now by the small, subsistence farmer. Now plantations and slaves increased there, and the political and economic outlook of the cotton area became more like that of the older coast. Of course the cotton area never produced only cotton. Corn was undoubtedly the most widespread crop, but it was mainly used upon the farm or plantation where it was raised and seldom sold outside the locality. Wheat, oats, and other small grains were raised along with potatoes, vegetables, peaches, apples, and livestock. While some planters emphasized cotton at the expense of food crops, the best ones always raised enough food for their slaves and work stock. Yeoman farmers tended to raise more foodstuffs, often with some to sell, but they also raised cotton.

Cotton prices remained high until the embargo of 1807 disrupted international trade. There was rapid recovery once the War of 1812 ended in 1815. By 1820 60 percent of the upland farmers grew cotton, and production increased from 1,000 bales in 1790 to 90,000 bales. The rapid increase in cotton cultivation was beginning to fasten slavery, which many had hoped was a dying institution, upon the South much tighter than before. Cotton also resulted in the rapid push for the remaining Indian lands in the state. In fact cotton was beginning to exert a greater force upon the economy of the state and the life of its people than they yet realized.

Manufacturing in Georgia between 1783 and 1820 was in the handicraft stage or else consisted of simple, first-stage processing. Artisans in Savannah, Augusta, Milledgeville, and other towns produced many items for local sale. There were spinners, weavers, tailors and dressmakers, wigmakers, bakers, furniture makers, tanners, shoemakers, silversmiths, jewelers, and other craftsmen. Almost none of these workmen made things except for the local markets, and many of the items they made were also imported from Europe or the northern states. This was a typical situation in a frontier area, but there were a surprising number of able artisans found in Georgia county seat towns by 1820. In simple or first-stage manufacture lumber, naval stores, flour and meal, and similar things were produced for local consumption or export. No real factories existed, but there were shops in which master workmen and apprentices worked together, or where plantation slave artisans labored. Many people also engaged in part-time household manufacture.

Merchandising was more important than manufacturing. Savannah remained the import-export center of the state, with the largest merchant houses located there. Despite the hopes of Brunswick, Darien, and St. Marys, Savannah continued as the only port of more than strictly local importance. Augusta was the first merchandising center in the upcountry, and it greatly increased in importance as more land to the north and west was settled. Milledgeville, both because of its location and because it was the capital of the state, developed as a middle Georgia merchandising center. To a lesser degree, county seats performed this service for their counties and nearby areas. Some larger planters continued to buy from the importing merchants in Savannah, but smaller planters in the upcountry, of necessity, traded with local merchants. One form of merchandising that declined or disappeared was the Indian trade, as the Indians moved out of Georgia or changed from hunting to agriculture as their main occupation.

Most Georgia businesses were individually owned, but some were partnerships. By 1820 only twenty-four business corporations had been chartered, each by special act of the legislature. Of these, thirteen were concerned with developing transportation, five were banks, two insurance companies, and one a textile manufacturer. Four were capitalized at over $1 million and six at under $100,000. Most businesses were much smaller and mainly local in operation.

Commercial banks in the United States began with the establishment of the Bank of the United States, a part of the Hamiltonian economic program, in 1791. James Jackson, then a member of the United States House of Representatives, joined James Madison in leading the unsuccessful congressional opposition to the bank. From 1791 until 1807 most Georgians would have been classified as believers in specie currency rather than the paper banknotes that were becoming the main circulating medium of the country. Banks in Georgia received a bad name by being linked in many people's minds with the Yazoo fraud. James Jackson continued his opposition to banks and helped to prevent any being chartered in Georgia for the next decade.

The state's first bank was the branch of the Bank of the United States established at Savannah in 1802, which soon saw its loans and the use of its banknotes as currency increase rapidly. With the growth of Savannah and Augusta as commercial centers and the success of the Bank of the United States, more Georgians came to see the benefits of commercial banks. Thus the assembly in 1810 chartered the Planters' Bank of Savannah and the Bank of Augusta. The state reserved one-sixth of the stock in these two banks for its own investment and increased this to one-half in the Bank of Darien, chartered in 1818. After 1810 the state invested much of its surplus income in bank stock. When Congress attempted to recharter the Bank of the United States in 1811, Senator William H. Crawford favored it, while Congressman George M. Troup opposed it. When the Second Bank of the United States was chartered in 1816, most Georgia congressmen voted for it and Crawford worked well with it for the next eight years as secretary of the treasury.

Milledgeville, besides being the capital of the state, was an increasingly important commercial center. Having lost its bid to secure a bank in 1813, it tried again in 1815 and immediately met opposition from Savannah and Augusta interests. As a compromise, the legislature created the Bank of the State of Georgia, with a capital of $1.5 million. Its main office was to be in Savannah, with branches in Augusta and Milledgeville immediately and eventually in Washington, Athens, Eatonton, Greensboro, and Macon. Two-thirds of the stock was reserved to the state, one-half of the remainder to Savannah and Augusta, and the other half to eight designated interior towns. This was a private commercial bank different from earlier banks in Georgia only in the branch bank provisions.

Several attempts in the decade 1810–20 to create a bank to make long-term loans to farmers and planters, primarily in new areas of the state, were defeated through opposition of the older areas. In order partly to fill this need and also to develop Darien's port facilities, the Bank of Darien was established in 1818, modeled to a considerable extent upon the Bank of the State of Georgia. One-half of the stock of $1 million was reserved to the state. Branches were to be located in Milledgeville and on the Ocmulgee and elsewhere as the directors saw fit.

Georgia banks, unlike those in many other states, did not suspend specie payment during the panic of 1819 and none failed. This was undoubtedly due to the rather conservative banking operations in the state, which had been so tightly controlled by the state government.

From 1782 to 1820 Georgia's economy grew rapidly, as would be expected in a frontier state increasing in population and in land available for settlement. The most dramatic growth was in new land for settlement and in increased agricultural production. Many white Georgians felt themselves held back by the continued presence of the Indians in the western and northern part of the state, but growth probably came about as rapidly as it could be advantageously handled by the state. Inadequate transportation facilities may have delayed economic development by 1820, and this would not be solved until the coming of the railroads in the 1830s and 1840s. While there was little manufacturing, that was to be expected in a frontier state. Overall Georgia's economic growth had been rapid and brought increased wealth into the state and nation.

X

Society and Culture on the Frontier
1782–1820

Wars always affect the way that people live, and the American War for Independence was no exception in the case of Georgia. First there was the disruption of life and economy incidental to combat and territory's changing hands between British and Whigs. Many people moved either permanently or temporarily, church congregations were scattered, clergymen left and were not replaced, schools were disrupted, marriages could not take place, and children were not born because of the separation of the parents.

The first major population change occurred when Tories fled at the beginning of the war. Movement into the upcountry, which had been going on rapidly since 1763, slowed when combat began. With the return of the British to Georgia at the end of 1778, many Whigs left, Georgia Tories returned, and Tories from other southern areas moved in. At the end of the war, this situation was reversed again. Some Tories who left returned as the hatreds of the war years abated. Once fighting stopped, people began coming into Georgia's upcountry again, while only a few new residents chose the older coastal area. Most of this new population came from the states to the immediate north, with a few from New England. Georgia had 82,000 people by 1790, 162,000 by 1800, and 340,000 by 1820.

The decline of the embryonic colonial aristocracy and the increased emphasis on equality for the common man that resulted from the Revolution slowly weakened the eighteenth-century idea of a stratified society. While the common man was elevated and the economic base of many coastal planter-aristocrats was lost, the beginnings of upland cotton culture by 1800 led to the creation of the cotton aristocrats, who were to dominate so much of the state up until the Civil War. Besides the few old upper-class families from the colonial period and representatives of such families that came to Georgia from Virginia, this new aristocracy came mainly from the yeoman farmer class.

Of course the great majority of whites continued to be small farmers, who usually lived in rural abundance but with simplicity and little sophistication. The towns had a small artisan class, which matched the yeomanry in social and economic standing. This large middle class usually had little formal education but was independent-minded and knew the value of its vote at election time. These people were in a very real sense the backbone of Georgia and her development. There were always the poor who were not able to achieve worldly success for varying reasons—physical, emotional, educational, or mental. They existed all over the state, generally located on the poorer soil. Some were given a slight amount of relief by local governments or charitable organizations, but most had to support themselves.

There were also the blacks, virtually all of whom were slaves. Because of the large number of slaves lost during the Revolutionary War and the economic disruption of the immediate postwar years, there was a shortage of slaves until the 1790s. Hence Georgians insisted at the constitutional convention in 1787 that the foreign slave trade be allowed to continue. In 1783, probably because of the slave insurrection in Santo Domingo, Georgia prohibited the importation of slaves from the Bahamas, the West Indies, and Florida. The state constitution of 1798 and the federal law of 1808 outlawed all foreign slave importation, but a trickle of blacks continued to be imported illegally. In 1789 Georgia also outlawed the importation of slaves from other states, and this law was reenacted in 1817, probably because it was not being enforced. It was never interpreted to prevent masters who were moving to Georgia from bringing slaves for their own use, however. The great importance of slaves was economic, and many whites did not realize the social effect of such large numbers of blacks in society. Little opposition to slavery, such as existed in the upper South, was obvious in Georgia.

Life of the blacks was considerably affected by the amount of time they or their ancestors had been in America, the size of their owner's plantation, and how closely they lived and worked with whites. New arrivals from Africa were soon put to work, but their social life changed much more slowly. Blacks who were closely associated with whites gave up some African ways more easily and adopted those of whites more quickly. The small number of slaves on most upcountry plantations to 1820 helped this process of change, as did the great decline in slave importation after 1800. Larger plantations and greater concentrations of blacks in the coastal area made for more independent social and family life. On large plantations slaves had a better chance to develop leadership abilities when used as drivers or as overseers. Slave artisans were also more common on larger plantations. Thus hierarchy among

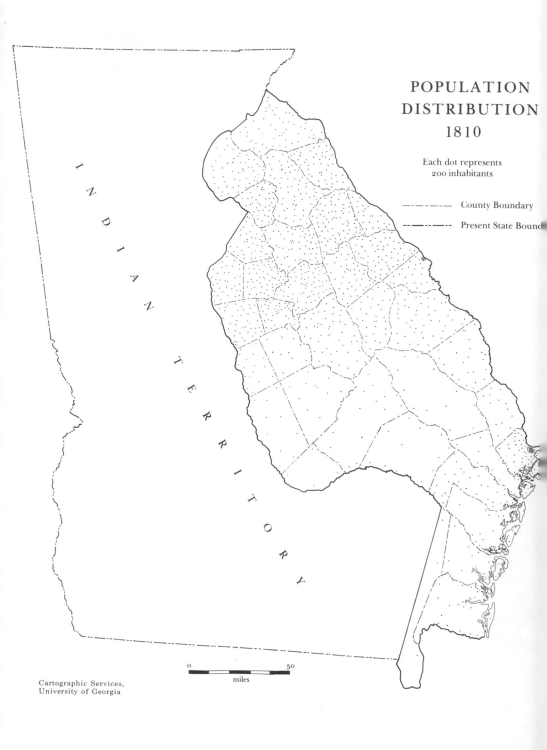

POPULATION
DISTRIBUTION
1810

Each dot represents
200 inhabitants

— · — · — County Boundary

━ · ━ · ━ Present State Bound

I N D I A N   T E R R I T O R Y

0   50
miles

Cartographic Services,
University of Georgia

slaves became obvious. As cotton culture increased in the upcountry, the number of blacks increased also, but the proportion was never as large as it was on the coastal area. Throughout this period, most slaves brought into Georgia came from other states to the north, and the percentage of blacks in the total population increased from 35.9 percent in 1790 to 44 percent by 1820. In the last analysis, the lives of slaves were controlled to a considerable degree by their personal abilities and by the type of masters and overseers for whom they worked.

Indians made up the other nonwhite group in Georgia. In 1780 most Georgia Indians showed little sign of the traits that were to secure for them the title of the "Civilized Tribes," but by 1820 great strides had been made toward adopting the white man's civilization to their own needs. In the 1790s the United States government began to formulate Indian policy and appointed agents to handle Indian affairs. In the Treaty of Holston of 1791 with the Cherokees, who made the most rapid progress in a new civilization, the United States promised to help the Indians to develop agriculture, household manufactures, and crafts such as blacksmithing and carpentry.

United States agents Benjamin Hawkins and Return J. Meigs (after 1800) urged agriculture and crafts on the Cherokees. The Cherokee interest in this approach was increased by whites and mixed-breeds who lived within the nation and by the Indian belief that as game declined it would be impossible to continue their old hunting and trading economy. Meigs did what he could to teach the Indians agriculture, furnish plows and other implements, and to get artisans to move into the nation to fulfill Indian needs and to teach the Indians trades. Women learned to spin and weave and cattle were raised. A number of visitors in the Cherokee country in the early nineteenth century commented upon the good farms and prosperity of the area.

Meigs encouraged white missionaries, who brought Christianity and formal education to the Indians. Mission schools began in a small way about 1800, with the Cherokees much more interested in education than in Christianity. By 1820 real growth of schools and churches began. Meigs was interested in a more centralized and stronger government and encouraged the Cherokee council along this line. By 1820 a real beginning had been made, but the final flowering with a written constitution did not come until 1827. By 1820 most Cherokees had become farmers and cattle raisers and had given up the old hunting economy. Once the Cherokees decided to accept the new ideas and methods, they adopted them rapidly.

The Creeks did not change their ways as rapidly as the Cherokees, but eventually they decided that it would be necessary. How much of this decision was due to Agent Benjamin Hawkins is not known, but his influence was important. Hawkins was one of the federal commissioners for the Creek treaty of Coleraine in 1796, became southern Indian agent soon thereafter, and in 1801 was appointed Creek agent. He established his agency upon the Flint River with a model farm, nursery for fruit trees, blacksmiths and other artisans, and a plantation of his own worked by slaves. Hawkins sought by example and gifts of plants, seeds, and implements to induce the Creeks to adopt the white man's ways.

Hawkins urged the Indians to engage in agriculture individually, rather than following the old communal method, but he succeeded mainly with the mixed-breeds and with those who owned Negro slaves. Indians took to livestock raising because of the decline in wild game and because it was easier than growing field crops. Some raised small amounts of cotton, and some women learned to spin and weave. The old hunting and trade economy was declining, but most Creeks adopted new ways slowly.

Throughout the first two decades of the nineteenth century, the importance of the older leading towns declined with the exhaustion of their fields, losses of population, changing economy and lifestyle, and the corruption of their way of life by increasing numbers of whites in the nation. By 1811 the federal road from the Oconee River into Alabama brought more whites into the nation. This prepared the ground for Tecumseh's appeal in 1812 to give up the white man's ways, eliminate the whites in the nation, and return to the old ways. But the decisive military defeats of 1813–14 made it clear that the old ways were doomed. The Creeks were now a broken people and no longer a threat to the whites. Change was essential. Some Creeks, especially the mixed-breeds, took up individual farming, entered into business partnerships with whites, and changed otherwise. The Creeks lost their best white friend and protector when Benjamin Hawkins died in 1816. The next year the nation adopted a law code drawn up from its traditional laws and customs, now written down for the first time. Missionaries had little success in converting or educating Creeks before their defeat in 1814, but thereafter some became more receptive. Despite repeated declarations that they would cede no further land, they continued to make cessions to whites.

Besides its effects on people and lifestyle, the War for Independence disrupted the few schools in Georgia. With independence there was renewed interest in education because of the feeling that self-government required an enlightened electorate. The state constitution of 1777 provided that schools should be founded in each county at state expense, but nothing was done to implement this policy until the war ended. In July 1783 Governor Lyman Hall strongly recommended that the assembly encourage education and religion. This body responded by creating three boards of commissioners (in Richmond, Wilkes, and Burke counties) to lay out county seats, sell lots, build academies, and oversee their operation. In 1785 the assembly chartered the University of Georgia and directed that its governing board have general oversight of all publicly supported schools in the state. The schools were given public land or confiscated estates, but there was no provision for continuing state support. Richmond Academy, the oldest school in the state, began operation in 1785, and other county academies opened within the next two decades. Bethesda reopened in 1788 but was soon burned. There was sometimes a little continuing public support at the local level. In 1817 the legislature created a free school fund of $250,-000, the income from which was supposed to be used to establish free schools. Apparently no schools were established under this law before it was revised in 1822. Essentially all schools, including county academies, were private after 1800. By 1820 there were about forty academies in Georgia, besides miscellaneous elementary schools. Initially academies had a heavily classical curriculum, but they added practical subjects and became terminal as well as college preparatory schools. Latin and Greek, English grammar, modern foreign languages, and mathematics remained their most popular subjects. For girls, there was less emphasis on Latin and Greek, and more on music and the arts. Many schools were coeducational, but not all were.

After being chartered in 1785, little else happened to the University of Georgia for the next fifteen years. The only funds available had to come from the 40,000 acres of land given it in 1785. Abraham Baldwin, a native of Connecticut with experience on the Yale faculty, wrote the charter and became the first president of the university. In the summer of 1801 it was decided to begin actual operation. Baldwin, by then a United States senator, resigned as president, and Josiah Meigs, formerly of Yale also, succeeded him. Classes began in temporary buildings in Athens, and the college prospered for several years. But Meigs and the Board of Trustees differed, and he resigned as president in 1810. During the next nine years, under two presidents, the university almost died, but in June 1819 a well-known educator, Moses Waddel, became president and better days soon arrived. The university received no state funds except special grants for buildings. The landed endowment was sold in 1815 and the money deposited with the state, from which the university henceforth received $8,000 a year as interest, its first regular income. In its first two decades, the university's enrollment was highest in 1806, with seventy students, while its income was usually under $10,000 a year. Yet, as the only college in the state, it embodied Georgia's hopes for improved intellectual opportunities.

Georgians undoubtedly were more concerned about religion than education. The Revolutionary War left Georgia's churches in disarray. Anglican clergy as well as Lutheran Christopher F. Triebner, of Ebenezer, were royalists and left by the end of the war. The Reverend John J. Zubly, of Independent Meeting House in Savannah, died in 1781, and the young Midway minister, the Reverend Moses Allen, a Whig chaplain, died while a British prisoner of war. The British burned the meeting house at Midway, and several other churches were destroyed or damaged by military action. At the end of the War, except for the Quakers and Baptists, churches and organized religion had practically ceased to exist in Georgia.

Early in 1783 Governor Hall and his council called upon the people to reorganize and repair their churches as necessary. In July the governor's urging of the assembly to encourage education and religion brought no immediate action about religion. A 1785 law provided for county ministers to be elected by the voters and paid by the state, with all denominations having equal liberty and toleration. Existing churches could receive their pro rata share of the tax money. There is no evidence that this attempt at a compromise between a state church and freedom of religion was ever implemented. Although never repealed, this law would have been invalid under the state constitution of 1798. Henceforth religious support in Georgia would be entirely voluntary.

Existing churches had a hard time securing and supporting ministers and rebuilding or repairing their buildings. A new building was erected at Midway in 1792; it still stands, the second oldest church building in Georgia. Gradually the churches were reinstituted and their scattered and sometimes divided congregations were brought back together. The disestablishment of the Anglican church by the constitution of 1777 reduced its status, so that there were only three parishes as late as 1820. Roman Catholics in 1796 were granted a lot in Savannah upon which to build a church. Meanwhile Catholics from Maryland came into upcountry Wilkes County in 1793 and founded the town of Locust Grove, where a church was soon constituted. The Congregationalists at Midway continued to obtain clergymen from New

England. In 1785 the Lutherans at Ebenezer secured the Reverend John Ernest Bergman from Germany, who remained their pastor until his death in 1824. Jerusalem Church and its clergymen lost their tight control over the Ebenezer congregation during the Revolution and never regained it.

The greatest religious change during the 1780s and 1790s was the growth of the Methodists and Baptists, first in the backcountry but soon throughout the state. Daniel Marshall, the colonial Baptist minister at Kiokee Church, died there in November 1784, and the next year the first recorded Methodist ministers arrived in the state. Both denominations grew very rapidly and soon became the state's strongest. The Baptists with their congregational control and emotional preaching were especially adapted to the frontier, but the Methodist circuit riders accomplished much the same results. The Georgia Baptist Association was separated from the South Carolina Association in 1784 or 1785, and Bishop Francis Asbury held the first Methodist conference in Georgia in upcountry Wilkes County in 1788. Other denominations grew much more slowly and mainly in the towns and older parts of the state. While slaves usually worshipped at their master's church or at special services approved by their masters, the First Colored Baptist Church, an organization controlled entirely by its own members, was created in Savannah in 1788. About 1800 a similar church was constituted in Augusta, but these were exceptions to the general rule.

Georgia churches remained a part of South Carolina administrative organizations until there were enough members to set up separate state groups. By 1820 only the Baptists were entirely independent of South Carolina. There were still many unchurched people in Georgia, either because of their personal inclination or because they lived in areas where regular church worship was not available.

In cultural affairs outside religion and schools, little had been accomplished in Georgia by 1820. The best-known literary work was Hugh McCall's *History of Georgia*, published in Savannah in 1811 and 1816, the first published history of Georgia. There were an increasing number of library societies and a few organizations that held debates or pursued other literary activities. One of the best-known debating societies was the Demosthenian Society, organized by students at the university in 1803. Savannah had a flourishing theater, as did Augusta, and theatrical productions were sometimes presented in other Georgia towns and at schools, with local or imported talent. At least one play, *The Mysterious Father: A Tragedy in Five Acts*, was written by William Bulloch Maxwell of Savannah and printed there in 1807.

Owens-Thomas House, Savannah, William Jay architect

Most plays presented in Georgia were English imports. Music was performed in churches and theaters by local groups and by traveling artists. Wealthy Georgians could have their portraits painted by visiting artists or upon visits to Charleston or elsewhere.

In architecture, most houses were small and utilitarian. There were a few houses built in the late colonial or Georgian style of architecture, undoubtedly reminiscent of houses the builder had known before coming to Georgia. Georgia's two best-known architects of this era both arrived late. William Jay came from Bath, England, and was in Savannah from 1817 through 1822, where he built some fine regency houses, several of which still survive. Daniel Pratt began about 1820 to build elegant plantation houses in the Milledgeville area. Savannah and Augusta, being the state's largest and wealthiest cities, had more well-done houses than other cities. Milledgeville, Washington, and the

Gordon-Blount-Banks House, Newnan (originally, Jones County),
Daniel Pratt architect

W. N. Banks, Newnan

eastern cotton belt began to build good houses by 1810, a number of which still remain today.

Wealthy Georgians who wanted fine furniture, carpets, silverware, draperies, and other furnishings for their houses usually imported from England or from the northern states, but there were skilled artisans who worked in Georgia, mainly for the local market. Fine textiles were imported, but cloth for ordinary clothing was often made in the state. Almost all clothing was made locally, either in the home or by local tailors and seamstresses. Georgians produced most of their own food, with such dishes as seafoods, pork and beef, sweet potatoes, and other traditional Georgia dishes already standard fare.

Georgia was still a frontier state in 1820. Many Georgians were interested in strong drink, hard work and play (often combined), physically vigorous religion, taming the frontier, getting rid of the Indians, clearing the land, and increasing their wealth. Many of "the finer things of life" would have to wait. At Savannah and Augusta and along the Savannah River the frontier had disappeared, and culture had arrived for those interested in it. But culture never kept up with the receding frontier. Instead it had to await the inclination of the people, the accumulation of wealth, and the passage of time.

PART THREE

1820–1865

by

F. N. BONEY

The Great Seal from 1799 to 1863

The Great Seal of Georgia during the Southern Confederacy

XI

The Politics of Expansion
and Secession
1820–1861

By 1820 Georgia's population of 189,570 whites and 151,419 blacks had
increased 35 percent in only a decade. All over the older areas of the
nation the red man was being driven west, and white Georgians coveted the Indian lands covering most of the northern and almost
half of the central part of the state. The Troup and Clark factions
both championed Indian removal, arguing only over tactics, and the
American acquisition of Florida in 1821 increased the irresistible
pressure on the state's Indians. President James Monroe supported
Georgia, and in January 1821 a treaty was negotiated at Indian Springs
that gave the state all Creek land from the Ocmulgee River to the Flint
River. Governor John Clark, who had narrowly defeated George M.
Troup by secret ballot of the legislators in 1819, quickly called the
legislature into session to distribute the new area through the state's
fourth land lottery and also to push for a similar land cession from the
Cherokees in northern Georgia.

Governor Clark again narrowly defeated Troup in 1821 as the two
contending factions continued the Georgia tradition of emphasizing
personalities rather than policies. Both favored slavery and both opposed protective tariffs and the national bank, but they passionately
disagreed on who should gain the responsibilities (and spoils) of office.
Concentrating on the local level and wooing the voters with stump
speeches, barbecues, and other popular attractions, the two emerging
parties competed in a rough, semifrontier environment where violence
and voting irregularities and fraud were not unknown. The Troup
followers tended to be numerous in the more settled, prosperous areas
of the state, and the Clarkites tended to concentrate in the poorer,
more frontier regions, but these were only vague tendencies in a fluid,
confused, highly partisan political milieu that defied logical explanation.

Clark declined renomination in 1823, and Troup defeated Matthew

Talbot for the governorship by the usual narrow margin in the legislature. The next year the legislators gave Georgia's nine electoral votes
to Troupite William H. Crawford even though a crippling stroke had
disqualified him for the presidency. Under the aggressive leadership of
Troup, his increasingly well-organized party made steady headway
against the wavering Clarkites. He moved quickly to consolidate his
hard-won power by pushing a very popular policy, Indian removal.

Troup aggressively concentrated on the Creeks, who still held most
of west central Georgia. In recent years these Indians had expanded
their traditional agriculture while deemphasizing their old hunting
ways. The Creeks refused to cede more of their land to Georgia. President Monroe was sympathetic to Georgia but unwilling to use force
to remove the Indians. Governor Troup with the full support of the
legislature and the people continued to pressure the federal government, which finally commissioned two Georgians to negotiate with
the Creeks. After several rebuffs and much blatant manipulation they
finally reached an agreement with Chief William McIntosh, the Scot-
Creek first cousin of Troup, and some other leaders of the Lower
(eastern) Creeks, who had no clear mandate from their people. The
Treaty of Indian Springs of 1825 ceded all of the Creeks' Georgia
land, and it was ratified by the federal government in the last days
of the Monroe administration. Governor Troup pressed the pliant
McIntosh for an immediate survey to prepare the whole area for distribution by lottery, but McIntosh and several other Indian leaders
who had signed the treaty were murdered by angry Creeks determined
to hold their lands.

New President John Quincy Adams doubted the propriety of the
new treaty, especially after learning that most Creek leaders opposed
any cessions of land. The mercurial Governor Troup, further angered
by what he considered the new administration's hostility to slavery,
quarreled fiercely with federal officials, insisting that the treaty was
valid, but he did delay the controversial land survey in response to
Adams's protests.

In the midst of this growing confrontation with the federal government, Troup ran for reelection in the state's first popular election of
a governor late in 1825. His opponent and old nemesis, John Clark,
was determined to revive his faltering party with a dramatic popular
victory. A bitter battle ensued with both factions attacking without
restraint. The two contestants differed little in actual policies, but
Governor Troup's forceful drive to expel the Creeks was probably decisive as he triumphed by a 20,545-to-19,862 margin. Although the

Clarkites actually gained a slight majority in the new legislature, they were shaken by their gubernatorial defeat and the departure of their leader to Florida in 1827, and their fortunes gradually declined.

Emboldened by victory, Governor Troup resumed his fight with the federal government over the Creek lands. Fully supported by both parties in the legislature, he reasserted the validity of the Treaty of Indian Springs and renewed his plans for a quick survey. However, despite a roar of protest from Georgia, President Adams negotiated a new treaty with the Creeks that ceded all of their Georgia lands except a small, narrow slice along the Alabama border. This Treaty of Washington of January 1826 was almost as cynical and corrupt as the original one, but Governor Troup was not satisfied. He denounced federal interference and began to survey Creek lands ahead of the deadline set by the new treaty. He also ordered a survey of the thin slice of Georgia land retained by the Creeks. Finally, he threatened to resist any federal military force and even alerted some state militia districts. The federal government had no real sympathy for Indians, so by the end of 1827 further negotiations had extinguished all Creek land claims in Georgia. The Creeks were finished; the Cherokees were next.

Georgia voters were not particularly impressed with the subtleties of states' rights doctrine, but they did like the way Governor Troup and his followers got things done, even when harassed by the federal government. Troup's decision to prepare for a return to the United States Senate did not seriously disturb his party, which gathered in legislative caucus in December 1826 and selected Congressman John Forsyth as its gubernatorial candidate. The increasingly disunified Clarkites finally renominated Matthew Talbot, but he died during the hectic fall campaign, and Forsyth won an easy 22,220-to-9,072 victory over scattered local opposition.

Legalistic and cautious, Governor Forsyth reluctantly cooperated when the legislature created the Central Bank of Georgia, a virtual government bank and treasury. The legislature also yielded the power to select presidential electors to the voters, who massively backed Andrew Jackson's successful bid for the presidency in 1828.

Although more moderate than his predecessor, Forsyth still favored Indian removal, so Georgia exerted increasing pressure against the stubborn Cherokees in the northwestern part of the state. He also shared his people's opposition to rising federal protective tariffs. The Indian and tariff issues dominated Georgia politics for years. Both caused more friction with the federal government, and the tariff controversy gradually eroded the shifting, personalized foundations of the Troup and Clark factions and stimulated the development of two new, more issue-oriented parties.

In 1829 retiring Governor Forsyth returned to the United States Senate, but the national politics that attracted him only sporadically affected Georgia's intense factionalism. His gubernatorial successor was another Troup man, Congressman George R. Gilmer, who won an overwhelming 12,316-to-6,798 victory over Joel Crawford of the disintegrating Clark party. Two years later in the fall of 1831 Gilmer and the Troupites lost to Wilson Lumpkin and the emerging Union organization by a count of 24,731 to 23,428. These two competent governors bore the brunt of the tariff and Indian controversies.

The anti-Indian legislature under Governor Forsyth had in 1828 ordered the replacement of Cherokee law with Georgia law, but major action occurred only after the gold rush of 1829 sent several thousand whites into Cherokee territory. New Governor Gilmer requested the withdrawal of all federal forces from the area, and President Jackson, a friend of Georgia and no friend of Indians, readily agreed. Congress's passage of the Indian Removal Act in the spring of 1830 dimmed the hopes of all Indians east of the Mississippi River. But the Cherokees, the most advanced of the southern Indians, were deeply rooted in northwest Georgia and determined to stay. Untutored but brilliant Sequoyah, probably the son of a white trader and an Indian mother, had given them a workable new syllabary, and they had their own newspaper, the bilingual *Cherokee Phoenix*, which was edited by Cherokee Elias Boudinot. White missionaries furthered the development of education as well as Christianity. Settling on the land as farmers and businessmen and even employing some black slaves, the Cherokees continued to adapt to white American standards by framing a constitution in 1827 that institutionalized their independence. And finally, relentlessly pressured by half a million Georgians, the approximately seventeen thousand people of the Cherokee nation carried their resistance to the United States Supreme Court.

This highest federal court had not yet fully consolidated its power within the national government, and Georgia, encouraged by the attitude of President Jackson and Congress, simply refused to recognize the court's authority over Cherokee affairs. Late in 1830 Georgia ignored a Supreme Court stay order and hanged George Tassel, a Cherokee convicted by a Hall County court of murdering another Indian in Cherokee land. The Cherokees persisted in their resistance and their distinguished counsel, former Attorney General William Wirt and Bank of the United States lawyer John Sergeant, presented the Supreme Court with *Cherokee Nation* v. *Georgia* in 1831. The hearing was brief because Georgia refused to send counsel. Chief Justice John Marshall was sympathetic to the Indians' plight, but he denied the right of the Cherokees to bring a direct suit against a state.

The following year the Marshall court received a more proper challenge to Georgia's Indian policy. Samuel Austin Worcester and Elizur Butler, northern missionaries sent to help the Cherokees, were arrested for defying Georgia law in Cherokee territory and sentenced to four years in the penitentiary by a state court. Retaining Wirt and Sergeant as counsel, they appealed to the Supreme Court. Governor Lumpkin refused to send counsel to represent the state in the famous *Worcester* v. *Georgia* case of 1832.

This time the Supreme Court rendered a definitive judgment: the laws of Georgia were invalid in Cherokee land and Worcester and Butler should be freed. The actual court order enforcing this decision was delayed as protests came from Georgia. Governor Lumpkin vowed "determined resistance" to the court's "unconstitutional encroachment," and President Jackson sympathized with Georgia. By this time Jackson had been reelected with overwhelming support in Georgia where his Indian removal policy was very popular, and the nullification controversy was threatening to destroy the Union. Worcester and Butler and their home office in Boston and Governor Lumpkin all feared that continuing controversy would drive Georgia into South Carolina's nullification movement, so a deal was arranged. The two missionaries withdrew their Supreme Court appeal, the governor pardoned them, and they eventually rejoined the Cherokees in the West.

Georgia had successfully defied the Supreme Court—but not the president or Congress—and the Cherokees were doomed. The state land lottery of 1832 had already assigned the Indians' lands to Georgia whites who were beginning to move in and take over, and President Jackson and Governor Lumpkin relentlessly pressured the despondent, divided Cherokees. Most supported their main chief, John Ross, in his resistance to removal. More Scot than Cherokee, the able Ross had favored adopting white civilization and had himself become a prominent planter with many slaves, but he could not stem the white tide. Finally in 1835 a minority faction of Cherokees under Major Ridge, his son John Ridge, and his nephew Elias Boudinot signed the Treaty of New Echota, agreeing to migrate to the west in return for $5 million from the federal government. These three leaders ignored the wishes of a great majority of their tribe and, like McIntosh of the Creeks, they were later murdered by their own people. But further resistance was hopeless, and in 1838 the United States Army rounded up the last twelve thousand Cherokees for the march along the "trail of tears" that claimed the lives of several thousand, including Ross's wife Quatie. A century of white-red struggle ended with the expulsion of the last major group of native Georgia Indians.

During most of this period Georgians were distracted by Indian affairs, but the rising tariff controversy emerged as the crucial issue in 1832. The legislature had denounced the Tariff of Abominations in 1828, but only after President Jackson signed the tariff of 1832 in July did a real crisis arise. John C. Calhoun's nullification crusade began to sweep through neighboring South Carolina. Georgians were antitariff and pro–states' rights but increasingly wary of nullification. South Carolina had sometimes seemed overbearing, and its opponent, President Jackson, was Georgia's ally against the Cherokees.

As political pressures increased both the Clark and Troup factions disintegrated, and first the Union party and then the State Rights party coalesced. As usual passion, personalities, and expediency played major roles in a Georgia political metamorphosis, but this time the tariff-nullification dispute led to a somewhat more rational party alignment. Most (but not all) Clarkites moved into the antinullification, pro–Jackson Union party, and many (but far from all) of the more numerous Troupites joined the rival State Rights party. Some of the emerging State Righters like Judge Augustine S. Clayton and Seaborn Jones were full-fledged nullifiers, but most were not.

Some old Troupites organized an extralegal antitariff convention that met in Milledgeville in November while the legislature was in session, but the people of Georgia rejected their anti-Jackson rhetoric. Nineteen of the state's eighty counties did not even send delegates, and after a few days of wrangling Congressman John Forsyth led a walkout of 53 of the 134 participating delegates. The remainder under the erudite John M. Berrien's leadership dutifully passed antitariff resolutions, and the much-ballyhooed convention was soon forgotten.

Meanwhile the legislature reiterated its opposition to protective tariffs but rejected nullification before South Carolina's convention could act. The Union survived partly because Georgia's quick decision for Jackson and the federal government helped deprive South Carolina of unified southern support in 1832. The following year the Union party nominated popular Governor Lumpkin for a second term. He opposed nullification. The emerging State Rights party nominated Joel Crawford, who dodged the issue. Lumpkin won by a 28,814-to-

27,379 margin, and his Union party gained control of the legislature. Georgia stood firm for the Union, but more tests were to come.

Both new political parties demonstrated a new discipline. Committees canvassed every county. Periodic district and state conventions set strategy, and loyal newspapers propagandized tirelessly. The new parties increasingly emphasized principles as well as personalities, and they drifted closer and closer to affiliations with national parties. The Union party inherited the old Clark faction's tendency to do well in the newer, less prosperous areas, and the State Rights party tended to show strength in the more settled, affluent areas where the Troup faction had been popular, but these tendencies never became hard-and-fast rules in Georgia politics, which remained fluid, inconsistent, and rather illogical throughout the antebellum period.

The Union party remained dominant for the next two years. Its best vote-getter, Congressman James M. Wayne, was appointed to the United States Supreme Court, but Congressman William Schley won the governorship in 1835 by a count of 31,122 to 28,520, while his party retained control of the legislature. The Unionists further prospered through the system of congressional elections, in effect from 1826 until 1844, which had one congressman in each congressional district but allowed each state voter to cast a ballot for one candidate in each district. A solid block of Unionist congressmen was elected in 1834, but the party's increasing affiliation with the national Democratic party boomeranged in 1836 when victorious presidential candidate Martin Van Buren of New York failed to carry Georgia in a campaign that was even rougher than usual.

By now the State Righters were cleansed of all traces of nullification, and they returned George R. Gilmer to the governorship in 1837 with a narrow 34,179-to-33,417 victory over weak incumbent Schley, but they failed to win the legislature. Facing a nationwide depression, Governor Gilmer and his State Righters championed government economy by weakening the much-criticized Central Bank of Georgia and granting only minimal state aid for railroad construction and public education. In 1839 the Union party called for positive action to combat the depression. Charles J. McDonald won the governorship by a margin of 34,634 to 32,807 and his Unionists retained control of the legislature.

Then once again rapidly evolving national politics intruded. In the presidential election of 1840 the State Rights party, increasingly nationalistic under Berrien's influence, allied with the national Whig party and swept the state with a tremendous ballyhoo campaign for William Henry Harrison. The Unionists-turning-Democrats were again carried to defeat by Van Buren's presidential candidacy, but in 1841 they evened the score against the State Righters–turning-Whigs by easily reelecting McDonald governor.

The new Georgia Whig party, roughly and imprecisely the descendant of the old Troup and State Rights parties, still tended to be strongest in the more settled, prosperous agricultural regions with relatively large slave populations and in the towns and cities serving these areas. Many (but not all) large commercial planters found a natural home in the Whig party. The new Georgia Democratic party, roughly and imprecisely the descendant of the old Clark and Union parties, still tended to have its greatest strength in newer and less prosperous regions.

Georgia Whigs gradually assumed the stance of their national leaders, supporting the tariff and the national bank, which was a complete reversal of Troup–State Rights policy, and Georgia Democrats gradually drifted toward the southern rights sectionalism of Calhoun, a repudiation of the Clark-Union kind of Jacksonianism. Yet the number of politicians changing parties did not greatly increase, and both parties tended to retain their traditional constituencies. They remained evenly matched, and their unions with national parties and their new emphasis on policy created a false appearance of permanence.

But for a while the Democrats and Whigs, both well-organized and competently led by prosperous planters and businessmen, lured the voters by using their enthusiasm and every expedient at hand. Georgians were exposed to a series of local, state, and national elections, complete with all the passionate rhetoric and stirring rallies of antebellum American politics. Even in brief interludes between elections the partisan press hammered away relentlessly. Both parties were strengthened by talented young leaders who would make their mark in the nation as well as the state. The Whigs gained two close but contrasting friends: sickly, scholarly Alexander H. Stephens of yeoman background, and robust, dynamic Robert Toombs of the planter elite. The beginning of regular congressional district elections in 1844 and a little gerrymandering by a Whig legislature gave these two Georgians firm foundations for distinguished careers in Washington. The Democrats countered with equally talented young leaders like Howell Cobb, a son of the elite who became a very able and ambitious congressman, and Herschel V. Johnson, the son of plainer folk who gained most of his fame on the state level until he ran for the vice presidency in 1860.

The political struggle continued as Governor McDonald and his

Democratic majority in the large, malapportioned legislature ineptly combatted the depression by cutting the budget and crippling the Central Bank. In 1843 the Whigs nominated able George W. Crawford for the governorship, and he defeated Democrat Mark Anthony Cooper by a 38,713-to-35,325 count as the Whigs also won control of the state's first biennial legislature. But in 1844 the Whigs were handicapped when the national party's presidential nomination went to Henry Clay, who opposed the immediate annexation of Texas. The Democratic candidate, expansionist James K. Polk, carried the state by a rather narrow margin in the wake of another massive ballyhoo campaign.

Governor Crawford's first term was effective enough to check this Democratic surge. He continued the liquidation of the Central Bank, secured congressional districts acceptable to the federal government, and cautiously pushed construction of the state-owned Western and Atlantic Railway by utilizing convict labor and obtaining credit from private banks rather than state government sources. Even though the federal government had not yet fully compensated Georgia for expenses incurred in campaigns against the Seminoles and their fugitive slave allies along the Florida border, economy-minded Crawford greatly improved the state's shaky financial status, and the voters reelected him in the fall of 1845 by a 41,059-to-39,140 count and allowed his Whigs to retain tenuous control of the legislature.

Governor Crawford continued to encourage cautious construction of the Western and Atlantic Railroad while reemphasizing the need to reduce the state debt. He reflected the general Whig tendency to run the state government more frugally than the Democrats in an age when education and other social services were poorly funded. One positive achievement of his administration was the creation of a state supreme court to hear appeals from county justice. In the usual partisan spirit the legislature elected two Whigs and one Democrat as the first justices for staggered, six-year terms.

Then national affairs again intruded. In March 1845 the United States formally annexed Texas as a slave state despite Mexico's protests, and in May 1846 President Polk led the nation to war. Georgians were soon in combat; some fell but more learned a new trade they might later practice on another enemy. Initial American wartime unity soon faded as more and more Whigs became disaffected. Georgia Whigs soon joined this growing antiwar movement, either openly or by implication. Aging Senator Berrien denounced the war, and Congressman Stephens supported him. One of Stephens's antiwar allies and closest personal friends in Congress was an ambitious young politician from Illinois named Abraham Lincoln.

Most Democrats in Washington enthusiastically supported their president's war, and antiwar Georgia Whigs found themselves on the defensive in their hawkish state. They were further embarrassed when the famous Wilmot Proviso, demanding the exclusion of slavery from all territory taken from Mexico, received much more support from northern Whigs than from northern Democrats. They condemned the proviso but tried to avoid discussing it, and many followed Stephens, Toombs, and Berrien in opposing the acquisition of any Mexican territory, but these expediencies compared poorly with the Democrats' confident expansionism.

The Democrats had sectional problems too, but in Georgia they exploited the Whigs' awkward position during the gubernatorial campaign late in 1847. Branding opposition to the war "disloyal," they nominated colorful Congressman George Washington Bonaparte Towns, who unleashed an aggressive southern rights campaign. The Whigs nominated aloof, inarticulate General Duncan L. Clinch, who was no match for a popular spellbinder like Towns. The Whigs managed to retain narrow majorities in both houses of the legislature, but they lost the governorship by a count of 43,220 to 41,931. In Georgia the Whigs and Democrats were so evenly matched that even the strongest trends netted only narrow victories.

Victory over the Mexicans in 1848 forced the United States to face the problem of defining the status of slavery in its newly conquered territories in the southwest. Sectional tensions increased rapidly, and in the North a new Free Soil party championed the containment of slavery. The unstable Whig party began to disintegrate even as it nominated General Zachary Taylor for the presidency. The disunited Democrats finally settled on Lewis Case of Michigan.

Again a state trend was reversed by a presidential campaign. The triumphant Democrats were saddled with the colorless Cass, and Georgia Whigs rallied behind Taylor, a hero of the war they had opposed. He was a southerner and a slaveholder, and he had enough charisma to defeat Cass in Georgia and in the nation. Many Georgians broke party ranks in the usual closely contested fall elections, which also sent four Democrats and four Whigs to Congress again. Democrat Cobb and Whigs Toombs and Stephens won reelection, although "Little Aleck" was almost killed during the campaign when he made the mistake of trying to cane a husky Democrat armed with a bowie knife.

Following Taylor's victory, Calhoun tried to draw all southerners in Congress into a new southern unity movement, but he had little success. Toombs, Stephens, Cobb, and to a lesser extent Berrien opposed him. Only Herschel V. Johnson and two other Democrats in the Georgia delegation backed Calhoun. Senator Johnson symbolized the slow but steady erosion of moderation in a Georgia Democratic party stung by the loss of a national election and federal patronage. Governor Towns and elder statesman Wilson Lumpkin were with Johnson; and, even more important, the Augusta *Constitutionalist* and the *Macon Telegraph* were leading a general shift of Democratic newspapers toward Calhoun radicalism. And a few Georgia Democrats like young Henry L. Benning and ex-Governor Charles J. McDonald had swung all the way to secessionism, the last resort in Calhoun's theory.

Still the growing rift between the southern rights radicals and the Unionist moderates led by Cobb did not prevent the Georgia Democrats from agreeing to support Calhounite Towns for a second term as governor in 1849. The Whigs overcame dissension too. Old Senator Berrien was gradually swinging from his traditional nationalism toward a southern rights position, but young Stephens and Toombs, who still rejected Calhounism, now dominated the state party, which was receiving much patronage from President Taylor. Closing ranks, the Whigs nominated Judge Edward Y. Hill for governor.

The state elections in the fall of 1849 could not be divorced from national affairs. Calhoun had continued to champion a separate southern political party, and by the spring of 1849 he had instigated a movement in Mississippi that culminated in the call for a southern convention to meet in Nashville in June 1850 to further southern unity. Meanwhile, by the summer of 1849 President Taylor had shown he was willing to allow free states to form quickly in the territories taken from Mexico. The sectional clash over slavery was escalating again right in the middle of the Georgia elections.

Both state parties denounced the Wilmot Proviso and stressed their loyalty to southern institutions, but most Democrats, and especially Governor Towns, emphasized southern rights and "resistance" to northern "aggression" more than the Whigs. Towns won reelection by a 46,514-to-43,322 count, and the Democrats also gained control of the legislature by a narrow margin. The Calhounites quickly expanded their control of the state Democratic party even though Towns's increased majority was probably more the result of his popular first administration than his southern rights rhetoric. The politicians were much more excited about the sectional struggle than the voters.

Certainly the new legislature that assembled in Milledgeville in November 1849 was aroused. For the first time the possibility of secession was formally discussed, and southern rights sentiment was temporarily ascendant. Governor Towns quickly pushed through a bill requiring a state convention if the Wilmot Proviso became law or California entered the Union as a free state. He also scheduled an April 1850 election of delegates to the Nashville Convention. Moderate opposition developed too slowly to be effective but did indicate the beginning of the breakdown of regular party lines early in 1850.

The new Congress in Washington underwent even worse contortions. A bitter, protracted fight for the speakership of the House finally ended in victory for Howell Cobb, leader of Georgia's Unionist Democrats. This occurred only after a few southern Whigs led by Stephens and Toombs backed him. Once again the beginnings of a new political alignment in Georgia were noticeable as increasing sectional controversy threatened to tear the Union apart.

Then in January 1850 Senator Henry Clay proposed a complicated compromise that included a tough new federal fugitive slave act and provided for California to become a free state and the rest of the Mexican cession to decide for itself about slavery. Calhoun opposed the compromise and so did Berrien of Georgia.

The long struggle to push Clay's compromise through Congress was well under way when Georgia held its spring elections for delegates to the Nashville Convention. After months of sectional tension and intense propaganda by the southern rights radicals only about twenty-five hundred Georgians even bothered to vote! Most Georgians were not seriously disaffected. The politicians, especially the southern rights radicals, had greatly underestimated the people's Unionism. A patchwork delegation of Georgians did attend the Nashville Convention, but, led by secessionists Benning and McDonald, it was not representative of the moderate masses back home.

But sectional controversy soon shattered both the Whig and Democratic parties in Georgia, where political alignments were always fragile. New factions for and against the compromise soon emerged from the wreckage of the old parties. The southern rights radicals, mostly Democrats, held a convention in Macon in August, and this was really the beginning of the new anticompromise Southern Rights party, which was composed primarily of supporters of Calhoun's southern unity concept and only a few outright secessionists. Evolving in opposition was the Union faction favoring compromise, composed of Cobb's moderate Democrats and most former Whigs under the leadership of Stephens and Toombs.

Cobb, Stephens, and Toombs, the Georgia Triumvirate, championed the Compromise of 1850 that Congress passed and new President Millard Fillmore signed into law in September. The Union was saved—if the South would accept this sectional deal. South Carolina was ready to secede but hesitated to go alone. The rest of the South wavered.

Again Georgia was on center stage at the height of a sectional crisis. As soon as the compromise became law, Governor Towns ordered a November election for delegates to a state convention, as the legislature had directed in its last session. This was to be Georgia's second crucial election in 1850, and both sides campaigned fiercely. The Southern Righters demanded "resistance," denounced the Unionists as cowardly "submissionists," and frequently appealed to the racism of the voters. The Unionists condemned their opponents as "disunionists" as they fought back vigorously. In the last phases of the canvass the Southern Righters became more moderate and the Unionists emphasized that the compromise was acceptable but not ideal. Nevertheless on 25 November Georgians still had a clear choice, a chance to set the pace for the rest of the uncertain South.

For the second time in 1850 the voters of Georgia rejected extremism, giving the Unionists an overwhelming 46,000-to-24,000 victory over the Southern Righters. South Carolina's secession crusade was stopped cold. Georgia moderation was certainly boosted by economic prosperity—cotton was selling well—but even more basic was the people's loyalty to the Union, which would be tested again and again over the next decade.

The Georgia convention assembled in December 1850 with a huge Unionist majority, which completed the formal organization of the new Constitutional Union party. The convention concluded with the passage of Charles J. Jenkins's famous Georgia Platform, which accepted the Compromise of 1850 but warned that the state would resist even to secession if the North violated the compromise or unduly hindered slavery in the territories.

The new political alignment in Georgia was even more fragile than usual as both new parties prepared for the 1851 fall elections. The Constitutional Unionists nominated Howell Cobb for governor, and the Southern Righters countered with Charles J. McDonald. Cobb defended the Compromise of 1850, and the fire-eater McDonald attacked it and championed the right of secession. Cobb did not deny the right but rejected the necessity of secession. The campaign was bitterly fought with the usual exaggerations and evasions, and the voters turned out in record numbers. Gubernatorial elections almost always drew the most interest in Georgia's highly personalized politics, and this contest attracted over twenty-five thousand more voters than the November convention balloting. Unionist Cobb overwhelmed McDonald by a count of 57,397 to 38,824, and the Constitutional Unionists also won an unusually large majority in the legislature and six out of eight congressional seats. For the third time in twenty months Georgia backed moderation, compromise, and the Union.

New Governor Cobb proposed Jacksonian reforms to a sympathetic legislature. The state's inadequate school system was improved. An academy for the blind was established and the state's overburdened insane asylum was enlarged. Cobb even tried unsuccessfully to provide some facilities for insane blacks. He virtually destroyed the Central Bank and kept all government funds in the state treasury. The currency was expanded and the state's annual revenues were increased from $290,000 to $377,000 by new ad valorem taxes levied on all property, including slaves. He vigorously backed the state's Western and Atlantic Railroad, which had just linked Atlanta and Chattanooga, with convict labor and government funds. Finally he expanded the state's bureaucracy through a crude spoils system and added a million dollars to the state debt.

But in the midst of Cobb's administration his Constitutional Union party began to disintegrate. It had remained an unstable coalition of Whigs and Democrats in roughly equal numbers who had combined in an emergency. Its success eliminated its reason for being, and its lack of a national affiliation left it without outside aid. The rival Southern Rights party was more stable since only a few Whigs crossed over to join the Calhounized Democrats. More important, the thrice-defeated Southern Righters expediently diluted their radicalism, and, led by increasingly moderate Herschel V. Johnson, they moved quickly to rejoin the national Democratic party.

With the Southern Righters now calling themselves Regular Democrats, the Constitutional Unionists were isolated as the presidential election of 1852 approached. Cobb and his old Democrats preferred to return to the national Democratic party and carry along enough old Georgia Whigs to regain control of the state party now dominated by former Southern Righters. Toombs, who was given Berrien's old seat in the United States Senate by the Constitutional Union legislature, and Stephens and most other old Whigs hesitated to join the old Democratic enemy, hoping that the national Whig party could somehow elect one more president.

The presidential election accelerated the realignment process. Cobb's Constitutional Union Democrats sent a delegation to the Democratic party's national convention that was accepted along with the Regular Democrats' delegation, but the Cobbites were clearly the outsiders. Many followed Cobb back to the regular Democratic party, but others, especially from northwest Georgia, hung back a while, no longer Constitutional Unionists but not quite Democrats again either. Both factions of Georgia Democrats eventually backed Franklin Pierce, but they entered separate slates of electors. A splinter group of hard-core Southern Rights Democrats backed elderly George M. Troup, who personally favored Pierce. This apparently quixotic move actually kept Johnson's Regular Democrats from making too many concessions to the returning Cobbites. Obviously the Democratic schism would long fester.

The old Whigs suffered more as their new Constitutional Union home crumbled. Many eventually supported the national Whig party's nominee, General Winfield Scott. Another faction led by Stephens and joined by Toombs backed Daniel Webster, who died nine days before the election. Stephens was hoping to so split the popular vote that the election would be thrown into the Constitutional Union legislature where a deal could be manipulated.

Thus Georgians had five slates of electors to evaluate in the presidential election of 1852. Many, especially discouraged old Whigs, did not vote. Georgians were accustomed to a rough, erratic, personalized brand of politics, but even they were disheartened to watch their expedient leaders darting about in search of patronage and power. The Regular Democratic electors won a majority with 33,400 votes, and Pierce carried the state. The other slate of Pierce electors drew 5,775 more votes, mostly from the northwest. The Scott Whigs gained 16,000 votes and Stephens's Webster Whigs polled 5,225. The Troup electors won 1,000 votes to cap off an election that marked the end of the Constitutional Union and Southern Rights parties.

In 1853 the Georgia Democratic party regrouped under the control of the former Southern Righters, who nominated Herschel V. Johnson for governor. The old Whigs' state organization was gone and their national party was disintegrating. Stephens wavered, so Toombs organized a temporary Union party convention that nominated urbane Charles J. Jenkins, author of the Georgia Platform, for governor.

Jenkins held the old Whigs together and made some headway among the Democratic small farmers of northern Georgia, but charismatic Johnson, aided by Governor Cobb, won a very close 47,638-to-47,128 victory. The Democrats also won control of the legislature and gained six of the state's eight congressional seats. Governor Johnson was not an activist, but economic prosperity enhanced his popularity as he increasingly shifted his attention to the national level where the Kansas-Nebraska bill of 1854 led to the emergence of a new Republican party opposed to the expansion of slavery.

Georgia could not escape the rising turbulence. Soon the Know-Nothing or American party developed in the vacuum left by the defunct Whig party. Its anti-Catholic, anti-immigrant platform had no great appeal in Georgia, but it did offer a refuge for old Whigs who would not join the old Democratic enemy. Aging former Senator Berrien, Jenkins, Judge Eugenius Aristides Nisbet, Francis S. Bartow, and young Benjamin H. Hill all joined this new crusade, as did some former Whig journals like the Columbus *Enquirer*, the *Augusta Chronicle*, the Savannah *Daily Republican*, and the Milledgeville *Southern Recorder*. In 1855 the Know-Nothings' summer convention nominated Garnett Andrews for governor and hailed the Georgia Platform and the Kansas-Nebraska bill, excluding the section enfranchising foreigners.

The surging Democrats renominated popular Governor Johnson and hailed the Georgia Platform (especially the resistance section) and the whole Kansas-Nebraska bill. Even under increasingly nationalistic Johnson, the Democrats remained sufficiently Calhounized to absorb a new Southern Union movement, but a new Temperance party entered this gubernatorial race, which degenerated into a mud-slinging contest with much religious bigotry. Governor Johnson was reelected by a vote of 53,478 to 43,228 for the lackluster Andrews and his Know-Nothings and 6,284 for the Temperance party. The Democrats also retained control of the legislature and again elected six of eight congressmen, including Cobb, who was finally back in the good graces of his party. Georgia's traditional well-balanced two-party system weakened as the Democrats consolidated their dominance.

Governor Johnson continued to stress economy and debt reduction in his second administration, but he watched national affairs closely. The rapid growth of the Republican party in the North alarmed many Georgians, but he resisted any radical reaction. Like Cobb, Stephens, and Toombs, Johnson was convinced that the national Democratic party was now the South's best defense. He was also ambitious for national office. He received some backing for the vice presidency at the 1856 Democratic national convention, which finally settled on James Buchanan of Pennsylvania and John C. Breckinridge of Kentucky, and he, like Cobb, traveled widely in the North supporting this ticket.

The powerful Democracy was favored to win the presidency again, but the Know-Nothings, who nominated former President Fillmore, and the Republicans, who nominated Savannah-born John C. Frémont, injected real issues into the hard-fought campaign. The Republicans had no appeal among Georgia's white, male voters, but the Know-Nothings, the fading remnants of Georgia's old Whig party, campaigned vigorously, even though many prominent members like Jenkins and Nisbet were defecting to the Democrats. The usual campaign excesses occurred, and feisty Stephens (Democrat) even challenged young Hill (Know-Nothing) to a duel, but Hill was able to make light of the affair for by this time the *code duello* was obsolete even in Georgia politics. Georgia Democrats won another decisive victory as Buchanan defeated Fillmore by a 56,000-to-42,000 count. He also won on the national level, though he attracted only 45 percent of the total popular vote. The Know-Nothings were finished, but the surging Republicans demonstrated that they might well capture the presidency in 1860—and force Georgia to make another agonizing decision.

The first year of President Buchanan's administration brought increasing sectional controversy and a sharp economic recession, but the big political event in Georgia in 1857 was the fall gubernatorial election. The dominant Democrats' June convention became deadlocked as the old Southern Rights faction rejected Cobb, now secretary of the treasury under Buchanan. Finally the delegates selected a thirty-six-year-old dark horse, Joseph Emerson Brown, a Calhounite from the Unionist northwest. The fading Know-Nothings picked their best man, thirty-four-year-old Ben Hill.

Both candidates were outstanding leaders who had risen from the yeoman masses, but the Georgia Democracy was so ascendant that Hill had no real chance to reverse the decision of the previous year's presidential election, as had been done so often in the past. Brown rolled to an impressive 57,067-to-46,295 victory as his Democrats again won six of eight congressional seats and retained control of the legislature, which quickly sent Democrat Toombs back to the Senate for a second term.

Governor Brown's administration marked the start of a new era in Georgia politics. Reelected in 1859, 1861, and 1863, his regime was ended only by a conquering Yankee army. Joe Brown was a thin, teetotaling, Baptist lawyer from the hill country who capped off a hard-won education at Yale. On the national level he was a staunch Calhounite who wanted the Georgia Democracy to be more independent of the national party. Under the proper provocation he would not hesitate to lead his people out of the Union, and in this he was only an extreme reflection of Georgia's growing disillusionment with a federal government that reeled from one sectional crisis to the next.

On the state level Brown was a Jacksonian activist who knew well the yeoman masses and became one of antebellum Georgia's greatest popular leaders. He quickly launched a crusade against state banks that suspended specie payment during the recession of 1857. He did not really win his fight against "high, commercial, moral, and legal crime," but the people hailed him as "Young Hickory," the foe of elites and special interests. He also championed public education and actually got the legislature in 1858 to appropriate $100,000 for schools from the profits of the Western and Atlantic Railroad. This state-owned railroad was thoroughly modernized and reformed by the efficient governor, and by 1859 it was generating annual profits approaching half a million dollars. This not only insured the continuation of public education funding but also allowed a reduction in the state's already low taxes.

In 1859 the Democrats quickly renominated their popular governor. The Know-Nothing party was finished, but its disspirited members briefly rallied in an Opposition party convention and nominated unimpressive Warren Akin. Brown won by a 63,784-to-41,830 landslide, and the Democrats retained complete control of the legislature and again won six of eight congressional seats even though Stephens, deeply pessimistic about the future, did not seek reelection.

Brown the Jacksonian had been reelected by the common white folk of Georgia, but now it was Brown the Calhounite who led his people as the American Union disintegrated. Even in his first administration he had supervised the state's takeover of the Georgia Military Institute in Marietta and had demanded that the Georgia Platform be fully honored, but he had failed to get the legislature to reform Georgia's "almost entirely neglected" militia system. But at the start of his second administration he even more forcefully advocated state subsidies for volunteer companies, and the legislature, enraged by John Brown's antislavery raid into Virginia, appropriated $75,000. Governor Brown was increasingly disaffected within the Union and not far behind him was the overwhelmingly Democratic legislature, swollen to almost three

George M. Troup

John Ross

Howell Cobb

Joseph E. Brown

hundred members as the state's population soared to 591,550 whites and 465,698 blacks and many new counties appeared.

The national Democratic party was one of the last institutions holding the Union together, but it was torn between the followers of President Buchanan and the backers of Senator Stephen A. Douglas of Illinois. The Georgia Democracy was also ridden with dissension, but its troubles had more to do with personal ambitions than abstract principles. Late in 1859 the Cobbites had staged a hurried party convention that selected delegates pledged to favorite-son Cobb. Then Brown and Stephens directed a second convention that selected uncommitted delegates. Both sets of delegates went to the Democracy's national convention in Charleston in April 1860.

There the national Democratic party finally ruptured. Douglas and his northern Democrats held to the party's 1856 doctrine of popular sovereignty, the right of the people of the territories to decide for themselves about slavery. Most deep southern delegates insisted on federal protection of slavery in the territories, and they (and some pro-Buchanan northerners) soon withdrew from the convention, with most (but not all) of the Georgia delegates following fire-eater Henry L. Benning in the walkout. A second convention at Baltimore failed to heal the breach as the southerners again walked out. The remaining delegates, including some southerners, nominated Douglas for the presidency and balanced the ticket with moderate Herschel V. Johnson of Georgia. The departed delegates, mostly southerners, held their own convention and nominated John C. Breckinridge of Kentucky. The surging Republicans, still championing the containment of slavery, chose a dark horse named Abraham Lincoln; and the remnants of the Whig and Know-Nothing movements in the border states rallied as the Constitutional Union party, nominated John Bell of Tennessee, and cried for the preservation of the Union.

The Republican Lincoln had no organized following in Georgia, but the other three candidates were vigorously supported. The shaky Opposition party had sent a delegation to the Constitutional Union convention, and under Ben Hill it backed Bell with the aid of the Milledgeville *Southern Recorder*, the Savannah *Daily Republican*, the *Augusta Chronicle*, the Columbus *Enquirer*, the Macon *Journal*, the Athens *Southern Watchman*, and other newspapers. Northern Democrat Douglas actually campaigned in Georgia, but his popular sovereignty policy and candid insistence that secession was unconstitutional alienated most voters despite the best efforts of his running mate Johnson and Stephens and a handful of journals like the Augusta

Constitutionalist and the Rome *Southerner*. Southern Democrat Breck-inridge was most popular, and he was backed by most of the Calhoun-ized Democrats, including Brown, Cobb, Toombs, and Benning, and mány influential newspapers like the Milledgeville *Federal Union*, the *Savannah Morning News*, the Columbus *Times and Sentinel*, the *Macon Telegraph*, the Athens *Southern Banner*, and the Atlanta *Intelligencer*. The campaign was bitterly fought, and Hill's last-minute efforts to unify all conservatives against the Republican menace were frustrated by old grudges and new ambitions.

A record turnout of over 106,000 voters rendered Georgia's incon-clusive decision: Breckinridge, 51,893; Bell, 42,886; Douglas, 11,580. The conservative supporters of Bell and Douglas were a majority, but the more radical Breckinridgers tallied the largest plurality by far. The election was thrown into the legislature which, as usual, was more radical than the voters. The legislators quickly awarded all of Georgia's ten electoral votes to Breckinridge, who had won only 48.8 percent of the popular vote. This gave the radicals a crucial boost as Lincoln's victory (with only 39.8 percent of the national popular vote) triggered the secession movement. Once again South Carolina tried to rally the disaffected as its hastily called convention voted unanimously on 20 December to secede from the Union. Once again as the secession tide swelled Georgia was forced to make an agonizing decision that could save or scuttle the Union.

As soon as the results of the presidential election were known, the Georgia legislature followed Governor Brown's advice and appropri-ated a million dollars for military expenses and called for the election of delegates to a state convention. In the intensive campaign that fol-lowed Breckinridge men spearheaded the immediate secession forces while many Bell and Douglas backers championed delay and action only in cooperation with the other southern states. A few secessionists probably believed what they often told the voters, that secession was only a temporary technique to force Yankee compromise in a restored Union, and a few cooperationists may have really thought that seces-sion would be more efficient as a cooperative effort; but basically the 2 January election was a struggle between immediate secessionists who wanted to leave the old Union forever and cooperationists who wanted to save the Union by another sectional compromise.

The secessionists had the advantage of advocating a dramatic, posi-tive solution in a time of unending tension and trouble. South Carolina had already seceded, and Alabama, Mississippi, and Florida were lead-ing a general southern movement in the same direction. In Georgia a majority of the political leaders and influential journals joined the movement. Governor Brown, the hero of the masses, was an avid secessionist, and so were Howell Cobb (who resigned from the Buchanan cabinet) and his younger brother Thomas R. R. Cobb and Toombs (who would soon deliver a fiery farewell speech to the United States Senate) and Nisbet and Benning and Bartow and elderly Wilson Lumpkin and a growing host of other politicians. Their campaign propaganda skillfully exploited the voters' racism, employing everything from vague rumors of slave insurrections to Brown's warning to the nonslaveholders that submission to Lincoln would mean abolition, ethnic equality, and intermarriage.

The more moderate cooperationists were thrown on the defensive and sometimes even intimidated. They were not united on policy and not entirely able to forget old feuds, and they spent much time denying that they were "submissionists" or crypto-abolitionists. They grew increasingly pessimistic as they realized that even the state's continuing economic prosperity was not diluting radicalism much this time. Still they made a fight of it. "Little Aleck" Stephens, who was much the same Unionist he had been in 1850, and his younger half-brother Linton were joined by Hill, Jenkins, Johnson, who had swung completely away from his 1850 Southern Rights stance, and many other Bell and Douglas men. Support also came from the Milledgeville *Southern Recorder*, the *Augusta Chronicle*, the Columbus *Enquirer*, the Athens *Southern Watchman*, the Thomasville *Southern Enterprise*, and a few other newspapers, but the defection of the influential Augusta *Constitutionalist* was ominous. Desperately Stephens appealed to his old friend Lincoln to speak directly to southerners, but the enigmatic new Republican leader remained silent.

Finally on a stormy 2 January 1861 Georgians made their decision; the secessionists won a 50,243-to-37,123 victory. But several factors obscure the results of these county elections for convention delegates. Many candidates did not make their position perfectly clear, and many voters, still inclined to emphasize personality as much as principle, chose a "good man" to solve complex problems. Even more than the usual number of voting irregularities caused additional confusion, and the traditional light turnout for special convention elections was accentuated by especially bad weather as almost twenty thousand fewer ballots were cast than in the 1860 presidential or 1859 gubernatorial contests.

Many Georgia voters were consistent in 1860 and 1861. Bell and Douglas men tended to favor cooperation even after Lincoln's victory, and Breckinridge men tended to favor secession, with the significant exception of the north Georgia farmers, who voted for Breckinridge but two months later refused to follow Brown and Cobb into the secession camp. Nonslaveholding counties tended to favor cooperation and slaveholding counties, especially traditionally Democratic ones, tended to favor secession. The towns and cities tended to be much more attracted to secession than the countryside. The moderate, rural cooperationist rather than the zealous, urban secessionist was most likely to find it too inconvenient to vote in the stormy weather, which was one crucial factor. Only two things were really clear: the secessionists had won control of the state convention and they had no massive mandate for drastic action.

Yet when the convention assembled in Milledgeville on 16 January, it acted quickly to follow South Carolina, Alabama, Mississippi, and Florida out of the Union. Among the 301 delegates was practically every important leader including the Stephens brothers, Toombs, Johnson, Hill, Nisbet, Bartow, Benning, and Crawford. Howell Cobb was an honorary delegate. Governor Brown, who had already ordered the seizure of abandoned federal Fort Pulaski and still refused to disclose the popular vote for convention delegates, was another influential honorary delegate, and commissioners from seceded states were also persuasive.

On the third day Judge Nisbet presented the fateful resolution that called for secession and also required a committee to draw up a formal secession ordinance. Johnson tried to stall by advocating a southern convention, and he was supported in debate by the Stephens brothers, Hill, and many other delegates; but the secessionists, reinforced by Thomas Cobb's assurance that Georgia could "make better terms out of the Union than in it," finally forced a vote on Nisbet's original resolution, which passed by the narrow margin of 166 to 130.

The conservatives under Johnson struggled to reverse this crucial vote. The next day, when the formal secession ordinance was presented by a committee headed by Nisbet, Hill moved to adopt Johnson's southern convention resolution instead, but this last diversion was defeated 164 to 133. The conservatives were clearly beaten, and a last vote on the formal secession ordinance passed 208 to 89, with the Stephens brothers and Johnson again voting in opposition before joining all the delegates in signing the ordinance in a tenuous display of unity.

It was done. Old Georgia, which had held firm in 1832 and 1850, finally yielded to the tides of disaffection sweeping through the Deep

South, ending any real chance for rational compromise and peaceful reunification. But many white Georgians were basically opposed to permanent secession; at heart they still loved the Union of their fathers. And beneath the divided whites were silent masses of slaves, 44 percent of the entire population. Georgia blacks had no deep commitment to a system that kept them in bondage, and soon the Yankees would offer freedom. Georgia was dangerously divided as it stood on the threshold of modern war. Disaster lay ahead.

XII

The Emerging Empire State
1820–1861

Georgia's economy expanded rapidly as most of its territory was distributed by six land lotteries between 1805 and 1832. Despite a strong laissez-faire spirit, the state government played a significant role in economic development. However, its own financial resources were limited because it sold its valuable lottery lands for a pittance (less than seven cents an acre) and relied on an outdated revenue system that included a tax on land and a poll tax. The improved general property tax system of 1852 levied ad valorem taxes on all real and personal property, both individual and corporate, including slaves. Both systems generated by far the most revenue from slave property, and the later one appreciably raised taxes. Nevertheless, antebellum Georgia taxes remained quite low as periodic recessions and depressions failed to halt for long the general economic advancement.

This rapid economic development led to the expansion of private, commercial banking, which provided some credit for agriculture. These banks also issued bank notes, which became the universal medium of exchange, the workaday paper money of the people. The panic of 1819 and subsequent depression were weathered by Georgia's relatively stable banks, but the conservative national bank branch at Savannah fell from favor, and the inadequate system of national currency meant that the economic revival of 1825–36 would be mainly financed by private banks chartered by the state legislature.

By April 1837 Georgia had twenty-one commercial banks and their sixteen branches with capital of $8,850,000, loans of $17,000,000, circulation (bank notes) of $8,700,000, deposits of $3,110,000, and specie reserves of $3,175,000. These banks were mainly concentrated in Savannah, Augusta, Macon, Milledgeville, and Columbus. The state government invested funds in some of these banks and regulated them all through charter provisions and other acts of the legislature. Georgia's private banking system was more stable than most others in an age of rather primitive finance.

In addition the state created the Central Bank of Georgia in 1828. It

served as the government depository, and its stock was all unappropri-
ated state funds. Its main mission was to furnish small, long-term agricultural loans that were not being adequately provided by the private,
commercial banks. It also issued bank notes, which served as currency.
Overall, the state-owned Central Bank was successful, especially in providing reasonable loans to the smaller farmers, but the legislative practice of dipping into the bank's capital to pay off government deficits
caused increasing difficulty.

The expanding economy's insatiable demand for credit led to the
formation of five railroad banks in 1835 and 1836, but these operated
just like other commercial banks and were usually not very useful in
financing the parent railroads. All banks were hurt by the panic of 1837
and the national depression that dragged on into the early 1840s. No
new banks were chartered in this gloomy period when all Georgia
banks twice suspended specie payments, and finally only eleven of the
stronger commercial banks survived. The mismanaged Bank of Darien,
which was heavily subsidized with state funds, deserved to die; but
many others, like all six banks in Columbus, were primarily victims
of financial circumstances.

The largest casualty was the state's Central Bank of Georgia. Continued government raids on its capital, especially to finance construction of the Western and Atlantic Railroad, and its own accumulation
of the notes of failing private banks weakened the Central Bank. Attempting to invigorate the depressed economy, it borrowed more funds
and issued new notes, which steadily depreciated. Political attacks on
the Central Bank increased, with the Whigs showing greater hostility,
and finally by 1842 the legislature ended its power to issue bank notes
and to grant new loans, although it could still renew old ones. From
1843 through 1847 Whig Governor George W. Crawford accelerated
the liquidation of the Central Bank, which finally withered completely
away in 1856.

The return of full prosperity in the late 1840s revived the great demand for credit, and in six years thirty-three new commercial banks
were chartered by the legislature. Savannah, prospering as the terminus
of the Central of Georgia Railroad, remained the banking capital of
the state, and the other major cities continued to be financial centers,
but nineteen of these new banks were located in the country, a rather
new development. At the grassroots level much credit was dispensed
by local merchants who were often also farmers or planters, but middlemen and agents and factors generally carried this credit back into the
state or northern banking system.

The panic of 1857 found the conservative Georgia banks again in relatively good condition, but they still suspended specie payment with the permission of the legislature, which overrode Governor Brown's passionate veto. Brown continued to criticize state banking procedures, and some additional restrictions were legislated in 1858 and 1859. Then the approaching war brought another specie suspension in 1860 as discussions of banking policy yielded to more important matters.

As Georgians surged out into the inviting new lands to the west, transportation and communication facilities became increasingly inadequate. The legislature appropriated funds for improving the state's major water routes, and by 1821 it had provided $500,000 for a permanent Internal Improvement Fund. This money was invested in the Steamboat Company of Georgia and various banks, and the limited profits were plowed into internal improvement projects. As people settled farther and farther from navigable streams, a maze of trails and roads developed, mainly oriented toward the nearest river or closest town, but most of these were poorly constructed and even more poorly maintained, and Georgia's road system remained woefully inadequate.

The canal craze sweeping the nation affected Georgia too. Grandiose schemes abounded, especially after New York completed its spectacular Erie Canal in 1825. Plans were formulated to connect the Tennessee River system with Georgia rivers flowing into the Gulf of Mexico and the Atlantic Ocean by a great central canal system. Such massive proposals obviously required thorough planning, so Georgia, following the example of other states, created a Board of Public Works in 1825 and hired Englishman Hamilton Fulton away from North Carolina as chief civil engineer. The board lasted only a year and engineer Fulton only a little longer, but they had time to conduct a comprehensive examination of the state's overall transportation requirements, especially its need to reduce the cost of shipping agricultural products to market. They made several foresighted recommendations: a primary seaport for export should be selected (probably Savannah), the main rivers should be made navigable for steamboats, and railroads rather than canals should be the main transportation arteries.

In general the dying board got its message across. Georgia did not follow states like Virginia and Pennsylvania in spending huge sums of money on obsolete canals. Only two coastal projects were seriously attempted. With considerable state aid and heavy investment by Boston capitalists the Brunswick Canal Company, employing first slave and then Irish labor, dug a twelve-mile connection from the deepwater harbor of Brunswick to the Altamaha River, but it never actually operated. The Savannah, Ogeechee, and Altamaha Canal, financed by state and city and mostly private funds, achieved the short connection between Savannah and the Ogeechee River but never progressed far on the long additional stretch to the Altamaha River. As the Board of Public Works had foreseen, the short canal linking the Ogeechee and Savannah rivers, which began operations in 1831, could not compete with railroads, and it was soon abandoned. In 1847 Augusta completed its own sophisticated, seven-mile canal, which furnished power to operate factories and improved access to the city from the Savannah River.

Traffic on the navigable rivers increased, especially after the Supreme Court's *Gibbons* v. *Ogden* decision in 1824 eliminated monopoly restrictions and steamboat builders learned to lessen the draught and generally improve the design of their riverboats. This stimulated the growth of fall line cities like Augusta, Milledgeville, Macon, and Columbus. On the Savannah, Chattahoochee, and Flint rivers steamboats continued to thrive into the 1850s, despite the competition of railroads. The state followed the Board of Public Works' advice about improving the navigability of the rivers for only a few years with decreasing funds. Then in 1829 it diverted most of its resources to a new "market road" project. For five years 190 state-owned slaves and $160,000 in state funds were used in cooperation with the major cities to improve the road network. However, this work was poorly done and few lasting benefits were achieved. Then by 1835 state internal improvement policy had changed again. The state sold its slaves and for the next five years turned again to projects to improve river navigation, pouring in $80,000 on top of the more than $300,000 spent previously for this purpose since 1815.

None of these limited internal improvement projects solved Georgia's transportation problems, but neither did any of them overly commit the state to obsolete systems on the eve of the railroad boom. Neither roads, including the plank roads of the 1850s, nor canals nor rivers were the real answer. Georgia's future lay with railroads, and Georgians were able to respond quickly when the opportunity came to bind the state together with twin ribbons of iron.

Georgia reacted quickly when South Carolina completed the Charleston and Hamburg Railroad in 1833. At that time the longest railroad in the world, it ran from the seaport of Charleston 136 miles to the town of Hamburg just across the Savannah River from Augusta. It clearly threatened to divert much Georgia commerce to Charleston, but the strongest initial reaction came not from Georgia's seaports but from interior towns like Athens and Eatonton, where transportation costs were very high. As early as 1831 Eatonton in the heart of the cotton belt had hosted two railroad conventions and championed an Eatonton-to-Augusta line, and in 1833 Athens promoted an Athens-Augusta railroad, hoping that this might be the first section of a long line through to the booming west. Then Savannah, the most threatened by South Carolina's new line, proposed a Savannah-Macon railroad, and Macon responded by projecting a Macon-Forsyth railroad that would simply run the new line from Savannah deeper into the cotton lands of the interior. The legislature granted charters to these three lines late in 1833: the Athens-Augusta line as the Georgia Railroad Company (by 1836 the Georgia Railroad and Banking Company), the Savannah-Macon line as the Central of Georgia Railroad Company (by 1836 the Central of Georgia Railroad and Banking Company), and the Macon-Forsyth line as the Monroe Railroad Company (which also gained banking rights but soon went bankrupt).

Wilson Lumpkin, who under the old Board of Public Works had surveyed possible canal or railroad routes to link Georgia's seaports with interior trade on the Tennessee River, was now governor, and his old enthusiasm for canals easily evolved into a railroad crusade. He stressed the need for a rail connection all the way from Savannah to the Tennessee River and advised state government subsidies for only one main trunk line within a larger, integrated system that would serve the transportation needs of the whole state.

The railroad craze continued beyond his administration. In 1836 a Macon railroad convention recommended that the state build a railroad from the Tennessee River to the Chattahoochee River in DeKalb County and that existing private lines be authorized and encouraged to construct branch lines to link up with the southern terminus of this new state railroad. Such a system would then not only improve transportation within the state but also tap the lucrative trade of the West through the old river system and other railroads that would someday snake across the nation. The legislature quickly agreed and chartered the state-owned Western and Atlantic Railroad in December 1836.

Actual railroad construction progressed rapidly in Georgia even after the depression of 1837–44 weakened the economy. Indeed the railroad boom helped combat the depression by providing scarce jobs and injecting funds into the sluggish economy. Approximately half of the $8.5 million spent on railroads during the depression came from city and state appropriations.

Construction of the Georgia Railroad began in 1834, with Athens and cotton planters along the proposed route showing much more enthusiasm than Augusta. Under the skillful direction of engineer J. Edgar Thomson, later president of the gigantic Pennsylvania Railroad, its new tracks moved west from Augusta to Madison and west by north to Athens in 1841. Support of the Central of Georgia Railroad was much greater in Savannah than in Macon, but action was stimulated by the progress of the rival Georgia Railroad, which in a competitive sense functioned as an extension of the Charleston and Hamburg Railroad. Construction of the Central of Georgia began at Savannah in 1836, and, with slaves gradually replacing white laborers during the depression, work continued. The new line reached Macon in the heart of the central cotton belt in 1843. The Central of Georgia constantly improved its trunk line, built some short feeder lines, partially financed (and at least partially controlled) longer new lines, and soon became one of the state's greatest business corporations.

The state's Western and Atlantic Railroad was shadowed by the depression for its first seven years. Most of the surveying of the 138-mile route was completed in 1837, and two thousand workers had done most of the grading by 1841. Then hard times forced a two-year delay with no rails yet laid. From 1843 through 1847 construction proceeded slowly but surely from the starting point south of the Chattahoochee near the White Hall post office. Named Terminus, then called Marthasville (for Lumpkin's daughter), the area was finally designated Atlanta. The Western and Atlantic was actually operating as far north as Marietta in 1845, and it reached Dalton in 1847, and a short branch got to Rome in 1849. The entire line to Chattanooga was in operation by 1851, and soon the East Tennessee and Georgia Railroad ran a supplementary line all the way from Knoxville to Dalton. The new Western and Atlantic required many improvements and alterations, and considerable sentiment for selling or leasing the whole railroad existed. Then in 1857 new Governor Brown appointed the efficient John W. Lewis superintendent, and the Western and Atlantic began to realize its potential as the main connecting link in a fast-growing regional railroad system that gave Georgia access to eastern as well as western markets by 1860.

While the Western and Atlantic moved north to the nascent rail center of Chattanooga, its booming southern terminus at emerging Atlanta was tied into the state rail system. The Georgia Railroad, now controlled by Augusta, pushed west beyond Madison and reached the new town in 1845. The early Monroe Railroad laid its original 25-mile line between Macon and Forsyth by 1838, but when it attempted to push on north to Atlanta during the depression, it went bankrupt. Reorganized by northern capitalists as the Macon and Western Railroad as the depression ended in 1845, it reached Atlanta in 1846 and in a practical sense gave the Savannah-based Central of Georgia Railroad the same connection to the new Western and Atlantic that its archrival, the Augusta-based Georgia Railroad, had achieved the previous year.

As the long depression finally faded away, a host of new railroad proposals appeared, but only a few ultimately succeeded. Primarily they were extensions of the Western and Atlantic–Georgia Railroad–Central of Georgia system that had already bound much of the state together. The rapid agricultural development of the southwestern part of the state led to the charter of two new lines in 1845: the Southwestern Railroad and the Muscogee Railroad. The Southwestern, bailed out of deep financial difficulties by the Central of Georgia Railroad and the city of Savannah, finally by 1860 had run a line all the way from Macon to Albany with a branch running west to Fort Gaines and Eufaula, Alabama, on the Chattahoochee River. Meanwhile, the Muscogee, cautiously subsidized by the city of Columbus, was unable to complete the line from that city to a linkup with the Southwestern Railroad. The Southwestern finally ran a line west from Fort Valley to close the gap in 1853. Soon the troubled Muscogee line was absorbed by the stronger Southwestern, which was in turn almost completely controlled by the mighty Central of Georgia Railroad.

The Atlanta and West Point Railroad was started in 1847 and when completed in 1853 joined the main Georgia rail system to a rapidly developing Alabama rail system at West Point on the Georgia side of the Chattahoochee. In 1852 Augusta finally allowed its own profitable Georgia Railroad and the old Charleston and Hamburg to connect, as railroads all over the state gradually began to integrate their lines. Two years later Augusta grudgingly welcomed a new line running 54 miles north from Millen on the Central of Georgia Railroad. This new Waynesboro Railroad was the first direct link between old rivals, Georgia's two largest private railroads. It was soon absorbed by the ever-expanding Central of Georgia, which also finally gave Eatonton its long-sought railroad by running a 37-mile spur line north through Milledgeville. By 1860 the Charleston and Savannah Railroad connected the two great rival seaport cities of the Southeast. The Macon and Brunswick Railroad was chartered in 1857 but had barely begun construction of a line down the Ocmulgee River from Macon toward Hawkinsville when the war started.

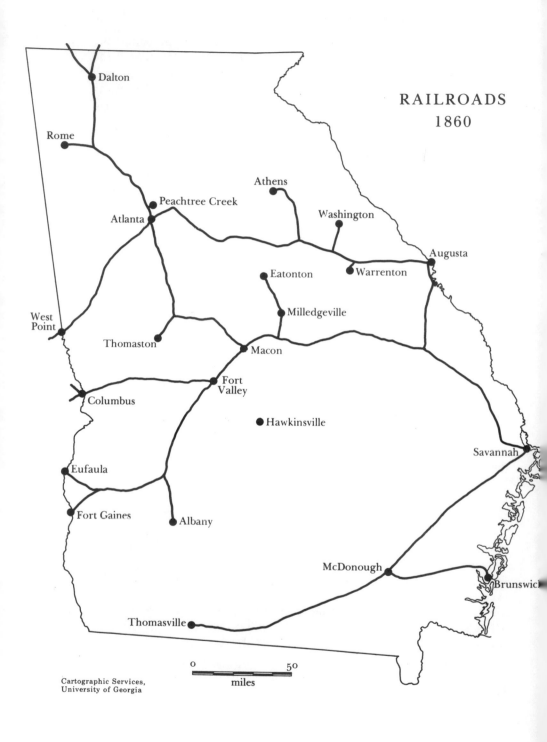

RAILROADS
1860

Dalton

Rome

Peachtree Creek

Athens

Washington

Atlanta

Augusta

Eatonton

Warrenton

West
Point

Milledgeville

Thomaston

Macon

Fort
Valley

Columbus

Hawkinsville

Savannah

Eufaula

Fort Gaines

Albany

McDonough

Brunswick

Thomasville

0   50
miles

Cartographic Services,
University of Georgia

One more major trunk line developed before the war, designed to tap the booming cotton fields of southwest Georgia and adjoining areas in Alabama and Florida. Albany and Thomasville both planned rail connections with the east, but the real competition developed between Savannah with its proposed Savannah and Albany Railroad chartered in 1847 and Brunswick with its even older Brunswick and Florida Railroad scheme. Both plans called for a line to Albany and an extension to the Gulf of Mexico. Brunswick's 1835 charter gave it some advantages, but mighty Savannah, which skillfully shifted its investment funds from old to new railroads to meet its needs, pursued an expanded plan for a Savannah, Albany and Gulf Railroad all the way to Pensacola, Florida.

In 1856 the state intervened before either city began major construction and chartered a new trunk line something like the popular Western and Atlantic Railroad. This new Atlantic and Gulf Railroad began at a point fifty miles inland from Brunswick where the Brunswick and Florida and the Savannah, Albany and Gulf railroads were to meet, and it ran toward Alabama where it was to link with other developing railroads to tap western markets. Financed with $1 million from the state and even more from the cities of Savannah and Thomasville and the largely Savannah-owned Savannah, Albany and Gulf Railroad, this new trunk railroad graded much of the route to the Alabama line and actually laid tracks as far as Thomasville before the war began. In the meantime Savannah and Brunswick ran their long-planned lines to the Atlantic and Gulf's eastern terminus at McDonald (eleven miles southwest of modern Waycross), and south Georgia had its railroad to the sea.

By 1861 Georgia had an extensive railroad system, the best in the Deep South and second only to Virginia in the whole South. Over fourteen hundred miles of tracks, mostly 5-foot gauge, crisscrossed central Georgia, spilled over into the northern and southern sections of the state, and linked up with other lines snaking out into the rest of the nation. The state's eighteen railroads were not thoroughly integrated, rates varied considerably, and a few cities still lacked crosstown connections between major lines. But gradually the large lines had absorbed or overawed most of the smaller ones and imposed greater efficiency. The major urban areas were linked, and the agricultural bounty of the countryside was more quickly and cheaply marketed. In Georgia and much of the rest of the nation this railroad boom which stimulated the whole economy was heavily subsidized by state and local government funds. Of the approximately $26 million invested in

Georgia railroads the state spent $7,151,509 (including over $6 million for the Western and Atlantic), the city of Savannah contributed another $2.7 million, and Augusta, Macon, Columbus, and Thomasville also invested considerable sums. Private funds came mostly from banks, other railroad companies, and individual capitalists. The money was well spent as Georgia's thriving railroads steadily reinforced a vigorous economy.

Agriculture was the mainstay of Georgia's economy, the occupation of the overwhelming majority of blacks and whites. Though not directly subsidized by government, it benefitted tremendously from the development of transportation facilities that opened up the rich interior for exploitation. By the 1820s upland cotton was becoming king. Increasingly, large plantations and many smaller farms concentrated on cotton all through central Georgia, especially in the lower piedmont, and by the 1830s the rich new lands of southwestern Georgia were also opened up for this primary money crop. Some lands were quickly worn out and abandoned as many Georgians moved west into Alabama and Mississippi and eventually Texas, especially in the 1840s, but Georgia remained a land of agricultural opportunity that attracted newcomers from the upper South and the North, and the population continued to grow steadily from 189,570 whites and 151,419 blacks in 1820 to 407,695 whites and 283,697 blacks in 1840 to 591,550 whites and 465,698 blacks in 1860.

Like other Americans Georgians were wasteful, unscientific farmers. Cotton was king, and the world market price of upland cotton fluctuated erratically from a high of 29¢ a pound in the inflation year of 1818 to as low as 5½¢ a pound in the depression of the late 1830s and early 1840s. But nothing could stop the expansion of cotton production that soared from 90,000 bales (at least 400 pounds each) in 1821 early in the cotton boom to 150,000 bales in 1826, which made Georgia the world's leading cotton producer. A six-year slump in cotton prices stimulated diversification into other crops, livestock, and even an unsuccessful effort to revive silk culture, but cotton production still crept upward and soared to 326,000 bales in 1839 before low cotton prices stimulated even greater diversification. This time agricultural reformers led a much more sophisticated shift to livestock, grasses, grains, fruits, and vegetables, and industrialization began to make significant progress too. But King Cotton could not be dethroned as the price per pound rose in the late 1840s to about 9½¢ and then leveled off at 11–12¢ in the 1850s. Georgia cotton production soared to half a million bales in 1850, second only to Alabama. The agricultural boom of the 1850s again emphasized cotton and in 1860 Georgia produced 701,840 bales, trailing only Alabama, Mississippi, and Louisiana.

Large plantations employing gangs of slave laborers specialized in cotton, but most farmers were not entirely squeezed out of this lucrative crop. Small farmers cultivating less than 100 acres, usually without the assistance of slaves, often planted cotton as a money crop to supplement the corn, vegetables, and rather scruffy livestock on their 31,000 farms, approximately half of the state's total farms in 1860 but nowhere near half of the acreage under cultivation. A few of these small farmers worked plots too small or barren for profit, and they sometimes drifted into tenant-sharing schemes in the 1850s, which left them little better off than the state's nearly twenty thousand landless white farm laborers; but the great majority of the small farmers did reasonably well. Middle-class farmers with 100 to 500 acres and up to thirty slaves usually cultivated sizeable cotton crops on their nineteen thousand diversified farms. Even in the heart of the cotton and black belts farms survived and often prospered in the shadows of the great plantations. A drop in cotton prices was not disastrous to these smaller agriculturalists, who raised most of what they consumed and could easily convert their cotton lands at least temporarily to other uses. Some of these conservative, hardworking, diversified farmers operated efficiently enough to gradually rise into the ranks of the planters in an economic system that retained considerable flexibility as it matured, especially in the newer areas of the state.

The great planters were a very small part of the white population. Even as late as 1860 only 3,594 of the state's 62,003 farms had over 500 acres; only 902 contained more than 1,000 acres. Only about thirty-five hundred Georgians owned 30 to 100 slaves, only 212 owned over 100, and only 23 owned over 200. One lone white Georgian owned more than 500 slaves. Very few whites lived on big plantations, but many blacks did. Although slaves lived a little above the subsistence level, their upkeep in food, clothing, and shelter was minimal in relation to their great value. Slaves worked not only as field hands and house servants but also in a wide variety of skilled and semiskilled occupations. Cooks, weavers, seamstresses, carpenters, blacksmiths, millers, drivers, sometimes even overseers—blacks participated in almost every conceivable occupation available in agricultural Georgia, despite the restrictions of the slave codes. When skillfully managed, plantation agriculture was quite profitable, and during slack periods many slaves, especially ones with special skills, could be lucratively hired out to work in a variety of enterprises, everything from nursing and

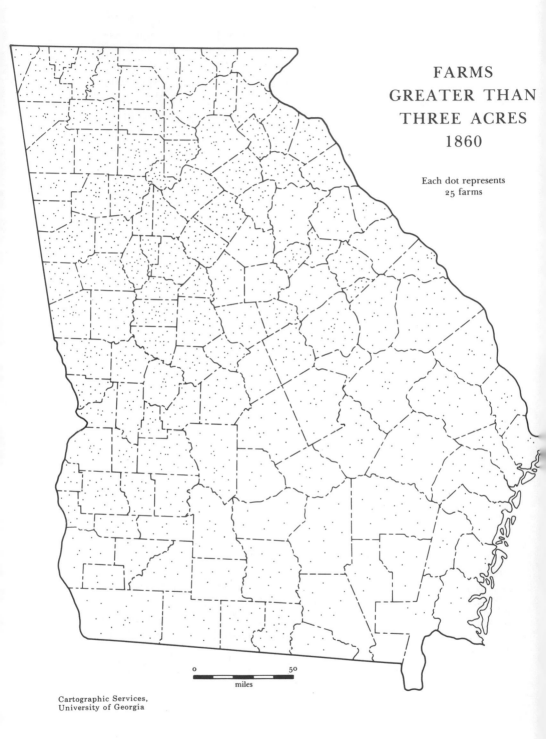

FARMS
GREATER THAN
THREE ACRES
1860

Each dot represents
25 farms

0   50
miles

Cartographic Services,
University of Georgia

babysitting to railroad building and lumberjacking. Except in a depression, it was usually easy to sell slaves for a good price, especially in the 1850s when able-bodied field hands sold routinely for $1,200 in an extensive trade that transported slave property to where it could be most profitably employed.

The planter elite was composed primarily of hardheaded businessmen skilled at managing a flexible, profitable system of slave labor. Many were self-made men who had advanced at least from the ranks of the lesser planters, and some had quickly clawed their way up from the masses. Only in the coastal area was "old wealth" frequently represented by gentlemen like Thomas Spalding of Sapelo Island and James Hamilton Couper of Hopeton. Most planters were plainer men who concentrated on producing cotton because cultivation of large estates with gangs of slaves directed by low-wage managers called overseers was more profitable than most other economic enterprises. Many of these agribusinessmen saw the wisdom of diversification, and some, like Robert Toombs, boasted of the self-sufficiency of their plantations, which raised not only cotton but also subsistence crops like corn, peas, beans, sweet potatoes, and livestock and often also included enough mills and workshops to acquire a semi-independent air. Always alert for profit, fully utilizing the credit facilities of the commission merchants in the cities, the big planters were shrewd opportunists. Some near growing urban centers successfully converted to large-scale "truck farming" with some of their produce even reaching northern markets, and many planters invested in Georgia's rapidly expanding industries.

Rivaling cotton as Georgia's main crop was corn, one of mankind's most efficient foodstuffs. For Georgians it was the staff of life, and it was raised not only by many planters and most farmers but also by many poor whites on remote, marginal lands. Fully 40 percent of the state's cultivated land was planted in corn, which totaled over 30 million bushels in 1850 and increased another 700,000 bushels by 1860 despite the cotton boom. Almost as universal were Georgia's 2 million swine, a rather scroungy tribe that usually roamed on its own but was sometimes penned and corn-fed in the cotton belt. Another increasingly common sight was the sturdy Kentucky and Tennessee mule, which became the basic work animal, especially in cotton culture.

Most of Georgia's other agricultural products were regional. Along the old seacoast high-quality, sea island cotton was grown, and rice cultivation staged a late antebellum comeback with almost 39 million pounds in 1850 and over 52.5 million pounds in 1860. This particular crop was worked by slave labor under the task system, which allotted each worker a daily assignment and required skillful supervision. Coastal Georgia trailed only South Carolina in rice production. The pine barrens and wiregrass regions mainly supported free-roving herds of mongrel cattle, sheep, and hogs among a thinly spread, predominantly poor-white population. Equally isolated was the mountainous northeastern section, where some wealthy planters withdrew to cottages in the summer. A few fertile valleys were cultivated, and some commercial apple orchards had begun, but the white mountaineers of the region generally practiced subsistence agriculture and hunted and fished frequently. The hilly northwestern part of the state, formerly the land of the Cherokees, was settled rapidly by yeoman farmers in the late 1830s—the population had passed 62,000 by 1840—and its diversified economy produced corn and wheat and livestock and some industry along the new Western and Atlantic Railroad. Some mountaineers lived much like their brethren to the east. In some fertile valleys a few large-scale operations developed, like Farish Carter's huge plantation with several hundred slaves in Murray County, but Cherokee Georgia remained overwhelmingly white.

The real heartland of antebellum Georgia was the central and southwestern regions, the land of cotton and corn and slaves, the center of black and white population and the new railroads and urban developments. From here came the main force of the statewide agricultural surge which by 1860 was producing bountiful harvests even in secondary crops: almost a million pounds of tobacco, more than a million bushels of sweet potatoes (a world record), over two and a half million bushels of wheat, almost a million pounds of honey, over a million bushels of oats, over a million and a half pounds of butter, increasing quantities of fruit, and even a trickle of domestic wine.

Georgia was blessed with plentiful land that produced even when abused, but late in the antebellum period it also benefited from an idealistic band of agricultural reformers, some native sons and some newcomers, who championed the concept of scientific farming that had flowered in Europe and spread to the North. The Planters Club of Hancock County, in the lower piedmont cotton belt, was founded in 1837 and became the most famous of numerous county agricultural societies. Among its planter members were Dr. William Terrell, who advocated crop diversification and endowed a chair of agriculture at the University of Georgia, and Richard S. Hardwick, who championed hillside ditching and other anti-erosion techniques. Hancock County's greatest farm expert was David Dickson, who pioneered contour plowing, crop rotation, the use of guano and chemical fertilizer, the devel-

EMPLOYMENT IN
MANUFACTURING
1860

Each dot represents
50 employees

miles

Cartographic Services,
University of Georgia

opment of skilled slave labor, and many other reforms, but he was not a member of the prestigious Planters Club, probably because of his black wife and mulatto children.

Reform made slow but steady progress against the stubborn conservatism of the rural masses. In 1845 the Agricultural Association of Georgia was organized with Governor George W. Crawford as its first president, but this organization had only limited effect. The main work was still done bit by bit at the grassroots level. James Camak, railroad promoter from Athens, conducted extensive agricultural experiments and developed the *Southern Cultivator* of Augusta into the state's best farm journal. The Reverend Charles Wallace Howard advocated grasses and livestock for northwestern Georgia, briefly edited the *South Countryman* at Marietta, and later edited the *Southern Cultivator*. Professional overseer Garland D. Harmon preached a passionate love of the southern soil wherever he roamed. Thomas Spalding, Joel Crawford, Linton Stephens, Charles J. McDonald, Bishop Stephen Elliott, John M. Berrien, Mark Anthony Cooper, William Schley, and many other prominent Georgians supported the agricultural crusade that was centered in middle Georgia.

Many newcomers made significant contributions to agricultural reform. Daniel Lee of New York succeeded Camak as editor of the *Southern Cultivator*, later edited the *Southern Field and Fireside* (also in Augusta), and also served as the University of Georgia's first professor of agriculture. Richard Peters of Pennsylvania and Jarvis Van Buren of New York came to Georgia to work on railroads; Peters stayed to pioneer scientific livestock breeding and Van Buren to improve apple orchards. Danish immigrant Robert Nelson championed peach orchards and better vegetables. Belgian Louis E. Berckmans and his son Prosper Jules Berckmans pushed fruit culture and landscaping from their Augusta nursery, and Rhinelander Charles Axt established a promising grape-wine operation in the 1850s near Crawfordville. Stimulated by the new science, agriculture was prospering on the eve of the Civil War.

Industrialization also made steady, significant progress in predominantly agrarian Georgia. Its roots ran back to the small workshops and mills on farms and plantations and in nascent urban areas where a nucleus of white managers and black and white skilled workers evolved. By the 1820s infant industries that supplemented the agricultural surge were developing sporadically. Local cotton gins and presses grew larger and more sophisticated and so did local mills, which by 1860 were annually producing wheat flour and cornmeal worth more than

Eagle Textile Mill in Columbus, 1851

Reeves Brothers Inc., Eagle and Phenix Division

$4,550,000, not counting another $772,000 worth of rice flour processed in Savannah.

The economic logic of bringing cotton mills to the cotton fields was irrefutable, and by 1829 Judge Augustin S. Clayton had established a profitable plant on the Oconee River near Athens. Others soon followed, making the little college town a textile and light industry center. Macon, Columbus, Thomaston, Augusta, and even little Sparta with one large mill became centers of a growing textile industry run by steam as well as water power. This new industry matured during the cotton boom of the 1850s, with some isolated plants in rural areas. A few towns like Eatonton lost ground as the total number of plants decreased from thirty-six to thirty-three but actual production increased by 70 percent. By 1860 Georgia led the southern textile industry with 2,813 workers, including 1,682 women, compared to 1,441 workers in Virginia, the runner-up. Increasingly Georgia was called "the New England of the South."

Other industries developed almost as rapidly, and many were largely scattered in the rural areas. Tanneries, slate and marble quarries, small copper and coal and iron mines, and turpentine distilleries added valuable products to the economy. Goldmining, especially in former Cherokee Georgia, went from haphazard, individual panning in the late 1820s and early 1830s to capitalistic mining corporations by 1835, and enough gold was produced to establish a federal mint at Dahlonega in 1838. By 1861 production had dropped drastically and the mint closed, but by then it had received over $6 million in gold and that was only an uncertain portion of the total production of antebellum north Georgia.

The lumber industry, which by 1860 was annually producing pine and cypress products worth almost $2.5 million, was mainly rural too. In 1834 a Maine company started a massive operation on 700,000 acres on the northwestern fringe of the pine barrens, where four large mills cut yellow pine boards that were shipped down the Altamaha River to Darien. Englishman Henry Stevens established a similar but smaller operation in Baldwin County near his pottery works. But native Georgians were not left out. A host of small sawmills scattered through the countryside turned out a large total product and additional big mills developed too. By the 1850s Savannah dominated the Georgia lumber industry and was one of the nation's busiest lumber markets with lumber yards, steam-powered sawmills, woodworking establishments, and a booming British export trade unencumbered by Yankee middlemen.

Savannah in 1855

Savannah was Georgia's main industrial center. With an 1860 population of 22,292 (38 percent black), it produced goods valued at almost $2 million and served as the main shipping port for the state's almost $19 million worth of foreign exports (mostly the 547,037 bales of cotton exported by Savannah that season) and also was the home of many commission merchants, factors, agents, and other general businessmen, including some of the state's wealthiest slave traders. The smaller cities of Augusta (population 12,493—32 percent black), Columbus (9,621—38 percent black), and Macon (8,247—35 percent black) all annually manufactured goods worth more than $1 million by 1860. Atlanta's industrial production was less than $500,000 at that time, but it had developed rapidly since its beginning in the late 1830s as the southern terminus of the Western and Atlantic Railroad. Machine shops for railroad maintenance began its industrialization, which soon included an iron plant that could roll or reroll 18,000 tons of rails annually. The only other rolling mill in the state was part of Mark Anthony Cooper's iron complex near Cartersville. By 1860 Atlanta had 9,554 inhabitants (20 percent black) and was already a city with a commercial and industrial future.

Georgia's growing urban areas produced a variety of other goods like shoes and boots and other leather goods, wagons and carriages, woolens, furniture and other finished wooden products, machinery and engines, bricks, newspapers and books and journals, and milled or processed foodstuffs. Georgia's overall industry, rural and urban, was expanding rapidly. By 1850 it included 1,522 establishments capitalized at almost $5.5 million and employing 8,368 workers and producing goods worth $7 million. By 1860 it had grown to 1,890 establishments capitalized at almost $11 million and employing 11,575 workers and manufacturing goods worth $17 million. The state's massive agricultural production still dominated the economy, but clearly the industrial revolution had reached Georgia.

Slavery was an integral part of this vigorous industrialism. Skilled and unskilled black labor was used in virtually every emerging industry, sometimes by itself and sometimes integrated with free white labor. Industrial slaves were often just as controlled and exploited as field hands, but some did acquire a degree of sophistication and professional pride far beyond anything envisioned by the slave codes. Nowhere was the flexibility and profitability of slavery better demonstrated than in Georgia industry, where approximately 5 percent of the total slave population was employed. Despite complaints from the emerging white proletariat, black labor became an essential part of Georgia's and the whole South's industrialization.

Planters eagerly invested their resources, both slaves and cash, in new industries, especially in periods of agricultural depression; but even during the cotton boom of the 1850s, practical planter business-men were among the main backers of industrial expansion. Local and state governments, equally probusiness and procapitalism, accepted incorporation and other forms of industrial promotion and were re-strained in their exercise of regulatory powers.

Even in the shadow of King Cotton, commerce and industry flowered in late antebellum Georgia. Many northerners and immigrants settled in the "Empire State of the South," but native Georgians held their own as growing numbers of wholesalers, retailers, shippers, processors, and insurers emerged. Entrepreneurs like Savannahian Gazaway Bugg Lamar prospered amidst the competition. A national and international economy that seemed to encourage a colonial status for the largely agrarian South worried some Georgians. Many dramatic attacks were made on the system. Periodic southern commercial conventions were a favorite forum, and the 1856 convention in Savannah marked the be-ginning of excessively anti-Yankee tirades. An even more spectacular challenge came in 1858 when Charles A. L. Lamar, the son of Gazaway, smuggled 409 African slave laborers into Georgia at Jekyll Island. Black slaves had been smuggled into Georgia periodically ever since the federal government outlawed the African slave trade in 1808 but never before in such a brazen, defiant manner. But these belligerent actions in the late 1850s were not so much economic protests as political agita-tion by the growing secession movement. Many white Georgians were doing too well to worry much about supposed inequities in the eco-nomic system, but politics finally intruded, and Georgia's increasingly diversified economy faced the stern test of modern war.

XIII

A Slowly Maturing Culture
1820–1861

Georgia emerged from a rough, frontier environment only in the last decades of the antebellum period, and its cultural and intellectual achievements at this time were limited. Only in the old tidewater areas had wealth matured for several generations, and primarily here a handful of polished, cultivated ladies and gentlemen emerged. Thomas Spalding, James Hamilton Couper, the Reverend Charles Colcock Jones, and John B. Lamar were deeply rooted in the soil, but a few of the upper class were newcomers like John M. Berrien and Thomas Butler King, who were northern born and educated, and Pierce Butler, who was more at home in Philadelphia than on his Georgia sea island plantations.

But these grandees were only a fraction of the state's small elite. Most wealthy Georgians, especially in the interior, were much more bourgeois than aristocratic. They were hospitable and unpretentious, and they lived comfortably but not luxuriously in large frame farmhouses rather than stately mansions. Most were ambitious agribusinessmen like David Dickson, Farish Carter, and Hartwell H. Tarver, who skillfully directed slave labor and had little time for leisure activities. A few were very prosperous professional men and merchants living in urban areas. Many were self-made men and proud of it; a few were in the process of falling from a class that did not long tolerate economic failure. A handful like Howell Cobb, Alexander H. Stephens, Robert Toombs, and Herschel V. Johnson were professional politicians, shrewd and well-educated but not really refined. The great majority of the small, diversified upper class shared the culture and the worldview of Georgia's great, sprawling middle class.

The Georgia bourgeoisie was a conglomeration of doctors, lawyers, merchants, artisans, and especially yeoman farmers who owned their own land and sometimes a few slaves too. It encompassed the great majority of white Georgians. Literate but usually not well-educated, these hearty, materialistic provincials lived plain lives centered on families and jobs and neighborhoods. Most enjoyed corn shuckings,

Home of Alexander H. Stephens at Crawfordville
Georgia Department of Archives and History

quilting bees, dances, horse races, traveling shows, barbecues, political rallies, militia musters, court days, church activities, hunting, fishing, and other traditional rural recreations; some in the urban areas attended the theater and joined literary and debating societies or other social and charitable organizations, but generally Georgians showed little interest in the finer arts.

More provincial and backward were the poor whites who owned little or no land, but the lowest mudsill of white society was a small, rather nebulous group known as "poor white trash." Inarticulate but visible, probably as much the victims of strong germs as weak genes, they received little sympathy from Georgians, black or white, and they were frequently the butt of the jokes and stories of their betters within a fluid, mobile socioeconomic system where the talented could rise and the inept could fall rapidly.

One major reason for Georgia's limited cultural development was the continuing lack of adequate education for the rural masses. Blacks were specifically forbidden by law to acquire education, and positive efforts to educate the scattered white masses on the land were unsuccessful enough to leave approximately 20 percent of the adult whites illiterate as late as 1850. This was a rather high rate of illiteracy by northern, especially New England, standards, but "advanced" European nations like England and France had much higher illiteracy rates among their free population, and Georgia did make some efforts at improvement. In 1822 $500,000 was added to the poor school fund, which was designed to give every white child at least a few years of basic education. This money was invested in bank stock, and its limited income was equally divided between the private old field schools and academies of the middle and upper class and the public poor schools, and thus it had little effect. Some cities and counties established their own free school systems, but many lower-class children in the poorer rural areas received little or no formal education. An attempt to organize a true public school system in the late 1830s was frustrated by conservative opposition and economic depression.

Despite calls for reform, Georgia continued to try to educate its white citizens in an erratic conglomeration of public and private schools of widely varying quality. Only in 1858 did liberal Governor Joseph E. Brown lead in the establishment of a broad public school system for all white children to replace the inadequate poor school system. Financed by large state bond issues and $100,000 annually from the state-owned Western and Atlantic Railroad, real public education was only beginning to develop on the eve of the Civil War, which consumed it.

Higher education was even more limited. Various religious denominations subsidized a few small colleges: the Methodists, Emory College near Covington in 1838; the Presbyterians, Oglethorpe College near Milledgeville in 1838; the Baptists, Mercer University at Penfield in 1839. By 1860 over forty self-styled colleges had emerged. Half of them had some religious affiliation, and a few like the Georgia Military Institute at Marietta and a business college in Atlanta were highly specialized, but most of these new institutions were really only secondary schools.

The University of Georgia at Athens was the state's most famous school, but weak financial support and a highly politicized board of trustees hampered its development, and it seldom had much over a hundred students—roughly the same enrollment as Emory or Oglethorpe or Mercer. It emphasized traditional classical education but professors like Joseph and John LeConte and Daniel Lee introduced more modern science. The university produced most of the state's political leaders, and in 1859 Joseph Henry Lumpkin and Thomas R. R. Cobb organized the state's first law school there.

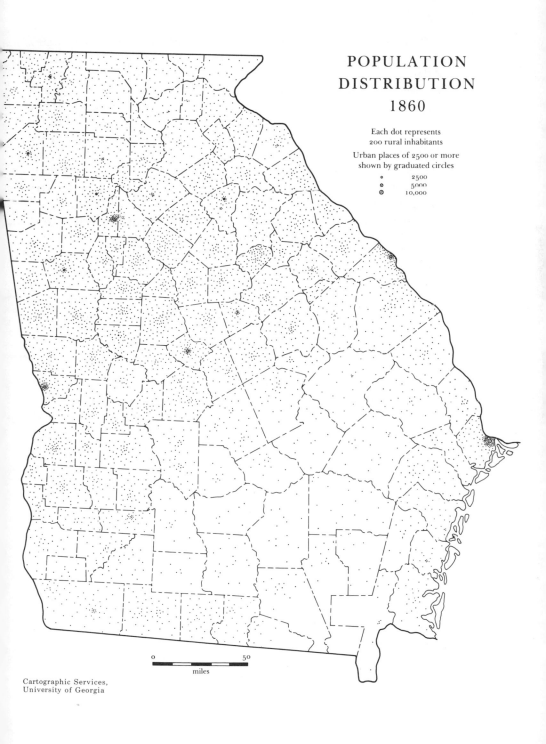

POPULATION
DISTRIBUTION
1860

Each dot represents
200 rural inhabitants

Urban places of 2500 or more
shown by graduated circles

    2500
    5000
    10,000

0   50

miles

Cartographic Services,
University of Georgia

Professional medical training had an earlier start when the state's first medical school was founded in Augusta in 1828, and Savannah and Atlanta established similar schools in the early 1850s. Doctors like Paul F. Eve, Richard D. Arnold, and Joseph Jones were outstanding, and surgeon Crawford W. Long's unheralded use of ether as an anesthetic in 1842 was a scientific milestone, but medical education was still in its infancy. Yellow fever and malaria and cholera epidemics still periodically ravaged cities like Savannah and Augusta, and the normal attrition of various diseases and infirmities and infections regularly killed off even more Georgians, especially the very young, the very old, and pregnant women.

Though handicapped in education too, white women made progress. Most of the scattered local private and public primary schools were coeducational. Some of the more advanced academies were, too, or offered separate complementary female courses emphasizing practical work like sewing and "ornamentals" like fine arts and French. At least thirty-five academies, seminaries, institutes, and colleges for women developed in the late antebellum period, but only one gained national recognition. Georgia Female College was chartered in 1836 in Macon, and under Methodist sponsorship it was renamed Wesleyan Female College in 1843. It flourished and in 1860 its student body of 173 was the largest in the state. This limited progress stimulated many calls for reform, but, as with many other aspects of Georgia education, little more was actually achieved. White women in Georgia found their limited education abruptly terminated when they married in their middle teens. In a society ignorant of contraception, most women were quickly absorbed in their new calling as wife of one and mother of many. A few ambitious, intelligent women chafed at the traditional kitchen-church-nursery restraints of American marriage; some like Eliza (Mrs. Farish) Carter actively assisted their husbands' business operations; most stoically accepted the status quo and a few gradual changes like the 1833 law that liberalized the rigid procedure for divorce.

The inadequate educational system and the general materialism of the raw new land created an atmosphere where businessmen, politicians, farmers, soldiers, and even adventurers could thrive but not artists and intellectuals. Only a few scholars emerged. The Reverend Adiel Sherwood's small but succinct *Gazetteer of the State of Georgia* was first published in 1827 and revised three times by 1860. In Savannah in 1839 Dr. William B. Stevens, avid manuscript collector Israel K. Tefft, Dr. Richard D. Arnold, John M. Berrien, and others organized the Georgia Historical Society. Stevens soon became a professor at the

Wesleyan Female College, Macon

University of Georgia, and, using copies of colonial records obtained in England by the state government, he wrote a two-volume history of eighteenth-century Georgia that was published in 1847 and 1859. Using similar manuscript materials, the Reverend George White contributed *Statistics of the State of Georgia* in 1849 and *Historical Collections of Georgia* in 1853, but his expunging of antislavery sentiments in some documents he reprinted reflected the rising sectionalism that was diverting some of the state's best talent into a rigid defense of slavery. Stephen F. Miller's two-volume *Bench and Bar in Georgia* (1858) presented flattering biographical sketches of thirty-two prominent Georgians. Even this handful of volumes was largely the work of northern immigrants. Three other books by outsiders particularly disturbed Georgians. Fanny Kemble's *Journal of a Residence on a Georgian Plantation in 1838–1839* (not published until 1863) and Lewis W. Paine's *Six Years in a Georgia Prison* (1852) and Emily P. Burke's more sympathetic *Reminiscences of Georgia* (1850) were written by critical visitors who explored some of the less attractive aspects of Georgia life.

Literary developments were only a little more impressive. Augustus Baldwin Longstreet's humorous and often realistic sketches of the rough-and-tumble adventures of ordinary Georgians were first published in newspapers and then in 1835 consolidated under the title *Georgia Scenes* before he became president of Emory College. Ohioborn William Tappan Thompson showed this same gut feeling for his adopted state in *Major Jones's Courtship* (1840) and other works in the Longstreet tradition. Francis R. Goulding's *The Young Marooners on the Florida Coast*, first published in 1853, was a popular adventure story. Thomas Holly Chivers and Richard Henry Wilde, a native of Ireland, and Henry Rootes Jackson were respectable poets. A number of literary periodicals and journals also appeared, especially as the demand for loyal "southern" literature increased in the late antebellum era, but most of these publications did not last long in provincial Georgia.

Other kinds of journals also appeared, and a few that specialized in medicine, religion, family affairs, or agriculture survived. But most literate Georgians preferred to read newspapers. Most Georgia newspapers were county weeklies, but the most influential journals were dailies published in the leading towns and cities. They were saturated with profitable advertisements and commercial announcements, including rewards for the capture of runaway slaves, and almost all were staunchly committed to some political faction. But even the most politicized papers with the heaviest concentration on legislative and congressional activities found space for a wide variety of other material: letters to the editor, poems and other literary efforts, local news and gossip, jabs at rival journalists, select and sometimes erratic coverage of foreign and national events often taken directly from other papers, and just about anything else an individualistic editor might choose to include except abolition writings. As the population increased and sectional tensions intensified, the major newspapers multiplied their circulation—and their ability to influence public opinion.

This rising sectionalism that would eventually tear the Union apart forced Georgians into an increasingly rigid defense of the "southern way of life." Angered by abolitionists' attacks from without and concerned about the possibility of slave insurrections from within, white Georgians refused to tolerate any direct criticisms of their "peculiar institution."

Journalists, politicians, and academics were joined by clergymen in this conservative crusade. Although many Georgians still had no formal religious affiliation, the churches grew rapidly, especially the more evangelical Baptists and Methodists, but also the Presbyterians and Episcopalians and to a lesser extent the Lutheran and Christian churches, while the Universalists barely survived. By 1850 Irish immigration led to the establishment of the Catholic Diocese of Savannah; by 1860 more than sixty-five hundred Irish immigrants lived in Georgia, most of them laborers in Savannah where the free population was one-third foreign-born. In the same city a small Jewish congregation grew slowly as a trickle of immigrants arrived from Germany. The spiritual leaders of these religious groups almost all held firm in the ranks of the defenders of the South. One, Methodist Bishop James O. Andrew, a reluctant slaveholder through marriage, became the center of a national Methodist argument over slaveholding officials which led to the formation of a separate Methodist Episcopal Church, South, in 1845 with Andrew one of its leaders. A similar controversy the same year among American Baptists over slaveholding missionaries led to a similar schism as the antebellum South slowly and sullenly closed ranks before a world that seemed increasingly hostile to slavery.

This conservative conformity in defense of slavery tended to spill over into other areas, making reform generally more difficult, especially when northern champions of change were so often vocal abolitionists. But not all reform was rejected in Georgia. Somewhat liberalized by a healthy influx of immigrants and Yankees, a state that was slowly struggling to establish a workable white public school system also founded the Georgia Institution for the Deaf and Dumb at Cave

Springs in 1847 and the Georgia Academy for the Blind at Macon in 1852. In 1837 the state founded an insane asylum for whites at Milledgeville not far from the state penitentiary, which was vainly trying to rehabilitate as well as punish criminals convicted of everything from assault and murder to horse and slave stealing. The penitentiary's workshops were not profitable and limited experiments with convict leasing only foreshadowed postwar abuses. Its facilities were vastly improved by the 1850s, and the over two hundred white male inmates, half under twenty-six years of age and one-third illiterate, and handful of white women and free blacks would have been much worse off in the old, crude county jails. Criminal law was gradually modernized by such actions as the abolishment of imprisonment for debt in 1823, and just before the Civil War Thomas R. R. Cobb efficiently codified the entire substantive common law of Georgia.

The Reverend Charles Colcock Jones wrote *The Religious Instruction of the Negroes in the United States* in 1842 as part of a movement to bring Christianity to more blacks, and a few hearty reformers even joined the American Colonization Society. Some Georgians supported the society only as a means of exiling free blacks to Africa, but others favored it as a device for freeing slaves who would become pioneers in Liberia. The society received scattered support in Georgia throughout the antebellum period, but not enough to effect significant change. Nevertheless, it did send twelve hundred black volunteers from Georgia to a new life of freedom in their ancestral homeland, and it also gave white humanitarians like Richard Hoff of Oglethorpe County, who freed over a hundred slaves, and Richard and Emily Tubman of Augusta and Alfred Cuthbert, Jr., of Eatonton an opportunity to demonstrate their opposition to slavery without unduly angering the overwhelming majority of white Georgians, who were determined to keep blacks suppressed and subordinate.

Almost half of Georgia's antebellum population was Negro slaves. They were primarily the property of their white masters, lacking all civil and political rights. The slave code of 1833 summarized their suppression. Slaves could not learn to read and write; they could not own property; they could not testify against whites in court; they could not travel without a pass; they could not bear arms, administer drugs, or work in printing shops. There was no such thing as a legal slave marriage or family, and only by a special act of the legislature could a slave gain his freedom. Slaves were hanged for murder, insurrection, arson, and rape of a white woman, and, unlike some southern states,

Georgia did not compensate masters for their destroyed "property." Lesser crimes were usually punished by whipping.

During occasional tense periods, whites strictly enforced these harsh laws and even resorted to lynchings, but most of the time slave laws were only haphazardly and erratically enforced. Vaguely worded laws restricting the importation of slaves from other states were massively ignored, and even the stern federal law against importing African slaves was periodically violated, even by prominent men like former Governor David B. Mitchell and Charles A. L. Lamar. Quasi-military units of adult white men were organized on the local level to enforce the slave code, but these slave patrols also functioned erratically.

Generally the individual master governed his slaves as he saw fit, especially in the rural areas where most blacks lived. Corrupted by excessive power, some masters atrociously abused their "niggers" while some others treated their "black families" with great kindness. Most masters fell between these extremes in a flexible, varied system designed to control blacks.

The great majority of slaves were not mindless, infantile Samboes. They rendered the surface subservience required and only covertly or indirectly resisted most abuses; but, more important, they retained considerable individuality within a system that was harsh but lacked the ruthless, total efficiency of the twentieth century. During busy seasons the arduous, disciplined workday often extended from sunup to sundown with a lengthy midday break, but after work and on Sundays, Christmas week, and other holidays slaves were usually free of direct white supervision.

This allowed a broad, active slave community to develop at the bottom of Georgia society. Some elements of West African culture survived in language, music, religion, and folklore, especially in isolated coastal regions, but much of the dominant white culture was also absorbed. Slaves spoke a dialect of English very similar to their masters'; many practiced a similar kind of Protestantism, sometimes within a predominantly white congregation but usually separately. Many slaves fashioned orthodox nuclear families headed by fathers, but these black families were always vulnerable to disruption by sale. Blacks shared the warm, lush southern environment with whites and ate the same corn and pork staples; they too were Georgians.

But they remained subordinate, the mudsill of Georgia society. Their housing was usually inadequate—sometimes no more than a bare, drafty cabin with a dirt floor—and their food, though often plentiful, was plain and monotonous much of the year. Their clothing was shoddy and scarce, and their medical care was usually minimal. Many, but not all, masters were practical enough to refrain from consciously abusing their valuable property, but the slave masses still lived only a little above the subsistence level.

Within stratified slave society the lightest burden rested on the very young who performed routine chores and the very old who were already worn out by a lifetime of hard labor. Unskilled and semiskilled laborers had the hardest row to hoe. House servants and skilled artisans had it better, and they were most likely to acquire some education, hire their own time, and otherwise violate the letter and spirit of the slave code. Vulnerable to the sexual aggression of an unscrupulous master, slave women faced unique difficulties. Outspoken Rebecca Latimer Felton may have exaggerated when she recalled that mulattoes were "as common as blackberries," but she was only articulating the annoyance of antebellum white women, who witnessed the evolution of a

Slave family picking cotton near Savannah

New York Historical Society

hardy new race of hybrid Georgians. This miscegenation sometimes led to lasting attachments. The slave Amanda was really the wife of prominent planter David Dickson as well as the mother of his children, and after the Civil War she legally inherited part of his estate. Irish immigrant and rich planter Michael Morris Healy and his beautiful mulatto slave-wife Mary Eliza lived happily and had ten children, and the eldest, James Augustine, eventually became a Catholic bishop in Maine.

A few slaves defied hopeless odds and openly resisted. Insurrectionary activity was rare—with rumor and reality impossible to separate—but individual attacks on whites were more common despite swift and often lethal punishment. The most numerous open resisters were runaways. Some simply hid out in the neighborhood and tried to negotiate a better deal, but a few maroons lived free for years in isolated areas. Some tried to get all the way to free country, and a few actually made it. The slave Fed escaped to England and in 1855 under his free name of John Brown dictated his autobiography, *Slave Life in Georgia*, detailing many of the brutal aspects of rural slavery. William and Ellen Craft of Macon found the same haven and published an account of their spectacular escape. Aron Bradley escaped from Savannah and returned after the Civil War to become a radical leader of the freedmen. But the great majority of blacks remained slaves, not satisfied with their lot but hopeful of a better tomorrow.

Free blacks composed the last small portion of Georgia's Negro population. Less than 1 percent of the state's black population, only thirty-five hundred persons in 1860, they were nevertheless a significant preview for the future. The passage of harsh laws in 1818, 1829, and 1859 handicapped these black noncitizens, but in normal times these laws, like the slave codes, were not strictly enforced. Most free blacks lived in coastal and urban areas, especially Savannah and Augusta; the majority were poor, working-class folk suppressed by a white majority that considered them at best a nuisance and at worst a threat to the whole slave system. A few were manumitted by proceedings that sometimes evaded or ignored the law, but most were born free, the children of free black mothers. Many were mulattoes, sometimes the offspring of their former masters. Family life was insecure and women were often heads of households. Some free blacks acquired literacy in spite of the law and only a few became African colonists. They earned their meager incomes as draymen, porters, cooks, farmers, artisans, seamstresses, washerwomen, and unskilled day laborers, but a handful prospered— men like Atlanta dentist Roderick Badger, Dahlonega miner-merchant James Boisclair, Savannah fisherman Anthony Odingsells, Macon merchant Solomon Humphries, Milledgeville blacksmith-preacher Wilkes Flagg, and farmers McPherson Bowman and William Lucas. This small vanguard could expand only after slavery was destroyed by a civil war that shook the entire fluid, maturing culture of antebellum Georgia to its foundations.

XIV

War and Defeat

Following secession the independent state of Georgia was swept along in the rush of events that led inexorably toward war. Briefly the secession convention set policy. As Georgia's representatives in Washington resigned, it officially severed all ties with the federal government but at the same time ordered continued enforcement of virtually all old federal laws. The convention also ordered the raising of two regiments of troops and other defense measures and appointed Toombs, Stephens, Hill, the Cobb brothers, Eugenius A. Nisbet, Francis S. Bartow, and three others as delegates to the convention of seceded Deep South states, which met in Montgomery, Alabama, on 4 February and organized the Confederate States of America.

Howell Cobb served as president of this convention, T. R. R. Cobb was the main architect of the new Confederate Constitution, and Toombs and Stephens were also prominent in the proceedings, but finally the presidency of the new nation fell to Jefferson Davis of Mississippi. Stephens won the vice presidency and a disappointed Toombs accepted the office of secretary of state.

Back in Georgia the secession convention that had adjourned on 29 January reconvened in Savannah on 7 March for a final sixteen-day session. It adopted the Confederate Constitution on 16 March without a popular referendum. Functioning as a legislature, it passed many acts and resolutions, including crucial ones on 20 and 23 March authorizing the transfer of military operations in Georgia to the Confederate government. It also sent commissioners to the border slave states to champion secession, and finally it replaced the obsolescent state constitution of 1798.

The new constitution of 1861 was largely the work of T. R. R. Cobb, who certainly had the necessary experience. It reduced the 293-man legislature to 212 members, mainly by expanding senatorial districts from one to three contiguous counties. It formalized the concept of judicial review and allowed the governor to appoint supreme and superior court judges while leaving local judicial offices elective. These and other minor adjustments modernized Georgia government. The voters were distracted by the coming of war, but they saw no real threat to their traditional democratic system in the new charter, which was ratified by a very light popular vote of 11,499 to 10,704 in July.

The unwieldy convention was not a really effective governing body in the last tense moments of peace. Much more forceful leadership came from popular Governor Brown. An ardent secessionist, he had seized undefended Fort Pulaski at the mouth of the Savannah River even before Georgia seceded on 19 January. After secession he moved much faster. On 22 January he ordered state forces to take the vital Federal arsenal at Augusta, which was full of scarce weapons. He seized the Federal mint at Dahlonega and also held several New York vessels at Savannah until he was doubly assured of receiving a promised arms shipment from that northern industrial state, all the while excluding Confederate authorities from the dispute. Following convention orders, he efficiently recruited two regiments of troops and collected army and navy equipment, but he was less enthusiastic about convention efforts to cooperate with the new Confederacy.

The new "Black Republican" administration in Washington puzzled and irritated Georgians, but until 12 April most still thought that war could be avoided. Then Confederate batteries at Charleston opened fire on Fort Sumter, and Lincoln called for volunteers to suppress the rebellion. Now it was all-out war for a Confederacy greatly strengthened by the addition of Texas, Virginia, North Carolina, Tennessee, and Arkansas. But the North still had a much larger population and a vast economic and industrial superiority. The South could win only by a swift, massive, unified war effort.

Northerners and southerners rushed to enlist in the new armies that would soon drench the nation in blood. Governor Brown's call for volunteers on 18 April brought an enthusiastic response. By October 1861, at least 25,000 Georgians were in Confederate service—a year later the total would reach 75,000 and, by the end of the war, approximately 120,000. But only manpower was plentiful. Clothing, equipment, and weapons were dangerously scarce, and Brown forbade anyone to take arms out of the state. Colonel Francis S. Bartow took his Georgia-armed Oglethorpe Light Infantry to Virginia and denounced Brown's parochial policy a short time before he fell in battle at Manassas leading his decimated regiment. This and other disputes between Brown and Confederate authorities over the control of military units and the right to appoint officers were ominous.

However, Brown was an efficient administrator, and, more important, he stirred the white masses to support Georgia's war effort. In November 1861 he ran for an unprecedented third term as governor. He was opposed by many prominent politicians and almost every major newspaper, and the popular secessionist Judge Eugenius A. Nisbet emerged as a rival candidate. The concurrent legislative elections sent a majority of Nisbet men to Milledgeville, but Brown's personal popularity was so great that he easily won reelection by a 46,493-to-32,802 margin, despite a rather light turnout of voters.

Governor Brown continued to clash with Confederate officials. He was loyal to the Confederacy but even more devoted to the old southern states' rights heritage, and he did not realize that many traditional rights and privileges would have to be subordinated to a centralized war effort if the Confederacy was to survive. This attitude was widespread in the conservative South, but only Brown carried it to a ruinous extreme.

In April 1862 the Confederate government initiated conscription. This was the first national draft in American history, and it was often ineptly and arrogantly enforced. Governor Brown was convinced that this new policy was unconstitutional and despotic, and he tried to maintain control of the state militia and other state troops, but the state supreme court sided with the Confederacy, and the legislature gave him only limited, erratic support. Grudgingly he yielded—and immediately began to rebuild the state forces with men too young or too old for Confederate conscription. As the war continued, the age limits of the draft were extended periodically. Each time this ate into Georgia's newest "army" and provoked renewed protest and resistance from Brown as he relentlessly labored to field some kind of separate state force of at least ten thousand men. Five times this peculiar process was repeated, and Brown further harassed conscription by exempting thousands of state employees, especially militia officers who became known as "Joe Brown's Pets." This official resistance made conscription harder and harder to enforce as some other states began to follow Georgia's example.

Governor Brown also led Georgia resistance to impressment—the seizure of private property at arbitrarily set prices by the Confederate army, a process that included the requisition of slave laborers for limited periods. Arbitrary arrests without traditional habeas corpus proceedings were employed more by the northern than the southern government, and spies and Unionists were an increasing problem for the beleaguered Confederacy, but Brown and the legislature still condemned this emergency procedure early in 1864. Brown also successfully squelched Confederate General Braxton Bragg's impolitic proclamation of martial law in Atlanta in the summer of 1862 and equally inept Confederate efforts to gain control of the vital Western and Atlantic Railroad in 1863 and 1864. He also argued over available space on blockade runners, draft exemptions for skilled workers, and the new Confederate tax-in-kind, which took part of farmers' crops. Brown's opposition was erratic and egotistical. Occasionally he cooperated with the Confederates, but more often he balked, and sometimes he engaged in startlingly vitriolic correspondence with President Davis.

He did not stand alone against the central government in Richmond. Stephens, the vice president of the Confederacy, spent much of his time at his Georgia home, denouncing the Davis "despotism" and helping his brother Linton repeat this theme in the state legislature. Toombs had quickly become bored as secretary of state and joined the army. Soon he quit the army and spent the rest of the war denouncing the Davis administration. To a lesser extent Herschel V. Johnson joined the chorus of dissent from his seat in the Confederate Senate, but he refrained from the more excessive Brown-Stephens-Toombs attacks, which increasingly crippled the Confederacy on the home front.

But Brown's ultimate ally was the white masses of Georgia, and in the fall of 1863 he confidently ran for a fourth straight term as governor. Again he was opposed by every major newspaper but the ever-loyal Milledgeville *Federal Union* and Atlanta *Intelligencer* and the newly converted Augusta *Daily Constitutionalist*. Most politicians continued to oppose him too, but many of the ablest nationalists like Confederate General Howell Cobb and Confederate Senator Benjamin II. Hill were too often away from Georgia.

With a straight face the governor presented himself as a staunch supporter of the Confederate government! Once again he triumphed as another light wartime turnout gave him 36,558 votes to 18,222 for suspected peace candidate Joshua Hill and 10,024 for outspokenly pro-Davis Captain Timothy M. Furlow. The opposition tried to draw enough Unionist north Georgians to Hill and enough old secessionists to Furlow to throw the election into the legislature where Brown would surely lose, but the governor garnered too many votes in the army and the cities. The Confederacy could not escape Joe Brown's states' rights extremism.

Strictly on the state level, the perspective of most Georgians, the Brown administration had a much more positive approach. The state mobilized many of its resources effectively. Needy soldiers and their families received $22 million. Another $4 million was spent for soldiers' clothing and additional funds for sick and wounded soldiers. The state had some success in combating a severe shortage of salt, which had previously come mainly from the North. Governor Brown's early efforts to stop the export of cotton were only partially successful, and by 1863 the state was actively encouraging blockade runners to try to take out cotton and bring back weapons. A popular movement to shift from the cultivation of cotton to foodstuffs was reinforced by additional legislation late in 1862, and cotton production dropped by almost 90 percent. The state also reduced the amount of corn and other foodstuffs being distilled into whisky, but even teetotaling Governor Brown could not entirely eliminate "white lightning," especially in his own northern hill country. Georgia did greatly increase its food production and became one of the chief suppliers for the army.

The state's industrial production increased rapidly too. At the local level women knitted and sewed much more, and many returned to the neglected system of carding, spinning, and weaving to meet their families' basic needs as well as part of the army's requirements for clothing and bandages and other equipment. This revival of cottage industry probably boosted morale as well as moderately increasing total output, but the significant increases in production came in heavy industry.

The industrial base established in the 1850s expanded rapidly but unevenly to meet the insatiable demands of a Confederate war machine increasingly cut off from European industry by the Federal blockade. The greatest expansion came in the manufacture of military equipment by state and Confederate plants and private companies fulfilling government contracts. Atlanta, Columbus, Macon, Augusta, and Savannah were the main industrial centers. Each had a Confederate arsenal and several also had state arsenals. The rail center of Atlanta became the regional headquarters for the Confederate quartermaster and commissary departments, and its large rolling mill was one of the few in the whole South. The Confederates erected a huge gunpowder mill in Augusta. Dalton, Rome, and Athens also developed extensive military industries as urban Georgia went to war.

Georgia's large textile industry operated at full capacity but did not expand, largely owing to shortages of machinery. By the middle of the war, state and Confederate agents had contracted for most production. Brown tried to stimulate home production by establishing a cotton card factory at the state penitentiary, which was already producing rifles, but shortages of materials hampered this new operation. Georgia's shoe factories were also increasingly tied up with army contracts, but neither soldiers nor civilians were adequately supplied at all times.

Georgians' efforts to increase iron production were largely unsuccessful, but many other small and a few large private industrial enterprises did develop in the expanding wartime economy. Difficulties were numerous. Capital was scarce unless a government subsidy was available. Machinery was often unavailable, and raw materials were often hard to obtain. Women and blacks relieved some labor shortages, but skilled workers, though usually exempt from the draft, were scarce enough to cause heated disputes between Confederate and state officials. However, a shrewd entrepreneur could overcome all handicaps and reap fabulous wartime profits. Some greedy businessmen became rank profiteers, fueling the runaway inflation that was wrecking the Confederate economy.

Overall the record of Georgia's manufacturers was impressive but still inadequate. They greatly expanded industrial production and helped carry Confederate armies through four years of modern warfare, but ultimately they could not match the awesome industrial might of the North.

Georgia's antebellum rail system was even more advanced than its industry, but it too faced an accelerating challenge. After much initial confusion, the railroads handled the greatly increased traffic in the state reasonably well for several years in spite of shortages of capital, labor, and materials. But gradually equipment wore out, leading to numerous accidents, disrupted schedules, and soaring rates. No new lines were started, but the aging system continued to function until Sherman's invaders destroyed much rolling stock and devastated long stretches of track in 1864. At the end of the war the only major line operating normally was the Western and Atlantic, which was rebuilt and maintained by the Union army.

The state's economy was sound in 1861, but it was gradually undermined by a relentless inflation that ravaged the home front in the last half of the war. Like the Confederacy, Georgia tried to finance the war too little with taxes and too much with bonds and treasury notes that circulated as money. The state's ad valorem taxes were not increased enough, and a profits and income tax enacted in 1863 was ineffective. The state-owned Western and Atlantic Railroad was the most reliable source of funds for the treasury. Counterfeiters, speculators, and profiteers added to the confusion. Hard money disappeared as the Confederacy, the state, banks, and even private businesses poured paper money into an economy that finally priced necessities beyond the reach of the masses. By early 1864 in Atlanta firewood was selling for $80 a cord; corn, $10 per bushel; felt hats, $150 each; oranges, $1 each; dress shoes, $100 per pair; flour, $120 a barrel; and Irish potatoes, $20 per bushel

—while a private at the front was still paid only $11 a month! Sherman's devastating invasion was only the final blow against an economy that was already crippled.

This terrible inflation relentlessly eroded the morale of the masses. No people went to war with more enthusiasm than white Georgians in 1861. The compromisers and conciliators and even many of the seven thousand northern-born residents were swept along in the initial euphoria that promised quick victory over the Yankees. Several early battlefield triumphs further increased unrealistic optimism, but pockets of at least passive Unionism remained, especially in north Georgia. Generally Brown handled the area's individualistic farmers with great tact, and many fought well for the Confederacy.

But as time passed, morale began to waver. Germs and bullets began to thin the ranks of the army. More and more fell: Colonel Bartow at First Manassas, General T. R. R. Cobb at Fredericksburg, and thousands of ordinary Georgians all around the South's slowly shrinking defensive perimeter. Following the savage slaughter at Antietam late in 1862, Lincoln's preliminary Emancipation Proclamation stirred old fears of slave insurrection made more terrifying by the absence of so many white soldiers. Then in 1863 the Fourth of July weekend brought disaster. Lee's army was mauled at Gettysburg, and on the Mississippi River Ulysses S. Grant forced the 30,000-man Confederate army at Vicksburg to surrender. Union armies advanced on all fronts as the blockade tightened relentlessly.

Conscription, impressment, inflation, numerous shortages, and fiery denunciations of Confederate authorities by the Brown-Stephens-Toombs clique intensified war-weariness in Georgia. Increasing dissension led to numerous desertions from the army and some disloyalty at home. Some areas, especially in north Georgia, temporarily defied Georgia and Confederate authority, and a peace movement centered in western Georgia made headway. In the spring of 1864, with Sherman's massive army poised to slash into Georgia, a special session of the legislature adopted the resolution of Brown and the Stephens brothers; it was a very vague call for peace negotiations based on the Declaration of Independence and states' rights and only part of a complex procedure that condemned the Confederates but praised President Davis. The legislators forcefully rejected Brown's efforts to call a peace convention in November 1864 and February 1865, but in the last chaotic months of the war the morale of the people crumbled and near anarchy prevailed in many areas.

Georgia's black population never shared the whites' enthusiasm for the new Confederacy. During the last stages of the secession crisis a wave of terror, including lynchings, kept them briefly cowed. After the war started the legislature considered (but did not enact) proposals to reёnslave all free blacks, and the slave code was tightened. Nevertheless, as more and more white men marched away to battle, some of slavery's old controls were gradually weakened.

Most slaves lived on much as they always had until Union troops arrived, but many Georgia blacks lived a new life during the war. Some were moved to new areas away from the enemy; others went with rebel armies as cooks, teamsters, and servants or as laborers impressed to work a few months on fortifications; others were shifted into burgeoning war industries. These disruptions of the black population (and many black families) were extensive enough to send a tremor through the whole slave system.

Some blacks remained docile and obedient, but others became increasingly restive and insubordinate. Open rebellion was still suicidal, but rumors of insurrection surfaced periodically, and individual blacks did occasionally strike out violently only to be eliminated by a court or a lynch mob. Runaways multiplied. At first they were only a trickle toward Union forces along the coast, but when Sherman came thousands of blacks voted with their feet for northern victory. By this time the Union was committed to destroy slavery, and the good news had gradually filtered down to the black masses. Freedom seemed near, and some slaves began to reveal more confident, assertive personalities.

Blacks faced even greater wartime privations than whites on the home front. Despite increasing shortages, many slaves, especially those under close supervision, labored on ceaselessly and made a real and often involuntary contribution to the rebel war effort in agriculture, industry, and transportation; at the same time others intensified their loafing, thieving, sabotage, and other forms of traditional resistance and aided the oncoming bluecoats when they could. On the brink of freedom black Georgia was in flux.

The crumbling Confederacy made one last, desperate bid to rally the black masses to its banner when on 20 March 1865 it finally imitated what the Union had been doing for nearly three years and recruited black troops. This dramatic offer of freedom for blacks who served honorably in the Confederate army came much too late— Appomattox was only twenty days away—and even then it was bitterly denounced by Brown, Cobb, and the Georgia legislature. For once Georgia blacks probably agreed with the white leadership, for Billy Yank was already bringing the freedom Johnny Reb offered too late.

Controlling increasingly restless slaves was only one home front problem for white Georgians, especially women thrust into the traditional "man's world" by the absence of their soldier menfolk. Women operated many farms and plantations and began to teach school in significant numbers for the first time. They supported "aid societies" and "wayside homes" for soldiers, and scores like Madame M. C. Cazier of Savannah shed their modesty and went into grim hospitals all the way up to Virginia to nurse the wounded. Many women began to make assorted soldiers' equipment as well as clothing for their own families. Bazaars, plays, dances, "starvation parties," and other social events were used to raise money for the cause and to entertain soldiers on leave. Traditional courtships were often sharply abbreviated amidst a flood of wartime marriages. A few southern belles were totally absorbed in these social activities, but most women fully appreciated the seriousness of a war that would leave many of them widows and spinsters.

Shortages became more and more severe as inflation priced the barest essentials out of reach for many. Women resorted to all sorts of expedients. They concocted many synthetic foods and occasionally even banded together to seize government or private supplies. Food riots in Atlanta, Milledgeville, and Colquitt and a rapidly increasing criminal and prostitute population demonstrated the terrible tensions in wartime Georgia society.

Perhaps the greatest challenge for Georgia's white women was the awful loneliness in isolated rural areas. They tried to resist this by working hard and writing long letters to loved ones at the front. These letters powerfully affected army morale, the positive ones encouraging renewed optimism and the negative ones encouraging a host of deserters. In the later stages of the war some rural areas were harassed by deserters and bushwhackers and then overrun by Union forces that sent great hordes of men, women and children, black and white, "refugeeing" into more secure regions like southwest Georgia.

Yet even amidst the growing confusion of war, Georgians tried to hold onto as much of their traditional life as possible. Many white men remained at their civilian jobs. Some were too old or young for the army; others avoided the draft by hiring a substitute, gaining an occupational exemption or a medical deferment, or some other expedient. Reinforced by new white womanpower and old black slavepower, they had some success in carrying on as usual.

Georgians had never been very intellectual, but they read with special interest the twelve daily urban newspapers that carried the latest war news as well as a wide variety of sixty other newspapers. Neither the state nor Confederate governments seriously threatened freedom of the press, and key workers were exempt from conscription— though some volunteered anyway. The patriotic optimism of most editors boosted home front morale. Early in 1863 the Press Association of the Confederate States was established in Augusta by publishers trying to reduce costs by sharing resources, but, hampered by shortages and inefficient transportation and communication facilities, Georgia's newspapers declined in size and quality and increased in cost. Subscriptions plummeted. Many newspapers eventually disappeared for the duration, and some editors and presses "refugeed" away from oncoming Union forces several times.

Journals and books continued to be published too. The sudden elimination of Yankee competition was an initial boost, but eventually deteriorating wartime conditions crippled or destroyed every commercial press in the state. One colorful new journal appeared early in 1862 when Joseph Addison Turner began *The Countryman* as the successor to a short-lived prewar quarterly called *The Plantation*. Turner included a potpourri of literary and journalistic material in his new periodical, which was actually printed at his plantation near Eatonton. Here his thirteen-year-old assistant, Joel Chandler Harris, first came into contact with the African folklore that later became the basis for his famous Uncle Remus animal stories.

A flood of patriotic songs, poems, and plays poured forth during the war, but perhaps only Dr. Francis Orray Ticknor's poem entitled "Little Giffen" had lasting merit. His picture of a tough young Johnny Reb who fought and fought and fell mangled and rose to fight on and finally to disappear in the maelstrom of battle still demonstrates the tragedy of modern war. More traditional were Richard Malcolm Johnston's *Georgia Sketches,* published in Augusta in 1864, describing humorous events in the lives of simple rural folk, and Major Charles H. Smith's "Bill Arp" stories, a "cracker" view of the Civil War that appeared periodically in newspapers and helped Georgians laugh away their troubles. Only after the war could the Arp adventures be collected in one book, *Bill Arp, So Called: A Side Show of the Southern Side of the War.*

Georgia's educational system was also crippled by the war. The young men attending the University of Georgia, Emory, Oglethorpe, Mercer, the state's medical colleges, and other advanced schools flocked into the army. Only Mercer University remained open, and it had only a skeleton operation by 1863. Conversely, some women's colleges remained open as the demand for trained womanpower increased, and Wesleyan Female College in Macon actually flourished.

Below the college level deterioration was also extensive. Georgia's new public school system, which Governor Brown had organized just before the war, collapsed quickly when its funds were shifted to relief of soldiers' families and other war activities. Public education was again the responsibility of the counties. Some of the wealthier, more stable areas provided adequate education, but for the state as a whole the old, uneven, uncoordinated system sputtered along erratically. By the time Union forces overran Georgia, some rural, poor white youngsters, especially the children of fallen soldiers, had been almost as deprived of formal education as the children of the slaves.

The state's churches functioned more effectively. Many ministers had opposed secession, but, once the war started, the great majority backed the Confederacy. Though exempt from conscription, some ministers became soldiers, and others served the troops as chaplains, hospital commissioners, and agents for organizations like the interdenominational Soldiers Tract Association of Macon. Periodic revivals swept through the army, bolstering morale. At home the work of ministers like Episcopalian Bishop Stephen Elliott and Methodist Bishop George F. Pierce spurred religious enthusiasm and morale until wartime disruptions curtailed many organized activities. Churchmen were active in a movement to liberalize the Georgia slave code, but no significant changes actually occurred. The defeat of the Confederacy left the white churches in complete disarray, faced with the totally un-American problem of explaining and justifying a lost cause that had seemed so righteous.

This total defeat was ultimately the verdict of the battlefield. The early fights raged far to the north and west. Soldiers from Georgia participated and paid the usual bloody price, but their home state seemed safe far from the carnage. The rapidly expanding Union navy soon dispelled this illusion as it maneuvered to blockade the Confederacy's vulnerable coastline. Early in November 1861 a Federal naval expedition captured Port Royal and Hilton Head islands on the Carolina coast, just a few miles north of Fort Pulaski at the mouth of the Savannah River. A Confederate "mosquito fleet" of a few riverboats under Commodore Josiah Tattnall was the only naval defense available, but President Davis did dispatch a desk general from Richmond named Robert E. Lee to coordinate coastal defenses for a few months before he returned to Virginia and a more active assignment.

The Union Navy methodically extended its operations down the

, and by March 1862 it had seized all of Georgia's sea islands, h became havens for runaway slaves from the mainland. It also hed aside Tattnall's "fleet" and isolated Fort Pulaski from Savannah. Then on the morning of 10 April Federal batteries of new, rifled artillery on Tybee Island unleased a devastating barrage that soon tore gaping holes in the fort's old-fashioned masonry walls, and on the afternoon of the following day Fort Pulaski surrendered.

Only twelve miles upriver, Savannah frantically prepared defenses, but a naval assault never came. The capture of Fort Pulaski had effectively closed Savannah as a port, so the Union navy was content to conduct periodic raids along the coast. In the summer of 1863 a Federal amphibious attack destroyed the town of Darien, but five separate naval attacks failed to take Fort McAllister, a simple, rugged earthwork reinforced with stone at the mouth of the Ogeechee River.

Union naval harassment along the coast continued, but soon Georgia had to face greater threats from the interior as Federal armies in the west moved forward steadily. At first it was only occasional raids on the vital Western and Atlantic Railroad. In April 1862 Union spy James J. Andrews and twenty Ohio soldiers passed through Confederate lines in civilian clothes, seized a small train seven miles north of Marietta, and steamed toward Chattanooga. Western and Atlantic officials pursued them, and after a wild chase the Yankees were caught near Ringgold before they could significantly damage the line. Andrews and seven of his raiders were hanged as spies. A year later a more serious threat to the line came when Colonel Abel D. Streight and sixteen hundred mounted infantrymen swung through northern Alabama and knifed into Georgia. Checked at Rome by a rag-tag collection of convalescing rebel soldiers and pursued back into Alabama by General Nathan Bedford Forrest and only six hundred raw recruits, Streight was bluffed into surrendering to a "superior force," and the Western and Atlantic escaped any injury.

Soon these minor clashes were forgotten. In September 1863 Union General William S. Rosecrans's powerful army captured Chattanooga and moved into northwestern Georgia. Confederate General Braxton Bragg rushed his troops up and late in the month won the bloody battle of Chickamauga. The Union army seemed safely bottled up in Chattanooga, but the inept Rosecrans was replaced by new and much more talented generals: Ulysses S. Grant, commander of all Union forces in the west, and William Tecumseh Sherman, his ablest aide.

Quickly Grant reinforced his troops in Chattanooga. On 23–25 November he attacked at Lookout Mountain and Missionary Ridge and

GEORGIA CAMPAIGNS
OF THE CIVIL WAR

Chattanooga

hicka-
auga

Dalton

SHERMAN'S ROUTE

Resaca

Rome

Kingston

New Hope
Church

Kennesaw Mountain
Marietta
Peachtree Creek

Ezra Church

Atlanta

Athens

Washington

Madison

Covington

Union
Point
Eatonton

Warrenton

Augusta

Jonesboro

Newnan

Griffin

Milledgeville

Sandersville

Barnesville

Forsyth

Millen

Thomaston

West Point

WILSON'S   RAID   Macon

Gordon

SHERMAN'S

ROUTE

SHERMAN'S ROUTE

Columbus

Fort
Valley

Ft. Pulaski

Andersonville

Hawkinsville

Americus

ufaula

Smithville

Savannah

Cuthbert

Ft. McAlister

Fort Gaines

Albany

Irwinville

Darien

McDonough

Brunswick

Valdosta

Thomasville

0   50

miles

Cartographic Services
University of Georgia

sent Bragg's forces reeling back into Georgia. Grant was soon ordered east to face Lee in Virginia, leaving Sherman with an army of almost one hundred thousand men to carry the war to Georgia in the spring of 1864. The discredited Bragg was replaced by General Joseph E. Johnston, who hurriedly prepared his approximately fifty thousand men for the coming invasion.

The last act began in May 1864. Grant moved forward in Virginia, ignoring terrible losses as he gradually wore down Lee's Army of Northern Virginia. A similar drama unfolded in Georgia as Sherman moved toward Atlanta. Using his superior numbers to outflank strong defenses at Dalton, he then inflicted heavy losses on Johnston at Resaca. The Confederates retreated down the Western and Atlantic Railroad, fighting again at New Hope Church late in May and then on 27 June at Kennesaw Mountain hurling back the Yankees with heavy losses. Sherman was handicapped by increasingly long and vulnerable supply lines through rough, ravaged country, but he was always able to outflank Johnston's smaller army and keep moving south.

By 9 July his army was on the north bank of the Chattahoochee River, ready to assault Atlanta itself. Although Johnston had fought skillfully and had inflicted heavier casualties than he had received, President Davis replaced him with General John Bell Hood, an aggressive but mediocre commander. With Lee driven into entrenchments at Petersburg, Davis would send no troop reinforcements to Hood, so Atlanta's defenses were hurriedly strengthened by thousands of impressed slaves, and Governor Brown's latest ten-thousand-man force of the very young and the very old was thrown into the line.

Hood arrived at Atlanta on 18 July. Two days later he began a series of headlong attacks that were repulsed with heavy losses. His army retired into prepared positions, and the forty-day seige of Atlanta began. Union artillery pounded the city as many civilians fled and the rest burrowed into the earth. Hood attacked again at Ezra Church on 28 July and was again repulsed with heavy losses. Meanwhile a raid by Union General George Stoneman and four thousand cavalrymen swung around Atlanta and headed for Macon and Andersonville, an overcrowded prisoner-of-war stockade where thirteen thousand of the thirty-one thousand inmates died. Quick Confederate reactions frustrated this sally and forced the surrender of Stoneman and seven hundred of his troopers. Hood tried one final attack at Jonesboro on 1 September, but his troops were again thrown back.

Battered and fearful of complete encirclement by Sherman's endless flanking movements, which had already cut the major railroads into

the city, Hood's army destroyed much war material and railroad equipment and evacuated Atlanta. On 2 September Sherman's troops
marched in. Only the fall of Richmond could have stunned southerners more, and in the North the news helped insure the reelection of
Lincoln. Despite Hood's protests, Sherman forced the remaining sixteen hundred civilians in Atlanta to leave, and at the same time Governor Brown furloughed his ten thousand state troops to keep them out
of the Confederate Army.

Seeking to exploit the gloom and dissension, Sherman initiated peace
negotiations with Joshua Hill and two other Georgia Unionists, but
Brown and Stephens rejected the idea of a peace conference at this
time. Alarmed by events in Georgia, Davis visited Hood's shaken army
and delivered fighting speeches to civilians too. In late October the
governors of Virginia, the Carolinas, Alabama, Mississippi, and Georgia
met in Augusta and determined to fight on. Nevertheless, disaffection
was spreading all over Georgia as Governor Brown began to call openly
for peace and General Sherman prepared to strike again.

After evacuating Atlanta, Hood's army of forty thousand men had
marched north into Tennessee, hoping to disrupt Sherman's supply
lines and draw him away from Georgia. Sherman briefly followed but
then swung back to Atlanta after sending General George H. Thomas
northward with sufficient forces to crush Hood's army near Nashville
by the end of the year. Then in mid-November Sherman launched his
famous "march to the sea."

He planned to sever all lines of transportation and communication
and live off the rich Georgia land, so he ordered all the main buildings
in Atlanta burned. In the ensuing holocaust only four hundred dwellings survived. Smoldering Atlanta ceased to exist as a railroad and industrial center as Sherman's five thousand cavalrymen and fifty-seven
thousand infantrymen marched southeastward against the token opposition of scattered militia units and General Joseph Wheeler's three
thousand Confederate cavalrymen. Sherman simply disappeared from
the sight of the North as he cut a forty- to sixty-mile wide swath
through the soft underbelly of the Confederacy.

Initially his army split into two large forces, the left wing moving
along the Georgia Railroad to Madison and then swinging south to
Milledgeville while the right wing feinted toward Macon and then
swung eastward to join the other wing near Sandersville. Rail lines,
bridges, factories, mills, and other wartime resources were destroyed
under the direction of responsible officers, and, despite strict orders to
the contrary, some private homes and property suffered too. Sherman's

Western and Atlantic Railroad depot, shops, and roundhouse, Atlanta, after Sherman's capture of the city in 1864

veterans were determined to enjoy "marching through Georgia," especially in scouting and foraging parties on the fringes of the main forces. Civilian property losses mounted rapidly as the army moved forward fifteen miles a day, but the increasingly carefree bluecoats generally refrained from rape and murder. Thousands of slaves flocked toward the Union army of liberation, often suffering great hardships in the general confusion. As usual cavalry units ranged widely and wildly, and Judson Kilpatrick's Yankees were man-for-man little more destructive than Wheeler's Confederate horsemen.

On 22 November Union troops entered the undefended capital of Milledgeville. Aside from destroying the penitentiary and other wartime industrial facilities and a little haphazard looting, they contented themselves with holding a mock session of the legislature, which repealed the ordinance of secession. By 24 November they were moving east again in the bitter cold.

During the last half of its march to the sea Sherman's huge army concentrated a little more and lumbered straight for Savannah as the destruction and pillaging continued unabated. By 10 December his troops were closing in on Georgia's largest city, and three days later they reached the mouth of the Ogeechee River and took Fort McAllister from the rear. Confederate General William J. Hardee's ten thousand nondescript soldiers evacuated Savannah to avoid encirclement, and on 21 December Union troops moved in, their long march completed in a little over a month. Triumphantly Sherman telegraphed Lincoln: "I beg to present you as a Christmas gift the city of Savannah, with one hundred and fifty heavy guns and plenty of ammunition, also about twenty-five thousand bales of cotton."

Savannah yielded all too graciously; Confederate Georgia was whipped. On 1 February 1865 Sherman's rested veterans moved north to crush resistance in the Carolinas while in Virginia Grant prepared for his final campaign against Lee, which would end at Appomattox on 9 April. The final blow was delivered in Georgia by Union General James H. Wilson and thirteen thousand crack cavalrymen. They knifed into western Georgia from Alabama, brushed aside General Howell Cobb's three thousand ragged militiamen, captured Columbus on 16 April, wrecked its industries, and then rode on to Macon where Cobb surrendered his troops and the city on 20 April. Early in May Governor Brown formally surrendered the state's last military forces.

Victorious Union forces fanned out across the state and arrested Brown, Stephens, Cobb, and Hill, but Toombs escaped to Europe and avoided his colleagues' brief imprisonment. Only Major Henry Wirz, the commandant at Andersonville, was executed for war crimes. Defiant Jefferson Davis had fled from Richmond early in April, and his shadow government held its last meeting at Washington in Wilkes County. Then on 10 May Union troops captured Davis near Irwinville deep in south Georgia.

It was over; Confederate Georgia was overwhelmed in a modern war it had never doubted it could win. Death and destruction lay heavy on the land, but Georgians were disunited in defeat just as they had been when they seceded and waged war. For white Georgians the future looked gloomy, but black Georgians looked forward to a brighter tomorrow. All Georgians faced the challenge of Reconstruction.

Sergeant Thomas Jefferson Rushin, Twelfth Georgia Infantry, missing in action at the Battle of Antietam

Georgia Department of Archives and History

PART FOUR

1865–1890

by

CHARLES E. WYNES

The Seal of the Radical Government, 1871–1872

*The soldier is shown with his sword in his left hand,
as a result of an error in copying.*

From 1872 to 1914 the Great Seal of 1799 was restored

XV

The Politics of Reconstruction, Redemption, and Bourbonism

Politics and reconstruction were not the chief concern of Georgians, nor of other southerners, in the months following the collapse of armed resistance in April 1865. To white Georgians, how to make a living amidst a civilization that had collapsed, and how to live with a formerly slave population now free, were foremost concerns; while to blacks, exercise of their new-found freedom was paramount. It was true, though, that these concerns had to take place in some kind of political framework, and as time went on that framework became of more importance and received more attention. But never at any time did politics become the all-consuming passion of southerners, including Georgians, white and black, that written history often leads one to believe. Life and making a living were the chief passions, as they had always been.

With the collapse of state government in 1865, disorder was not uncommon in many parts of the state. The idle, both black and white, together with army stragglers, often simply pillaged what they wanted. Augusta had bread riots, and in Wilkes County the United States Army, which had quickly spread over the state, had to restore order by resort to force. Meanwhile, it was not at all clear where local civil authority began and the authority of the army ended. Ultimately, a policy of "the military authority should sustain, not assume the functions of civil authority," prevailed. Yet southerners eagerly awaited word from the new president, Andrew Johnson, on the question of restoration of both full civil authority, and of the Union, which nearly all seemed to accept as not only inevitable but as their due.

Congress did not reassemble until November 1865, and in the interlude President Johnson announced on 29 May his own plan of reconstruction. This plan revealed that Johnson, like his predecessor, Lincoln, interpreted reconstruction as a presidential, not a congressional, function. And surprisingly, to northerners and southerners alike, Johnson showed himself to be quite as lenient and compassionate as Lincoln.

The Johnson plan called for the appointment by him for each southern state of a native, Unionist provisional governor, whose responsibility it would be to register the voters and call for the election of delegates to a constitutional convention. Only those persons who had taken an oath of allegiance to the United States might vote; nothing was said, to the relief of the whites, about Negroes' voting. The president later suggested the idea of a very limited suffrage for Negroes, but nothing came of it until after congressional reconstruction began, in 1867. Once assembled, the conventions had to do three things: abolish slavery, repudiate state debts incurred while waging the war, and annul—not merely repeal—the ordinances of secession.

On 17 June 1865 the president named James Johnson (no relation), a respected lawyer and one-term, prewar congressman from Columbus who had opposed secession and quietly sat out the war, as provisional governor of Georgia. Provisional Governor Johnson shortly called for the October election of delegates to the convention, with the convention itself to convene later that same month.

The convention that assembled was one of "average talents." Although twenty-two of the delegates had been members of the secession convention all but one of the twenty-two had opposed secession. In sum, it was a collection of moderates, men who more often than not had opposed secession and then gone reluctantly with their state. By the end of the first week in November, the convention had completed its work but not without evidence of foot-dragging in meeting the conditions laid down by the president, a fact that did not go unnoticed in the North. The ordinance of secession was repealed, not declared null and void as required, slavery was abolished in a reluctant article of little grace, and the wartime debt was repudiated by a narrow margin only after agonizing debate. All in all, the resulting constitution was not greatly different from the old one.

In the November general elections, Charles J. Jenkins, from Richmond County but a native of South Carolina who had played a leading role in the constitutional convention, was chosen as governor. In fact, he did not even have an opponent. The new legislature was conservative in tone, but among its members there were fewer antisecessionists and Union sympathizers than had been present in the constitutional convention. When the legislature turned to the election of Georgia's two United States senators, it chose Alexander H. Stephens, former vice president of the Confederacy, and Herschel V. Johnson, a former Confederate senator, both of whom had opposed secession but whose choice was sure to inflame the North.

Meeting in Milledgeville on 4 December (the capital was not moved to Atlanta until 1868), the new legislature promptly turned its attention to the question of the newly freed Negro. President Johnson had stipulated that in addition to abolition of slavery in the new constitution, legislative ratification of the Thirteenth Amendment, which freed the slaves, must follow. Accordingly, after beating down some sentiment for ratification with reservations, the amendment was approved with near unanimity.

Unlike most of the other former Confederate states, Georgia's legislature acted more circumspectly regarding the so-called black codes for dealing with the Negroes; its members had seen the storm of northern criticism that some of the other states' black codes had already reaped. Accordingly, with the exceptions that blacks were not to serve on juries or to testify in court against whites, nor to intermarry with whites, Georgia accorded to Negroes, at least on paper, a full bill of civil rights. Of course they still could not vote, but at that time Negroes could vote in only six northern states, for that matter.

Having been led by President Johnson to believe as much, Georgians now fully expected to be restored to the Union without further ado. Such was not to be, for on the same day that the newly chosen Georgia legislature assembled, 4 December 1865, the Thirty-ninth Congress of the United States met in Washington. Already gathered there were the senators and congressmen from some of the southern states that had completed the Johnson requirements for restoration of the Union. However, far more was at stake than the question of simply restoring the Union. Many senators and congressmen from the North, as well as their constituents, felt that President Johnson had exceeded his constitutional authority when, without consulting Congress, he had taken the question of reconstruction unto himself as a presidential function. Others, not unreasonably if sometimes vindictively, felt that the South should be further punished in some fashion for secession. Still others saw the Negro being reenslaved by the often harsh black codes that most of the southern states had enacted and were angered at the foot-dragging of some of the former Confederate states on the ratification of the Thirteenth Amendment. Then, too, many in the North wanted to see some act of contrition on the part of the South; when they saw waiting to be sworn in as part of the South's congressional and senatorial delegations former military and civil officials of the Confederacy, they considered this an act of defiance. The result was that the southern senators' and congressmen's names were omitted from the roll call when the Congress assembled and their states were left unrepresented.

Rapidly thereafter the course of Reconstruction passed into the hands of Congress and out of those of the president. To the fore now came Senator Charles Sumner of Massachusetts and Representative Thaddeus Stevens of Pennsylvania, two of the leading architects of what would become known as Radical, or Congressional, Reconstruction. Congressman-elect Horace Maynard of Tennessee commented that "Thad Stevens had the whole Southern Confederacy in his breeches pocket and meant to keep it there for a good while to come." Then on 14 December, the same day that Governor Jenkins was inaugurated in Georgia, where he gave a statesmanlike address for which the *New York Times* praised him, the Joint Congressional Committee of fifteen members was constituted and Reconstruction took on a new face as well as new leadership.

From the Joint Committee on 30 April 1866 came an additional proposed amendment to the constitution, the Fourteenth, which Congress passed and sent out to the states, including the former Confederate states, on 8 June. Briefly, this amendment defined citizenship so as to include Negroes and guaranteed to all citizens equal protection of the laws; while it did not confer the suffrage upon anyone, it nevertheless declared that states might have their congressional representation reduced in proportion to the number of citizens denied the right to vote—a sort of "carrot and stick" approach to encourage the South to enfranchise blacks. It also barred from officeholding persons who as officials had taken an oath of allegiance to the United States and subsequently engaged in rebellion, until Congress by a two-thirds vote removed such disability.

Alone among the former Confederate states, Tennessee almost immediately ratified the Fourteenth Amendment, and seemingly, for her "good example," was restored to the Union in July 1866. Whether this meant that had Georgia and the remaining southern states ratified the amendment they too would have been readmitted to the Union without further ado is unknown, but it is doubtful. Tennessee was a special case for many reasons. At any rate, one after another, the southern states rejected the amendment, Georgia doing so in November 1866.

The year 1866 also saw race riots in Memphis and New Orleans, President Johnson's abortive political campaign known as the "swing around the circle," and consolidation of the Radicals' position in the North, with the result that by the winter and spring of 1867 the Joint Committee and Congress were prepared to take over Reconstruction. With Thaddeus Stevens proclaiming that for two years the South had been in a "state of anarchy," Congress passed over presidential veto on

2 March the first and major Reconstruction Act. Now, real Reconstruction had come to Georgia and the rest of the South.

The new legislation, which placed the Johnson state governments in a "provisional" status subordinate to military authority, provided for the division of all the former Confederate states that had not ratified the Fourteenth Amendment (only Tennessee had) into five military districts, with Georgia part of the Third District—together with Florida and Alabama. Each district was to be commanded by an officer of at least the rank of brigadier general, appointments that the president dutifully if grudgingly made. Major General John Pope was placed in command of the Third District on 1 April 1867, and shortly thereafter he took up his duties in Atlanta, two years after the end of the war.

One of the chief duties facing the district commanders was a new registration of voters. All adult males, black as well as white, upon swearing to an oath of allegiance might register. Registrants might then vote for selection of delegates to a constitutional convention, where a guarantee of Negro suffrage had to be written into the constitution. When a state had ratified the Fourteenth Amendment, Congress might then, upon certification that the requisite three-fourths of the states had approved the amendment, restore the state to its normal relationship to the Union and put an end to military occupation. It was a bitter pill to white southerners and a far cry from the promise held out by both Lincoln and Johnson.

Governor Jenkins had meanwhile hurried to Washington, where he futilely sought to get the Supreme Court to issue an injunction against the new Reconstruction Act, while at home Benjamin H. Hill, in the presence of General Pope, counseled Georgians to register but to vote "no" on the calling of a constitutional convention. Neither action helped the state in the eyes of either General Pope or the North.

The April 1867 registration of voters, amidst charges of corruption and Union favoritism toward Negro registrants, resulted in a total of 102,411 eligible white voters and 98,507 Negro voters. The election for the convention, which was held from 29 October to 2 November 1867—thus giving the inexperienced black voters greater opportunity to exercise their franchise—was generally boycotted by the whites and resulted in a lopsided 102,283 votes for the convention to 4,127 against.

The 169 delegates chosen assembled in Atlanta on 9 December 1867. General Pope had ordered the convention to assemble in Atlanta instead of in the capital, Milledgeville, because allegedly the innkeepers there had vowed that they would not house the thirty-seven Negro delegates. Although overwhelmingly Republican in makeup, the delegates constituted a basically conservative body. True "carpetbaggers," or white, northern outsiders, numbered fewer than ten members, while the overwhelming majority, some radical and some not so radical, were the supposedly abominable "scalawags," native whites who were willing to cooperate with the Radicals. In actuality Georgia's scalawags, like those elsewhere in the South, were a mixture of old-line Whigs and Jacksonian Democrats, the former long without a party to call home, and the latter long resentful of the planter-lawyer domination of their party. This body of generally reasonable men builded well, and the constitution they wrote was perhaps a better framework of government than the Bourbon-Redeemer constitution of 1877 that replaced it.

One of the most popular provisions of the new constitution, with Radicals and conservatives alike, was relief for debtors, namely the cancellation of many debts contracted before 1 January 1865, and of all those debts in connection with support of the recent rebellion. In education, the new constitution called for the establishment by the first session of the General Assembly of a free public school system for *all* the children of the state. (The constitution of 1865 under the Johnson plan of reconstruction had called for a public school system for white children only.) Also, of course, the constitution of 1868 fulfilled the demands of the Reconstruction Acts, notably by conferring the suffrage upon Negroes. Led by such men as Rufus B. Bullock, the first governor under the new constitution, Amos Tappan Akerman, later attorney general of the United States in the cabinet of President Grant, H. K. McCay, and Benjamin F. Conley, all of whom were northerners by birth but who had settled in Georgia before the war, the convention finished its work in early March 1868, after three months of labor and deliberation.

General Meade, who had succeeded General Pope in January 1868, ordered that the new constitution be presented to the voters and that state officers and congressmen be chosen in an election to be held 21–23 April. Meade had meanwhile found it expedient to remove Governor Jenkins and to appoint in his stead Brigadier General Thomas H. Ruger. The Republicans in March had nominated Rufus B. Bullock, a leading figure in the constitutional convention, for governor. Bullock, one of the more notorious Radicals, would later apparently turn out to be the scamp many thought him to be, but he was also a former Confederate army officer of the Quartermaster Corps. He had originally come to Georgia in 1859 from New York and settled in Augusta. Bullock had the backing of ex-Confederate governor Joseph

E. Brown, who counseled cooperation with the Radicals in Congress, apparently because he believed it to be the wisest policy and not just for personal gain, as often charged. In opposition, the Democrats put forth the esteemed General John B. Gordon. In a bitter and vituperative campaign, the constitution was approved by a vote of 88,172 to 70,200, while Bullock was chosen governor over Gordon, 83,527 to 76,356. The vote probably meant that some moderate Republicans who favored the constitution voted for Gordon in preference to Bullock. In the legislature, while the Republicans won a clear but narrow majority in the House, in the Senate the Democrats and the Radical Republicans were about equally divided, with a handful of moderate Republicans holding the balance of power, which they usually used to support their party. There were 29 Negroes among the total of 172 members in the House, and 3 Negroes in the Senate of 44 members.

The new legislature met on 4 July 1868 and on 21 July ratified the Fourteenth Amendment. Joshua Hill from Madison, with the help of moderate Republicans, was chosen over former governor Brown for the long term in the Senate, and Dr. H. V. M. Miller from Rome over Bullock henchman Foster Blodgett for the short term. Congress had meanwhile, on 25 June, approved Georgia's readmission to the Union as soon as the Fourteenth Amendment was ratified. Since this was not done until 21 July, although Georgia's congressional delegation and two senators hurried to Washington, Congress had adjourned before they could be seated.

Meanwhile, Georgia was about to start paying for the fact that there, so far, the principles of conservatism had triumphed more than in any other state in the lower South. Off and on during the summer of 1868 the Georgia House of Representatives had tinkered with the question of eligibility of some of the Negro members, while at the same time some of the white members, as former Confederates, sat unchallenged and in plain defiance of both the Reconstruction Acts and the Fourteenth Amendment. Finally, in early September, all the known Negro members of both houses were expelled, in all twenty-eight; four members of the House were so light-skinned that there was some question about whether they met the "one-eighth Negro blood" definition, and they were left alone. The legislature took this action on the grounds that possession of the right to vote did not imply the right to hold office as well. Conservative whites who had opposed the individual Negro members were then seated in their stead.

It was plain that the Radicals in Congress were not going to stand for any such display of white southern intransigence as this, especially when it was aggravated by the state's voting Democratic, for Horatio Seymour and against General Grant, in the presidential election of 1868. So, though the Georgia members of the House were seated briefly, in late 1868, after March 1869 they were barred from their seats, while the Georgia senators were not seated at all. Georgia thus remained in a "Reconstruction limbo" until 22 December 1869, when Congress, after hearing testimony of Ku Klux Klan and other racially inspired violence, took the advice of Governor Bullock and reinstituted military rule in the state. There was added the stipulation that before Georgia could be restored to the Union she must ratify the Fifteenth Amendment in addition to the Fourteenth, which she had already ratified. The Fifteenth Amendment stipulated that the right to vote should not be denied to anyone on the basis of "race, color, or previous condition of servitude," and thus prevented the southern states from ever removing from their constitutions by amendment the provision for Negro suffrage; it also brought suffrage to Negroes in the vast majority of northern states for the first time.

General Alfred H. Terry was made the new military commander, though Bullock was permitted to function as provisional governor. In January 1870, the expelled Negroes had their seats in the legislature restored, while in proceedings that became known as "Terry's Purge" some twenty-nine white conservatives were removed for ineligibility and replaced by their Republican runners-up in the election of 1868, thus giving to the legislature the political complexion that both Bullock and the Radicals in Congress wanted. The next month, February, the Fifteenth Amendment was ratified, and in July 1870 Congress, for the second time, restored Georgia to the Union. Finally, in February 1871, for the first time in a decade, Georgia was fully represented in both houses of the Congress of the United States. Ironically, however, the Senate refused to seat the two senators chosen by the Bullock-Terry legislature in early 1870, Republicans Henry P. Farrow and Richard H. Whitely. Instead, the seats were awarded to Joshua Hill and H. V. M. Miller, who had been chosen by the conservative legislature of 1868. Also seated was Georgia's lone Negro congressman, Jefferson Long of Macon.

In the meantime, the Bullock administration and the legislature as reconstituted by General Terry were gaining a reputation for being the most wasteful, corrupt, and generally all-around unfit that the state had ever had, or has had since. While there is some truth in many of the charges made against the Bullock regime, his administration was not nearly so bad as some have made it out to be, and even its harshest critics have conceded that, compared to some of the other former Confederate states, Georgia was fortunate. As for Bullock, he seems to have been condemned as much for his friends and their alleged embezzlements as for any of his own. And of course, corruption in Georgia must be viewed as part of a then-current "national disease" of corruption—present alike in the nation's capital, especially during the Grant years; in northern cities like New York, where the peculations of the Tweed Ring made those in Georgia look like a crooked card game between two near-broke cotton merchants; and even in the statehouses of some northern and western states.

Scandals there were, but the Bullock regime did not last long enough for them to become very great. Though technically in control of the state from its first restoration to the Union in June 1868, it was nevertheless not until January 1870 that Bullock got reasonably firm control over the legislature. Then in December of that same year, the Democrats won control of both houses of the legislature. Also, it must be remembered that the investigation of all the alleged scandals was conducted by a Democratic legislature. Bullock did not even stick around to defend himself. The Democratically controlled legislature that had been elected in December 1870 did not take office until 1 November 1871, and on 31 October it was announced that Bullock had resigned his office and had already left the state. Benjamin F. Conley of Augusta and an old ally of Bullock, as president of the Senate, assumed the governorship. But the Democrats, on doubtful constitutional grounds, rammed through a law, over Conley's veto, calling for a special election in December 1871, to fill the remaining portion of Bullock's term, which ended 1 January 1873. In a special convention, James M. Smith, newly elected speaker of the House, was nominated by the Democrats. The nominee of the Republicans, James Atkins, declined the honor, so the election went by default to Smith. Smith, a Columbus lawyer who had opposed secession but later served in the Confederate army, was sworn in as governor on 12 January 1872. With the Democrats in control of both houses of the legislature, Georgia was now "redeemed" with Radical Reconstruction a thing of the past. But before it was put to rest the Democrats set out to reveal just what Bullock had left behind.

The main scandals seem to have lain in the areas of greatly increased administrative expenses and in the expenditure of funds gained from the sale of railroad bonds for purposes other than those for which they were intended. The state also endorsed at least $5.75 million in bonds for seven different privately owned railroads, three of which had the same president, Hannibal I. Kimball, Governor Bullock's closest associate and a man of whom it has been said, with some reason, that he probably was the real power in Georgia during the Bullock years. Meanwhile, the state-owned railroad, the Western and Atlantic, now headed by another associate of Bullock, Foster Blodgett, went some three-quarters of a million dollars in debt in a two-year period as it became a gold mine of jobs, both fictitious and real, and a genuine source of plunder for those who knew the right people. There was more, much more, especially as to charges. Yet, when in 1874, Kimball, who had like Bullock fled the state, returned to Georgia of his own volition and challenged his accusers to indict him, none did so. As for Bullock, in 1876 he was arrested in New York state and returned to Georgia for trial. It took the state two years to get around to trying him, during which time he might have fled again, but did not. At his trial in Atlanta some of his former chief accusers dramatically reversed themselves, and the jury acquitted him after but two hours of deliberation.

Bullock was a bad governor and a weak man, perhaps often taken in by friends who were smarter than he, while Republican rule in Georgia was not exactly an example of fiscal responsibility. But in both the regional and the national context of the times Georgia was lucky— lucky that her rulers were not more inept and unscrupulous than they were in an age noted for that type of leader, and lucky that the amount of waste and corruption was not greater than it was.

The role of blacks in the Radical Republican legislature of Georgia was a very limited one, more so than in most of the other southern states. This was so due mainly to the fact that, after only two months in office, they were removed from and denied their seats for almost a year and a half, from September 1868 to January 1870. Less than a year later, in December, the Democrats won control of the legislature, and the state was "redeemed." Thereafter, both their numbers and influence waned, until they were a nullity. At the local level, here and there through much of the state, there were black holders of public office, usually minor ones. At all levels, though, as long as they were in office, whether during or after Reconstruction, the quality of their overall performance was probably no better and no worse than that of white officeholders.

Never having known the alleged Negro rule of which their descendants would make so much, and having known Radical Republican rule but briefly, the generation of white Georgians of the 1870s and 1880s set out to drive Negroes from the polls, unless they could be, as many were, induced to vote Democratic. Meanwhile, stultifying one-party rule was fastened upon the state, with the state Republican party being steadily driven into oblivion. So, as happened in other southern states, notably Virginia, "independentism" or factionalism within the Democratic party itself was the only thing that, for a few years, prevented elections from becoming a Democratic rubber stamp.

Increasingly the dominant faction in the Democratic party came to be known as Bourbons, a term of opprobrium first applied by the Radicals to all those who opposed congressional reconstruction. Clinging to the old values, they were supposed to "have learned nothing and forgot nothing." Quite the contrary. In fact, the term "New Departure Democrats" is a much more accurate one. Of mixed Whig and Democratic antecedents, virtually all of them accepted the end of slavery as a not unmixed blessing, though they continued, usually for political purposes, to laud the Confederacy and the "Lost Cause." Likewise, instead of glorifying the "agricultural ideal," they sought rather to "Yankeefy" Georgia and the South, as promoters of a "New South" of commerce and industry. The "little man"—usually the farmer, whether a tenant of some kind, or the small, independent landowner, black and white— became the forgotten man of Georgia and the rest of the South, except at election time. Then the old bogey or specter of "Negro rule" was raised to keep white men in line, lest they divide and place the Negro in a position of holding the balance of power. Economic coercion and intimidation caused the Negro to vote Democratic, or terror tactics kept him from voting at all. Georgia and the rest of the South were to know upwards of twenty years of this type of political leadership before the little man revolted in the crusade known as Populism.

If further proof were really needed that the Democrats were truly in the saddle following the Georgia election of 1870, the elections of 1872 provided it. That year Governor James M. Smith was reelected by a majority of 60,000 out of 145,000 votes over the Republican candidate, Dawson A. Walker of Whitfield County, while the Republican minority in the legislature was further reduced. And, whereas in 1868 a total of thirty-two Negroes had been elected to the General Assembly, in 1872 only four were chosen, all in the House. Also, in spite of the fact that no party or no group was a real threat to the Democrats, the election was a bloody and violent one, in keeping with the heritage from Reconstruction.

For the next several years, beginning in 1873 and lasting through 1878, Georgia, like the rest of the nation, was to wrestle with the woes of economic depression. And until that depression was past, the New Departure Democrats could hope for little real progress toward the

New South, the pursuit of which would dominate the decade of the 1880s. Accordingly, these years were used primarily to consolidate the Democrats' hold upon the state, which meant a struggle between them and the Independents who split from their own party, often to be aided and abetted by white Republicans and less frequently by black Republicans in their attempt to restore genuine two-party government to the state. In Georgia, the Independents tended to be from a Whiggish background, but in general they represented all those who, for whatever reason, were unhappy with the oligarchy that controlled the Democratic party.

Although the election of 1870 had witnessed the appearance, unsuccessfully, of the first Independent candidates, the term "Independent" had appeared earlier, in 1868. However, the Independent movement in Georgia is usually dated from 1874, when Dr. William H. Felton won a seat in Congress from the fourteen-county Seventh District in north Georgia, later to become known as "the Bloody Seventh." It was fitting that the Independent movement should begin in north Georgia, the most disaffected region of the state before the war, with pockets of Unionism during the war, and a "scalawag center" during Reconstruction.

By the time of the elections of 1876, the state Democratic party was torn by internal dissension, while depressed economic conditions resulted in an inordinate number of would-be officeholders in search of jobs. Obviously all of them could not receive the party's endorsement, so that they often served to increase the number of Independents. For example, the race for the governorship was almost unseemly, with some fifteen possible candidates mentioned even before Governor Smith announced that he would not be a candidate for reelection. Surprisingly, the nominating convention was harmonious, with Alfred Holt Colquitt of Baker County but a native of Walton County receiving the nomination. Colquitt, a former Confederate major general, was a graduate of Princeton University.

The Republicans were more hopeful than they had been in years, due to the growing disarray in the Democratic party and to the fact that 1876 was also a presidential election year. They nominated for governor Jonathan Norcross, a native of Maine who had come to Georgia in the 1830s, become a Whig, and served as the mayor of Atlanta before the war. Hurt by the federal Civil Rights Act of 1875, not to mention the depression, Republican Norcross was trounced by Colquitt, 111,297 to 33,433. It was estimated that upwards of twenty thousand Negroes even voted for the paternalistic, lay preacher

Colquitt, while as many more did not vote at all—some from fear, some from indifference, and some from resignation to the fact that "the bottom rail was always going to be on the bottom." Dissatisfied Democrats and Republicans combined successfully, however, to return Independent William H. Felton to Congress from the Seventh District.

If Republicanism in Georgia was not through it was at least on its last legs by 1876, as it would be many years before a regular Republican would again be nominated for governor. Increasingly, the Republicans turned to support of Independent candidates, who now became the only threat to complete Bourbon control.

The remaining chief symbol of Republicanism and Reconstruction— the constitution of 1868—the Bourbons did not seem to be especially interested in removing. In truth, that constitution was more in keeping with Bourbon beliefs than the one that replaced it. But to many Georgians, it was, in the words of the unregenerate Robert Toombs, "the handiwork of negroes, thieves, and Yankees," and it had to go. Here was a visceral reaction from the people that Bourbon leaders and the greatly weakened Republicans, who of course admired the constitution as their handiwork, could not control. Finally, in a public referendum on 12 June 1877, a constitutional convention was approved by an extremely narrow margin. Not a single Negro delegate was chosen.

Since the Bourbons had not favored the convention, the result was that anti-Bourbon and conservative, agricultural interests were in command. Neither Governor Colquitt nor Joseph E. Brown nor John B. Gordon, the so-called "Bourbon Triumvirate" who together dominated the governorship and the two Senate seats for most of the period 1876-90, was present. The constitution that resulted and that the people overwhelmingly approved by referendum on 5 December 1877 reduced the authority of the state government, especially that of the executive and the judiciary, while that of the thinly populated, rural counties was increased. It was an inelastic document, written by farmer interests, and was ill-suited to the needs of a modern state, with the result that it was soon shingled with amendments. It was not, however, a genuinely reactionary document since it continued many of the features of the constitution of 1868, such as the guarantee of separate property rights for women. Mainly, though, the constitution of 1877 embodied a reaction against both "carpetbag rule" and "big government." Even so, it lasted in much-amended form until 1945.

Meanwhile, the spirit of Independentism continued to grow, until by the elections of 1878 politics in Georgia was marked by much of the bitterness of the Reconstruction years. By that date, so complete was one-party control of the state that in Georgia, as in some other southern states, it was inevitable that both philosophical and internal party differences should foster Independent movements. One party, especially when it was controlled by a relative few, could never adequately give opportunity to all the politically ambitious. Bitterness was aggravated by the increasing tendency of Republicans to support the Independents. To many Democrats, Republicans were Radicals, and by association Independents became much the same.

The years 1878–82 represented the height of the Independent revolt. In the congressional elections of 1878, not only was Dr. Felton returned to Congress for a third time over the regular Democratic nominee, he was also joined by Henry Parsons from the Fourth District and Emory Speer from the Ninth, while there were some grounds for believing Alexander Stephens from the Eighth to be an Independent, too. It was clear that the Independents were going to make a major play for the governorship in the elections of 1880. Adding fuel to the fire was the fact that John B. Gordon, one of the "Bourbon Triumvirate" of Gordon, Colquitt, and Brown, who had just been reelected to the Senate in 1878, suddenly resigned in 1879, to be replaced by the wily and distrusted Joseph E. Brown, who was appointed by Governor Colquitt! The popular hero Gordon came home to campaign for the reelection of Colquitt and to accept a lucrative railroad position in the state, while Brown was in office again. "Bargain and corruption" was the statewide cry.

In the nominating convention of 1880, the Independents were able to keep Colquitt from getting the required two-thirds vote, but since no one else could get it either, Colquitt was presented to the people as the "recommended candidate."

The Independents quickly sought to get Dr. Felton to oppose Colquitt, but when he declined they made the unfortunate choice of former United States Senator Thomas M. Norwood of Savannah but a native of Talbot County. With no war record, and at least tainted with a financial scandal involving state bonds, Norwood was also no friend of the Negro. In a speech at Emory he had once said about the Negro: "Cut him down. Why cumbereth he the ground?" But with the Republicans offering no candidate of their own, and with the white vote thus split between Colquitt and Norwood, Negroes played a larger role in the election of 1880 than they had in any election since 1870. But it was the paternalistic Colquitt whom they supported, thus helping him to win reelection by a majority of more than fifty-four thousand votes, or almost two-to-one. It was a bitter, violence-marked campaign that made even clearer to the Bourbons the necessity for nullifying any white opposition so that the Negro could never again hold the balance of power. Perhaps as an omen of what was to come, Dr. Felton lost his bid for reelection to Congress that year.

Up to this point, cooperation between the Independents and the Republicans had been a haphazard, off-and-on sort of thing. Now, with Felton taking the lead for the Independents and General James Longstreet for the Republicans, Bourbon opponents sought the basis for an alliance which, they hoped, might not only bring them control of the state but control of federal patronage from the Republican administration in Washington as well. Complicating this dream, however, was dissension among the Republicans, between the "lily-white" faction, who believed that the presence of Negroes in the party could only serve to put the mark of Cain upon them—"the party of the nigger"—and the "black and tans," who believed in an interracial party.

The governorship, of course, was the main prize that the coalition of Independents and Republicans sought. Since the new constitution halved the governor's term, the next election was in 1882. Determined to avoid the mistake of 1880, when the Independents had put forth the weak and unattractive Norwood, this time they sought a real name. And who could be a better one than the former vice president of the Confederacy and now congressman from the Eighth District, Alexander H. Stephens? Panicking at the prospect of such opposition, the regular Democrats sought to get Stephens as their own candidate! Coyly the old man led both sides along until the Independent leaders publicly recommended him as their candidate; then Stephens disavowed the offer. Earlier, General Lucius J. Gartrell from Atlanta, to the chagrin of Independent leaders, had put himself forward as a candidate for the governorship, so the Independents were left with only Gartrell while Stephens, claiming to stand for "true Democratic principles," sought to unify the party of the Bourbons.

In the October 1882 elections the Independents generally did poorly, with Stephens defeating Gartrell by a vote of 107,253 to 44,896. In the later congressional elections, the regular Democrats swept every district. The Negro vote had generally disappointed the Independents, with the result that some of them, too, began to talk of the desirability of getting rid of the Negro vote altogether.

With the election of 1882 the Independent movement in Georgia was finished, and Stephens, more than anyone else, was responsible, though in truth it would probably have failed soon anyway. Once again what opposition there was to Bourbon-Democratic rule was the Republican party, a much healthier prospect for the Democrats. Now, when fighting Republicans, they could always bring out all the old emotional issues of Reconstruction and "Negro rule." But Republican opposition was next to no opposition at all, and the remainder of the decade of the 1880s meant unchecked Bourbon control. Governor Stephens, however, did not have long to participate in this period of oligarchic control, as age (he was seventy-one) and illness caught up with a lifetime of frailness, and he died in office on 4 March 1883. James S. Boynton of Griffin, as president of the Senate, succeeded him and served until Henry D. McDaniel of Monroe was elected, without opposition, on 24 April 1883 to finish out the term. Fewer than twenty-four thousand Georgians even bothered to vote. The next year, 1884, Governor McDaniel was reelected without opposition and at the same time given an almost solid, Democratic legislature to work with. Amidst the apathy born of one-party rule, one observer commented on the general lack of political interest among both whites and blacks, that while other states enjoyed politics, "Georgia will attend almost exclusively to gathering her crops."

So went state elections during the remainder of the 1880s, with Bourbon Triumvirate member and popular hero General John B. Gordon elected governor in 1886 and reelected in 1888, both times without Republican opposition. When Gordon was sworn in as governor, both the remaining members of the Triumvirate, Brown and Colquitt, were representing the state in the United States Senate in Washington. Independentism as a political movement was dead; Republicanism was a nullity, interested only in federal offices; while the Democracy had become an oligarchy. As for the Negro, while he remained a political issue, largely to keep white men together, he had by the end of the 1880s ceased to be a political force to be reckoned with.

Inevitably, though, there had appeared, first in 1887, a third challenge to Bourbon, Democratic control—the Farmers' Alliance. First founded in Texas, by the mid-1880s the Alliance had spread throughout the South and West. Like the earlier Granger movement, the Alliance sought by cooperative marketing arrangements and the spread of scientific methods of agriculture to improve the economic plight of the farmer, and also like the Grange, the Alliance early realized that only political power for the farmer was going to lead to improvement in his lot. To the southern white farmer, though—there was also a Colored Alliance—a separate political party was not the answer, for the old, obvious reason of fear that it would leave the Negro holding the balance of power. So the white farmers set out to capture control of the Democratic party, or at least to make sure that that party's candidates measured up to Alliance principles. This meant a program of increased state and federal regulation of monopolies, a federal subtreasury or crop support plan, more equitable distribution of the tax burden, more and better public schools, abolition of the convict lease system, and better-regulated and more honest elections, among other demands. In a remarkable display of political verve, by 1891 the Alliance had captured control of the Democratic party in Georgia. In fact, though, the Democratic party had only absorbed the Alliance, whose members, when they realized that fact, fell out among themselves over the question of joining a national, separate party, the Populists. The fight between this new party and the Democrats would dominate the decade of the 1890s and also see the Negro restored to a significant, if not a major, role in Georgia politics.

While Reconstruction is much more keenly remembered in the state's political history, the years of conservative Democratic rule from 1871 to 1890, but especially after 1882, were far more important. The period of Radical Republican rule, which was only about four years including the military phase, was too short to leave little more than the bitterness engendered by the fight for redemption and reduction of Negro political influence. The Bourbon years were something else. These New Departure Democrats, marked by a chamber-of-commerce mentality more popularly known as the "creed of the New South," played on the old values of the Lost Cause, white supremacy, and states' rights in order to promote their New South views. Under them, Georgia, like the rest of the South, was run by an oligarchy of businessmen, industrialists, and big farmers, not by planters and lawyers as of old. Ironically the constitution of 1877 repudiated many of their business values—government aid to private interests, especially the railroads, tax exemption for business, and the like. But it was also a laissez-faire document, permitting the weak government that business and industrial leaders liked. Freedom from regulation was prized even more than government aid.

Yet, realizing that Georgia was still a land of farmers, in 1874 the Bourbons gave the state the nation's first state department of agriculture. They also provided for a state railroad commission, fertilizer inspection laws, lien laws and usury laws. But none of these measures slowed the increase of farm tenantry. Meanwhile, many of the New Departure leaders continued to pursue agricultural interests, especially in farm supply houses, and usually from their homes in town even when they owned much rural land. They were capitalistic promoters, not agrarian planters. The Negro issue kept small-farmer support behind them.

The Bourbons were also tight-fisted, and by repudiating much of the state debt left by the Radical Republicans and practicing fiscal efficiency, they came close to giving the state a dollar's worth of services for a dollar spent. Among these services was an improved but still wholly inadequate public school system and expanded care for the mentally ill, the blind, and the deaf and dumb. Meanwhile, Bourbon leaders often personally profited from their position of controlling the system, notably through the convict lease system and the lease of the state-owned Western and Atlantic Railroad.

A mixture of liberalism and conservatism, of good and bad, of statesmen and crass politicians, the worst thing the Bourbons did for the state was to saddle it with a stultifying one-party system, while they played upon the white supremacy issue. In the words of Judson C. Ward, the leading interpreter of the Georgia Bourbons, "Perhaps the greatest condemnation of the advocates of the New Departure is the heritage they left Georgia of intolerant, bigoted, one-party control; and a weak, parsimonious government unwilling to support in adequate fashion the state's public services."

XVI

Postwar Economic Development

Georgia, like all the other southern states, had always been primarily a producer of agricultural commodities, and so she would remain until well into the twentieth century. Not only was Georgia the fourth-ranking state in cotton production when the Civil War began, she was also a significant producer of corn, wheat, oats, and rye, and had more livestock than any other southern state. Many of her farmers were progressive and not only knew of but practiced such scientific concepts of farming as contour plowing and terracing, while others experimented with new breeds of animals, including Brahman cattle from India, which were more resistant to heat and insects. This "agricultural empire" state also had in 1860 more railroad track mileage than any other southern state except Virginia, and in that year produced almost seventeen million dollars' worth of manufactured goods.

The war, however, put an end to all such immediate progress. After the war Georgia soon found herself in the agricultural doldrums that beset all American farmers; her industry had to begin anew, and often her railroad tracks had to be completely rebuilt. But it was the revolution in labor spelled by the end of slavery that turned the Georgia economy upside down.

In the spring of 1865 following Appomattox the average Georgian, black and white, was almost completely absorbed with how he was going to make a living in a vastly changed state. But for a while, both races—not just the Negro, who often went roaming to "test" his freedom—seemed uncertain and reluctant to face the new problems connected with making a living. Amidst this state of confusion and often physical devastation, the Freedmen's Bureau fed thousands of both races, largely in the towns and cities. The bureau also sought to get the blacks employed and evolved a system of written contracts for the protection of both employer and employee. The average white Georgian, because of his almost complete lack of knowledge and contact with free Negro labor before the war, was skeptical about the freedmen as laborers; others even thought they would be hopeless as free laborers, and that all the South must look to immigrant labor from the North and from abroad. The idea of importing such laborers was a will-o'-the-wisp, though. Aside from a few Irish in the rice fields along the coast, the immigrants never appeared, yet the dream of obtaining them did not die out until the early twentieth century. So, black and white were driven to depend upon one another, since the one held nearly all the land and the other represented the only likely source of cheap labor.

The contractual arrangement for labor led to a great deal of experimentation. Some contracts called for so much money a week, or a month; some stipulated that half that amount was to be withheld until the crop was in; others provided no wages and promised only a percentage of the crop, in which case maintenance of the laborer and his family was usually provided, with that expense to be deducted from his share of the crop. Cash wages varied, depending upon the wealth of the owner, the state of the money market, and the area of the state concerned. But in the early Reconstruction years, wages usually varied from about eight to fifteen dollars a month, with the higher wages paid in the newer cotton lands of the southwest portion of the state.

More and more, though, beginning during Reconstruction, did the practice of compensating the laborer with some portion of the crop become the accepted way of life for farm laborers, black and white, who were too poor to own their own land, and they were the vast majority. There thus was born and became near-universal in Georgia, and in all the lower South, a system of marrying land, labor, and capital known as sharecropping. In time, sharecropping would take on the onus of a curse, particularly as viewed by outsiders; in fact it was, or became, a system that beggared all the South—landowners, laborers, and merchants alike—with only the rest of the world that consumed the cheap cotton the gainer. But in Georgia, as in the rest of the South, sharecropping was born as the result of peculiar economic conditions—concentration of landholding, shortage of capital, and a vast pool of penniless, uneducated labor of both races. Also, the average laborer, particularly blacks in the early days of Reconstruction, preferred sharecropping to "wage slavery," because it gave a man some control over his "own" piece of land and even afforded him a measure of autonomy that he could not otherwise hope to know. Unfortunately, though, the system eventually caused the entire family, not just the head of the household, to be regarded as a labor unit, because the more "hands"—that is, the number of family members—one had, the more land he could crop, especially cotton, which demanded little skill. On the other hand, this family unit concept must have strengthened the family structure more than slavery.

Sharecropping, as it developed in Georgia and the rest of the South, was but a part of a larger problem of farm tenantry. At the top of the "hierarchy of tenantry" was the cash tenant, who simply rented the land, usually with a house, while he himself furnished all else in the way of tools, seed, fertilizer, and mules. As rent, he paid a fixed cash sum agreed upon in advance. The next lower form of tenantry was the "standing rent" plan, whereby the tenant agreed to pay the landlord for the use of house and land by a stipulated number of pounds of cotton, for example. All else he furnished himself. In a good crop year he might make out very well, whereas in a bad year nearly everything might go to pay the rent. Then there was the system of "thirds and fourths," whereby in return for use of only the land and a house the tenant paid with one-third of the grain or one-fourth of the cotton produced. Finally, there was the straight sharecropper or "cropper," who looked to the landlord for land, house, mule, tools, seed, everything. He, together with his family, contributed only the labor and usually the crop was divided fifty-fifty, with the landlord keeping the books. Within this broad framework the possibilities for variations were almost endless, depending upon the extent of the tenant's contribution: whether just labor, or a mule and tools as well as labor, or even a portion of the cost of the seed and fertilizer as well. The vast majority of Georgia tenants, however, both white and black, were usually straight fifty-fifty sharecroppers, or at best some slight variation on that system. The "thirds and fourths" system began to die out by the 1880s, giving way to the "cropper" plan; "standing rent" did not really catch on until the turn of the century.

Part and parcel to Georgia tenantry was the crop lien system. Both landlords and tenants needed credit, the landlord for tools, seed, and fertilizer, and the tenant for the ordinary staples of life until the crop was gathered and sold. With the general shortage of banks in Georgia, the crossroads or town merchant came to supply the credit needs of owner and tenant. As early as 1866 the state's first lien law was passed, giving the merchant a lien upon the landowner's share of the crop for tools, seed, and fertilizer bought on credit. The same law also secured to landlords a lien upon the tenant's share of the crop for making those items available to him, plus the proverbial "meat, meal, and molasses," denim, calico, tobacco, sugar, and coffee that the tenant had to have before the crop was sold. Sometimes, too, landlord and merchant were one and the same individual, thus allowing him to benefit from the high prices charged the poor-risk tenant. A bad crop year might then mean that the tenant's portion of the crop did not "pay

Sharecropper's wife plowing
Farm Security Administration

$100
REWARD!

Atlanta, Ga., July 22, 1887.
Escaped from our camp on A. & H.
Railway, this day,

WARREN THARPE,
BLACK NEGRO CONVICT.

Age, 30 years; crime, burglary;
from Houston county; term, 20
years; weight, 150 to 160 pounds;
height, 5 feet 8 inches; color hair,
black; color eyes, black; right arm
off above elbow; prominent white
teeth.

The above reward will be paid
for his arrest and delivery to us in
Atlanta.

Chattahoochee Brick Co.

out," resulting in his share of next year's crop being twice mortgaged. The result for the tenant was often a hopeless cycle of poverty, degeneracy, and disease even unto the second and third generations. Less often recognized, though, was the fact that a bad crop year might also wipe out the in-debt landowner and merchant, who likewise was in debt to the bank that had supplied him credit, or to the wholesalers represented by the salesmen or "drummers" who plied the highways and byways of the South. Georgia's and the rest of the South's sharecropping system was like the tar baby of her own Joel Chandler Harris's Uncle Remus tales. All who touched it became stuck.

Another result of tenantry, whether sharecropping or rental, was the apparent, but only apparent, breakup of large landholdings, which gave the appearance of democratization of landowning. For example, a very large prewar plantation might, after the war, be farmed by dozens of sharecropping families, each having its own piece of land; some of the land might be rented, while another part might be worked by "hands" drawing straight wages from the landlord. In 1880 the United States Bureau of the Census, either foolishly or out of ignorance, counted each sharecropper, renter, or cash-tenant portion of land as a separate farm, leading to the wholly erroneous impression, in comparison with the census of 1870, that in Georgia and the rest of the South a revolution in landholding had taken place within a decade!

But whatever form of tenantry or private ownership was involved, cotton—even more than before the war—remained "king," in spite of the fact that it cost more than twice as much to produce as it had in 1860. It was useless to point out that such practice meant that one of the richest agricultural regions of the nation would not even supply its own basic food needs, while its capital was drained out to meet them; that infrequent rotation of crops either meant ruin of the soil or greater use of expensive, commercial fertilizers; that dependence upon one crop to such an extent meant either feast or famine for a whole state or region, depending upon world demand. Tradition, an almost religious conviction with no basis in fact, that black Georgians were incapable of learning any other type of farming (they had, for generations) and general fear of the unknown as well as fear of competition, all militated against agricultural diversification. Of course, in a region short of credit, cotton made the best kind of collateral. It was easy to store; it would keep indefinitely while one waited for the market to rise if he could afford to; and the "cropper" who usually grew it could neither eat it, steal it, nor readily sell it. Land was so cheap that rarely did creditors want it as collateral, while one of the chief sources of prewar

Typical cotton gin scene

collateral in Georgia, slaves, was no more. So cotton remained king, whether it brought about eleven cents a pound, as it did in the mid-1870s, or about six cents, as it did in the mid-1890s.

Where agricultural diversification did take place between 1865 and 1890, it was largely in the area of livestock, chiefly because it demanded less labor. A few Georgia stock farms reported demand for all the breeding stock they could deliver of Jersey cattle, Merino sheep, Angora goats, Essex, Berkshire, and Poland-China hogs, and even Shetland ponies, while other Georgia farmers imported blooded bulls to cross with native cows. All this, of course, had also been done before the war. Now, commencing all over again in 1865, not until the turn of the century did the number of cattle reach the million mark that had first been achieved in 1850!

Since livestock required hay, state production of that commodity increased some fourteen times between 1870 and 1890; interest in wheat and oats was sporadic, even though both required little labor. Corn acreage increased steadily, but corn had the disadvantage of requiring about as much hand labor as cotton. Rice production never recovered after the war and continued a steady decline. By the early 1870s, peaches had become a commercial crop, and in the 1880s Georgia developed and gave to the world the superior Elberta and Georgia Belle peaches. Truck farming and pecan growing were also tried, and tobacco gained in significance. But all to what avail? True, the state, especially the northern portion, became less dependent upon outside agricultural sources, while the basis of future major crops, notably peaches and pecans, was laid. But all the while the percentage of the state's cropland devoted to cotton continued to increase, from 31 percent in the late 1860s and early 1870s to about 41 percent by 1880, and better than 42 percent by 1890. During the 1880s alone, cotton production increased more than 50 percent. By 1890, certainly there was no agricultural New South in Georgia; whether there was an industrial and commercial New South was another question.

Necessary to agriculture and commerce-industry alike, but especially to the latter, was the existence or the construction of a viable transportation system, which in that day meant railroads. On the eve of the Civil War, with 1,420 miles of track, Georgia had more railroad track mileage than any other southern state except Virginia. Five years later, at the end of the war, this network of rails lay in a shambles. Almost immediately after the end of hostilities, rebuilding of the old lines and construction of new ones was begun. Short of capital, the railroad companies soon turned to the state for aid, and in 1866 the legislature authorized the governor to endorse bonds issued by the Macon and Brunswick Railroad. No other endorsements were made by the Johnson Reconstruction government, but beginning in 1868 increased demand for such state endorsement of railroad bonds led the Republican legislature of the Bullock era to guarantee in all some $5.75 million in bonds. (Some sources claim that the total was upwards of $7.75 million.) Later, under Democratic control, the state repudiated a large part of this amount. However wise, or unwise, the policy of state endorsement may have been, it helped get railroad lines either built anew or running again. By the time state aid ceased, under the Democrats in 1872, some 740 miles of new track had been added to the 1,420 miles of damaged lines existing in 1865, which probably represented overexpansion given the general economic condition of the state during Reconstruction. Cessation of state aid, the national depression of 1873–78, and probable overexpansion in the years 1865–71 explains why only 561 miles of track were laid in Georgia during the rest of the 1870s. But the booming decade of the 1880s saw 1,958 miles of new track laid, again representing overexpansion.

The state was also in the railroad-owning business, in addition to endorsing the bonds of private companies. The Western and Atlantic Railroad had been state-owned before the war, and it became a major beneficiary of state funds as soon as civil authority was restored. The Bullock regime turned the Western and Atlantic into a plaything, and a refuge for political hacks and scoundrels as well. Even Republicans became disgusted, so a bipartisan vote of the legislature in 1870 authorized lease of the Western and Atlantic to private interests. Governor Bullock leased the line to a company headed by the chameleon-like, former Democratic governor, Joseph E. Brown, then a Republican. Fraud was later charged, but even the Democrats, after they returned to control, decided that the matter was not worth reopening. For the next twenty years the state collected $25,000 monthly rental under the conditions of the lease, half of which went toward payment of state revenue bonds and half into the public school fund. In 1889, in preparation for expiration of the lease in 1890, the legislature drew up a new lease, providing for rental of $35,000 to $45,000 monthly, depending upon whether the lease was for a minimum of twenty years or a maximum of fifty years. The Nashville, Chattanooga, and St. Louis Railroad won the lease, with a bid of $35,001 for a period of twenty-nine years. There had, by agreement, been only one other bid, a minimum one of $35,000 by the Richmond and West Point Terminal Railway and Warehouse Company, for the same period.

In commerce and in manufacturing the war had been even more disruptive than in agriculture, despite the fact that neither was dependent upon slaves for its operation to the extent that agriculture was. The blockade and the war caused merchants often to have little or nothing to sell, while labor problems, disrupted markets, and the fact that they were often military targets crippled or destroyed most industries.

Commercial revival was, of course, the quicker of the two to take place. Starved by the material privations of war, Georgians, for all their poverty, were quick to snap up the goods on newly restocked shelves. Interestingly, northern suppliers often were eager to extend the necessary credit to southern merchants. Also numerous were northern "carpetbagger merchants," who in fact probably brought much more to Georgia than they took out, in the sense that they offered a real and needed service. It was claimed that there were soon three to four times as many drygoods and grocery stores as in 1860. Meanwhile, clerking seemed to have become one of the most popular ideals of young men in search of a livelihood.

Such were conditions in all the towns, especially the major ones, but in none so much as Atlanta. But from the beginning the economic base of revived Atlanta was more secure. Located outside the heart of the plantation country, Atlanta was not so tied to the vagaries of the cotton market, as for instance were Macon and Augusta. Instead, Atlanta, with her excellent rail connections, early became a distribution center for northern grain, meat, and manufactures as well as the banking and insurance center of the state.

Such commercial revival continued whether the government of the state was that of presidential reconstruction or that of military and Radical Reconstruction. Revival in manufactures and railroads was underway, too, but necessarily at a slower pace. Both were hampered by the larger amounts of capital needed, as opposed to that needed by grocery or drygoods stores, for instance. Georgia, like all the South, had always suffered from a shortage of banking capital, while the war had more completely destroyed that basic sector of the business and manufacturing economy than any other. Outside sources had to be looked to, and from them, generally in the North, some aid came. But northern bankers and businessmen in the postwar 1860s and the early 1870s were as cautious, if not reluctant, as their counterparts would be today about investing in an area marked by political, racial, and labor turmoil, one undergoing political, social, and economic reconstruction. Then, just as stability in Georgia and the South was improving, the nation was hit by the financial panic of 1873 and the resultant depression, which lasted until 1879. So in truth, though some recovery took place in the postwar years of the 1860s and 1870s, the industrial revolution that Henry Grady and other New South disciples talked about and worked for belongs to the decade of the 1880s and the early 1890s, until depression struck once again.

Before the war, Georgia's chief factory industry had been cotton mills. So it was natural that with the return of peace the cotton mills were among the first to be restored. Even so, little was accomplished in 1865–66, but the census returns of 1870 revealed that Georgia had almost the identical number of cotton mills that she had had in 1860, thirty-four in place of thirty-three. In the same period, the number of flour and grist mills increased some three times, while that of sawmills increased about 20 percent.

Such industries as tar and turpentine and marble and granite, which would in time become almost synonymous with the name of the state, were insignificant during the whole Reconstruction period. In truth, Georgia yet remained an almost exclusively agricultural land, exemplified by the fact that in 1872 all the manufacturing establishments in the state were carried for tax purposes at $6.25 million. But that was more than in 1860. Or, put another way, according to the census of 1870, 76 percent of the work force of the state was engaged in some form of agriculture and only 6 percent in manufacturing, mining, and mechanical pursuits combined. The remaining 18 percent was in trade and transportation, the professions, and domestic service.

Perhaps, though, such characterization of Georgia's industrial progress during Reconstruction is not wholly fair. After all, these years, including as well virtually all of the decade of the 1870s, were years of search for political and financial order, of depression and bitter party in-fighting. Likewise, the Bourbons, whose name would become synonymous with the new order and a New South of industrialism, did not get firm control until the elections of 1882.

Just as industrial recovery during Reconstruction was most noted in the area of textiles, so did that industry dominate the industrial expansion of the 1880s. Interestingly, while in the South in general most of this expansion was an "up by the bootstraps" southern operation, in Georgia, northern capital apparently played a bigger role.

Symbolic of the fact that cotton was king industrially, even as it still was king agriculturally, was the huge International Cotton Exposition, held in Atlanta in 1881. But this "world's fair" was more than an exposition of cotton. It was a declaration to the rest of the nation, even to the world, that Georgia was no longer mired in the slough of Reconstruction politics, nor any longer married to one-horse agriculture. Hopefully, it meant the dawn of a new age, and it and the crusade for industry that followed took on the emotion and promise of both economic and social salvation. In the charge to Georgia towns, great and small, "Get out and get yourself a cotton mill," Georgians, together with other southerners, almost literally found a second religion, fundamentalist Protestantism being the first, of course. But the textile industry remained concentrated in the fall-line towns and cities, especially in Augusta, Macon, and Columbus. Impressive growth there was, from the thirty-four mills in the state in 1870, capitalized at $3,433,265 and turning out products valued at $3,648,973, to fifty-three mills in 1890, capitalized at $17,664,675 and producing goods valued at $12,635,629. Nor was all the cloth produced of the rougher and cheaper grades commonly associated with the South, because Georgia was also a leading producer of the higher-priced bleached yarns.

The decade of the 1880s was also a growth period for others of the old industries such as lumber, flour and grist mills, tanneries, distilleries, and brick yards. And along with the lumber industry, the related naval stores industry began to come into its own, so that by the end of the century Georgia led the nation in this rough, low-paying industry that demanded little skill.

New industries likewise came into being while others expanded, so that for the first time statistical comparison became viable. There was the fertilizer industry, a natural since Georgia was using more commercial fertilizer than any other state in the Union. In 1880, where there had been only three fertilizer factories in the state, producing a quarter of a million dollars' worth of the chemical for Georgia farmers, by 1890 there were forty-four factories, producing more than five million dollars' worth, including some for export. Similarly the cottonseed-oil industry began to come into its own, with seventeen processors in 1890 where there had been none in 1880.

Geologists even today would probably agree that Georgia has never developed her mineral potential to anything like the degree possible. In the late nineteenth century, in spite of increased activity, she scarcely scratched the surface. Coal and iron ore were both being mined in north Georgia: 154,644 tons of coal in 1880 (all from Dade County), and 72,705 tons of iron ore (all from Bartow, Dade, and Polk counties). But in 1890, the United States Bureau of the Census, citing figures for the year 1889, did not think that Georgia even rated a separate listing by state for either coal or iron ore produced. Instead, it listed Georgia and North Carolina production as combined: 226,156 tons of coal, and 258,145 tons of iron ore, scarcely impressive when compared to the 1880 figures. Some basis of comparison may be gained, however, by comparing Georgia production of these two minerals with that of neighboring Alabama, a leading producer of both. In 1889 the Alabama figures were 3,572,983 tons of coal and 1,570,319 tons of iron ore.

Of course there were other minerals than coal and iron, notably marble and granite, which would in the twentieth century become major industries, but in 1889 the granite produced was valued at only $752,481 and marble at only $196,250. By way of comparison, in that same year both the state's tanneries and wagon factories, not to speak of bakeries and distilleries, each turned out more than a million dollars' worth of finished products. And none of Georgia's New South "boomers," so far as is known, ever touted the state as either a wagon manufacturer or a baker of breads and cakes.

By 1890, on the eve of another great, national depression, what did Georgia's industrial advancement of the 1870s and 1880s, especially the latter, mean to her and her people? Was there a "New Georgia" even as people talked of a "New South"? The anwer is a mixture of the good and bad, of the positive and the negative.

First, Georgia's industrial economy was in many ways still a colonial one. Much of the capital for development and expansion, especially in industries other than textiles but not excluding that one either, had come from outside, and back to the outside much of the profits went. Georgia industries were not industries of great refinement, and they usually demanded little skill. For example, cotton cloth, even of the better grades, was generally shipped to the North before being made into consumable items, while most of the iron ore left the state in the form in which it came out of the ground.

Another consequence of industrialization was a marked increase in urbanization. By 1880 Atlanta, with a population of 37,409, was the state's most populous center (it was 65,533 by 1890), but the older cities of Augusta, Macon, Columbus, and Savannah had also made major gains. Urban growth, of course, created new problems (not the least of which was political underrepresentation) that would absorb much of the state's energies in the twentieth century and ultimately markedly change the state itself. Small towns and villages—often wholly owned company towns, especially by textile mills—either sprang up rapidly or expanded with equal vigor. Industrial development, and the concomitant growth of towns and cities, meant the development of a whole new class of workers, often straight off the farm and as likely as not to be women and children. All were uneducated and unskilled, which meant that they were poorly prepared for their life and ill-equipped to deal with their employer, who might be an impersonal corporation, and this in a region where employer-employee relationships were customarily deeply personal. So, while tens of thousands of Georgians, black and white, became little more than serfs on the land in the system of sharecropping, other thousands—always white—coughed out their lives in the lint-filled atmosphere of the cotton mills.

Meanwhile industrial "progress" there was, at least in absolute terms. But all the time Georgia and the South were running harder and harder to keep from falling further and further behind. In 1860, when the South was scarcely thought of as industrialized, she had 17.2 percent of the manufacturing establishments in the nation and 11.5 percent of the capital. Shortly after the turn of the century her percentage of the manufacturing establishments had slipped 2 points, to 15.3, while her share of the capital remained almost static at 11 percent. Georgia was a part of this picture. On another and finer scale, Georgia, which produced in terms of dollar value .00897 percent of the nation's manufactured goods in 1860, by 1890, after the "boomer," New South decade of the 1880s, had slipped slightly, to .00727 percent. By 1900 the percentage was up to .00817, still less than that of 1860.

XVII

Education, Life, and Culture

Politics and economics did not encompass the whole world of postwar Georgians, of course. There were important matters of education and schools; of religion and churches; of race and race relationships; of crime and prisons; and even of the latest adventures of "Br'er Rabbit" and "Br'er Fox" from the pen of Joel Chandler Harris, together with the humorous tales of Charles H. Smith, better known as Bill Arp. After all, when the state lay devastated by war or when, later, cotton was bringing but six cents a pound, it was important to have something to laugh about.

Georgia emerged from the Civil War, as she had entered it, without a real system of public education. Nor did this make her an exception among the other southern states, for public education as it is understood today did not come to the South until the days of Reconstruction. For slaves and for the few free blacks, before the war there was, of course, virtually no opportunity for schooling; for the wealthier whites, at least, there were private schools; and for the poor an inadequate "poor-school fund" to aid the children of those willing to declare themselves paupers. While whites may have seen some advantages in keeping the slaves in abject ignorance, such was not the case when blacks became freedmen and soon thereafter voters as well.

The legislature of Georgia, in December 1866, while presidential reconstruction was yet in effect and with the encouragement of Governor Jenkins, passed a bill providing for the establishment of a system of free public schools for whites between the ages of six and twenty-one. But the general poverty of the state and the problem of finding suitable buildings led to a provision that the act should not go into effect until 1 January 1868. By then presidential reconstruction had been replaced by congressional reconstruction and the act was never implemented.

The constitution of 1868 provided that the first legislative session following ratification of the constitution should provide for "a thorough system of general education to be forever free to all children of the State." As a start in financing such a system, the constitution also provided that poll tax receipts and liquor taxes, among others, should be set aside as a common school fund. The General Assembly was authorized to enact a general property tax for further financing, if necessary. This was first done in 1872. Other tax sources were added from time to time, for instance the proceeds from convict leasing after 1881.

In spite of the constitutional mandate to the legislature to establish a public school system at its first session, it was not until the third session, in October 1870, that the General Assembly responded and the school system was created. Governor Bullock immediately appointed as the first commissioner of schools the former Union army officer and then Freedmen's Bureau official in Georgia, General John Randolph Lewis from Pennsylvania. General Lewis apparently sincerely tried to do a good job, but he failed, perhaps in part because of the opposition he met as an outsider. The fact was, though, that under Commissioner Lewis and the Bullock regime the public school system never became operational, while funds voted for the purpose were diverted elsewhere. When the state was "redeemed" from Radical rule the new Democratic governor, James M. Smith, appointed Gustavus John Orr to succeed Lewis as commissioner of schools, in January 1872. A career educator and professor of mathematics at Oglethorpe College at the time he was appointed, Orr was from Jackson County and had attended the state university before graduating from Emory College in 1844. For the next fifteen years, until his death in 1887, Orr was the single greatest resource of the Georgia public school system, and he can truly be called the "father of the common school system in Georgia." In the process he became a national figure in educational circles, and in 1881 was elected president of the National Education Association.

From the beginning, separate schools were maintained for the two races. The basic school law of 1870, written during the regime of Governor Bullock, called for the two systems to be "equal" as to facilities, but in 1872 under the Redeemers, the law was changed to read "equal so far as practicable."

The school system for both races was not without its critics. Schools were expensive, indeed the most expensive function engaged in by the state, so there were critics who for reasons of economy said that the state should not even be in the education business. A few others made the same criticism, for philosophical reasons, while still others questioned the wisdom of educating the poorer classes, especially poor blacks. But since the constitution of 1877, which replaced the "radical" document of 1868 that had provided for establishment of the public

Sidney Lanier, the poet

Gustavus J. Orr, father of the
public school system in Georgia

University of Georgia Libraries

schools, likewise provided for "a thorough system" of public education separate by race, criticism of the state's being in the education business soon thereafter practically ceased.

By law, though, a "thorough system" of public education meant only the provision of primary schools and a school term of only three months. But by 1890 the school term had been increased to four months, with efforts being made to increase it to six months. Such a system was not "thorough"; it was not even adequate to the needs of that day. But with both races eager for education, the total enrollment steadily increased, from 49,578 in 1871 to 190,626 in 1877 and 209,276 in 1889. In sum, the Bourbons began, kept alive, and steadily improved the public school system. Inadequate it remained, though, both for inculcating the masses with the rudiments of education and for preparing the "cream of the crop" to take advantage of the opportunities for higher education available within the state as well as outside. In addition to the state schools, there were in some of the larger towns and cities public schools supported by the city or county government. Private schools also continued, often as a supplement to publicly supported schools. All secondary schools were private.

As with nearly everything else in the state, the Civil War had played havoc with higher education. The state university in Athens had closed down during the war and did not reopen until January 1866. The private colleges shared the same fate, though most of them soon reopened too, among them Emory, Mercer, Wesleyan, and Oglethorpe. Oglethorpe, however, barely limped along until, following a disastrous fire in late 1869, it moved the next year from Milledgeville to Atlanta. But two years later it failed altogether and was not refounded until 1913. Mercer, originally located at Penfield in Greene County, moved to Macon in 1871. Among the new colleges for whites opened in the period were Shorter at Rome, in 1873, as the Cherokee Baptist Female College; Brenau at Gainesville, in 1878, as the Georgia Baptist Seminary; Reinhardt at Waleska, by the Methodists, in 1883; and Young Harris in Towns County, also by the Methodists, in 1886.

The University of Georgia continued in a hand-to-mouth existence for many more years. Its only regular state support was $8,000 annually. This situation was improved somewhat when, in November 1866, the legislature passed a "GI Bill" providing for the payment by the state of $300 a year to the university—as well as to Emory, Mercer, and Oglethorpe—for each indigent and maimed Confederate veteran under thirty years of age enrolled. This grant or loan was to be "repaid" by each recipient's teaching a year in Georgia for each year that he received such aid. Sadly, this humane and forward-looking legislation was repealed in March 1869.

It was the federal government, however, that provided the greatest financial boost for the University of Georgia. By the Morrill Act of 1862, passed while Georgia was out of the Union, each state was eligible to receive 30,000 acres of public lands for each United States senator and representative to which it was entitled, with the proceeds from the sale of the land to be used to encourage "agricultural and mechanical education." Georgia received her share in 1871, some 270,000 acres, the scrip for which was disposed of for ninety cents an acre, resulting in a principal of $243,000, with the interest alone to be expended, and that never exceeded $17,000 a year. But since the state university was largely a liberal arts college with a heavily classical curriculum, provisions for a more "practical" curriculum had to be made. This was done in 1872 with the establishment in Athens of the Georgia State College of Agriculture and Mechanic Arts, said to be separate from the university, but in fact it really was not. Two years later, in 1874, the Medical College at Augusta was made the Medical Department of the university; it did not become a separate institution until 1949.

At the same time the state embarked upon a well-meaning, but some said mistaken, attempt to bring higher education physically closer to the people through the establishment of several other state educational institutions. The first of these was the North Georgia Agricultural College, located in Dahlonega and incorporated in 1871. There rapidly followed other regional institutions, called branches of the university, and all of them sharing in the small income from the public land endowment: the South Georgia College of Agriculture and Mechanic Arts at Thomasville, in 1879; the Southwest Georgia College of Agriculture and Mechanic Arts at Cuthbert, also in 1879; the Middle Georgia Military and Agricultural College in Milledgeville, in 1880; and an A & M College in Hamilton, in 1881.

Although most of the new institutions were colleges of mechanic arts as well as agriculture, the state still lacked a genuine engineering and technological institute, one that might develop and educate the kind of talent so necessary in a growing industrial era. So in 1885, over the objections of the university, which feared the "disintegrating process" of multiple educational institutions—all inadequately supported—the General Assembly provided for the establishment in Atlanta, as a part of the university but with a separate faculty and board of trustees, of the Georgia School of Technology. This institution, later to be known as "Georgia Tech," opened in the fall of 1888.

With the greatly increased interest in "practical training," fostered by both the Morrill Act of 1862 and by the changing needs of the times, there was also increased interest in such training for women. So in 1889 there was established in Milledgeville the Georgia Normal and Industrial School (later known as the Georgia State College for Women, and today, no longer just for women, as Georgia College).

Before the Civil War there were, of course, no institutions for the education of Negroes, and in that day, as well as after the war, Negroes were not allowed to attend the white institutions. Nor were white Georgians eager to provide the opportunity for higher education for blacks; elementary education was controversial enough. Not until 1890 was the first state-sponsored institution of higher education for Negroes founded, the Georgia State Industrial College for Colored Youths, now known as Savannah State College, located at Savannah. And, had it not been for the pressure of the federal government, this institution would not have been chartered when it was. In 1890, the second Morrill Act made available to all the states additional funds from the sale of public lands, but only if the state provided for agricultural and mechanical education for *all* its citizens. Savannah State was quickly authorized.

Until after 1890, then, black Georgians who aspired to more than the rudimentary education available in the four-months-a-year common schools had to look to private institutions if they would stay in the state. Fortunately there were a number of these, most of which were founded and largely supported by outside capital. Among them was the Atlanta University, chartered in 1867 and sponsored by the American Missionary Association. It was 1872, however, before the college department opened, with the first bachelor's degrees awarded in 1876. Morehouse College was founded in 1867, by the American Baptist Home Missionary Society, in the city of Augusta, under the name Augusta Institute. It was moved to Atlanta in 1879 and awarded its first college degree in 1883. Clark College was founded as Clark University in 1870 under sponsorship of the Methodist Episcopal Church, North, and commenced offering college-level work in 1879. Spelman College was created in 1881 as the Atlanta Baptist Female Seminary by Miss Sophia B. Packard and Miss Harriet E. Giles, but not until 1897 did it become a full-fledged college, after John D. Rockefeller had befriended it. Morris Brown College was founded in Atlanta in 1881 by the African Methodist Episcopal Church of Georgia and began offering college-level work in 1894. Paine College was established in Augusta in 1881 as the Paine Institute, sponsored by the Colored Methodist Episcopal Church and the Methodist Episcopal Church, South, as an interracial endeavor but named after a white man and long dominated and largely supported by whites. Finally, in the period prior to 1890, there was the Gammon Theological Seminary, established in 1883 as a part of Clark University but made a separate institution in 1886 with the impressive endowment, for a black institution in that day, of $200,000. In 1890 that amount was doubled, to $400,000, nearly all of the entire amount coming from Elijah H. Gammon of Batavia, Illinois.

In sum, blacks in Georgia found that it was often years after their founding before their "colleges" offered college-level work, and that, unlike the whites for whom the state was providing higher education closer to home on a regional basis—excepting one private institution, Paine, in Augusta—it was necessary for them to go to Atlanta to private institutions until classes commenced at Savannah State in 1892. Also, until Savannah State was founded, the only support the state provided for Negro higher education was $8,000 yearly from the Morrill Act funds, which after 1874 was assigned to Atlanta University. Beginning in 1891, these funds, or a total of one-third of all Morrill Act funds, were assigned to Savannah State instead.

Just as the problem of education for Georgia blacks was born of the state's defeat in the Civil War, so was the problem of what to do with her black lawbreakers. In slavery, discipline had been handled by the slaveowners, except for such serious charges as murder, where the state might try, condemn, and execute the accused. At least, then, there was no real problem of black imprisonment. Overnight, with the coming of freedom, all this was changed and the state was faced with not only the continuing, expensive, and vexing problem of what to do with white offenders, but with black ones as well. Meanwhile, the tribulations of the Reconstruction process itself and those of the two races' learning to live together under a new relationship added to the incidence of lawbreaking. The result was that amidst improvement and increase in most other social services offered by the state, notably education, the prison system in Georgia, and all the rest of the South, collapsed.

Just as necessity and peculiar conditions together were the parents of the innovation of sharecropping, so were they the progenitors of the convict lease system. Faced with the problem of a growing prison population and a railroad system that lay largely in ruins, it was not an "evil" proposal, whether made in Georgia, Louisiana, or Texas, that able-bodied prisoners be leased as cheap labor to the financially pressed

Negro college near Savannah

railroads by equally financially pressed states. All parties, except the prisoners, of course, would gain: the railroads could earn greater profits with such cheap labor, while the state could turn an expensive, money-losing proposition into a money-making one. Thus it was that one southern state after another just seemed to fall into the convict lease system, with Georgia among the first. In Georgia, the presidential reconstruction state government created it; the first prisoners were leased out during the period of military reconstruction; the Radical government of Governor Bullock continued it; and when the economy-minded Redeemers took over, they saw no reason to change it.

The Georgia legislature, in December 1866, provided for the establishment of a system whereby the state's prison population would be leased to private companies, which would in return for the prisoners' labor provide both maintenance and security, thus relieving the state of all expense. But before the first prisoners were leased military reconstruction came to Georgia, with the result that Provisional Governor General Thomas H. Ruger leased out the first one hundred convicts, in May 1868, to the Georgia and Alabama Railroad operating out of Rome. Then in June 1869, under Radical Governor Rufus Bullock, the entire penitentiary population at Milledgeville was turned over to Grant, Alexander, and Company, a railroad construction firm, which paid the state nothing for them but did free it of the expense of operating the penitentiary.

With little or no state inspection or supervision provided for—not that such inspection either would have or did make any significant difference—living and working conditions of the leased prisoners from the beginning could be described only as frightful. As soon as the Democrats won control of the state they launched an investigation of the system and found that prisoners were being worked such long hours that they were getting inadequate sleep. Even the drinking water provided was sometimes found to be both inadequate and unclean, while discipline was cruel and inhumane. Later in the century, other investigations would find that sometimes prisoners were kept in rolling, open cages, to which the men were chained at night without sufficient bedding or protection from the elements. The diet was wholly inadequate, and the mortality rate frightful. Only the disabled, the elderly, most women—but not all, since they could be used as camp cooks—and the very youthful escaped leasing; but for those who did life was often little better in the inadequate prison camps. Unless one lived to serve out his sentence—sometimes deliberately made longer, it was charged, in order to bring in more revenue to the state, when payment was provided—there were only two other means of release, physical escape and death. And the escape rate was about as high as the appalling death rate. Finally, with white lawyers, white judges, and usually all-white juries, it was not surprising that black Georgians, both as to numbers and as to treatment, were the chief victims of the convict lease system.

In power, the Democrats not only kept but refined the system, chiefly by charging for each convict leased and providing for longer—and thus more attractive—leases of from five to twenty years. In 1874, former governor and state supreme court justice, and later United States senator, Joseph E. Brown leased one hundred convicts for five years at eleven dollars per year for use in his Dade County coal mines. Two years later, Brown, as president of the Dade Coal Company, together with two other concerns, leased the entire available prison population for twenty years for a total of $25,000 a year. But Brown was not the only Bourbon Democratic figure who enriched himself through this evil system, which as a powerful political figure he helped to perpetuate.

Such a prison system was, of course, never without its critics. At one time or another it was condemned by such a diverse cross-section of Georgia critics as John B. Gordon, the conservative Bourbon governor; William II. Felton, the leading political Independent—he called it an "epitomized hell"; and Thomas E. Watson, the state's leading Populist. Still it persisted, until 1908.

How much racial integration, or segregation, there was in either the prisons or the work camps of the lessees is not certain. It is a fact, though, that not until 1891 did the General Assembly enact the first statute requiring segregation by race of convicts. The absence of such a statute, of course, does not mean that before its passage integration was the order of the day, but it does indicate that by 1891 it was felt that a law providing for separation of the races while imprisoned was needed. This was either to make sure that a universal practice was continued— which is unlikely—or to assure that segregation became universal, because it was not—which seems much more likely.

Actually, the whole picture of racial relationships in this period— from the end of the Civil War down to the 1890s—is just as clouded. Although it was not until 1891 that Georgia first provided for segregation on the railroads by statute, this does not mean that until then integration was the general practice. Quite the contrary, it was not. But it does mean, in Georgia as elsewhere in the South, that until the early 1890s there was no written, monolithic, and unvarying code of racial relationships. Therefore, uncertainty—on the part of both races—as to what would be permitted and inconsistency as to segregation or integration were the order of the day. In this atmosphere of uncertainty and in the absence of segregation statutes, between 1865 and the early 1890s white Georgians and black Georgians did upon numerous occasions meet face to face in situations where thereafter until the 1960s they would not meet again.

Early in the Reconstruction years, once white Georgians realized that the Radicals had more in mind than simple restoration of the South to the Union, they resolved that Georgia should remain a "white man's country." And that simple pledge by the Democrats, plus the threat of Negro rule if the Republicans were restored to office, in large degree determined the relationship between the races. Not surprisingly then, there was a natural resentment or fear on the part of white Georgians of what might happen if and when they met blacks, usually former slaves, seated beside them on trains and streetcars, or in restaurants and hotels. To most whites, such contact held threats of what they vaguely and generally called "social equality"; to the blacks, and a few others, once the Civil Rights Act of 1866 and the later Fourteenth Amendment became law, they represented only "civil rights" for other citizens who happened to be black. Even so, the determination to demean and set aside in a separate world a whole people does not seem to have been present in the 1860s, 1870s, and 1880s, as it was later.

In rail travel in Georgia, the only universal means of public transportation, the general practice seems to have been to deny to Negroes access to the first-class cars, even when they had paid first-class fares. Instead, they were assigned to the second-class cars or the smoking car, where incidentally there was often integration. Some lines, in accordance with an 1870 state law, furnished separate first-class cars for Negroes; some lines segregated all classes of travel; a few made no attempt at segregation whatever.

At the same time, at least in Atlanta and Savannah, the two largest cities, the streetcars were generally integrated—the inconsistency before 1891 spoken of above. The railroad segregation law of 1891 provided for "separate but equal" railroad accommodations, but generally the "equal" part was simply ignored. The same law sought to separate the races on the streetcars "as much as practicable," a much more difficult task. But the law did not cover Pullman sleeping cars, and until 1899, when this loophole was closed, Negroes could and did upon occasion use them.

Integration in the restaurants, hotels, bars, and such establishments was less of a problem, for the simple reason that Negroes were less likely to seek such service than they were to use public transportation facilities. Even very poor blacks were likely to be found on the trains, where, if they were going some distance, they probably carried a basket lunch. Relatively few were those who walked in off the streets of Atlanta or Savannah seeking a meal in an establishment frequented by whites. Fewer still, and they were generally out-of-state travelers, sought lodging in the white hotels. And when either service was sought, generally it was denied. Here, then, there was less inconsistency, and less occasion for it. Even so, startling as it may have been to witness a Negro quietly being served and as quietly eating in a restaurant or hotel dining room, it was scarcely the kind of news likely to make the newspapers. On the other hand, loud denial of service, often followed by the Negro's being bodily thrown out of such an establishment, made the newspapers. Hence, it is really impossible to learn just how much integration there was.

In one area, however, the Georgia Negro chose to segregate himself, and for the good reasons of pride and self-respect. That area was the church. Before the Civil War slaves, especially on the larger plantations, had generally either attended the same services as their owners, sitting separately in a balcony or gallery, or a separate service might be held for them by the white minister, or by a black one.

In freedom, the Negro fled this arrangement for the same reason that he deplored "gang labor"; it was a reminder of his former condition. But perhaps even more important in bringing about separation was the Negro's natural desire to have some say in the operation of his church and the choice of his minister. And as long as he stayed in the white church he was going to have neither. So rapidly Negroes set up their own churches, generally, out of necessity, with untrained and uneducated ministers. At times the native whites assisted them in establishment of their churches, but often such aid came from northern missionary and other sources. Often Georgia whites did nothing to discourage Negroes from leaving their churches. The vast majority of the new Negro congregations were either Baptist or Methodist, as were the vast majority of white congregations in Georgia.

White churches, too, had their problems after the war. Congregations had become scattered or broken up, church buildings were often rundown and neglected, and congregations were without ministers. Also, either before or during the war, all the major Protestant denominations had seceded from the northern wing of their faiths. Was there to be reconstruction in this area as well as the political, or were they to continue their independence? As early as November 1865, the House of

Bishops and Deputies of the Episcopal Church in the Confederate States, meeting in Augusta and with Georgia churchmen among those strongest in favor, voted for reunion. Meanwhile the Methodists, as the Methodist Episcopal Church, South, continued to enjoy their independence until 1939, while the Presbyterians and Baptists yet remain apart. The result was that not only did the scars of the prewar antislavery debate last longer in the churches than anywhere else, but the churches also became the first formerly "integrated" southern institution to become almost wholly segregated. Meanwhile, whether reunited or separate, but always segregated—except for an occasional nurse or old "uncle" or "auntie"—in an atmosphere of growing urbanism, industrialism, and materialism, Georgia churches and church membership, especially among the Methodists and Baptists, rapidly increased in number among both races. In the New South that was Georgia, there was room for both God and Mammon.

Just as there was the realm of the spirit for most Georgians, so was there also the realm of the intellect, of culture, of creativity—and not just in the schools and colleges—for a much smaller number of Georgians. The war had given them something to glory in; defeat and the bitterness of Reconstruction had given them something fondly to look back upon—the prewar South. Both gave them something to write about. And the writing about the days of old emboldened them to meet the new.

Among the very first southerners to join the written affray of constitutional issues already settled on the battlefield was the former vice president of the Confederacy, Alexander H. Stephens, who between 1868 and 1870 published his ponderous, leaden, and discursive two-volume study, *Constitutional View of the Late War Between the States.* Of greater moment and of infinitely more variety were the historical works of Charles Colcock Jones, Jr., of Augusta but a native of Liberty County, who, beginning shortly after the Civil War and continuing until his death in 1893, poured forth a stream of books, monographs, and lesser studies ranging from the early Indians to colonial Georgia to the Civil War, with ventures into the history of the cities of Savannah and Augusta, Negro folklore, and biography along the way. Another historian was the versatile Isaac W. Avery, native of Florida, lawyer, able managing editor of the *Atlanta Constitution*, secretary to several Georgia governors, and author, in 1881, of *The History of the State of Georgia from 1850 to 1881.*

Richard Malcolm Johnston, a native of Hancock County and before the war a member of the faculty of the University of Georgia, warmly

stirred the memories of his and an older generation with his *Dukes-
borough Tales* (1871), sketches of life in the small village he had
known as a boy, a village that had already ceased to exist. Later, in
1897, he published in the same genre a collection of stories, *Old Times
in Middle Georgia*, all of which had earlier appeared in northern
magazines.

But it was the poet Sidney Lanier, a native of Macon and an ailing
veteran of the Civil War, who could best pluck the heart strings of
lovers of the mountains of north Georgia and those of coastal devotees
as well, with such poems as his rollicking "Song of the Chattahoochee"
and the haunting "Marshes of Glynn." More importantly, his poetry
endured, and he is still considered one of the great American, not just
southern, poets of the late nineteenth century. Tragically, he died of
tuberculosis in 1881 at the age of thirty-nine, while in Lynn, North
Carolina, where he had gone seeking respite from the disease. For several years before his death he had been living in Baltimore, where he
played the flute in the Peabody Symphony and, beginning in 1879,
lectured at the Johns Hopkins University. About the same time another
poet, Paul Hamilton Hayne, a native of Charleston and perhaps of less
stature than Lanier, was writing out the last years of his life in a
tumbledown shack near Augusta, amidst both the physical and intellectual poverty of his sharecropper and sawmill-worker neighbors.
There were one or two others who really were poets, among them
Francis O. Ticknor, M.D., a native of Jones County who later settled
outside Columbus, and many others who thought they were poets, and
no novelists worthy of the name. A red-haired, freckled, and painfully
shy young man from near Eatonton in Putnam County—himself destined to become one of the best known of all Georgia's authors—
assessed his state's and his region's literary efforts rather harshly. Joel
Chandler Harris, writing in the *Atlanta Constitution* in 1879, declared,
"The truth might as well be told: we have no Southern literature
worthy of the name." Of course, Harris overstated his case, but it was
nevertheless true that the Sidney Laniers, the Paul Hamilton Haynes,
and the Joel Chandler Harrises were pearls in a sea of pablum and
saccharine Victorian prudery that passed for American, not just southern, literature, especially in the decade of the 1880s.

Harris, writing New South editorials by day from the offices of the
Atlanta Constitution—which he served for almost a quarter of a century—and "Old South" Uncle Remus tales from his home, "The Wren's
Nest," by night, would have it said of him by the southern intellectual
emigré Walter Hines Page, "What strange habitations does genius

choose among men." This illegitimate son of a wandering Irishman was a genius, and he was a master of both the English language and contemporary Negro dialect who, through the literary device of a mythical Uncle Remus, related to a little boy the stories of a whole world of animals who talked, acted, and schemed much like the denizens of the real world. Its best-known inhabitants were, of course, "Br'er Rabbit" and "Br'er Fox." Beginning in 1879, these stories first appeared in the *Atlanta Constitution*, with the first bound collection, *Uncle Remus: His Songs and Sayings*, appearing in 1880. Nine more Uncle Remus volumes followed. But Uncle Remus was not all, for Harris also wrote stories about the southern aristocrat as well as poor whites, mountaineers, and slaves—among them, *Mingo and Other Sketches in Black and White*; *Daddy Jake the Runaway*; and *Other Stories Told After Dark*. Northern readers were fascinated, and the *New York Evening Post*, among other newspapers, eagerly reprinted Uncle Remus stories from the pages of the *Atlanta Constitution*.

Also appearing in the *Constitution* about the same time (from 1878 to 1903) were the weekly "letters" of Bill Arp (Charles Henry Smith). Smith was a native of Gwinnett County who practiced law for many years in Rome before moving to Bartow County and finally to its county seat of Cartersville. His Bill Arp letters had been appearing in various newspapers since 1861 when, from the ranks of the Confederate Army, he had written his first, to "Mr. Linkhorn," president of the United States. Over the years, especially after he joined the *Constitution*, Arp evolved from a political satirist to a country sage. Georgians and the readers of some seven hundred weekly newspapers, mostly in the South but including a few outside the South, loved him as both, but especially as the teller of down-home, funny stories that southern countrymen could best appreciate. To Georgia and much of the South, Arp was a sort of early-day Will Rogers who, from one of his early "letters," left us this: "I'm a good Union man—'so called'—but I'll bet on Dixie as long as I've got a dollar."

For ten years (1879–89) during the period that the *Atlanta Constitution* had both Harris and Arp, and, after 1888, Frank L. Stanton, author of the lyrics to "Mighty Lak' a Rose," on its star-studded staff, it was edited by the even better-known Henry Woodfin Grady, a native of Athens and the man whose name is most often associated with the term "New South." Grady was a charming, perceptive, and persuasive promoter, as well as an able reporter and editor—a promoter of harmony between the sections, North and South, and of commerce, industrialization, and economic independence for the South. He made the *Constitution* the voice of the New South, and when he died in 1889, of pneumonia following a speech in Boston, the nation, not just the South, mourned him.

But even before Grady became editor of the *Constitution* in 1879, it had for several years been Georgia's leading newspaper. Founded in 1868 by Carey W. Styles, it instantly became an "anti-Radical" sheet in the days of Reconstruction, which, of course, added to its popularity. Over the next few years, the *Constitution* had a succession of owners, until in 1876 it was acquired by Evan P. Howell, to remain in the Howell family for three generations. At least until 1883, when the *Atlanta Evening Journal* was founded by Colonel E. F. Hoge, the *Constitution* was the undisputed leader of Atlanta's newspapers. The same year it was founded the *Journal* sprang into prominence as a result of a fire that destroyed Atlanta's Kimball House, at that time the South's largest hotel. The *Journal* completely "scooped" the *Constitution*'s coverage of the fire by bringing out a special edition and placing some five hundred newsboys in the streets to sell them. For almost seventy years the two papers would remain great rivals.

Outside Atlanta other major metropolitan papers included the *Augusta Chronicle,* the state's oldest newspaper, dating from 1785, which did not miss a single daily edition even during the height of the Civil War. In Columbus, there was the *Enquirer* and, after 1874, the *Enquirer-Sun*, the result of a merger. Macon had two major newspapers, the morning *Macon Telegraph* and, after 1884, the evening *Macon News*, while Savannah had the staunchly conservative, but independent, *Savannah Morning News*.

Meanwhile county weeklies, the countryman's standby, were growing like mushrooms after a rain all across Georgia. Virtually wiped out by the war, by 1869 there were 59 weeklies in the state and 225 by 1890. These were the only newspapers that a majority of Georgians ever saw. And the editors of these papers, at least some of them, saw Georgia's and the South's problems in a different light from that of the editors of the metropolitan dailies. The Henry Gradys and other New South editors were desperately courting capitalists and industrialists of all kinds and welcoming them to the South, while as publishers they were growing fat on advertising. In contrast, the small-town editors, writing for their rural subscribers, were likely to be found railing against one of those advertisers, the fertilizer trust, for example, as an enslaver of the farmer, or at the banks for allegedly scheming to deprive him of his land. The decade of the 1890s would see such grievances explode into the Populist revolt that would threaten both the New South "boomers" and the hegemony of the Democratic party itself.

Meanwhile, by 1890, a whole generation of Georgians born since the war had grown to maturity, while much of the generation that had fought both the war and Reconstruction had died. Also the first full, generally prosperous decade since before the war was coming to an end, with a new and major depression rapidly approaching. Even the brief "literary flowering" of the late 1870s and the 1880s in the South was ending, including that in Georgia. The decade of the 1890s was to have a character and flavor all its own that made it stand out in the life of the nation, of the South, of Georgia. Profound changes were to come to them all.

PART FIVE

1890–1940

---

by

WILLIAM F. HOLMES

The Great Seal of 1799

In 1914 the date was changed to the year of Independence

XVIII

Economic Developments
1890–1940

During the first four decades of the twentieth century, Georgia's economy changed, but it changed so slowly in the rural areas that by 1940 many country people continued living, in some ways, as had their grandfathers. In 1940 the rural population stood at 65 percent, and Georgia's annual per capita cash income of $317 ranked among the lowest in the nation. A number of ailments afflicted the economy, one of the most serious being the domination of King Cotton, which until the 1920s accounted for over half of the total value of Georgia's agricultural production. The planting of so many acres in cotton contributed to overproduction that frequently resulted in low prices. Repeated planting of cotton year after year sapped the soil's fertility, so that only by using large quantities of fertilizer could farmers grow cotton on worn-out land. The cost of fertilizer, along with the many manual laborers required for hoeing and picking, made cotton an expensive crop to produce. Finally, the great attention given to cotton prevented many farmers from becoming self-sufficient in producing foodstuffs.

Many things worked against diversification. Force of habit kept some farmers growing cotton because that was the only money crop they had ever planted. Many had neither the education nor financial resources necessary to change from cotton to other crops. Truck farmers, fruit growers, and dairymen had only a small urban population nearby to consume perishable products. Although railroads expanded greatly in Georgia, most farmers did not have easy access to shipping facilities for perishable goods. As late as 1930 only 6 percent of the state's farmers lived near hard-surfaced roads.

Inadequate credit facilities created another problem. In the 1890s many counties did not have banks, and the existing banks rarely did business with small farmers. The inadequate banking facilities forced the few farmers who could get long-term credit to pay dearly for it. Banks and mortgage companies required that loans be payable upon

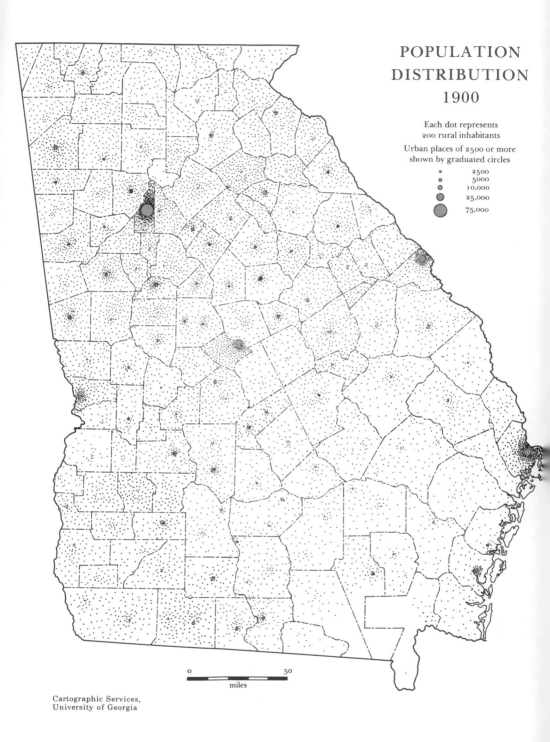

POPULATION
DISTRIBUTION
1900

Each dot represents
200 rural inhabitants

Urban places of 2500 or more
shown by graduated circles

2500
5000
10,000
25,000
75,000

miles

0   50

Cartographic Services,
University of Georgia

demand, granted them for short periods of time, charged high renewal fees, and imposed an annual interest rate of 10 percent.

A more serious problem confronted farmers who sought short-term credit. In the wake of the Civil War the crop lien system emerged as a source of short-term credit; over the years that system expanded until by the 1890s it entrapped between 80 and 90 percent of the cotton growers. In order to obtain credit, a farmer secured a lien on his ungrown crop from a furnishing merchant who supplied credit in the form of needed goods—food, cloth, seed, and fertilizer. The merchants themselves were not wealthy, and their loans to small farmers and tenants were relatively high-risk ventures. Consequently, merchants attached high interest rates—ranging from 25 to 75 percent—for supplies that they advanced under the crop lien system. Merchants also insisted that farmers to whom they extended credit grow cotton; perishables might spoil, livestock might die or be stolen.

The high interest rates that many landowners had to pay for credit, coupled with frequent periods of low cotton prices, drove farmers deeper and deeper into debt. As their indebtedness mounted, many had to mortgage their lands to get extensions of credit, and eventually the sad day came when some lost their lands through mortgage foreclosures. Each year an increasing number of farmers made the transition from landowner to tenant, the level of tenancy rising from 53 percent in 1890 to 65.6 percent in 1910 and peaking at 68.2 percent in 1930. Tenants either paid a cash rental or became sharecroppers who divided their crop with a landlord in return for the right to work part of his holdings.

The large number of tenants, many of whom received little supervision from their landlords, created additional problems within Georgia's agricultural system. Tenants frequently moved from one farm to another and consequently devoted little attention to curbing erosion, repairing buildings, or planting fruit trees. Actually it would have been surprising for them to have done otherwise. Tenants had no legal claim on any improvements they made in the land or buildings, and the landlord had the right to raise their rent or evict them at some future time.

The slow pace of industrial growth in Georgia forced most people to rely upon the land for their livelihood. The constant pressure of people against the land caused the number of separate farm units to increase from 224,000 in 1900 to 310,132 by 1920. During that same time the rural population increased by 278,000 people, and the average size of farms fell from 117 to 82 acres. Most of the small farms were

FARMS
GREATER THAN
THREE ACRES
1900

Each dot represents
25 farms

0   50
miles

Cartographic Services,
University of Georgia

neither self-sufficient nor prosperous. By 1920, for example, the typical tenant farmer cultivated about twenty-one acres, devoting much of this to cotton. Yet a study made seven years earlier, in 1913, estimated that for a farm family to be reasonably self-sufficient it would be necessary to devote 22½ acres to foodstuffs.

The persistence of primitive agricultural practices contributed to low crop yields. For many years state and federal agricultural agencies tried to persuade farmers to follow more enlightened practices and to diversify their crops. Some farmers, especially large landowners, successfully adopted the new methods, but a far greater number either did not have access to agricultural agencies or they lacked the education necessary to implement the new methods. As a result, the old ways persisted and each year more of the soil lost its fertility. Some of the larger and abler farmers prospered, but most people, black and white, made only meager livings and frequently knew poverty.

The 1890s were an especially hard time for farmers. A major financial panic hit the country in 1893, followed by a depression that lasted until near the close of the decade. During the depression cotton prices plunged to less than 5¢ a pound and not until 1898 did they exceed 7½¢ a pound. The hard times of the 1890s forced merchants to restrict credit, and as a result many farmers had to become more self-sufficient by devoting greater attention to gardening and livestock. Some tried to produce new commercial crops. Dairying, truck farming, and the commercial production of peaches, watermelons, and pecans secured permanent footholds. Attempts to develop livestock, tobacco, and seed farms on a commercial basis did not succeed in the 1890s.

After the turn of the twentieth century cotton prices rose, and during most of the next two decades they remained high. In response to the improved prices, farmers devoted more and more land to cotton, going from 3.5 million acres in 1900 to a peak of over 5 million acres in 1916. Between 1900 and 1916, in fact, the value of Georgia's cotton crop tripled. When America entered World War I in 1917, Georgia farmers —large landowners and tenants alike—experienced greater prosperity than at any time since the 1850s.

The expansion of Rural Free Delivery of the mails and the increase in automobiles and telephones in the rural areas added to the impression that farming in Georgia had become more prosperous by World War I. The war, moreover, stimulated the commercial production of corn, wheat, hay, Irish potatoes, sweet potatoes, tobacco, oats, peanuts, and livestock. Despite these favorable developments, Georgia agriculture changed little in the first two decades of the twentieth century.

Marietta, Georgia, 1908

Cotton production increased so greatly that the movement for agricultural diversification hardly made a dent in the state's cotton economy. Cotton culture remained unmechanized, and few people tried to use more enlightened methods of farming. Nor did the war alter those basic trends of an increasing number of small farms and a rising rate of tenancy. By the end of the war in 1918 most farmers lived as they always had in unpainted houses, traveling in wagons over unpaved roads, lighting their homes by oil lamps, and drawing water from wells by hand.

In 1920 the wartime prosperity suddenly ended. During the next decade a series of economic crises hit farmers so quickly and so hard that they permanently altered the old agricultural system. First came an abrupt postwar drop in cotton prices from 35¢ per pound in 1919 to 17¢ by 1920. At the same time cotton seed dropped from $31 to $10 per ton, and corn went from $1.07 to 66¢ per bushel. At no time during the next two decades did farm prices regain their wartime level. On the heels of this collapse of farm prices came the boll weevil, an enormously destructive insect often described as "a cross between a termite and a tank." The weevil first arrived in southeast Georgia in 1913. During the next six years it spread slowly over the state, but the high cotton prices of the war years largely offset its effect. In 1919 weevil damage became serious; between 1921 and 1923 it became disastrous and reduced thousands of rural families to hunger and destitution. Cotton yields fell 30 to 45 percent below normal each year, with the total crop dropping from an average of 1.75 million bales a year to 588,000 bales in 1923. Between 1920 and 1925 nearly 3.5 million acres were removed from farming and left idle; the farm population declined by 375,000 and the number of farms fell from 310,132 to 249,095. By 1925 droughts and insecticides had reduced weevil damage greatly, but never again did Georgia cotton production attain its pre–boll weevil level. Gone were the days in which farmers planted cotton on 4 to 5 million acres; gone too were the days of 2-million-bale crops.

While Georgians were still struggling to adjust to the price decline of 1920 and the ravages inflicted by the boll weevil, the Great Depression hit the nation in 1929. Between 1929 and 1932 farm prices fell 60 percent, and the gross yearly cash income of each farm person in Georgia went from $206 to $83. For the first time since the 1890s cotton dropped to 5¢ a pound. Many had to stop farming because they no longer had the credit to purchase seed and fertilizer. In some ways the farmers' lot had changed little over the past forty years. In the 1890s they had experienced the ravages of a bitter depression, although prosperity revived to a degree after 1900. By the early 1930s, after more than a decade of hard times, most rural Georgians longed for reforms that might ease their plight.

Major changes began with the implementation of President Franklin D. Roosevelt's New Deal. In an effort to reduce the overproduction of major agricultural staples, the Roosevelt administration implemented a program in 1933 under which farmers agreed to restrict production in return for subsidy payments. In 1936 the government modified the program so that farmers received subsidy payments for planting soil-conserving crops in place of staples. While the New Deal farm program exerted its major influences in Georgia on cotton, it implemented identical programs for tobcaco, corn, hogs, peanuts, and wheat.

The New Deal farm program did stimulate some beneficial developments. Soil conservation measures contributed to the preservation and rejuvenation of much of the state's land. The program also helped reverse two trends that had long weakened Georgia agriculture, namely, the growing number of small farms and the rising rate of tenancy. Beginning in 1935 and continuing in the years thereafter, more and more Georgia farmers came to own the land they worked and the size of the average farm increased. This resulted from the fact that the New Deal's program helped primarily the top third of Georgia's farmers—those who owned sizable amounts of land—while forcing many tenants and marginal farmers off the land. Whereas big farmers could receive subsidy payments for withholding part of their land and still produce an abundant crop on the remainder of their holdings, small farmers did not own enough land to make the system profitable. Many eventually sold their lands to larger farmers. Tenants suffered more severely. As large farmers curtailed production, they no longer needed as many laborers and consequently dismissed many tenants.

Although the New Deal mainly helped the top third of Georgia's farmers, it made some efforts in behalf of the lower two-thirds by offering rehabilitation loans, purchasing submarginal lands, and sponsoring resettlement projects. Some small landowners living on fertile soil had the opportunity to work themselves out of debt and gain a more solid economic footing by receiving rehabilitation loans. In return for these loans, they had to practice better farming techniques and make home improvements. The federal government also purchased sizable quantities of land that had lost fertility and converted it into pastures, forests, and parks. At the same time, it resettled most of the people whose lands it purchased on individual farms with better soil on the condition that they work in close cooperation with county extension agents in programs of home economics and farm management. Beginning in 1937 a small number of tenants received long-term, low-interest loans to buy farms of their own.

In addition to those people resettled on individual farms, the New Dealers also established four model farm communities: Pine Mountain Valley, Irwinville, Wolf Creek, and Briar Patch. Of these the most important was at Pine Mountain, a project especially close to the heart of President Roosevelt, who owned a farm in the vicinity. The original plan rested upon a utopian vision that included decent homes, gardens for subsistence, recreational and cultural opportunities, and employment in cooperative agriculture and industrial enterprises. Such a planned community would offer people from both the cities and the country a way to escape from poverty by engaging in cooperative methods of self-support. Unfortunately, Pine Mountain, like the other New Deal communities, never fulfilled the goals of its founders. Plans for a diversified agricultural system did not materialize, and the industrial operations remained small and unsuccessful.

Actually none of the New Deal programs were ever large enough to ease the hard lives that most rural people experienced in the 1930s. Individual rehabilitation loans proved the most successful, but the funds for such loans were never large enough to meet the demands of those who needed them. Over the next three decades many of Georgia's rural poor would leave the farms for the urban centers of the nation. There some found prosperity, while others came to know a new kind of poverty in the streets of American cities.

The Roosevelt administration did help to ease a problem that had plagued farmers for so long—the need for better credit facilities. Actually, improved farm credit began earlier in the century, but the most important advances came as a result of New Deal legislation. In 1916 the Federal Land Bank system introduced long-term, low-interest loans for farmers. Until the 1930s federal funds for the Land Banks remained so limited that they provided relief for only a small number of farmers. Under the Roosevelt administration funding for the Land Banks greatly increased, and during the next two decades they played a major role in revolutionizing long-term rural credit. Not only did the Land Banks provide a great deal of the mortgage credit, but they also established standards that other lending agencies eventually accepted. By 1940 the average interest rate for farm mortgages in Georgia stood at 5.5 percent, about half of what farmers had paid in the 1890s.

The government also helped to undermine the crop lien system. Under the Farm Credit Act of 1933, local production credit associations, backed with federal funds, began financing short-term loans for such things as livestock, crop production, and the repair of machinery. Georgia farmers quickly accepted the new system, the amount of loans under it going from $3.5 million in 1935 to more than $25 million by 1950. Though the production credit agencies never had enough funds to dominate the short-term credit market, they set standards that most other lending agencies were obliged to emulate. By mid-century most Georgia farmers had far better short-term credit facilities than had their predecessors fifty years earlier.

The increase in the number of commercial banks also saved some of the more successful farmers from the high costs of mortgage companies and merchants. Soon after the turn of the twentieth century the number of banks in Georgia began to increase and by 1914 reached a peak of 798. Many of those banks had such limited resources, however, that they could not withstand the agricultural collapse that began in 1920. During the ensuing decade 368 banks in Georgia suspended operations. Despite those setbacks, the new banks did help to ease the credit system. Commercial bankers came to understand agricultural problems better, and by 1940 approximately four hundred banks operated in Georgia, more than twice the number at the beginning of the century.

In one other important area the New Deal affected rural Georgia. Until the establishment of the Rural Electrification Administration (REA) in 1935, 97 percent of Georgia farms did not have electricity. By offering low-interest loans to electrical cooperatives, the REA enabled farmers to build power lines throughout the rural countryside. Between 1935 and 1950 forty-three REA cooperatives constructed over fifty-two thousand miles of line and electrified most of the farms in Georgia.

In 1940 Georgia remained a rural state, but developments had begun during the past twenty years that were altering farm life. The New Deal, of course, exerted an important influence. Although it did little to improve the lot of tenants and submarginal farmers, its programs of acreage restriction, subsidy payments, expanded credit facilities, and soil conservation all contributed to a better life for the larger farmers. The New Deal also encouraged the diversification of agriculture, a development that earlier had been stimulated by the depression of the 1890s, World War I, and the agricultural collapse of the 1920s. By 1930 cotton constituted 50 percent of the value of the state's crops, whereas in 1920 it had accounted for about 66 percent. By 1940, after the implementation of the New Deal acreage-reduction program, cotton represented only 40 percent of the state's farm income.

As King Cotton's position weakened, new crops came to play important roles in the lives of Georgia farmers. Tobacco production increased during World War I and continued to expand in the face of the boll weevil threat of the early twenties. By 1927 it had become Georgia's second most important crop, planted on 77,000 acres; by 1939 its acreage had nearly doubled. The war and the boll weevil also stimulated peanut growing, so that by the 1930s Georgia led the nation in peanut production.

During many years between 1890 and 1930 Georgia also led the nation in peach production. Following the crash of 1929, peach production fell sharply and by 1935 Georgia lost her position as America's leading peach state; in 1943 she ranked fourth among the states as a peach producer.

By that time other food crops played a larger role in the state's agricultural economy. Between 1900 and 1940 pecan production increased from 27,000 pounds annually to 23 million and Georgia became the nation's leader in that field. Watermelons became a major crop throughout the first half of the twentieth century. After 1920 there was a steady increase in the commercial production of tomatoes, beans, cabbage, cantaloupes, cucumbers, lettuce, onions, English peas, Irish potatoes, sweet potatoes, and pimentos. Nurseries also developed so that by the end of World War II Georgia farmers annually shipped to the North a billion tomato plants and hundreds of millions of onions, broccoli, cabbages, peppers, lettuce, and other seedlings. The growth of urban areas during the twentieth century stimulated the production of trees, shrubbery, and flower plants.

The onslaught of the boll weevil boosted the development of commercial livestock. The number of dairies and creameries grew and by 1940 the state had slightly over two thousand dairy farms. Hog production, long important, increased sharply after 1920. Until World War I the eggs and chickens raised in Georgia were largely for home consumption. The war encouraged the commercial production of eggs, and thereafter it steadily increased. The production of broilers, a more important part of the poultry industry, began in the 1920s and by 1940 Georgia was on the way to becoming one of the largest broiler-producing states in the Union.

Cotton remained Georgia's most important crop in 1940, but its position had fallen sharply during the past two decades. New crops

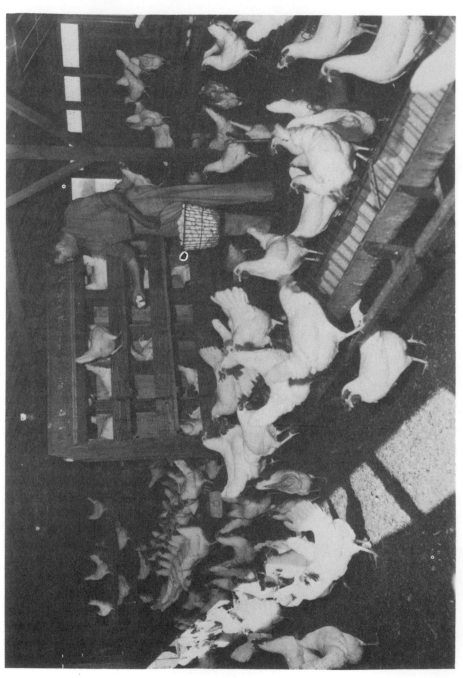

Laying hens, 1930s

had become firmly established, and agriculture had entered a healthier era. By that time, moreover, industrialization had begun to exert a greater impact, and Georgia's economy was in the early stages of assuming a closer balance between farming and manufacturing.

Cotton textiles continued as Georgia's leading industry throughout the half-century from 1890 to 1940. During those years hundreds of textile mills moved from the northeastern states to Georgia and the neighboring states of the Southeast. The South had definite advantages in luring mills: proximity to raw materials, abundance of cheap electrical power, newer machinery, and a milder climate. Far more important, however, were the cheap wages, long working hours, and absence of labor unions that characterized the southern work force. Prior to World War I Georgia mills produced mainly yarn and cheaper cloth, which they often shipped to the North for final processing. After 1920, Georgia mills began turning out larger amounts of finished products, including ready-made clothing.

Some textile mills were located in cities and larger towns, but others were found in small towns. The workers consisted chiefly of people directly off farms who often lived in mill villages where the company owned the houses, churches, schools, and stores. In 1890 a visitor described rural mill villages as consisting of "rows of loosely built, weatherstained frame houses, all the same ugly pattern and buttressed by clumsy chimneys. . . ." Inside the bare floors were marked with "the tread of animals" and the "muddy outline of splayed toes of all shapes and sizes" of barefoot people. The workers labored about seventy hours a week and received such low wages that children, some less than ten years old, worked along with their mothers and fathers to provide enough income to support the family. Life in mill villages resembled farm life in some ways. In place of merchants who advanced supplies against ungrown crops, a company-owned store advanced supplies against future wages. Workers frequently were paid in scrip redeemable only at the company store.

Mill villages improved as the twentieth century advanced. By 1940 over 60 percent of the workers still lived in company-owned houses, but in place of row after row of drab-looking frame structures, the homes in many mill villages displayed a variety of colors and shapes. Many had electricity, running water, and inside toilets. The number of company-owned stores had declined, and scrip was no longer widely used as a means of payment. The maximum working hours had been reduced to forty a week, but wages still remained so low that many wives and older children had to work to help support the family. In fact, throughout the years from 1890 to 1940 textile mills provided one of the major opportunities for lower-income white women to gain employment outside the home.

As railroads expanded into southwest Georgia in the late nineteenth century, lumber mills and naval stores operations grew rapidly. With the decline of forest resources in North Carolina by the 1880s, many lumber operators moved into Georgia and thereafter lumber production greatly increased in the state. In 1901, Charles H. Herty, a chemist at the University of Georgia, discovered a new method of extracting turpentine that enabled the naval stores industry to increase so rapidly that by 1928 Georgia led the nation in producing turpentine, tar, rosin, and pitch. Later, in the 1930s, Herty perfected a more economical process for making newsprint from southern pines. By 1940 large paper mills were operating at Savannah and Brunswick.

Although they did not develop on the scale of textiles, lumber, and naval stores, some other industries made important contributions to Georgia's economy. The outbreak of World War I in 1914 created new demands for foodstuffs, and within a short time modern meat-packing plants opened at Moultrie, Atlanta, Augusta, and Savannah. World War I also stimulated the development of commercial canning plants, especially those processing sweet potatoes and peaches. During the course of the early twentieth century more fertilizer plants were built throughout the state so that by 1943 there were 143 of them. Cottonseed mills began developing in the late nineteenth century following the discovery that cottonseed oil mixed with certain animal fats made a good substitute for lard. In the twentieth century the mills expanded as cottonseed oil was used in manufacturing soap, fertilizer, cattle feed, and rayon. Mineral products included marble, granite, slate, and clay. Georgia was one of four states that produced bauxite, the ore from which aluminum is made.

Atlanta became the home of Georgia's most famous industry. In 1886 John Styth Pemberton, a man who had long dabbled in patent medicines, devised a drug, consisting of extracts of cocoa and kola nuts, for the relief of headaches. Soon Asa Griggs Candler, a druggist, bought the rights of Coca-Cola. After selling the drink in his store for several years, he became convinced that it could become a successful soft drink; accordingly, in 1892 he formed the Coca-Cola Company and during the next twenty-five years he directed it into the most successful soft-drink company in the world. In 1919 the Candler family sold the company for $25 million to a syndicate consisting of three banks, one of which was the Trust Company of Georgia, presided over

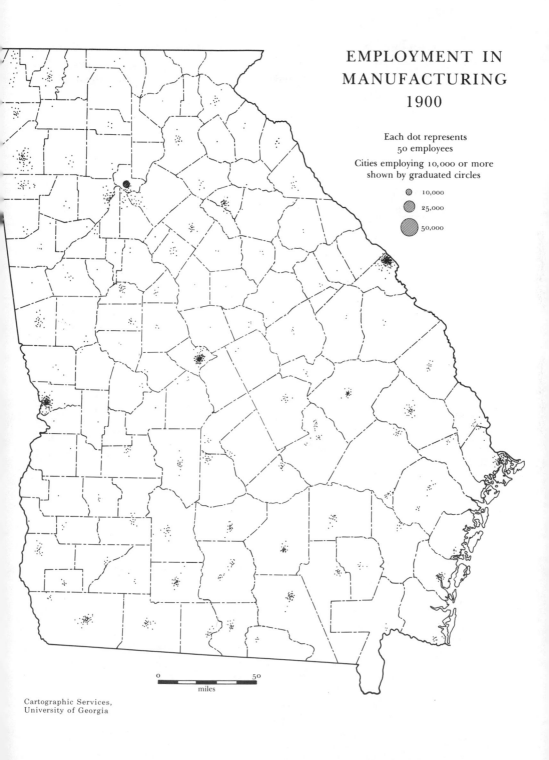

EMPLOYMENT IN
MANUFACTURING
1900

Each dot represents
50 employees

Cities employing 10,000 or more
shown by graduated circles

10,000

25,000

50,000

0   50
miles

Cartographic Services,
University of Georgia

by a tough, shrewd financier named Ernest Woodruff. In 1923 Ernest's son, Robert, took over the presidency of the company, and under his direction Coca-Cola changed from a national into an international product sold around the world.

The development of organized labor affords some insight into the kind of industrialization that occurred in Georgia. Trade unions did not begin developing in the state until the 1890s. Most of the activity during the next half-century was confined to skilled workers in building trades, metal works, printing trades, and railroad operations. Textile workers tried on a number of occasions to organize, and at times they resorted to strikes that ranged from ones at local mills in the 1890s to a widespread strike that closed many mills across the state in the summer of 1934 and that was eventually broken by the state militia. The attempts of textile and most other workers to unionize in Georgia failed. By the time of the Great Depression only 3.2 percent of Georgia's industrial workers belonged to unions, and most of those lived in the Atlanta metropolitan area. Despite the favorable attitude of the New Deal toward organized labor and the rapid

Family of textile mill workers

University of Georgia Libraries

growth of unions throughout the nation in the 1930s, organized labor in Georgia made little additional progress by 1940.

A number of conditions worked against the development of strong labor unions. The rural tradition of many workers along with their ingrained individualism, apathy, poverty, and suspicion of outsiders made it extremely difficult to achieve permanent unionization. Textile mill owners frequently worked to maintain a paternalistic atmosphere that encouraged workers to appreciate their jobs and to defer to the leadership of the owners. Many workers belonged to fundamentalist churches that encouraged an other-worldly perspective and opposed unions. Finally, community sentiment was often hostile to unions and sometimes condoned the use of violence against labor organizers.

The pattern of industrial growth in Georgia coincided closely with national periods of growth and recession. Expansion that had begun in the 1880s came to a close with the depression of 1893; not until the end of that decade did industrial growth resume and then it continued for two decades, the most intense period coming during World War I. Like farmers, manufacturers were hurt by the sudden postwar price drop of 1920. Although industrialists did not suffer as much as farmers during the 1920s, manufacturing did not expand so rapidly as it had in the previous decade. In fact, not until 1939 did Georgia industry regain the peak of production it had achieved in 1919. Several developments contributed to the slow industrial growth of the 1920s. First, throughout the decade the state's leading industry, cotton textiles, suffered nationally from low prices and cutthroat competition. Second, many Georgia banks had invested heavily in Florida real estate, and when the Florida land boom collapsed in 1926 some Georgia banks failed. Soon afterward came the crash of 1929, when far more banks, as well as industries, went bankrupt.

Whereas the New Deal's farm program exerted a profound impact on Georgia, its programs for industry had little effect. The National Recovery Administration (NRA) aimed to increase employment, raise wages, and lower working hours by encouraging businessmen to draw up codes to regulate their specific industries. The NRA codes usually reflected the interests of the nation's largest businesses and were designed to help people living in heavily industrialized states. The many Georgia workers employed in agriculture and domestic service were not affected by the codes. In addition, most Georgia industries, except for textiles, were so small that they could not, and in some instances would not, pay the wages that NRA codes stipulated.

Since the NRA did not have the authority to enforce its codes, the agency exerted little influence in Georgia.

As Georgia's industry grew slowly, so too did her urban population. During the half-century between 1890 and 1940 the number of people moving from farms and villages to cities and larger towns increased slowly but steadily, so that urban population rose from 14 percent of the total population in 1890 to 34.4 percent by 1940. The development of transportation facilities contributed greatly to urban growth, for cities developed along the major railroads and highways of the state. From 1890 to 1920, when railroads provided the chief means of transportation, railroad mileage in Georgia increased from 4,532 to 7,591. After that railroads declined, the mileage dropping to 6,334 by 1940. That decline resulted largely from increasing competition from automobiles, trucks, and buses. In 1916 Georgia had a total of 46,025 motor vehicles, but as the state's highway system expanded during the next quarter-century the number of vehicles rose to 502,603 by 1940.

In addition to improved transportation facilities, Georgia's cities and larger towns grew as a result of their ability to attract industry. By the 1920s, for example, Dalton advertised low assessments on manufacturing property and Gainesville offered free sites and tax exemptions to prospective companies. Among the cities that enjoyed the most success in attracting industry were Savannah, Georgia's principal port, which developed companies producing naval stores, sugar, and paper; Columbus, which had textile mills and iron foundries; and Augusta and Macon, which relied heavily on textile mills and clay works. Rome, Griffin, LaGrange, Gainesville, Dalton, Canton, and West Point became textile centers.

Atlanta experienced the state's most vigorous urban growth, leaving all other Georgia cities far behind as the city's population rose from 65,533 in 1890 to 302,288 by 1940. Railroads, more than anything else, made Atlanta by enabling the city to serve as a wholesale and retail distribution center. Industry also developed rapidly in Atlanta, where factories produced textiles, fertilizer, furniture, cottonseed oil, paper, and agricultural implements. By the 1920s Atlanta had become the convention center of the Deep South as well as the banking and insurance headquarters of the region. By that time, moreover, Atlanta had many tall office buildings and several skyscraper hotels, which enabled the city to attract the branch offices of many national firms and the home offices of many southern firms.

The rapid economic growth that characterized Atlanta's history

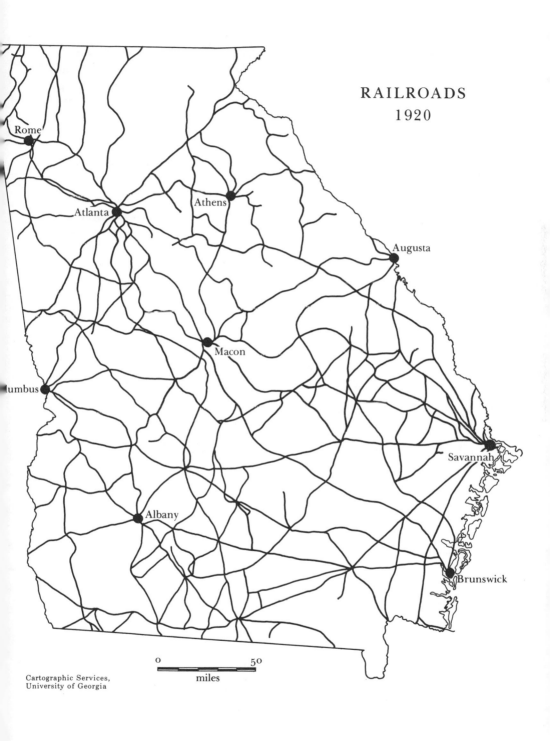

RAILROADS
1920

Rome

Atlanta

Athens

Augusta

Macon

umbus

Savannah

Albany

Brunswick

0   50
miles

stood in sharp contrast to developments in most other parts of the state. While the growth of industries did create jobs and give balance to the agricultural economy, by 1940 Georgia still had not become a major industrial state. In 1930, for example, industry provided employment for about 15 percent of the state's work force. Of greater importance, most of the industries that developed were the kinds that paid low wages to workers and contributed little to the state in the form of revenue. Throughout the nation textile workers received low pay, but the Georgia mills, like those in other southern states, paid 30 to 40 percent lower than in other parts of the country. By 1929 the average annual wage for industrial employees in Georgia was only 55.4 percent of the annual wage per employee for the nation. Thus the state's industrial system, like the agricultural, left some people impoverished and many others living well below national standards. The hard times and economic frustrations that so many Georgians experienced strongly shaped the state's history in the years before World War II.

XIX

Civil Rights
1890–1940

Between 1890 and 1940 black people experienced conditions that set them apart from white Georgians. Though they shared many things in common with whites, they differed so markedly in some ways as to warrant separate attention. That was especially true in the 1890s, when blacks became the victims of laws designed to relegate them to a position at the bottom of the social system. In 1891 the General Assembly passed Georgia's first Jim Crow law requiring railroad companies to furnish separate coaches for blacks and whites. In that same year the state had all prisoners in convict lease camps segregated by race. During the course of the decade Augusta, Atlanta, and Rome provided that blacks and whites be buried in separate cemeteries, and some cities also passed ordinances demanding that blacks sit at the rear of streetcars. At the close of the decade the state expanded its segregation laws to include railroad sleeping cars.

It is difficult to assess the full impact of these laws. First, they may have merely recognized unwritten rules that blacks and whites had long understood and followed. Certainly, the enactment of segregation laws represented a hardening of white attitudes toward blacks and marked the beginning of an era in which blacks experienced new restrictions. Many blacks recognized the dangers that the new laws posed, and they strongly protested them. While the legislators debated the state's first Jim Crow law in 1891, officers of the Colored Farmers' Alliance addressed the General Assembly and urged that the measure not be passed. In 1899 a delegation of prominent black leaders asked Governor Allen D. Candler to veto a law segregating Pullman cars. But the strongest forms of black protest occurred at the local level. When Atlanta tried to segregate streetcars in 1892, blacks staged such an effective boycott against the company that the measure was not enforced at that time. During the course of the next decade blacks in Augusta and Rome also resorted to boycotts to protest Jim Crow laws. The most sustained protest occurred in Savannah, where the city council passed a statute in 1906 requiring streetcar companies to segregate blacks and whites. The black community reacted quickly with an organized boycott that lasted throughout 1907, causing the streetcar company to lose nearly $50,000. Despite the sustained protest, white resistance remained strong; gradually the will to resist waned, and by 1908 blacks began to use the segregated cars. The failure of the Savannah boycott marked the demise of effective black protests throughout the state. By that time a harsher and more uncompromising racial code had developed in Georgia, and blacks had less freedom than they had known two decades earlier.

Throughout the first half of the twentieth century white Georgians continued to pass Jim Crow laws, both at the state and local levels. Larger cities enacted most of the segregation measures. In the 1920s Atlanta adopted an ordinance forbidding black barbers to serve white women. As late as 1942 Albany passed an ordinance that segregated ticket booths and ticket lines at movie theaters. It would be a mistake, however, to judge race relations solely on the basis of laws. The surprising thing is how few Jim Crow laws ever existed. Most rural areas did not have them. The segregation system was always more pervasive than the laws indicated; local customs and police forces played a far larger role in maintaining white supremacy. The Jim Crow laws passed after 1890 did tighten restrictions on blacks and sometimes closed areas to which they formerly had access.

A number of conditions contributed to the harsher attitudes that whites developed toward blacks during the 1890s and early twentieth century. By that time so-called scientific views of Negro inferiority became widely accepted throughout the Western world, and the experiences of America and European nations in colonizing nonwhite people strengthened the doctrine of white supremacy. Within the United States northern liberal opinion that earlier had exerted a check on racism began to wane, and white supremacy became the American way. In the 1890s the federal courts reflected the changing national attitude concerning black people by upholding laws requiring segregated public facilities. Developments within Georgia further contributed to the hardening of racial views. The Populist campaigns of the 1890s posed the first serious threat to Democratic control since Reconstruction and revived fears of blacks playing more active roles in public life. Then between 1890 and 1910 a new generation came to the fore, many of whom did not subscribe to the paternalistic views held by their predecessors. Some moderate whites after 1890 did ask that blacks be treated fairly and humanely, but they did not challenge segregation and they assumed blacks to be inferior to whites.

By the early twentieth century it became increasingly difficult for whites to take a moderate position on the race question, as the case of Andrew Sledd so well illustrates. In July 1902 Sledd, a young Latin professor at Emory College, published in the *Atlantic Monthly* an article entitled "The Negro—Another View." Though he made it clear in the article that whites should not treat blacks as their social equals, Sledd did criticize the worst aspects of racial segregation and strongly denounced lynching. When news of the article's publication became known in Georgia, a strong public outcry forced Sledd to resign from the college and leave the state.

The harsher racist feelings that became so strong by the early twentieth century also manifested themselves in a movement to eliminate black voting and officeholding. Actually Negro political participation had been lower in Georgia than in other southern states for many years. While fraud and intimidation kept some blacks away from the polls, the constitution of 1877 had supplied the most effective disfranchisement device by providing that only men who paid their cumulative taxes could vote. The cumulative aspect was particularly important, for once a poor person got behind in his payments, he practically disfranchised himself for life. Throughout the late nineteenth century, the tax requirement not only disfranchised many blacks but also many poor whites.

The Populist uprising stimulated a move for greater disfranchisement. Many white Democrats wanted to eliminate forever the possibility of blacks' voting, especially for a third party. They first attempted to achieve that goal by adopting white primaries. By the 1890s some counties had already adopted Democratic primaries to choose party nominees; after the advent of Populism more county primaries became white primaries. In 1900 the state Democratic party, which two years earlier had adopted the primary for selecting nominees for state office, restricted its primaries to whites. Blacks could still vote in the general elections, but that meant little in a one-party system where the meaningful contests occurred in the primaries. Blacks recognized this, and in Augusta and Savannah they protested the implementation of white primaries. Their protests were in vain. By 1900 about one in ten of the qualified black Georgians voted.

Just before the turn of the century, Thomas Hardwick, a young legislator, began urging that Georgia follow the example of other southern states by adopting a literacy test and grandfather clause to disfranchise the few remaining black voters and to end forever the possibility of blacks' participating in the general elections. Hardwick introduced such legislation in 1899 and 1901, but on each occasion his bills met overwhelming defeat. Whites then apparently believed the cumulative tax and white primary had solved the problem.

During the next five years, however, voices urging disfranchisement became stronger and stronger, one of the loudest being that of the former Populist leader Tom Watson. In 1906 he and Hardwick joined forces and agreed to support Hoke Smith for the governorship on a platform calling for railroad reform and Negro disfranchisement. Smith accepted their support and in the ensuing campaign he made disfranchisement the major issue. Following Smith's victory, the General Assembly proposed a constitutional amendment for a literacy test, property qualification, and grandfather clause as the means to end black voting. The literacy test required that voters be able to read and explain any paragraph of the federal or state constitution, while the property qualification required ownership of 40 acres of land or property assessed at $500. The grandfather clause enfranchised men who had served in the United States or Confederate military forces and their descendents; no one could register under that provision after 1914.

Before this amendment could become effective, the voters had to ratify it in the general election of 1908. In that contest many black leaders warned their people of the danger that confronted them, and in some places they conducted campaigns to have as many blacks as possible register for the coming election. These efforts had little effect. By that time the cumulative tax, the white primary, intimidation, and political apathy had greatly reduced black voter turnouts. In some rural counties prior to the election, night riders terrified blacks to keep them away from the polls.

In the face of such opposition it was not surprising that the voters approved the disfranchisement amendment; the surprising thing was that it passed by a vote of only 79,968 to 40,260. Many whites may have believed there was little need for the measure since so few blacks still voted. Others may have feared that the literacy test would disfranchise poor whites who would not want to experience the indignity of admitting that they could neither read nor write. Such fears were well-grounded, because fewer whites registered to vote after the amendment's ratification. It came close to eliminating black voting altogether. Some blacks continued to vote in places like Atlanta after 1908, but for all practical purposes black political participation had ended in the state until after 1940.

Despite the loss of their political power, blacks continued to make economic progress early in the twentieth century. From 1890 to 1940 there existed a small core of black professionals—doctors, lawyers, ministers, nurses, dentists, and teachers. From the 1890s onward the increasing number of blacks moving to cities and larger towns created a need for more Negro businesses. Consequently, black-owned grocery stores, drug stores, clothing stores, restaurants, real estate agencies, funeral homes, and barber shops arose to fulfill demands within black communities. Most of the black businesses were owner-operated retail stores, whose profit margins remained small. There were, of course, some exceptions. Alonzo Herndon, who came penniless to Atlanta in 1876 and eventually became a successful barber, merged eight small insurers in 1905 to form the Atlanta Mutual Insurance Company. In 1917 it had one hundred branches and over seven hundred employees. By the 1960s it had become one of the largest black businesses in America.

Professionals and businessmen represented rare exceptions among black Georgians. Between 1890 and 1920 the majority of black workers were farmers, while the second largest group—chiefly women—were domestic servants. Most of the black farmers served as tenants and agricultural laborers. In the black belt, which at that time had the largest number of Negro laborers, nearly 90 percent of the blacks were tenants. For a while some black farmers did make progress in becoming landowners: acreage owned by blacks increased from 586,664 in 1880 to 1,838,129 by 1920. Yet blacks, who made up over 40 percent of Georgia's population prior to 1920, never owned more than a small percentage of the state's farm lands. Aside from working as farmers and domestic servants, blacks did all types of physical labor and some found employment in crafts and manufacturing, serving as carpenters and joiners, blacksmiths and wheelrights, masons, barbers, painters, plasterers, printers, woodworkers, and dressmakers. Only a small number of blacks worked for railroads as operating personnel or for textile mills, jobs jealously monopolized by whites. In 1909, for example, white workers staged one of the few successful strikes of the period against the Georgia Railroad to prevent the line from employing additional black firemen.

After 1920 blacks began to experience economic losses on all fronts. The agricultural depression that came as a result of a postwar drop in cotton prices and the ravages of the boll weevil hurt all farmers; but blacks, most of whom were marginal farmers and tenants, suffered more severely. Between 1920 and 1925 the total number of black farmers who owned their lands dropped from 130,181 to 84,187. The

A black farm home, late nineteenth century

economic troubles that began in the 1920s also caused whites to take over many jobs formerly held by blacks: elevator operators, tradesmen, wagon drivers, bell boys, and filling station attendants. As a result of discrimination in apprenticeship and trade union practices after 1920, blacks had more difficulty gaining admission to skilled crafts. Also in an age of growing technological sophistication, blacks found their skills in carpentry, blacksmithing, plumbing, and other such fields becoming obsolete; having neither the opportunity nor the funds needed to stay abreast of recent developments, they were relegated more and more to repair work. With the Great Depression that came in 1929 many of the small, marginal black businesses went under. Thus by the 1930s most blacks continued to make a living as agricultural laborers and domestic servants. The proportion of blacks in crafts and nonfarm occupations had fallen sharply and their share of the work was small in comparison with what it had been in 1890.

Blacks did derive benefits from the New Deal programs of the 1930s, for some obtained jobs on work relief programs while others received vocational and literacy training. But blacks did not profit from New Deal programs as much as whites. That resulted partly from the fact that local whites directed some of the agencies, such as the Civilian Conservation Corps (CCC). The CCC in Georgia did not exclude blacks, but it never approached giving them a proportionate share of the jobs. On the other hand, federal officials in charge of the National Youth Administration tried hard to see that blacks received a fair share of that program's benefits. A more important reason for the New Deal's failure to improve the economic position of blacks resulted from the fact that most of its programs were not designed primarily to help workers near the bottom of the economic scale.

In a society in which whites discriminated so sharply against blacks, some state institutions, such as the penal system, affected blacks more than whites. Between 1890 and 1940, blacks constituted the overwhelming majority of Georgia's prison population. The state leased felony convicts to private companies, contractors, and individuals who needed cheap labor. In 1897 the General Assembly did provide that women, the disabled, the very young, and the aged be imprisoned on a state farm at Milledgeville. But the state made no attempt to rehabilitate prisoners.

Over the years many people had protested the corruption and brutality of the lease system, but reform did not come until 1908, when a movement developed to expose corrupt dealings between high prison officials and lessees. In an effort to arouse public support, reformers

Adult education group, Atlanta, WPA

emphasized the mistreatment of white prisoners, although at the time 86 percent of the state convicts were black. A legislative investigation revealed, among other things, that the Durham Coal and Coke Company worked prisoners seven days a week, requiring each man to mine a certain amount daily and whipping those who did not meet their quotas. Such findings spurred ministers, citizens' committees, and labor leaders to call for reform; mass protest meetings were held in Atlanta, Macon, and Griffin. In response to the public outcry the General Assembly in 1908 abolished the lease system. By shifting prisoners from the control of private interests to work under the direction of public officials on county roads and highways, the state greatly reduced the opportunities for private corruption. But the lot of prisoners changed little. After 1908 prisoners were sometimes housed in port-able metal cages, shackled, and closely watched by armed guards as they worked on state roads. Investigations of the early 1930s revealed conditions as barbaric as those that had existed under the old lease system.

During the administration of Governor Eurith D. Rivers, in 1937, Georgia made new attempts to improve the prison system by creating the Board of Penal Administration solely for the purpose of supervising the management of the work camps. The Prison and Parole Commission had the task of annually reviewing records of all prisoners and considering pardons and paroles for all except capital offenders. Until that time only an application from an attorney representing a prisoner got consideration for parole. In response to Governor Rivers's leadership the state also abolished the use of chains, sweat boxes, and other forms of extreme punishment. Despite these efforts, the conditions of most prisoners had changed little by 1940, because the state did not have adequate funds to implement the reforms.

Early in the twentieth century federal officials discovered cases of blacks' being held as peons, a form of debt servitude. At the county level a person convicted of a misdemeanor could pay a fine or serve on a chain gang. Frequently planters, lumbermen, and mine owners paid the fines of prisoners and then required them to work off the fines. In addition, Georgia had a contract law designed to prevent tenant farmers and laborers from breaking contracts. Although a violation of federal law, peonage proved difficult to identify and prosecute in rural areas. The peon, at the bottom of the social scale, was pitted against men of wealth and power at the top; juries usually displayed little sympathy for the peons. Federal authorities successfully prosecuted some cases, the most notorious occurring in Jasper County in 1921 where a white planter murdered eleven black laborers in a desperate attempt to destroy evidence that he had held them as peons. As late as 1939 the Georgia Baptist Association declared that peonage still presented a major problem in the state.

Violence that whites inflicted on blacks provided another manifestation of the inferior position that Negroes held. Violence took many forms, the most heinous being lynching. Between 1890 and 1940, when Georgia frequently led the nation in lynching, most of the victims were black. Complete and reliable statistics on lynchings do not exist, but the best estimate for Georgia is that between 1889 and 1930 at least four hundred and fifty lynchings occurred. The number of lynchings varied from year to year, going from twenty-seven in 1899 to none at all in the mid-1920s. Among the worst episodes of lynch law was one that occurred in 1905 at Watkinsville, where a mob took seven blacks and one white from the local jail and killed them. In Brooks and Lowndes counties in 1918 crowds of armed whites lynched eleven blacks and drove over five hundred from the region.

Whitecapping represented a more clandestine form of group violence directed against blacks. Whitecap organizations usually consisted of small groups of whites who attempted to gain control over Negro laborers by terrorizing them; sometimes they tried to take over the farms of black landlords by driving them off their holdings. Whitecaps attacked blacks near Fort Valley in 1893, in Floyd County in 1900, and in Forsyth County in 1912.

The most serious instance of racial violence occurred in 1906. One month after the Democratic primary in which Hoke Smith had aroused racial animosity by calling for the total disfranchisement of blacks, a race riot broke out in Atlanta. The immediate cause of the riot resulted from highly exaggerated and sensationalized reports that Atlanta newspapers published of alleged attacks by black rapists on white women. On the evening of 22 September, in response to such reports, crowds of whites began roaming the streets and attacking blacks at random. By the following day the state militia restored order, but it did not last long for violence again erupted and continued for three more days. In the course of that riot twenty-five black men died, about one hundred and fifty blacks were seriously wounded, and hundreds suffered lesser injuries. Dozens of whites also sustained injuries and at least one white man was killed.

Black Georgians responded to white discrimination after 1890 in a variety of ways, ranging from acceptance of prevailing conditions to emigration to Africa. Following a speech that he delivered at the

Cotton States Exposition in Atlanta in 1895, Booker T. Washington became the leading spokesman for the accommodationist point of view. Through his writings, speeches, and work at the Tuskegee Institute in Alabama, Washington urged blacks to avoid antagonizing whites and to shun involvement in politics; instead they should work hard, practice thrift, and acquire ownership of their homes. The surest means by which blacks could improve themselves economically was by becoming skilled craftsmen and self-sufficient farmers. Washington insisted that blacks did not desire social equality with whites. Ultimately, Washington hoped, blacks would have the full rights of American citizens, but for the time being he believed that they should content themselves with a secure, though inferior, position in society. Until his death in 1915, Washington exerted considerable influence among Georgia blacks, although few subscribed completely to his philosophy. Benjamin Jefferson Davis, who founded the Atlanta *Independent* in 1903, became Washington's closest adherent in Georgia, but Davis's complete espousal of the accommodationist position proved to be as exceptional as did those who urged the most rigorous forms of protest.

At the other extreme were two Georgians who believed blacks and whites could not live together peacefully in a true spirit of equality. Bishop Henry McNeal Turner of the African Methodist Episcopal Church conceded that Negroes in America would be forever relegated to a caste below that of whites and he urged blacks to emigrate to Africa. For many years Turner worked for voluntary colonization of American Negroes in Africa, but he never obtained adequate funds to accomplish his purpose. Bishop Lucius H. Holsey of the Colored Methodist Episcopal Church proposed a plan along similar lines by urging that the federal government set aside some western territory to serve as a separate state where Negroes could enjoy first-class citizenship. Though few blacks actually tried to follow the schemes of Turner and Holsey, they did represent serious protests against conditions prevailing in the late nineteenth century.

Early in the next century other forms of black protest developed that opposed the accommodationist position of Washington and the separatist positions of Turner and Holsey. William E. B. Du Bois, a sociology professor at Atlanta University, took issue with Washington's emphasis on vocational education and material success. Du Bois insisted that the pursuit of a liberal arts education could give rise to a class of black leaders, which could serve as a vanguard for racial advancement. He also criticized Washington's opposition to political involvement and protest, arguing that only by voting and agitating for their legitimate rights could blacks hope to win full citizenship. A number of other Georgians followed Du Bois's demand for full equality for blacks. The *Voice of the Negro*, a monthly magazine published in Atlanta from 1904 to 1906 under the editorshop of J. Max Barber, called for an end to all forms of discrimination. At that same time William Jefferson White, black editor of the *Georgia Baptist* of Augusta, urged that only by actively protesting could blacks win their civil rights. In response to a call by White, about five hundred black Georgians met in the Equal Rights Convention at Macon in 1906 and adopted a resolution denouncing Jim Crow laws, lynchings, and the convict lease system.

Throughout the long period from 1890 to 1940 most blacks in Georgia took a position somewhere between those of Washington and Du Bois. They tried to help themselves, complained about specific grievances from time to time, and usually avoided antagonizing whites. Following Hoke Smith's victory in 1906 and the enactment of the disfranchisement statutes in 1908, strong black protest declined for a number of years. In 1917 the first Georgia branch of the National Association for the Advancement of Colored People (NAACP) was formed in Atlanta in response to an attempt by city officials to eliminate one grade from the black grammar schools. The Atlanta branch of the NAACP organized the black voters so effectively that they blocked the ratification of a school bond issue and eventually persuaded the school board to build a new black high school. During the next two decades branches of the NAACP appeared in some other Georgia cities and helped to keep alive some semblance of the protest tradition.

In addition to openly protesting, blacks also expressed their dissatisfaction by moving. Until 1915 those blacks who moved went from one part of the state to another, or from Georgia to states of the southwest such as Mississippi, Louisiana, and Texas. For many years the number of blacks leaving did not exert a profound impact upon the state, for with the birthrate remaining high, Georgia's black population increased from 978,357 in 1890 to 1,173,075 in 1910. Conditions changed markedly after 1915, when blacks began leaving in large numbers for cities of the North. World War I caused an expansion in northern industry and also reduced emigration from Europe; in response to those developments, blacks went north to get better jobs and higher wages. By the early 1920s the boll weevil had devastated so much cotton that thousands more left for the North. The census of 1930 revealed an 11.2 percent decline in Georgia's black population over the past decade. At that time blacks accounted for only 36.8 percent of the state's population, the smallest since 1790.

While many blacks moved out of the state, many remained and tried to live as best they could under the prevailing system. Denied access to many parts of white society, they increasingly developed institutions to serve their own needs. Since the Civil War the church had become one of the most important institutions within the black community. The overwhelming majority of blacks joined Baptist or Methodist churches where ministers with little formal education preached an emotional, other-worldly gospel. Only a few became Presbyterians, Episcopalians, Roman Catholics, or Congregationalists. Though the poverty prevailing among members of rural churches prevented them from undertaking many charitable activities, they did serve both the religious and social needs of many people. Most city churches differed little from their rural counterparts.

Almost as important as churches in the black community were beneficent societies that offered their members sickness and death benefits as well as social opportunities and a chance to serve in leadership roles. Some also afforded their members valuable business training. In rural areas practically every black person belonged to a beneficent society; in cities as much as 75 percent of the population belonged. Until the 1890s most beneficent societies remained small and local; after that date national organizations, such as the Negro Masons and the Grand Order of Odd Fellows, overshadowed local groups. In many cities and towns blacks organized clubs and societies with purely social aims. In Savannah the Pleasure Club sponsored festivals, parades, and band concerts; many young married women in Macon belonged to the Art and Social Club; in Atlanta the Gate City Club and the Laboring Men's Pleasure Club were gambling halls and saloons.

After 1900 many black fraternal orders, as well as private individuals, became more aware of social problems facing blacks and worked to ease them. In 1890 Carrie Steele, an ex-slave, founded Georgia's first Negro orphanage in Atlanta; that same year Spelman Seminary established the Leonard Street Orphanage in Atlanta for girls. Increasingly black groups in Georgia cities founded homes for the aged, kindergartens, and day nurseries. Perhaps the most enterprising black social organization was the Atlanta Neighborhood Union founded in 1908 under the leadership of Lugenia Hope, wife of John Hope, the president of Morehouse College. The union first surveyed conditions in one of the largest black residential areas of Atlanta and found the chief ills to be poor housing, unsanitary conditions, lack of recreational facilities, family disorganization, and delinquency. To improve conditions the union established a health clinic, a boys' club, a girls' club, and vocational classes for children. The union also lobbied with local governmental agencies for improved schools, streets, and sewage facilities. By 1915 the union had expanded its services to the entire city.

Even though blacks developed institutions to meet their needs and protested some of the injustices they experienced, they failed to remove the barriers that whites had established against them. Segregation laws and disfranchisement statutes remained in effect until well after World War II. Nevertheless, early in the century changes began to appear in the attitudes of some whites toward blacks, changes which portended developments that became stronger as the century advanced. Immediately after the Atlanta race riot of 1906, former governor William J. Northen and a small number of other concerned whites in that city formed an interracial league consisting of prominent leaders from both the black and white communities. Through joint discussions they attempted to develop better communication between the two groups in the hopes of preventing future outbreaks of violence. Northen urged the formation of interracial leagues throughout Georgia, and in behalf of that cause he personally traveled to over half of the counties in the state. In response to Northen's appeals many interracial committees were formed, but after initial interest faded, most of them disappeared.

During the next two decades several white Georgians spoke out openly against some of the abuses that blacks suffered. In 1914 Lily H. Hammond, long associated with Paine College in Augusta and active in the affairs of the Methodist Church, published *In Black and White*. Hammond did not advocate social equality, but she castigated her fellow whites for acquiescing in existing penal conditions, Jim Crow facilities, and the high rate of lynchings. Shortly before leaving office in 1921, Governor Hugh M. Dorsey issued *A Statement . . . As to the Negro in Georgia* in which he listed 135 cases of peonage, lynching, and cruelty toward blacks that had been called to his attention during the past two years. "To me it seems," the governor concluded, "that we stand indicted as a people before the world." Though Dorsey's courageous attack on racial injustice did not result in immediate reforms, it signified a slight shift in white attitudes. During the next two decades racial violence in Georgia declined sharply over what it had been between 1890 and 1920.

A few years before Dorsey's statement a small group of people in Atlanta had begun considering ways to improve race relations. Under the leadership of Will W. Alexander, former Methodist minister and

YMCA worker, some blacks and whites organized the Commission on Interracial Cooperation in 1919. The commission added a Woman's Department in 1920, and under the leadership of Mrs. Luke Johnson of Griffin, Georgia, interracial committees were organized among women in every southern state. A conservative organization in that it accepted racial segregation, the commission worked to end lynchings and served chiefly as an educational force working to moderate harsh racial views. As the commission spread throughout the South, the Georgia chapter became one of the strongest. In 1923 it secured twenty-two indictments against alleged lynchers and four convictions; during the previous thirty-seven years there had been only one such indictment in Georgia. Though frequently cautious and shy, the commission took a stand at times during the 1920s and 1930s against racial injustice when no other agency would. In 1944 the Southern Regional Council, an organization that eventually worked for the abolition of racial segregation and disfranchisement, replaced the Commission on Interracial Cooperation.

Blacks were not the only victims of bias and prejudice, for between 1910 and 1930 currents of anti-Catholicism and anti-Semitism ran strong in Georgia. Tom Watson, the former Populist leader, became a major spokesman for both causes. In 1908 he initiated his attack upon the hierarchy of the Catholic church in an article that he wrote for his own publication, *Tom Watson's Magazine*. Why he launched that crusade is not clear. Earlier he had urged Catholics to support the Populist cause and had even sent his daughter to a Catholic school in Washington, Georgia. He may well have come to believe that the Catholic church posed a threat to the nation, or he may have been looking for an emotional cause that could strengthen him politically. He certainly hit upon a live issue that evoked much favorable response from his readers; for the next nine years, until the government banned his publication from the mail during World War I, he maintained a steady crusade against the Catholic church. Watson's attacks helped to generate a strong anti-Catholic movement throughout the state as many weekly newspapers supported the cause.

The movement manifested itself in state politics in 1915, when the General Assembly passed an act empowering grand juries to inspect convents to determine if any of the occupants were being held against their wills. If the jurors found people imprisoned, they were to liberate them and have the guilty parties prosecuted. The passage of that act convinced some Catholic laymen that the time had come to fight back, and they organized the Catholic Laymen's Association for the purpose of refuting attacks on the church. Soon it took the offensive, answering the charges made by Watson and other anti-Catholic spokesmen. Through pamphlets, speeches, and letters to newspapers it presented the Catholic side. The campaign proved highly effective and after 1925 overt anti-Catholic sentiment largely died out in Georgia.

The most serious manifestation of anti-Semitism arose in response to the brutal murder in 1913 of Mary Phagan, a fourteen-year-old girl employed by an Atlanta pencil factory. Authorities immediately arrested the factory superintendent, Leo Frank, a Jew and a northerner. Though the case against Frank rested on highly circumstantial evidence, strong public opinion prevailed against him. Atlanta newspapers sensationalized the case, and the crowds present during the trial openly favored Frank's conviction. After the jury declared Frank guilty, the court sentenced him to hang. Higher courts, including the United States Supreme Court, reviewed the case, but each tribunal upheld the conviction on the ground that it had been legally obtained. Still many people, including over ten thousand Georgians who petitioned the governor, believed Frank innocent of the murder. A national movement arose to save him.

Shortly before leaving office in June 1915, Governor John M. Slaton carefully reviewed the evidence in the case, concluded there was reasonable doubt of Frank's guilt, and commuted his sentence to life imprisonment. Public reaction was so adverse to the governor's decision that the following night a crowd of over five thousand marched on his home. Sixteen militiamen sustained injuries in protecting Slaton from the mob. During the next two months Tom Watson continually called for Frank's life. On the night of 16 August 1915 twenty-five armed men, calling themselves the Knights of Mary Phagan, seized Leo Frank from the state prison, drove seventy-five miles across the state to Mary Phagan's home town of Marietta, and hanged him.

Some of the phobias against Catholics, Jews, and Negroes found an outlet in the second Ku Klux Klan, which had its national headquarters in Atlanta. On Thanksgiving night in 1915, about three months after the lynching of Leo Frank, William Joseph Simmons, accompanied by some of the Knights of Mary Phagan, climbed to the top of Stone Mountain and founded the hooded order. Simmons, a longtime promoter of fraternal societies, intended for the Klan to be a secret society that defended 100 percent Americanism. By limiting membership to native-born, white Protestants, the Klan appealed to those attracted by anti-Catholic, anti-Semitic, and anti-Negro campaigns. Klan members on the Fulton County Board of Education tried unsuccessfully to remove teachers and principals who were Catholics. While the Klan did foster hostility against minorities, it gave far more attention to upholding traditional moral values that it believed endangered: hard work, sobriety, and marital fidelity. In Macon, for instance, Klansmen seized and flogged people it accused of adultery, bootlegging, drunkenness, and prostitution. In Georgia most victims of Klan violence were whites suspected of breaking the moral code.

Until 1920 the Klan remained small with a state membership of less than two thousand. Then Simmons joined forces with Edward Young Clarke and Elizabeth Tyler, both skilled in the techniques of fund-raising and advertising. Under their direction the Klan quickly grew into a powerful organization and during the next five years acquired a national membership reported at 5 million. In Georgia the Klan drew members from a wide variety of sources, including salesmen, shopkeepers, city clerks, lawyers, physicians, judges, ministers, and farmers. It became a powerful force in state politics, including among its members and sympathizers a governor, a commissioner of agriculture, and a chief justice of the Georgia Supreme Court. It also had many supporters in the General Assembly and in local governments.

From the outset reports circulated that the Klan engaged in violence to achieve its ends, but it took some time before public opinion mounted against the order. Much of the credit for awakening the public to the dangers of the Klan belonged to a small group of Georgia journalists, one of the most important being Julian Harris, the son of Joel Chandler Harris. Through the columns of his Columbus *Enquirer-Sun,* Harris took up the fight against the Klan two years before another state paper dared to tackle the issue. Harris reported Klan violence and printed the names of public officials who belonged to the secret order. Harris first reported the story in Georgia that Governor Clifford Walker had addressed a national Klan meeting in Kansas City. Despite attempts to intimidate him and to sabotage his press, Harris persisted in his unremitting campaign against the Klan. By the mid-twenties other newspapers had begun to attack the hooded order, and the public became concerned over the high rate of Klan violence. By that time, moreover, anti-Semitism and anti-Catholicism had largely ceased to have appeal in Georgia. As more and more prominent individuals spoke out against the secret society and as the organization began suffering from internal dissent, Klan membership in Georgia declined rapidly between 1925 and 1930, falling from a high of 156,000 to 1,400.

The onslaught of the depression in 1929 gave rise to several devel-

opments that threatened civil liberties in Atlanta. In the summer of
1930 the Blackshirts, an organization consisting of unemployed whites,
former Klansmen, and restless youths, arose in Atlanta for the purpose
of driving Negroes from the city and thereby creating jobs for whites.
For a short while the Blackshirts inflicted violence on some Negroes.
Soon, however, civic leaders, ministers, and newspaper editors began
speaking out against the Blackshirts, and the public became alarmed
over their activities. After the city refused to grant the group a charter
and after one of its leaders was convicted of passing a fraudulent
check, the Blackshirts ceased to exist.

Atlanta was also the site of the Angelo Herndon case. In the summer
of 1932 police arrested Herndon, a young black communist, for allegedly having distributed leaflets calling for a rally of the unemployed.
Though the rally had resulted in a peaceful demonstration, city officials became concerned during the Depression over the activities of
labor organizers and spokesmen for radical causes working among the
unemployed. A grand jury indicted Herndon for having violated an
insurrection law passed in 1866. Herndon was declared guilty at his
trial, but eventually the United States Supreme Court ruled in 1937
that the Georgia insurrection law unduly interfered with freedom of
speech and assembly and furnished no reasonable standard of guilt.
That decision represented a significant advance in the cause of free
speech and civil liberties in Georgia, for at that time Atlanta officials
had indicted a number of other people for violating the insurrection
law.

In the years between 1890 and 1940 justice did not always prevail,
but always some struggled to improve conditions. Catholic laymen
openly met attacks upon their religion and within a short time they
helped to reverse the tide of anti-Catholicism. Newspaper editors and
civic leaders fought successfully against the Ku Klux Klan and the
Blackshirts. In instances such as the Angelo Herndon case the federal
courts guarded the rights of individual citizens. Many blacks also protested the injustices from which they suffered, but prior to World War
II they did not succeed in overcoming their second-class citizenship.

XX

Populism and Progressivism
1890–1920

Between 1890 and 1940 the Democratic party dominated the political system prevailing in Georgia. Since Democrats automatically won election, the important contests came earlier between rival candidates for the party's nominations. On the local level some counties had used primaries to select nominees since the 1870s, while other counties had used conventions. Until 1898 candidates for state office were chosen at state conventions, composed largely of county political leaders. After that, the party selected nominees in primary elections.

With both conventions and primaries, the county-unit system played an important role in determining which candidates won Democratic nomination. Under that system a county had two unit votes for each representative in the lower house of the legislature. The constitution of 1877 provided that the 6 most populous counties in the lower house had three representatives each, the next 26 two each, and the remaining 105 one each. The creation of new counties after 1877 did not alter this pattern of representation, and power remained securely in the hands of the rural counties. The system greatly reduced the importance of minority votes, because the candidate who won the popular vote of a county got all of that county's unit votes. The county-unit system prevailed as a party custom from 1876 until 1917, when the Neil Primary Act gave it full legal sanction.

Between Reconstruction and World War II Georgia Democrats received their most serious challenge during the Populist uprising of the 1890s. The roots of that revolt lay in the economic and political conditions that farmers confronted in the late nineteenth century. Since the Civil War, Georgia farmers had experienced problems resulting from rising costs, falling cotton prices, poor credit facilities, high railroad rates, an inadequate money supply, mortgage foreclosures, and a rising rate of tenancy. As neither the federal nor state governments came forward with programs to alleviate their problems, many farmers eventually decided that they had to unite to help themselves.

An important attempt to ease agrarian burdens began in 1887, when the Farmers' Alliance arrived in Georgia, offering farmers the benefits of a fraternal lodge as well as a program of economic self-help through cooperative enterprises. During the next three years the Alliance set up local cooperative stores and a state exchange through which members could buy farm supplies at reduced prices. In 1889 Georgia Alliancemen supported a regional boycott against a jute cartel that controlled the supply of bagging used to cover cotton bales. The success of that boycott helped to swell the ranks of the Georgia Alliance so that by 1890 it had over two thousand lodges and more than 100,000 members. The Alliance cannot be understood only in terms of its programs. By combining the features of a fraternal society, a cooperative, and an evangelical church it became a deeply emotional force among rural people hoping for a better life.

As economic conditions worsened by 1890, the Alliance turned increasingly to political reforms, some of the more important being the free and unlimited coinage of silver, economy in government, prohibition of alien ownership of lands, abolition of the convict lease system, and government ownership of railroads, telegraphs, and telephones. In rural schoolhouses and country churches Alliance spokesmen urged members to vote in the coming elections only for Democratic candidates who promised to support Alliance reforms. In the ensuing elections it appeared that the Alliance had won a resounding victory. Not only did William J. Northen, an Alliance member, win the governorship without opposition, but Alliance candidates won six of Georgia's ten congressional seats and such a majority in both houses of the General Assembly that it came to be called "the Farmers' Legislature."

The victory proved deceptive, because some men won office by claiming to be the farmers' friends without actually being committed to Alliance reforms. This soon became apparent when the legislators selected one of the "Bourbon Triumvirate," John B. Gordon, as United States senator even though he openly opposed some of the Alliance programs. The legislators then proceeded to enact moderate reforms by broadening the authority of the state railroad commission to include telegraph and express companies, limiting the maximum working hours of railroad employees to twelve a day, extending the state's fertilizer inspection system, and establishing a state agricultural and mechanical college for Negroes. But those measures fell short of fulfilling the hopes of many hard-pressed farmers who had expected more from "the Farmers' Legislature." In addition, the assemblymen went against Alliance principles by strengthening the crop lien system, increasing the number of convicts leased, and raising taxes.

The failure of the Alliance legislature to enact stronger reforms contributed to the organization's demise. The cooperative programs, moreover, had not offset the problems resulting from low cotton prices and the prevailing credit system. As a result, the Alliance declined rapidly and by the fall of 1891 the order had lost most of its strength. Yet the Alliance had increased awareness among farmers of their common problems and had presented a set of reforms that many believed could help them. Since the Democrats had failed to enact those reforms, some Alliancemen concluded that they could achieve them only through a third party.

By now western farmers had already organized the People's party and within a short time it began to take root in Georgia. The state's most important Populist leader was a first-term congressman, Thomas E. Watson, a young man who rejected the New South creed of Henry Grady and instead believed in an agrarian order for the South. He liked farmers and felt at home among them. His success as a criminal lawyer resulted in no small part from his understanding of rural juries and his ability to speak their idiom. Once, while defending a client accused of stealing a hog, he said of the accuser, "I presume from what he says, that he could with all ease tell you the sex of a hog, male or female, merely by smelling of the gravy." By the 1880s Watson realized how the social and political status of farmers had declined since the days of his own childhood; he believed power and prestige now rested with industrialists and financiers.

Although Watson never joined the Alliance, he supported its platform in 1890 when he ran successfully for Congress. Once in office he remained loyal to Alliance principles and actively worked for every plank in the order's platform. In 1891 it appeared that the Democrats in the House would elect Charles F. Crisp, a Georgian, as speaker. Since that would bring great prestige to the state, Georgia congressmen came under considerable pressure to vote for Crisp, a conservative representative who opposed most Alliance reforms. Watson, alone among Georgia congressmen, refused to support Crisp. Instead he accepted the nomination of the People's party for the speakership. Newspapers throughout the state condemned Watson for abandoning the Democratic party; but, because he championed the farmer's interest, he became an inspiring leader for thousands of country people.

During the next six months many followed Watson's lead, and in July 1892 the Georgia Populists held a state convention at which they nominated W. L. Peek, a "real dirt farmer," for the governorship and also named candidates to run for some congressional and legisla-

Thomas E. Watson
Georgia Department of Archives and History

tive posts. They also endorsed the party's national platform, which in addition to reiterating most of the Alliance programs, called for a graduated income tax, low-interest loans for farmers, an eight-hour day for labor, and the direct election of senators.

While some former Alliancemen became Populists, others did not. Country people, especially small landowners who felt keenly the pressure of the crop lien system and low cotton prices, made up the rank and file of the Georgia People's party. Most townspeople, including county seat residents, remained Democrats and tended to look upon the Populists with disdain. A surprising number of large landowners joined the new party. Even though some landless tenants supported the Populists, the movement offered them little except the general hope for improved economic conditions. In the main, therefore, Populism represented a movement of small landowners, who did not strive to overthrow the prevailing political and economic system but wanted to ease some of the major problems that they had long experienced. The movement divided many rural neighborhoods, as within families some members became Populists and others remained Democrats.

With the Democrats facing their first major challenge in two decades, the election of 1892 became an exciting one that sometimes resulted in open violence. Such strong emotions erupted primarily because the

Populists seemed to threaten the prevailing social and economic views that Democratic leaders had long upheld. In addition, there were many potential black voters, and both Populists and Democrats fought for their support. With whites then divided between two parties, blacks could possibly determine the outcome of the elections. For that reason, the Democrats accused the Populists of endangering white supremacy.

Some insight can be gained into the relation between white Populists and black voters by observing Tom Watson's 1892 congressional campaign. Watson asked blacks to vote for him on the basis of common interest. The reforms advocated by the People's party could ease the economic burdens of black farmers as well as white farmers. Watson also condemned lynching, at the time a major problem in Georgia, and declared that black and white people should be allowed to vote freely and have their votes counted honestly. Watson did not, however, advocate social equality between blacks and whites. Instead, he asked the two groups to join forces to solve common economic and political problems, but he expected blacks and whites to go their separate ways in attending schools, churches, and social functions.

Some blacks accepted Watson's appeal. H. S. Doyle, a Negro minister, made sixty-three speeches for Watson in the Tenth Congressional District, and in return for his work received threats from the Democrats. Once, near the end of the campaign, he fled to Watson for protection. Watson sent riders into the surrounding countryside to ask for help. In response, over two thousand Populists gathered at Watson's home and stood guard for two days and nights. Other white Populists followed Watson's lead in appealing to black voters.

Georgia Democrats had experienced political coalitions between black voters and white independents in the Bourbon era, but they viewed the threat of the 1890s far more seriously because Populism represented a larger and stronger movement. The Democrats responded to the Populist challenge by accusing them of being in secret alliance with the Republicans and of working to bring blacks into political power. Many Democratic spokesmen engaged in bitter slander, charging that the Populists threatened Georgia with "anarchy and communism." The Democratic campaign became so intense that it sometimes led to Populists' "being turned out of churches, driven from their homes, and refused credit" at stores.

While condemning the Populists for endangering white supremacy, many Democrats did exactly what they accused the Populists of doing. Party leaders such as Governor Northen, who like many former Alliancemen had remained a loyal Democrat, spoke to black gatherings and urged them to vote the Democratic ticket. The Democrats employed other methods to control black voters, especially in the Tenth Congressional District where Tom Watson exerted such great influence. Since Watson was the most charismatic of Populist leaders, the Democrats hoped that his defeat would contribute to the collapse of the entire Populist movement in Georgia. In some places on the night before elections Democrats sponsored revelries for Negro plantation hands at which they served barbecue, whiskey, and beer by the barrel; the following day Democrats marched blacks to the polls in squads and had them vote repeatedly. In Augusta, a Democratic stronghold, the number of votes cast almost doubled the number of registered voters. Occasionally the Democrats resorted to physical violence and possibly killed as many as fifteen black people during the election of 1892.

It would be a mistake to attribute Democratic victories solely to the corrupt practices in which they engaged. Most blacks who voted, voted Democratic. Under Governor Northen's administration the Democrats had established a state college for Negroes, and the governor himself had consistently denounced lynching and called for penal reforms. If Northen and his fellow Democrats remained in office, black people could expect a continuation of these policies. They could not be so sure about the Populists. Despite the promises of third-party leaders, blacks knew that the Populists had in their ranks many poor whites whom they suspected of harboring intense anti-Negro sentiments.

Competing against the entrenched Democratic party and unable to win the majority of black votes, most Populists—including Tom Watson—went down to defeat in 1892. Only fifteen Populists won seats in the General Assembly. The new party's prospects remained slim until the following year, when a serious economic depression hit the nation. As the depression deepened, Populist strength grew. In the state elections the following year the Populists posed a more serious threat to the Democrats than they had in 1892. Tom Watson again ran for Congress. For governor, the party nominated James K. Hines, a Harvard-educated lawyer, former solicitor general, and superior court judge, who had long supported the principles of the Alliance and the People's party. The Democrats rallied behind the leadership of their gubernatorial nominee W. Y. Atkinson, former speaker of the state House of Representatives.

The tactics employed by both parties closely resembled those used two years earlier. This time the depression drove more white voters to

the Populist side. The third party also won more black voters, many
of whom found the highly respectable Hines an attractive candidate.
At the time blacks did not have as clear a notion of Atkinson's stand
on race relations as they had had with Governor Northen. In the 1894
elections intimidation and fraud again played a decisive role in ac-
counting for Tom Watson's defeat. In other parts of the state the
People's party made substantial gains. Even though Atkinson defeated
Hines, the Populists captured 44.5 percent of the vote and carried 46
of the state's 137 counties. All told, the Populists elected five state
senators and forty-seven representatives.

The gains that the Georgia Populists made in 1894 did not last
long. During the next two years developments inside and outside the
state undermined the entire Populist movement. For one thing, Georgia Democrats had many shrewd leaders who worked hard to offset the
Populist threat. Though they never put forth as strong a reform program as the Populists called for, the Democrats did present themselves
as the farmer's friends and enacted laws advocated by small farmers.
Under Governor Northen in 1892 the Democrats in the General Assembly passed a law that provided for stricter regulation of railroads
and a law that established stiff penalties for those convicted of tamper-
ing with election returns. In 1895, after the Populist challenge had
become more serious, Democratic legislators enacted measures to make
supreme court judgeships elective offices, to protect farmers in the
sale of their produce against the activities of unscrupulous middlemen,
and to safeguard consumers against those who tried to reduce competition in the production or sale of manufactured goods. More importantly, between the summer of 1895 and 1896 the Georgia Democratic
party shifted its position on the highly emotional money question and
endorsed the free and unlimited coinage of silver. By supporting free
silver, the Democrats managed to adopt a more conciliatory attitude
toward the Populists and thereby lured some of them back into the
Democratic party.

On the national level, too, those believing that the free and unlimited coinage of silver could end the depression and restore prosperity
won control of the Democratic party by 1896. By seizing that issue,
the Democrats stole the most attractive plank in the Populist platform.
In addition, the Democrats selected William Jennings Bryan, a man
of immense popularity throughout rural America, as their presidential
nominee. Believing Bryan to be their best hope, the Populists also
nominated him for the presidency. They could not, however, accept
the Democratic vice presidential nominee, Arthur Sewall, a banker.

Instead they nominated Tom Watson for that office. Watson's nomination did not offset the fact that by supporting the Democratic presidential nominee, the Populists abdicated their role as a third party.

In the state elections, the Georgia Populists adopted a platform similar to those of the past, the major difference being they now endorsed prohibition. For the governorship they nominated Seaborn Wright, a lawyer from Rome who had long supported the prohibition cause. The Democrats renominated Governor Atkinson and accepted the Populist challenge by supporting local option in place of statewide prohibition. This campaign closely resembled the two previous ones, the major difference being an attempt by some Populist leaders to win more support among their fellow whites. While still defending the right of blacks to vote and deploring lynchings, Populist spokesmen occasionally attacked such national black leaders as Fredrick Douglass and Booker T. Washington.

Those attacks cost the Populists the black votes they had won two years earlier. Blacks either abstained from voting or supported Democratic candidates running for state offices. At the same time, many whites who were strongly attracted to Bryan and free silver simply voted the straight Democratic ticket. As a result of these developments, the Populists lost fifteen counties that they had won in 1894. Their representation in the General Assembly dropped from fifty-three to twenty-nine. The party never regained its lost strength. In the future, especially after economic prosperity began returning in 1897, more and more members abandoned the People's party; some stopped voting, others drifted into the Republican and Democratic parties.

Despite the excitement and turbulence of the Populist era, the movement achieved little in Georgia. Throughout the 1890s government remained in the hands of conservative Democrats who refused to enact the reforms that the Populists espoused. Black people gained little from the political struggles of that decade. While never considering blacks as social equals, white Populists did offer them the hope of improving their economic lot and guarding their right to vote. By branding the Populists as traitors to white supremacy, the Democrats used the race issue to keep their own party members in line and to divide white Populists. Thus the Populist attempt to build an interracial coalition on the basis of common economic problems failed in no small part because conservative Democrats aroused racial tensions to preserve their political power. In response to the Democrats' attacks, the Populists increasingly appealed to antiblack sentiment by strongly denouncing anything that hinted at social equality between blacks and whites. The political climate of the Populist era heightened racial tension and helped prepare the way for black disfranchisement in the next decade. The Populist demise also ended a serious attempt to develop a viable two-party system. In its wake Georgia politics returned for many years to the confines of the Democratic party.

Following the demise of Populism, Georgia politics entered a quiet, colorless period that lasted for almost a decade. After Governor Atkinson completed his second term in 1898, he was succeeded by Allen D. Candler, a former legislator, congressman, and Georgia secretary of state. Candler served two terms as did his successor, Joseph M. Terrell. During Terrell's administration, some legislators and newspaper editors, especially those from cities and larger towns, began to call for better public schools, child labor laws, stricter regulation of railroads, and abolition of the convict lease system. Governor Terrell sympathized with some of those reforms, but he never gave them dynamic support by taking a program to the people and fighting for it. As a result, until 1906 reform sentiment in Georgia remained loose, disconnected, and leaderless.

Throughout the nation during the first two decades of the twentieth century, so many reforms developed that historians have labeled the period the Progressive Era. In Georgia, as in other states, reformers were active on diverse fronts but they never united their efforts in a single movement. Rebecca Felton worked in behalf of a number of causes, including women's suffrage; Bishop Warren A. Candler supported educational reforms; and Hoke Smith devoted much attention to railroad regulation. Though the Georgia progressives supported some of the same reforms as had the Populists who preceded them, the two groups differed greatly. Whereas the Populists had represented the interests of small farmers, the progressives worked chiefly in behalf of businessmen, professional groups, and more prosperous farmers. The progressives also lacked the radicalism that had characterized the Populists, for they espoused more moderate reforms. Finally, the Populists had tried to unite black and white voters in order to solve common economic problems, but many progressives wanted to end completely black voting and officeholding.

The cities of Atlanta and Augusta offer good examples of Georgia progressivism. In both, reform leaders strove to make their cities more prosperous, efficient, and livable. Wanting their cities run like model business corporations, they endorsed programs that they hoped would improve business conditions: paving streets, building sewer lines, improving fire and police protection, and beautifying the cities with parks and plazas. They also tried to eliminate political corruption and to curb vice. Middle- and upper-class whites directed these reforms largely in accord with their own interests; only indirectly did their programs affect those who worked in cotton mills, lumber mills, and as domestic servants. In fact, the progressive forces in Augusta tried to achieve better government by having business leaders dominate the organization of the local Democratic party, thus eliminating as far as possible the political influence of blacks and poor whites.

On the state level the Democratic primary of 1906 helped to unify reform sentiment. In 1905 Clark Howell, editor of the *Atlanta Constitution*, announced his candidacy for governor. He praised the Terrell administration and promised to maintain prosperity in Georgia by giving a "square deal" to capital. To many, he appeared as a logical successor to Terrell. Soon Hoke Smith, with the backing of Tom Watson, emerged as the gubernatorial candidate of the reform forces. Watson, who still commanded the loyalty of many former Populists, had abandoned his earlier view of uniting black and white farmers in a common political program and now held that whites could never divide politically unless they first disfranchised blacks. This view could greatly enhance Watson's own political power, because his ex-Populist followers could become the balance of power within the Democratic party. Accordingly, in 1905 Watson collaborated with Thomas Hardwick, a state legislator, and devised a plan calling for black disfranchisement and railroad reform. After Hoke Smith embraced that platform, Watson and Hardwick supported him.

In some ways it was surprising that Watson and his followers should rally behind Hoke Smith, a man who earlier had represented the antithesis of Populism. A highly successful lawyer and secretary of the interior during President Grover Cleveland's second administration, Smith embodied in his career many of the ideals of the New South creed. He had long been associated with the state's major urban center, Atlanta, rather than with the agrarian interests Watson represented. By the early 1900s, however, he had begun to identify with the newly developing reform forces and had become a leading spokesman for improved public schools and stricter railroad regulation.

Smith began his gubernatorial campaign in the summer of 1905, and during the next thirteen months he traveled throughout the state calling for a stronger railroad commission, a law to regulate lobbying, better public schools, and the disfranchisement of black voters. By combining appeals for reform with scathing anti-Negro statements, he won a decisive victory over Clark Howell in the Democratic primary of 1906.

In many ways Hoke Smith's administration served as a catalyst for reform, including some that he had not previously advocated. Though not an issue in the preceding campaign, prohibition became the first reform that surged to the front. By 1907, 125 of the state's 145 counties had adopted local-option laws prohibiting the sale of alcoholic beverages. A serious race riot that occurred in Atlanta shortly after Smith's primary victory in 1906, which some erroneously attributed to the consumption of whiskey by blacks, gave new strength to those calling for a statewide prohibition law. Smith cooperated with the powerful prohibition forces, led by the Women's Christian Temperance Union and the Anti-Saloon League, and in 1907 a prohibition law passed with little opposition. The law had many weaknesses, however, and during the following decade the General Assembly enacted additional statutes until by 1917 Georgia had one of the most rigid prohibition laws in the nation. But enforcement of prohibition proved to be very difficult, and bootlegging became a major problem for Georgia law officers.

Another issue not discussed in the 1906 campaign was penal reform. In the summer of 1908 some of the state's leading newspapers along with farm and labor groups and religious leaders launched an intense campaign against the convict lease system. In response to that outcry, the General Assembly established a system under which county and state authorities employed convicts on public roads. Private interests could no longer exploit state convicts.

Governor Smith enjoyed moderate success in securing measures for which he had campaigned. Legislation was passed giving the railroad commission more power to enforce its rulings and expanding its jurisdiction to include gas lines, electric power companies, and street railways. But even with its increased authority, the commission failed to obtain lower freight rates. The governor did not persuade the General Assembly to pass legislation forbidding railroads to grant free passes to public officials, nor did he convince the legislators to impose higher taxes on railroads operating in the state. The lawmakers did respond to Smith's appeals for a law requiring candidates to disclose their campaign expenses and prohibiting corporations from making campaign contributions. Smith also obtained a 30 percent increase in appropriations for public schools. Finally, he fulfilled his major campaign promise by leading the fight for a constitutional amendment that disfranchised black voters.

Reform sentiment declined after Smith's first administration and never regained its former strength. In 1908 Joseph Mackey Brown, son of former governor Joseph E. Brown and a spokesman for conservative business interests, defeated Smith for the governorship. His administration did not support reform. Hoke Smith won the governorship again in 1910, but he did not hold the office a year before being elected to a vacancy in the United States Senate. After Smith left for the Senate in 1911, reform forces in Georgia no longer had a strong leader around whom to rally. The men who held the governorship during the next decade—Joseph Mackey Brown, John M. Slaton, Nathaniel E. Harris, and Hugh M. Dorsey—did not espouse the general cause of reform.

Even without strong leadership, reformers took important steps after 1910 to improve Georgia's public educational system. Laws and constitutional amendments were passed that raised the standards for teacher certification, increased the powers of the state board of education, provided for the establishment of public high schools, and increased the financial support for public schools. But other attempts at reform enjoyed little success during that decade. Child labor constituted a serious problem, one closely tied to the textile mills where children, some less than ten years old, received wages of fifty cents in return for working twelve hours a day. In 1914 the General Assembly passed a child labor law, but it proved so weak and so poorly enforced that in 1920 Georgia led the nation in children employed between the ages of ten and fifteen. In 1916 the legislature passed a compulsory school attendance law, but it only required students between the ages of eight and fourteen to go to school for a total of twelve weeks a year. It also allowed local school boards to make any exceptions they saw fit, and consequently many potential students, especially black children, were not affected by the law.

The cause of women fared a little better than that of children. Despite the work of such leaders as Rebecca Latimer Felton and Frances Smith Whiteside, most Georgians—male and female—displayed little interest in women's suffrage. In 1919 Georgia became the first state to reject the Nineteenth Amendment, which gave the women the right to vote. Later that year, however, enough states did ratify the amendment, and in 1920 white women in Georgia began voting for the first time. The winning of the suffrage encouraged women to became more active in public life. In the 1920s they formed organizations, such as the

Child labor in Georgia, 1913

University of Georgia Libraries

League of Women Voters, which sponsored programs ranging from instruction in ballot marking to detailed studies of state and local governments.

Actually women had assumed more active roles in public life well before they secured the vote. By the late nineteenth century middle-class women had more time to themselves because of smaller families, better health care, canned food, and ready-made clothes. Those developments encouraged women to assume new roles outside the home as teachers, journalists, librarians, nurses, cashiers, and saleswomen. Many also became active in church missionary organizations, temperance societies, and club work; as a result they became increasingly concerned with a wide range of social problems and some actively worked in behalf of reforms. In Augusta Mary DeBardelaben organized the Civic Improvement League that provided a settlement house program, Sunday school, and kindergarten for blacks. Celeste Parrish contributed to improved public education by establishing a teacher-training program, based on the progressive education methods of John Dewey, at the State Normal School. The Methodist Missionary Council urged women to work for the abolition of child labor, reduction of illiteracy, an end to the convict lease system, and prison reform. In 1921 a combination of women's groups secured the enactment of a children's code, a child-placement bill, and a training school bill. They tried but failed to persuade the legislature to ratify a national child labor amendment and to limit the hours that women worked in cotton mills.

The state's revenue system partly accounted for Georgia's lag in providing better social services and public facilities. At the time, Georgia derived most of its revenue from an ad valorem tax assessed on land at a uniform rate regardless of how the land was used. Intangible property, including stocks and bonds, largely escaped taxation. Such a tax system did not supply adequate revenue to enable the state to provide its people with better schools, public health facilities, and roads. Reforms, such as a low inheritance tax, enacted in 1913, did not relieve the situation; major changes in the tax system did not come until later.

During the Progressive Era the federal government helped to meet the rising demand for better roads that resulted from the increased use of automobiles. In 1916 states could obtain federal funds on a matching basis to assist in the building of roads, and Georgia created a state highway commission to help coordinate state and federal activities. The destruction of the convict lease system, moreover, supplied a source of cheap labor for work on roads. By 1920 the state had begun building a modern highway system.

The Progressive Era in Georgia can be viewed as an attempt to modernize the state. Better schools could enable people to raise their standard of living. The regulation of railroads—most of which were owned by out-of-state interests—could help local merchants, shippers, and farmers. Good roads served the interests of industrialists, road builders, merchants, farmers, and railroads. Such measures primarily benefited middle- and upper-class white people. The Georgia progressives did not attempt directly to improve the lot of tenant farmers and industrial laborers, as the weak child labor law of 1914 so well illustrated. In many ways the Georgia progressives pursued the goals of Henry Grady's New South creed. Grady had called for greater industrialization as the best means to bring the South into line with the more affluent parts of the country and to that the progressives added the means of good schools and good roads.

XXI

The 1920s and the New Deal

During the decade following the end of World War I, state officials in Georgia continued to work for improved highways and better public schools, thereby making the transition from the Progressive Era to the 1920s almost unnoticeable. The most important changes resulted from the retirement of Hoke Smith and the death of Tom Watson early in that decade. During the course of the 1920s, a new set of leaders emerged who eventually played major roles in state politics: Walter F. George, Richard B. Russell, Eugene Talmadge, and Eurith D. Rivers.

In the Democratic primaries of 1920 Thomas W. Hardwick and Thomas E. Watson, both of whom had earlier led the movement to disfranchise black voters, made political comebacks. Hardwick captured the governorship, and Watson defeated Hoke Smith for a United States Senate seat. As governor, Hardwick worked for more constructive programs than any chief executive since Hoke Smith. To reduce corruption in primary elections, he secured legislation providing for secret ballots and private voting booths. To improve public education, he urged that there be at least one consolidated high school in each county. Convinced that Georgia government had become too large and cumbersome, he called for sweeping reorganization of the state administration, including the abolition of some agencies and the consolidation of others. The legislators did not respond to his appeal. He also failed to secure a state income tax as well as legislation to insure more humane treatment of prisoners.

Hardwick's political demise came as a result of his fight with the Ku Klux Klan. By the early 1920s, the Klan had become so powerful in Georgia that few public officials dared speak out against it, despite the widespread belief that the secret order frequently perpetrated terrorism. Among major Georgia politicians, Hardwick was the first to denounce Klan violence. If Klansmen did not voluntarily unmask, he promised to obtain legislation forbidding them to wear masks. In response to Hardwick's activities, Klansmen actively worked during the 1922 gubernatorial primary for the candidacy of Clifford Walker. Running on a platform opposing a state income tax and calling for rigid economy in governmental spending, Walker won the election.

Shortly after the Democratic primary of 1922, Tom Watson died. Governor Hardwick appointed Rebecca Latimer Felton, eighty-seven years old, to fill the vacancy temporarily. She held office for only a day but earned the distinction of becoming the first woman to serve in the United States Senate. In a special election to fulfill the remainder of Watson's unexpired term, Hardwick ran against Walter F. George, a state supreme court judge. Still confronted by Klan opposition, Hardwick suffered another defeat.

Clifford Walker served two terms as governor; Lamartine Hardman, a physician and former legislator, succeeded him in 1926 and proceeded to serve two terms. Unlike Walker, Hardman did not sympathize with the Klan, but they pursued similar policies during their administrations. Both favored rigid governmental economy and worked against large-scale public spending. Both tried to remove John N. Holder as chairman of the state highway department. By the 1920s that agency had become one of the most powerful sources of patronage in state government, and the governors fought for control of it. Holder, who enjoyed considerable power in the General Assembly, successfully rebuffed the attempts to oust him. Partly because of the conflict between Holder and the chief executives, highway construction advanced slowly in Georgia during the 1920s.

In 1930 Richard B. Russell, the "boy wonder" of Georgia politics, ran for governor against Holder and Eurith D. Rivers, a legislator. Son of the chief justice of the Georgia Supreme Court, Russell had won a seat in the state House of Representatives in 1920 at the age of twenty-three and had gone on to serve five terms, the last two as speaker. He based his gubernatorial campaign upon a call for reorganization of state government as a means of achieving greater efficiency and economy. Russell won in 1930 and the next year fulfilled his campaign promise. The Reorganization Act of 1931 reduced nearly one hundred agencies in the executive branch to nineteen, thereby helping to consolidate and simplify administrative procedures. In a further effort to improve the operation of state government, the General Assembly passed the Budget Act of 1931, which gave the governor more control over the expenditure of state funds. This measure, along with the Reorganization Act, concentrated more power in the hands of the governor.

During the Russell administration Georgians, like other Americans, suffered from the Great Depression that began in 1929. The severity of the Depression eventually led to a whole series of federal programs designed to bring relief and recovery, most of which began after Franklin D. Roosevelt won the presidency of 1932. Since many of the new federal programs would require the cooperation of state governments, the Georgia elections of 1932 were critical. Governor Russell ran for the United States Senate against Congressman Charles R. Crisp, a veteran of twenty years in Congress and chairman of the powerful Ways and Means Committee. In a hard-fought contest, the young governor again demonstrated his political adroitness by defeating Crisp.

Ten candidates entered the gubernatorial contest to replace Russell, and seven remained in the fight until the end. Among the better-known candidates were Thomas W. Hardwick and John N. Holder, but the strongest contender was the commissioner of agriculture, Eugene Talmadge. The descendant of a family of large landowners, Talmadge had divided his adult life between farming and practicing law. He was steeped in the ways of rural Georgia and managed to establish a rapport with country people that few politicians have ever equaled. An individualist and a hardworking man, he expounded on the values of fundamentalist religion, defended white supremacy, and projected an image of himself as a spectacular person. Let "no one doubt his strength and driving force," one observer pointed out. "When he arches his neck, spraddles his legs and starts a charge, nothing stops him. . . ." As Talmadge said of himself, he sometimes went "whole hog."

Despite his popularity with the rural people, Talmadge had little insight into the problems facing Georgia farmers. He believed that by hard work and thrift alone a person could master his own fate; he opposed programs calling for greater government spending and economic regulation. Such views, especially during the Great Depression, ignored the plight of tenant farmers as well as many landowners. In his 1932 gubernatorial campaign, Talmadge promised to establish a uniform $3 automobile tag, to abolish the ad valorem tax, and to reduce utility rates. He won the election largely on the basis of his personality and ability to communicate with the voters.

In 1933, after the legislature refused to enact the proposals that Talmadge had made in his campaign, he achieved much of his program by executive action. He decreed $3 automobile tags and reduced ad valorem taxes from 5 to 4 mills. When the Public Service Commission refused to reduce utility rates, Talmadge removed the members from office and replaced them with men who did his bidding. By his bold actions, Talmadge claimed to have helped the average Georgian. Actually he created more excitement than savings for the people. Most motorists saved $5 to $10 on their automobile tags, but large trucking firms and bus companies saved thousands of dollars each year. All property owners gained something by the reduction in ad valorem taxes, but large landowners benefited most. In addition, Talmadge's actions lowered the funds available for public schools and highways, and only the infusion of millions of dollars in federal funds after 1932 kept some schools open and highway construction advancing. Industrialists, especially textile mill owners, benefited from the utility reductions, but most rural families did not have electricity or telephones. Nevertheless, the majority of voters ignored these weaknesses in the governor's programs, because to them Talmadge remained their friend who had "kept his promises."

In light of Georgia's limited financial resources and Governor Talmadge's programs, the state government did little to help the thousands of people whom the Depression left unemployed and impoverished. During the early years of the Depression churches, organizations such as the Salvation Army, and some local governments gave limited assistance to the poor. But they did not begin to meet the needs of Depression victims. Instead, help came from the federal government. Between 1933 and 1940 the Roosevelt administration created a series of agencies that pumped millions of dollars into Georgia for a broad range of public works programs including malaria control, rural sanitation, hot lunches for school children, nursing services, art projects, and historical research. It also directed the construction of libraries, roads, schools, parks, hospitals, airports, and public housing projects. By the early 1940s the federal government had spent a total of slightly over a quarter of a billion dollars in Georgia. Its programs gave relief to many people and supplied the state with much-needed roads, buildings, and services. In addition, the relief programs brought many people into direct contact with the federal government for the first time, thereby reducing their dependence upon local leaders for direction and charity.

Considering the widespread poverty existing in Georgia and the state's long-standing attachment to the national Democratic party, it would not have been surprising for Georgia to support the New Deal. But the state government did not willingly cooperate with many of the early New Deal programs, because Governor Talmadge vehemently opposed them. As a result, many conflicts developed between the governor and federal officials, and one of the first involved the relief programs. Talmadge objected to the hourly wages paid on public works projects. He wanted the wages set in accord with prevailing community standards, or even lower, in order to force people to return to work for private employers when jobs became available. He also feared that high relief wages would undermine the supply of farm laborers. Appealing to white supremacy, he warned that under the relief programs some black people would make more than white farm laborers. On this issue the governor prevailed, for federal officials set wages for relief work and highway construction in accord with local rates; during the harvest season they curtailed their programs to insure farmers an adequate supply of cotton pickers.

Talmadge did not succeed in controlling the money spent under the relief programs. Early in his administration he appointed an old friend, Herman P. De La Perriere, a man totally inexperienced in relief work, to administer the distribution of federal funds. Besides providing relief, the governor wanted to use the federal funds to increase his own political strength, so he frequently bypassed relief administrators and dealt directly with county commissioners. As a result, early in 1934 President

A hitchhiking family, Macon County, Georgia, 1937
Farm Security Administration

Roosevelt appointed Gay Bolling Shepperson, a professional social worker from the Georgia Department of Welfare, to direct the relief programs in Georgia. A strong, determined person, she proved herself an excellent administrator. By staffing the state and county relief offices with trained social workers, she angered Talmadge, who charged that she ran the agencies with out-of-state personnel. Despite his protests, the governor never regained control over the spending of relief funds in Georgia. Once he had become fully aware of this, he charged that the New Deal was "nothing but a combination of 'wet nursin,' frenzied finance and plain damn foolishness."

During his first administration, Talmadge also spoke out against other New Deal programs, but his criticisms were not strong enough to make them the major issue in his 1934 campaign for reelection. Talmadge still maintained his great popularity with the rural people, who applauded his $3 tag policy and his bold actions. Even though he had alienated organized labor by demanding that relief wages remain low in Georgia, he had greatly increased his popularity among conservative business interests. Many businessmen recognized a valuable ally in a governor who favored low taxes and who spoke against government regulation, welfare spending, and the interests of organized labor. Judge C. C. Pittman, Talmadge's major opponent in the contest, proved no match for the governor, who easily won reelection, carrying 156 of Georgia's 159 counties.

Following his reelection, Talmadge intensified his attacks upon the New Deal and President Roosevelt. In the spring of 1935 the Georgia governor went on a national speaking tour, in which he warned of "communist" tendencies in the New Deal and urged that Roosevelt not be renominated for a second term. Early the next year he and John H. Kirby, a wealthy Texas businessman, sponsored a convention in Macon for the purpose of stimulating opposition to Roosevelt. Talmadge's fight against the national administration made little headway in Georgia, where President Roosevelt and the New Deal became increasingly popular. Talmadge's smashing victory in 1934 may have caused him to become overconfident; perhaps he either misjudged the sentiment for Roosevelt or ignored it. In any event, opposition began building against Talmadge because of his attacks upon the Roosevelt administration.

That opposition first manifested itself in the legislative session of 1935. Talmadge then vetoed measures to enable Georgia to participate in the old-age pensions and unemployment benefits of the newly created Social Security Administration. He also vetoed bills providing for free school textbooks and a seven-month school term. Altogether, at that session he vetoed seven proposed constitutional amendments, one hundred local measures, and fifty-three general bills. In response to the governor's vetoes, an opposition faction, which wanted Georgia to participate in New Deal programs, coalesced behind the leadership of House Speaker Eurith D. Rivers. In the hopes of forcing Talmadge to call a special session at which New Deal measures could be reconsidered, Rivers' faction blocked the passage of an appropriations bill. But Talmadge declared, "There ain't gonna be no special session," and proceeded to run the state government on the former appropriations law.

In Georgia's 1936 primary elections, Talmadge's opposition to the New Deal became a key issue. The governor, who could not succeed himself, entered the senatorial race against Richard Russell. At the time, he endorsed Charles D. Redwine, president of the state Senate, to succeed him as governor. Of the pro–New Deal candidates who ran against Redwine, Eurith Rivers proved the strongest. Not since the Populist era had a political campaign compared in excitement and intensity to the 1936 one. More people voted than usual, and in that contest Georgia resembled a two-party state as the electorate polarized into a Talmadge camp and a Roosevelt camp.

Richard Russell conducted a vigorous campaign in which he attacked Talmadge and drove him onto the defensive. Describing himself as a Roosevelt supporter, Russell declared that the New Deal helped the average man. Talmadge fought back hard and in the course of the campaign the two candidates attacked each other with every weapon available. The gubernatorial contest followed a similar course. Redwine intended to continue Talmadge's policies, while Rivers promised to bring the New Deal to Georgia. By cooperating with federal agencies, Rivers maintained, the state could obtain old-age pensions, improved health facilities, expanded highway construction, and rural electrification. In the end, Russell and Rivers prevailed as each captured about 60 percent of the vote.

In its 1937 session, the General Assembly responded to Rivers's leadership by passing a barrage of legislation that permitted greater state participation in New Deal programs. It seemed as though the lawmakers suddenly made a mighty effort to provide better public services than at any time in the past. First, the state created new agencies to facilitate cooperation with federal programs. The Georgia Housing Authority obtained federal funds for slum clearance and the construction of public housing projects for the poor. The Soil Conservation Service encouraged farmers to curb erosion and increase the productivity of their lands by establishing soil conservation districts; during Rivers's administration Georgia placed about two-thirds of her land in conservation districts. The Department of Natural Resources encouraged conservation and promoted the development of the state's natural resources. The State Bureau of Unemployment Compensation enabled Georgians to receive federal unemployment insurance. By making major changes within the organization of the State Highway Department, Governor Rivers complied more fully with federal standards for road construction; after that, federal highway spending increased greatly in Georgia.

The Rivers administration also moved on other fronts in its effort to improve the quality of life within the state. Not only did the General Assembly provide the funds necessary to enable Georgians to participate in the Social Security system, but it also passed legislation providing for better administration of the program. A 1937 act created a much stronger Department of Public Welfare, made it mandatory for all counties to maintain welfare departments, and set minimal standards for the local agencies. After that the aged, blind, disabled, and dependent children received better public assistance than ever before. By persuading the General Assembly to increase sharply state appropriations for public health, Rivers managed to get matching federal funds, thereby enabling Georgia to expand its public health facilities. Finally, Rivers obtained legislation that made possible the full implementation of the Rural Electrification Administration (REA), which allowed most farmers to enjoy the benefits of electricity. When he took office, Georgia only had one REA cooperative with 357 miles of line; by the end of Rivers's administration Georgia led the nation in the number of REA cooperatives.

In addition to cooperating with the New Deal, Rivers worked for educational and penal reforms. For the first time the state provided free textbooks for public school children and guaranteed every school a minimum term of seven months. Rivers succeeded in improving the treatment of state prisoners, although he made little headway in his efforts to implement rehabilitation programs.

During his first administration, Rivers achieved many of his goals and, in some ways, brought the New Deal to Georgia. But from the outset a tragic flaw undermined his efforts. In 1937 he either did not realize or failed to tell the people that his new programs would require an increase in state expenditures that could be met only by raising taxes. Had Rivers worked for tax increases at the beginning of his administration, when he enjoyed wide public support, he might have obtained them. But he did not, and soon his programs suffered from inadequate funding. Once aware of this, Rivers fought hard for more revenue, but he obtained only slight tax increases that did not come near providing adequate funding for new programs. In fact, the programs became so expensive that public opposition began mounting against them by 1938 when Rivers ran for reelection against two former Talmadge supporters, Hugh Howell and J. J. Mangham. In that year, however, a senatorial campaign overshadowed the gubernatorial contest, and it influenced the course of Rivers's second term.

In his bid for reelection in 1938, Senator Walter F. George faced Eugene Talmadge and Lawrence Camp. Talmadge, still a Roosevelt foe, attacked both George and Camp for supporting the New Deal. Camp, a former state legislator and federal district attorney, ran as a New Deal candidate. George's position proved a bit more complicated. During the previous six years he had supported most of the Roosevelt programs, but he had opposed the administration on enough key measures that he had incurred the president's ire. In 1938 Roosevelt urged voters in a number of states not to vote for Democratic members of Congress whom he considered lukewarm in supporting his programs. Aware of Roosevelt's great popularity, Senator George tried to avoid an open confrontation, thereby giving many the impression that he was straddling the fence. Consequently, early in the contest Talmadge ran strong while George's campaign languished.

After Roosevelt delivered a speech at Barnesville on 11 August 1938, things suddenly changed. With the senator sitting uncomfortably behind him on the stage, the president lashed out at him, declaring that George had not supported the Democratic party. George responded to the challenge, not by attacking Roosevelt personally, but by appealing to states' rights and white supremacy. He warned that the president had intervened in the affairs of a sovereign state and that some of his programs might encourage social equality between blacks and whites. Actually Roosevelt's speech helped George by knocking the props from under Talmadge's charge that the senator blindly supported all New Deal programs. After the Barnesville speech, George's campaign surged and he went on to win in the primary. A majority of the electorate deeply resented an outsider—even a highly popular president—coming into their state and telling them how to vote. As one tobacco farmer explained, "We Georgians are Georgian as hell!"

Rivers won reelection too, but only by a narrow margin. Though he carefully avoided taking part in the senatorial contest, he was so closely identified with the New Deal that he suffered because of the president's intervention. Rivers's weaknesses became more apparent in his second administration, which, in many ways, proved a disaster. The shortages in state revenue became more pressing, and the General Assembly refused the governor's requests for increased taxation. Rivers had to cut expenditures throughout state government. By 1939 the state school for the deaf had to close, some eighteen hundred patients had to be released from the state mental hospital at Milledgeville, and those receiving welfare checks dropped from fifty thousand to thirty thousand. Many feared that public schools would close early in 1939. Determined to prevent that from happening, Rivers used highway funds to keep the schools open, but that led to a long, drawn-out fight with the chairman of the highway department. Soon reports of corruption within the Rivers administration caused the governor to lose more public support. In 1940 Eugene Talmadge returned to office, winning the governorship on a platform promising economy in government and liquidation of the state debt.

Between the Populist uprising and World War II, the most meaningful attempts to bring social and economic reforms to Georgia occurred under the New Deal. Even then the state did not enjoy the full benefits of the federal programs. For four years Governor Talmadge fought against the New Deal; when Governor Rivers tried to implement reforms in Georgia, he could not obtain sufficient revenue to fund the new measures. The New Deal did help Georgia, though. Without the welfare and public works programs of the 1930s, the Depression years would have been much harder for many people. The New Deal also brought the state better highways, more public buildings, and improved health facilities. Rural electrification and soil conservation enhanced the quality of farm life. Yet, Georgia continued to face many serious problems. By 1940, to cite one example, Georgia ranked seventh among the twelve southeastern states in the number of people receiving old-age pensions, but she stood first in the number of applications pending. The New Deal, while definitely bringing benefits to Georgia, did not eliminate many of the social and economic problems that had long existed.

XXII

Social and Cultural Developments

The poverty and rural atmosphere prevailing in Georgia during the half-century between 1890 and 1940 caused social and cultural developments to occur more slowly than in the wealthier parts of America. But change did come. Georgia's public educational system moved toward more mature development, and health care improved significantly. As the twentieth century advanced, the rural way of living, so dominant at the outset, gradually declined as a new style of life evolved in the cities and larger towns. This transition was no doubt a factor contributing to the Southern Renascence that made southern fiction the most praised in the nation. Georgia writers contributed to this literary revival.

William Nathaniel Harben, a native of Dalton, ranked among the best local writers of his age. In works such as *Northern Georgia Sketches* (1900), *Ann Boyd* (1906), and *The Cottage of Delight* (1919) Harben described the lingering frontier tradition of the mountains as well as the commercial spirit developing in such places as Atlanta. Many of his works offer rich insight into the social history of north Georgia in the years between the Civil War and World War I.

During the early twentieth century Corra Harris became one of Georgia's most prolific writers. Her first novel, *A Circuit Rider's Wife* (1910), told the story of a young Methodist minister, William Thompson, a weak man who relied upon his wife, Mary, for strength to sustain him in his work on the rural circuit. In that novel, as in some of her other works, Mrs. Harris supported the basic beliefs of traditional Christianity and strongly criticized modernist trends as well as the leadership of the church. *Recording Angel* (1912) depicted the shortcomings of life in a small Georgia town, and *Co-Citizen* (1915) told the story of a campaign against political corruption. Her eight remaining novels dealt with marital problems.

An early death ended the promising literary career of Frances Newman of Atlanta. In 1924 the O. Henry Memorial Society presented a special award for her short story "Rachel and Her Children," which appeared in H. L. Mencken's *American Mercury*. Her two novels, *The Hardboiled Virgin* (1926) and *Dead Lovers are Faithful Lovers* (1928), received a good deal of critical acclaim, but they had little appeal among the general reading public.

During the 1930s several Georgia novelists did achieve great popularity, and two of them won Pulitzer prizes. In 1933 Caroline Miller won the award for *Lamb in His Bosom,* in which she described the lives of white yeoman farmers who practiced subsistence agriculture in an isolated community of south Georgia during the antebellum period. As a work of fiction the novel suffered from many weaknesses; its strength lay in the picture it gave of pioneer life.

The second Pulitzer Prize won by a Georgia novelist went to Margaret Mitchell for her long, romantic story of Georgia during the Civil War and Reconstruction—*Gone With the Wind* (1936). In contrast to Caroline Miller, Margaret Mitchell focused her novel upon the world of the great plantation owners. The book enjoyed instant success and became one of the fastest-selling novels in the history of American publishing. The popularity of *Gone With The Wind* was further enhanced by a lavish motion picture version produced by Metro-Goldwyn-Mayer. When the world premier was held in Atlanta on 15 December 1939, one reporter estimated that more people welcomed Clark Gable, Vivien Leigh, and other members of the cast than had participated in the Battle of Atlanta.

Erskine Caldwell, one of Georgia's most prolific authors, wrote stories that shocked many readers because of the explicit detail in which he described the degeneracy of tenant farmers and cotton mill workers. His real fame began with the publication of *Tobacco Road* (1932) and *God's Little Acre* (1933). Many of his best works, especially some of his short stories, are tall tales characterized by a robust, bawdy tomfoolery. Caldwell was also a social critic whose accounts of tenant farmers and cotton mill workers aroused the consciousness of many readers to the plight of the poor.

Though never rivaling the popularity of Margaret Mitchell or Erskine Caldwell, other Georgia writers produced works that enjoyed considerable success. Harry Stillwell Edwards of Macon published a number of novels, but he made his reputation with a little book he wrote at the age of sixty-four. *Eneas Africanus* (1919) told the story of a black man who became separated from his former master in 1865 and for the next eight years wandered in a humorous pilgrimage through the South. Nunnally Johnson, a native of Columbus, wrote the scripts for such important motion pictures as *The Grapes of Wrath, Tobacco Road,* and *The Three Faces of Eve.* Laurence Stallings, a playwright, drama critic, and novelist, became best known for three plays he wrote in collaboration with Maxwell Anderson: *What Price Glory* (1924), *First Flight* (1925), and *The Buccaneer* (1925).

The writing of poetry received encouragement from the Poetry Society of Georgia, a statewide organization founded in Savannah in 1923. The society offered prizes for well-written poems, occasionally published anthologies of the best poems by its members, and sponsored readings by famous poets. Perhaps the most distinguished poet born in Georgia —but one who left the state at an early age—was Conrad Aiken, who won a Pulitzer Prize in 1930 for his *Selected Poems*. Many people greatly enjoyed the simple, optimistic, patriotic lyrics of Frank L. Stanton, a columnist for the *Atlanta Constitution*. Best known for "Mighty Lak A Rose" (1901), Stanton published much of his verse in five volumes between 1892 and 1904.

One of Georgia's most talented poets was Ernest Hartsock, who before his death at the age of twenty-seven published three volumes of poetry: *Romance and Stardust* (1925), *Narcissus and Iscariot* (1927), and *Strange Splendor* (1930). While teaching at Oglethorpe University he also edited a bimonthly journal, *Bozart*. Beginning with the first issue in October 1927, Hartsock devoted the journal to publishing serious poetry as well as critical articles on poetry, music, and art. While Hartsock lived, he maintained high standards and received praise in national literary publications. After his death in 1930, the quality of the journal steadily deteriorated.

Georgia produced a number of able historians and biographers who contributed to the writing of the history of the state and the nation. Ulrich Bonnell Phillips, a native Georgian and one of the foremost authorities on the history of the antebellum South, devoted two of his early books to Georgia subjects: *Georgia and State Rights* (1902) and *The Life of Robert Toombs* (1913). Among his works that explored the history of the entire South were *American Negro Slavery* (1918) and *Life and Labor in The Old South* (1929). Ellis Merton Coulter taught at the University of Georgia for many years and wrote such books as *College Life in the Old South* (1928), *Georgia, A Short History* (1933), and *Thomas Spalding of Sapelo* (1940). In 1924 Coulter assumed the editorship of the *Georgia Historical Quarterly*, a journal founded in 1917, and for the next half-century he directed the work of that publication. John Donald Wade, an English professor at the University of Georgia, wrote two valuable historical biographies: *Augustus Baldwin Longstreet* (1924) and *John Wesley* (1930).

A number of black Georgians described some of their experiences in published works. Volumes of poetry were written by Thomas Jefferson

Flannigan, Victor Wellborn Jenkins, Frank Marshal Davis, and George Douglas Johnson. Walter White wrote two novels: *Fire in the Flint* (1924) told the story of a Negro doctor who was lynched by a white mob in a small town; *Flight* (1926) examined the life of a Negro woman who passed for white.

William E. B. Du Bois, one of America's foremost black writers, lived for many years in Georgia while teaching at Atlanta University. When he first came to Atlanta in 1897, the university had just begun a series of studies on Negro life in America. Du Bois assumed leadership of the project and directed the publication of sixteen of the twenty studies, which became known as the *Atlanta University Publications*. Those studies represented one of the first serious attempts to examine conditions prevailing among free black people in the South. Du Bois also wrote many books, one of the most popular being *The Souls of Black Folk* (1903).

In the 1930s some works appeared that described social conditions in Georgia. *I Am A Fugitive From A Georgia Chain Gang* (1932), by Robert E. Burns, and *Georgia Nigger* (1932), by John L. Spivak, pleaded for penal reforms by describing the brutality prevailing on chain gangs. Arthur F. Raper, a sociologist who worked in Georgia in the 1920s and 1930s, produced three valuable books on race relations and rural conditions: *The Tragedy of Lynching* (1933), *Preface to Peasantry* (1936), and *Tenants of the Almighty* (1943). Beginning in the spring of 1936 and continuing for the next decade, Lillian Smith and Paula Snelling edited a little magazine that appeared under three successive titles: *Pseudopodia* (1936), *The North Georgia Review* (1937–41), and *South Today* (1942–45). Dedicated to a critical examination of the life and culture of the South, the magazine appealed chiefly to those southerners who were concerned with such problems as the effects of racial segregation upon their region.

Prior to 1940, Georgia writers accomplished more than did people working in the visual arts and music. Until the 1920s there was little opportunity to acquire artistic education in the state, and consequently a number of Georgia artists studied in New York and Europe. Among the more accomplished were Edward Kemeys, a sculptor, William Posey Silva, a landscapist, Kate Flournoy Edwards, a portraitist, and Annie Laura Blackshear, a painter. During the 1920s fine arts departments were established at the University of Georgia and Emory University; in 1926 the High Museum of Art opened in Atlanta. Some of the more successful artists who worked in Georgia during the 1920s and 1930s were Lamar Dodd, Hal Woodruff, Marjorie C. Bush-Brown, Julian H. Harris, R. George Mamey, and Edward S. Shorter.

By the early twentieth century a number of people were working to encourage the development and appreciation of formal music. Oratorios were sometimes sung in the larger urban churches; opera companies and symphony orchestras gave performances in the principal cities. The Georgia Federation of Music Clubs, formed in 1918, sponsored concerts and study programs and also encouraged the formation of junior music clubs. By the 1920s music departments had become active at the University of Georgia, Emory University, Wesleyan College, and other colleges.

Georgia became the home of two clubs that played significant roles in the social and cultural life of the nation. In 1891 the first garden club with a constitution and by-laws was organized in Athens, and from there the idea spread throughout the nation. Garden clubs worked to stimulate interest in garden design, horticulture, flower arrangement, roadside development, and conservation. Another important club was founded in Savannah in 1912, when Juliette Gordon Low organized the first Girl Guide troop in America. The movement grew quickly and developed into the Girl Scouts of the United States of America.

Newspapers played an important role in the cultural and educational life of many people. Since Georgia was a rural state, county weeklies enjoyed great popularity. A few country people saw no other newspaper regularly, but city dailies also circulated in many rural areas.

The state's public education system changed greatly between 1890 and 1940. At the outset Georgia had a system of common schools that included grades one through seven and a five-month annual school term. The constitution of 1877 had restricted the use of state funds to elementary schools and the state university, and consequently Georgia had few public high schools. In an effort to enable some areas to improve their educational programs, the General Assembly passed legislation in 1889 that allowed county school boards to arrange as many school districts as they deemed necessary; a school district could, provided the voters approved, obtain revenue from local taxes to supplement state funds. Most county school boards proceeded to establish many small school districts, each of which worked solely for its own interests.

As a result of these developments, the wealthier school districts—usually those in cities and larger towns—had improved their educational programs by the beginning of the twentieth century and had even established high schools. White children in some black belt counties with large Negro populations also enjoyed better schools because local education officials spent most of the state school fund on the white schools. But most white children who lived in rural areas did not fare well. They walked miles to attend school in one-room buildings, where teachers had little formal education beyond the elementary level. The school term fell into two sessions, one of which began about mid-July just after the crops had been hoed and plowed for the last time. For the next two months children studied reading, writing, arithmetic, spelling, geography, history, and grammar. In the early fall, farm children left school to harvest crops. After they had picked cotton and gathered corn, they returned to school for the winter months.

Early in the twentieth century Georgia began improving its educational system. One of the first steps was the establishment in 1906 of agricultural and mechanical arts schools in each of the eleven congressional districts. These schools offered high school education, but they differed from most conventional secondary schools by providing agricultural and industrial arts training in place of foreign languages. The A and M schools never fulfilled the expectations of their founders, for they always suffered from insufficient funding. In addition, after 1911 Georgia began developing more high schools, and, beginning in 1918, high schools could obtain federal funds for agricultural education. These developments eliminated the need for the district A and M schools, and between 1924 and 1933 the state abolished some of them and transformed others into junior colleges.

Beginning in 1911, Georgia adopted a number of reforms to improve both the quantity and quality of its public schools. In that year the legislature passed a law expanding the powers of the state board of education by making it responsible for the policies governing public schools, the courses of study, and the selection of textbooks. The same law also established a statewide system of certification for public school teachers. During the next thirty years Georgians witnessed a steady rise in the level of teacher training, especially in the number who attended college. In 1912 and 1919 the voters ratified amendments to the state constitution that made high schools part of the public educational system and required every county to levy a local tax for their support. After that public high schools grew quickly. In 1920 the state had 169 accredited four-year high schools for whites and by 1938 the number had increased to 431, including at least one in each of the 159 counties. Beginning in 1930, in some places where there were not enough pupils to warrant four-year high schools, the state established two-year high schools, and within a decade Georgia had 125 such schools. The state also began providing funds to enable the poorer, rural school districts to establish consolidated high schools and thereby develop educational programs closer in quality to those of the wealthier school districts. In 1919 the legislature appropriated $100,000 for this purpose and during the next decade the amount steadily increased until in 1930 it reached $500,000.

Georgia took one of its most important steps toward improving educational opportunities in 1937, when the General Assembly passed legislation that guaranteed a seven-month school term throughout the state and provided free textbooks for every student from the first through the eleventh grades. The reforms of 1937 led to an increase in state appropriations for public schools; between 1936 and 1940 the expenditures rose from $7,948,137.53 to $16,083,848.68. By 1940 Georgia's public schools stood on the threshold of a new and better era.

Since the opening of the state's first public schools in 1872, Georgia had maintained separate schools for blacks and whites. White officials controlled the entire educational system and saw to it that black schools generally remained inferior to white schools. Negro students usually attended school for a shorter time each year than did whites, although this varied greatly across the state. In some rural counties school terms for blacks lasted only half as long as those for whites, but in cities and larger towns the two groups had terms of equal length. Black teachers usually were not as well trained as white teachers. In 1901, for example, only 20 percent of the black teachers in public schools had received any pedagogical training, whereas 80 percent of the white teachers had received at least some formal instruction. In 1910 white teachers in Georgia made an average monthly salary of $44.29 compared to $23.23 for blacks. During the next two decades the situation became worse: by 1929 the average monthly salary for whites had increased to $97.22, but the average for blacks then stood at $38.24. Far fewer black students had the opportunity to receive instruction beyond the elementary level than did whites. In 1914 only one four-year public high school for blacks existed in the entire state, in Athens.

The inferior conditions in black schools resulted largely from the way in which public officials divided educational funds between white and black schools. The state apportioned school funds to counties on the basis of their entire school-age population. County school boards then had the authority to divide the state funds, along with supplementary local funds, as they desired. They always distributed funds in favor of white schools. In counties with large black populations,

Negroes often experienced greater inequity in the disbursement of funds. In 1910 counties with a Negro population ranging from 10 to 25 percent divided the school fund on the basis of $5.77 for each white child and $2.42 for each black child; in counties with a black population between 50 and 75 percent, school authorities spent an average of $12.34 for each white child and $1.50 for each black child. Most counties did not spend public funds to build schoolhouses for blacks, and as late as the 1930s many black teachers in rural areas taught in churches, lodges, and deserted houses, where students sat on benches and held books on their laps.

From the 1890s, when Booker T. Washington popularized the idea, into the 1930s industrial education formed the basis of the curriculum at many black schools. Such programs encouraged students to take sewing, housekeeping, carpentry, blacksmithing, and, above all, agriculture. Men such as Washington hoped it would develop character and knowledge of mechanical skills among blacks and cause whites to have greater respect for Negro labor. Because the idea fit in well with prevailing beliefs in thrift and hard work, industrial education was encouraged in both black and white schools. However, in black schools it received more emphasis.

By the early twentieth century some black educational leaders had become highly critical of industrial education. Most Negro schools had neither the equipment nor the personnel to develop sound industrial education programs, they argued; moreover, the skills that blacks acquired were on the most elementary level and some, such as blacksmithing, were rapidly becoming obsolete. Most graduates of industrial education programs became teachers, not workers. For these reasons, the black leaders concluded, industrial education amounted to little more than an excuse for inferior education for blacks. Though those criticisms contained much truth, industrial education was the price that black schools had to pay for white toleration and support. Many whites believed blacks to be capable of only industrial education; others believed it would enable blacks to become more productive while keeping them in permanently inferior positions.

Northern philanthropists also encouraged the teaching of industrial education in black schools. Until the 1920s much of the financial support for black schools came from philanthropists, most of whom gave funds only to schools that emphasized industrial education. The philanthropists did make important contributions, however, because without their help many black Georgians would have received little formal education. Some of the important out-of-state agencies included the John

F. Slater Fund, which worked in cooperation with county authorities in establishing training schools that offered advanced instruction in industrial education and prepared teachers for work in rural elementary schools. The Anna T. Jeanes Fund made contributions for extending the length of the school term and supplemented the salaries of teachers employed to supervise industrial education in black schools. Between 1917 and 1940 the Julius Rosenwald Foundation worked with local officials in constructing over three hundred school buildings and vocational shops; the foundation supplied one-third of the funds provided state and local authorities raised the other two-thirds.

During the first four decades of the twentieth century, the state made more effort in behalf of public education for blacks. In 1911 Georgia established the Division of Negro Education, a state agency that attempted to facilitate cooperation between public officials and private philanthropic foundations. By the 1920s the number of black students attending public schools had increased sharply, rising a total of 73 percent in that decade. The number of black secondary schools increased, and black teachers in city schools began receiving more formal training. For blacks, as for whites, a turning point in public education came in 1937, when the state provided free textbooks and a seven-month school term. Even after that, however, black schools continued to lag behind white schools. In 1940 blacks had access to accredited four-year public high schools in only 48 of Georgia's 159 counties. By that time the state's investment in buildings, grounds, and teaching aids for each black child stood at $35.00, compared to $142.00 for each white child. Though Georgia had begun to make a greater effort to educate her black children by 1940, white and black students had not begun to enjoy equal educational opportunities.

Like elementary and secondary schools, higher education in Georgia experienced important changes between 1890 and 1940. In the 1890s the University of Georgia was a small institution that offered students a classical education, as it had earlier in the century. It had resisted innovations—such as an elective curriculum and more emphasis on science—that many other American universities had begun to adopt. Enrollment remained small and the university received much criticism, especially from agrarian spokesmen who charged that the school did not provide quality education for farmers.

A major turning point for higher education in Georgia came in 1899 when Walter B. Hill became chancellor of the university. Like some other college administrators of that age, Hill believed it no longer acceptable for a state university to be only a traditional liberal arts college catering to a small number of students. Instead, he believed a university should be more flexible and offer a broad variety of programs. Accordingly, under Hill's leadership the university made many changes, some of the more important ones being: the establishment of a summer school to offer instruction to public school teachers; liberalization of entrance requirements to enable students other than those trained in classical courses to gain admission; the securing of larger and regular state appropriations; and establishment of schools of forestry and pharmacy.

After Hill's death in 1906, David C. Barrow assumed the chancellorship and continued to lead the university in the direction that Hill had begun. During the Barrow administration, 1906 to 1925, the university expanded its operations to include the College of Agriculture as well as Schools of Education, Commerce, Journalism, and Graduate Studies. Women first attended summer school in 1911 and gained full admission in 1919. The faculty worked to liberalize the curriculum, thereby making it more flexible and attractive to a wider range of students. State appropriations for the university steadily increased.

As the university grew, so too did other public institutions of higher education. Georgia School of Technology (Georgia Tech), which had opened in 1888 to provide training in science and engineering, rapidly developed a strong educational program and by 1940 had become one of the South's best technical schools. Some of the other publicly supported institutions of higher education that served the state were Georgia State College for Women at Milledgeville, North Georgia Agricultural College at Dahlonega, the State Normal School at Athens, the Medical College at Augusta, South Georgia College at Douglas, Georgia Southwestern College at Americus, West Georgia College at Carrollton, and Middle Georgia College at Cochran.

During the first three decades of the twentieth century public institutions of higher education expanded until by 1930 they numbered twenty-eight, each with a separate board of trustees. In 1931, when the General Assembly passed legislation to reorganize state government, all public colleges and junior colleges were incorporated into the University System of Georgia and placed under the direction of a single board of regents. The new board proceeded to reduce the number of schools so that by 1943 the University System consisted of seven senior institutions, six junior colleges, and two experiment stations.

A number of private schools, many church connected, provided college education in Georgia, some of the better ones being Wesleyan College and Mercer University in Macon, Shorter College in Rome,

Brenau College in Gainesville, and Agnes Scott College in Atlanta. What became Georgia's most distinguished private university, Emory, was formed from an existing college in 1915 by the Methodist Episcopal Church, South, with the aid of a substantial endowment given by Asa Griggs Candler, the founder of the Coca-Cola Company. The school's undergraduate program began in 1919 when Emory College in Oxford moved to the new campus in Atlanta. Emory University also came to include schools of theology, medicine, law, business administration, and library science, as well as two junior colleges, one at Valdosta and one at the old Oxford campus.

The Berry schools near Rome were the most distinctive private schools founded in Georgia during the early twentieth century. In 1902 Martha Berry, the daughter of a wealthy cotton planter, opened a one-room school for poor mountain children. Under her leadership the school grew quickly and soon became a boarding school. To pay their tuition and to help meet operating costs, the students devoted part of each week to manual labor and part to training in academic subjects and in industrial education. Miss Berry worked to get financial support from philanthropists and secured especially generous grants from Henry Ford. In 1926 Miss Berry began a junior college and in 1930 a four-year college.

Public colleges for Negroes developed slowly, because many white Georgians strongly opposed spending public funds for black higher education. In fact, Georgia made its first effort in behalf of establishing a public college for blacks largely in response to pressure from the federal government. When Congress passed legislation that increased federal funds available to land grant colleges in 1890, it required that black schools receive a share of the funds. Rather than forfeit the federal funds, the state chartered the Georgia State Industrial College for Colored Youth (later renamed Savannah State College). From its opening in 1891 until after World War I, the Savannah school received little financial support and operated largely on its share of federal funds. In 1923 a national survey of black colleges revealed that the state gave the school so little financial support that federal officials threatened to terminate all federal aid to education in Georgia. The report also revealed that Savannah State was actually an elementary and secondary school, for only a few students took college-level courses. In response to pressure by the federal government, state financial support for the school increased so that by 1930 it provided about half of the funding. During the 1930s Savannah State added more liberal arts courses to its curriculum, and the number of college-level students increased.

In 1917 the legislature chartered the Georgia Normal and Agricultural College in Albany for blacks. Until the 1930s it remained little more than a high school offering courses chiefly in industrial education. In 1943 the school changed its name to Albany State College; by that time it had dropped agriculture from its curriculum and had become a four-year teacher's college. To provide more agricultural education for blacks, Georgia assumed control of a small college at Forsyth in 1922. In 1939 the state abandoned the Forsyth campus, merged the college with the Fort Valley High and Industrial School and named it Fort Valley State College.

Until after World War II most blacks seeking a college education in Georgia attended private schools. Blacks in Georgia were more fortunate than those in most other states, because a sizable number of private black colleges had existed since the Reconstruction era. Paine College operated in Augusta, while Atlanta was the home of Atlanta University, Clarke College, Spelman College, Morris Brown College, and Gammon Theological Seminary. Yet until about the end of World War I the private colleges for blacks, like the public ones, actually devoted most of their attention to offering elementary and high school education. This resulted in large part from the weak elementary and secondary schools available for blacks; the colleges had to devote much attention to doing what lower schools did not have the resources to do. In 1917 the Federal Bureau of Education released a report on black colleges in America that graphically illustrated the problem. Many institutions that had long prided themselves on being colleges and universities were classified in the report as secondary schools.

Although this report angered many black educators, it also prompted some to take steps to improve the situation. During the 1920s and 1930s every private Negro college in Georgia followed the earlier example of Atlanta University and abolished elementary programs. Most of them also dropped their high school departments. In place of industrial education, they gave more and more attention to liberal arts courses, teacher training, and the biological and physical sciences.

The most significant reform affecting higher education for blacks took place in Atlanta, where in 1929 three private black colleges worked out a plan for cooperation. Under this new system, eventually known as the Atlanta University Center, Spelman College took responsibility for instruction of undergraduate women, Morehouse for undergraduate men, and Atlanta University for graduate and professional study. During the 1930s Clark College and Morris Brown College joined the center. By 1940 the schools cooperated on many fronts: not only did they have a high degree of faculty and student interchange, but they also cooperated on the use of classrooms, laboratories, and athletic fields. Later in the 1940s the Atlanta School of Social Work and the Gammon Theological Seminary joined the center. By that time Atlanta had become the nation's leading center for black higher education.

Georgia's public health facilities developed more slowly than did the educational system. In 1937 a survey revealed that only 170 out of 593 incorporated towns in Georgia had public sewer systems; less than one-fourth of the state's rural homes had any means of sanitary sewage disposal. The State Board of Health had existed since 1903, but it had suffered from inadequate funding. The Ellis Health Law of 1914 placed the responsibility for public health with the counties, but by 1936 only 36 of the state's 159 counties had full-time health departments. Many people suffered because of insufficient diets, poor sanitary facilities, and inadequate medical attention. Because they lacked the education and the financial means to improve themselves, they remained poor and unhealthy.

Serious illnesses plagued many people during the early twentieth century. Malaria, which sapped people of their strength and left them to suffer periodically from chills and fever, had afflicted Georgians since the founding of the colony; as late as 1940 Georgia ranked among the top three states in deaths from that disease. Since 1910 health authorities had known that the problem could be solved by destroying the breeding places of mosquitoes and by screening houses, but Georgia lacked the funds for malaria control until the federal government supplied them in the 1930s. By 1950 malaria in Georgia had practically been eliminated.

Many people suffered from hookworm, a disease that rarely killed but that weakened its victims, robbed them of energy, and made them susceptible to other diseases. People contracted hookworm as a result of going barefooted in unsanitary areas. Early twentieth-century studies in some rural counties revealed that as many as 53 percent of the people were infected. In 1909 the Rockefeller Foundation established the Commission For Exterminating Hookworm, and within five years 76,776 Georgians received treatment. During the next thirty years, as public health officials educated people about the nature of the disease, as improved sanitary facilities spread, and as fewer people went barefoot, hookworm faded as a major problem.

Other diseases also plagued many Georgians. Pellagra afflicted its victims with a painful skin rash and took many lives. As a result of experiments conducted early in the twentieth century, Dr. Joseph Goldberger proved that pellagra resulted from protein dietary deficiency. His findings led to a sharp reduction in the disease between World War I and World War II. During World War I public health officials discovered that venereal disease was widespread in Georgia. Though state and federal health agencies worked to reduce the problem, Georgia had the third highest rate of infection in the nation by 1939. The state enjoyed far more success in reducing tuberculosis. Early diagnosis, along with the establishment of a state tuberculosis sanatorium early in the twentieth century, eliminated it as a leading killer by the 1930s.

Georgia's major advances in public health began in the 1930s when the New Deal made federal funds and work relief forces available. By 1940 federal funds had enabled every county to receive public health nursing services, tuberculosis diagnostic x-ray clinics, and sanitary engineering. As a result of the increased funding in the 1930s and the earlier work against such diseases as hookworm and pellagra, Georgia's health record improved by 1940. Disease rates were then lower than at any time in the state's history, and Georgia was entering an era of improved public health.

During the first half of the twentieth century more and more people moved from the countryside to the towns and cities of Georgia. But that change came slowly, and as late as 1940 the state remained predominantly rural with most people living on farms or in small towns. From the 1890s until well after the turn of the twentieth century, some farm families managed to supply most of their needs. They grew their own vegetables, fruits, grains, and livestock. Women made many of the family's clothes and laundered them with homemade soap. Men and boys hunted rabbits, squirrels, quail, and possum for sport as well as to supplement the family diet. For fishermen the streams abounded with catfish and carp, the lakes with bream and bass.

Tenant farm families and many small landowners—those struggling to keep from falling into tenancy—were not as self-sufficient; they were too hard-pressed just trying to make a commercial crop from year to year. Because of the unfavorable economic conditions prevailing from the 1890s through the 1930s, more and more people fell into this category. In most rural counties by the 1930s a few farm families lived well, but the vast majority did not. They had little money and depended upon their landlords and merchants for subsistence; they produced only a small portion of the meat, milk, eggs, and vegetables that they needed for their tables; they lived in unattractive and uncomfortable dwellings that had scant household furnishings; they worked in the fields with outdated agricultural tools. In short, they lived hard lives. But most people tried to make the best of what they had, and they were by no means totally dissatisfied with their lot. "Folks that look back at the old times now think it was a hard life," one farmer later recalled, "but then it was just the way of living. Most folks thought they were doing pretty well."

Country people labored on their own farms throughout the week, but when the need arose they helped one another and whenever possible they came together to socialize. If a farmer became ill and unable to work, friends usually helped by keeping his crops in good order. During times of serious illness, neighbors ministered to the sick. When death struck, friends laid out the corpse and sat up with the grieving family the night before the funeral. After a farmer had harvested his crops, he might ask friends to come to his house for a corn shucking. Women got together for quilting bees, while teenagers gathered for box suppers, candy-pullings, and games.

Most country people, young and old, enjoyed music. On Saturday nights many listened and some danced as banjo players and fiddlers rendered such "foot-patting" tunes as "Little Brown Jug," "Turkey in the Straw," and "Sally Goodin." They also liked somber tunes about sorrowful, dramatic events. For many years a favorite song told the story of little Mary Phagan, who was murdered in Atlanta in 1913.

> Little Mary Phagan, she went to town one day.
> She went to the pencil factory, to get her little pay.
> Leo Frank, he met her, with a cruel heart, you know,
> And said, "Little Mary Phagan, you go back home no more."

When the early radio stations and recording companies made possible the development of commercial country music in the 1920s, such Georgia performers as Fiddlin' John Carson, Gid Tanner, and Riley Puckett became popular throughout the rural South.

Protestant churchgoers frequently held song fests and "all day meetings with dinner on the grounds" for spiritual edification as well as social pleasure. In the rural tradition people sang songs at a fast tempo; for that reason as well as because rural music was vocal harmony to be sung, not listened to, country spirituals became the most sociable of musical devices. In many places people held annual singing conventions that lasted from one to four days and attracted hundreds of people.

Most rural churches were either Baptist or Methodist. Though some

A country store, Jasper County, Georgia, 1913

rural ministers had attended college, many had just received a "call" and "gone to preaching." They made low salaries and usually served three or four churches that they alternately presided over. People usually gathered each week for Sunday school, there being classes for adults and children. When the preacher came, he devoted his sermon to the need for strict morality and personal salvation, to describing the joys of heaven and the horrors of hell. Some special Sundays the congregation had dinner on the grounds. Every mother then brought the best she could afford: fried chicken, ham, fish, biscuits, cornbread, vegetables, pies, and cakes. People moved from table to table, sampling food from as many different families as possible and eating "enough to help them plow for a week."

Saturday loomed big in the lives of country people, because that was the day many went to town. At noon farm people left their work and soon the roads leading to town were lined with moving people, some on foot or horseback, some in wagons or automobiles. By mid-afternoon the business section of the town was crowded with people who purchased food and clothing, while others milled about exchanging gossip and discussing current crop conditions. As sundown came, most families began making their way home. Then men could be seen carrying sacks of flour on their shoulders, while their overall pockets bulged with tobacco and small packages. During the evening many country people remained in town. They gathered at stores where they made their supper of soda crackers, slices of cheese, and cans of sardines, which they washed down with carbonated drinks flavored strawberry or lemon or sarsaparilla.

More and more between 1900 and 1940 automobiles, motion pictures, and radios enabled the town to increase the influence it exerted on the country. Then too, World War I forced many farm boys to leave home for the first time and to travel to large cities in America and Europe. Increasingly as the century advanced country people made trips to places such as Atlanta and Columbus. Some returned to their country homes, but the cities lured others into becoming permanent residents, especially during hard times that rural areas experienced in the 1920s and 1930s.

During the early twentieth century the towns of Georgia developed a social life of their own. From the 1890s onward baseball was a popular sport, and many towns had teams that played on weekend afternoons. In the 1920s and 1930s many high schools had organized baseball and football teams. People also entertained themselves in more informal ways. On warm summer evenings they sat on front porches in swings and rocking chairs visiting with neighbors. Men played checkers at courthouses and stores; in private homes and clubs they played poker and dominoes. Well-to-do women played bridge in the afternoons and evenings. Many people, affluent and poor, attended motion picture theaters, the whites sitting downstairs and the blacks in the balconies. In the fall they went to fairs held annually. There they observed agricultural exhibits, drank red lemonade, rode Ferris wheels, and gazed at human freaks and big snakes.

Most church members in the towns, as in the rural areas, were either Baptists or Methodists. In the towns, however, there were also Presbyterian and Episcopal churches and occasionally Lutheran, Catholic, and Jewish congregations. Though town ministers usually had more formal education than those in the country, they too emphasized the need for personal salvation rather than the social gospel.

As the twentieth century advanced, new devices and new ways of doing things affected town and country life. By 1910 automobiles had ceased to be novelties, and commercial bus lines operated over much of the state by the 1920s. In many towns chain grocery stores had appeared by the 1920s and they initiated a trend that would revolutionize the food retail business and signal the decline of the local grocer. Public utilities continually expanded. By the 1920s more and more independent telephone franchises had become incorporated into the Southern Bell System; the Georgia Power Company supplied an increasing number of towns with electricity. WSB of Atlanta, the South's first radio station, began broadcasting on 15 March 1922. During the next two decades more radio stations opened in towns across the state, and people became accustomed to receiving immediate reports of current news from throughout the world.

Increasingly between World War I and World War II rural life declined. As rural churches ceased to play the dominant role in the social life of country people, their membership declined. By 1940 many country church buildings had become run-down, and others had been abandoned. All-day singings no longer attracted as many people. Paved roads and automobiles then made it easier for rural people to get to town, where they could sit in a dark, air-conditioned theater and watch a new motion picture, direct from Hollywood. The rural way of life was dying by then and giving way to an urban age.

PART SIX

1940
TO THE PRESENT

by

NUMAN V. BARTLEY

The Great Seal of 1914

XXIII

Prosperity and Problems:
The Economy during World War II
and After

Like other Americans, Georgians responded enthusiastically to the war effort triggered by the Japanese bombing of Pearl Harbor in December 1941. Some 320,000 men and women, approximately one of every ten people in the state, served in the armed forces, an impressive number given the fact that the inductee rejection rate in Georgia was considerably above the national average. Of those who donned uniforms, 6,754 failed to return. Losses were heaviest in National Guard units, which were pressed rapidly into service.

The war was probably most immediate to coastal Georgians who could see the wreckage and oil spills that accumulated on the beaches as a result of German submarine sinkings in the Atlantic Ocean. Governor Eugene Talmadge's adjutant general, Lindley W. Camp, organized a volunteer home defense force, composed mostly of those too young or too old to serve in the regular services, to defend the area from German espionage efforts or even, some feared, German invasion.

As masses of Georgians went away to war, even greater numbers of other Americans came to the state to train for combat. The army had more training facilities concentrated in Georgia than any other state except Texas. Every major Georgia city housed a substantial military installation of some type. Among them, Fort Benning, founded during World War I near Columbus, was the largest infantry training school in the world; Warner Robins Air Service Command was a $30 million Air Corps base located near Macon that at its peak employed fifteen thousand civilians; Camp Gordon was an army training center near Augusta; and Hunter Field near Savannah provided training for Army Air Corps crewmen.

The military bases pumped federal dollars into Georgia, and war production expenditures spurred further economic activity. The Bell Aircraft Company in Marietta employed some twenty thousand workers; shipbuilding facilities at Savannah and Brunswick boomed; large

The B-29 assembly line at the Bell Bomber Plant near Marietta during World War II

ordnance plants sprang up in Macon and Milledgeville; and numerous
Georgia firms received hefty war contracts. In Georgia as in the nation,
World War II accomplished what the New Deal had been unable to
do; it generated the payrolls and production that brought to an end
the Great Depression and touched off an era of prosperity.

Georgians were soon enjoying greater affluence than they had ever
known before. Per capita personal income in the state leaped from less
than $350 per year in 1940 to over $1,000 in 1950. In relative terms,
Georgians in 1940 got by on approximately 57 percent as much as
other Americans; by 1950 the state's citizens were approaching 70 percent of the national average. This growth continued at an impressive
though relatively slower pace during the 1950s and 1960s. Even when
measured in real, noninflated dollars, the income of a typical Georgian
doubled between 1950 and 1970. By the latter year per capita income
had reached 84 percent of the national level.

Much of Georgia's newly found prosperity was the result of the
rapid growth of manufacturing in the state. The industrial base that
had been gradually and often painfully laid in an earlier era fed on
wartime demand to launch into what one scholar has called "the period of great acceleration" during the decade of the 1940s. The 1950
census, for the first time in Georgia's history, showed more people
employed in manufacturing than in agricultural pursuits; increasingly
during the postwar years, the income derived from industrial and
commercial activity dwarfed that received from agricultural sources.
By the late 1950s manufacturing payrolls, governmental employment,
and wholesale and retail trade all provided Georgians with more personal income than did farming.

The cities, especially the Atlanta metropolitan area, were the cutting
edge of economic change. Not only did finance, commerce, and administration center in the cities, but there too factories concentrated.
In 1958 three counties in the Atlanta metropolitan area, Fulton, De-
Kalb and Cobb, accounted for 25 percent of all manufacturing employment in the state, and a study of industrial development during
the 1947–58 period found that well over one of every three new jobs
created by the expansion of manufacturing opened in these three
counties. Generally, the cities attracted a relatively more diversified
industrial base that met significantly higher payrolls than those common in the rural and small-town counties. The leading industry in
the Atlanta area was transportation equipment, a high-wage, capital-
intensive category that rested on the Lockheed Aircraft Corporation
(the state's largest employer during most of the postwar period) and

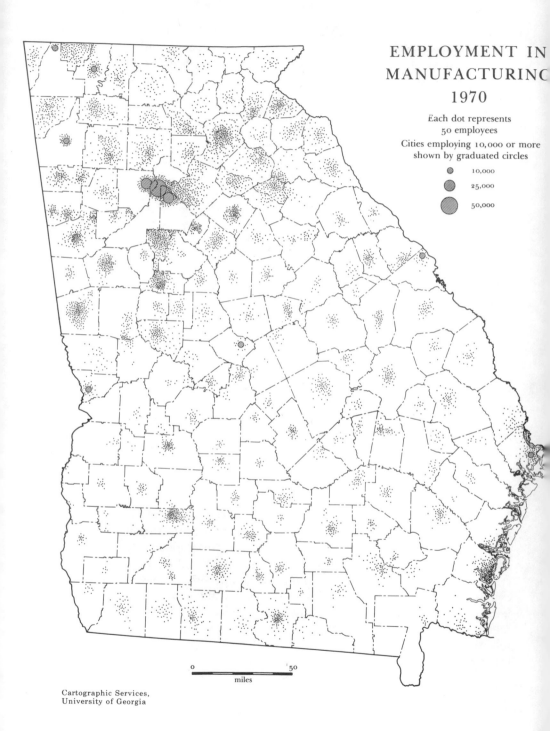

EMPLOYMENT IN
MANUFACTURING
1970

Each dot represents
50 employees
Cities employing 10,000 or more
shown by graduated circles

10,000
25,000
50,000

miles
0   50

Cartographic Services,
University of Georgia

several automobile assembly plants. Not surprisingly, manufacturing wages in the Atlanta area were considerably higher than those in the state as a whole. In 1960 the average Atlanta area industrial worker made $81.35 a week, which was not far below the $89.72 national average and well above the Georgia norm of $65.40. By 1970 manufacturing wages in the Atlanta metropolitan area had passed the national average.

Atlanta also was the banking, financial, and administrative hub not only of Georgia but of the Southeast and consequently captured a major share of the new jobs created by such rapidly expanding service occupations as government, finance, and insurance. Even in 1940 the per capita income in the Atlanta area was approximately equal to the United States average, and by 1950 it was well above the national norm and far above the level typical in Georgia. In 1970 the Atlanta metropolitan region contained one-third of Georgia's people, 38 percent of its jobs, and 42 percent of its personal income. As Neal R. Peirce has concluded in a recent study, "the real reason for Georgia's rise and regional preeminence—and the reason an old sobriquet, Empire State of the South, fits better than ever—can be summed up in one word: Atlanta."

During the 1960s the Atlanta area grew far more rapidly than did Georgia. The "Forward Atlanta" program, devised by businessman Ivan Allen, Jr., while he was president of the city chamber of commerce and launched when he became mayor in 1961, proved enormously successful. New office buildings, factories, warehouses, and shopping centers sprouted throughout the metropolitan area, leading one business executive to observe that "this has been Atlanta's decade." The city more than ever became the financial, administrative, and communications center of the Southeast, the hub of the regional railroad and interstate highway systems and the home of the nation's second busiest airport. Of *Fortune* magazine's list of the nation's 500 largest industrial firms, 440 had offices in Atlanta and 8 were headquartered there. No longer could critics jest that Atlanta had contributed only two things to the world: Coca-Cola and the modern Ku Klux Klan. Atlanta also possessed the state's most congested slums, a crime rate that has spiraled since the mid-1960s, and some of the nation's worst traffic jams. City leaders expected the latter problem to be alleviated with construction of a rapid transit system, which has been approved by voters in Fulton and DeKalb counties and is scheduled for operation in the 1980s.

Other cities in varying degrees shared in the Atlanta success story.

Chatham County (Savannah), with its port facilities, the Hunter Army Air Field–Fort Stewart military complex, more than two hundred factories, and increasingly during the postwar years a thriving tourist industry, was in terms of population and per capita income the largest and most prosperous county outside the Atlanta metropolitan area. The fall-line cities of Augusta, Macon, and Columbus enjoyed economic booms based on industrial and commercial growth and the payrolls generated by nearby military installations. The Augusta metropolitan area received an additional economic boost with the construction of the Savannah River Atomic Energy Commission facility during the 1950s. None of these cities could, however, match the population growth of almost 80 percent experienced by Albany between 1950 and 1960. The coastal city of Brunswick, which was the gateway to a number of nearby island resorts, benefited from the tourist boom. In north Georgia, Rome developed a diversified industrial base; Dalton expanded its tufted textile industry; and Gainesville became a center for poultry processing.

As trade, factories, construction, and money concentrated in the urban areas, so too did people. By 1970 just over 60 percent of Georgia's 4,589,575 people lived in urban communities, with about half of these concentrated in the Atlanta metropolitan area and the other half residing in the other major cities. The vast bulk of the remaining 40 percent who were rural dwellers were not farmers; they lived in rural areas and worked in nonfarm occupations, often in neighboring cities and larger towns.

Paralleling the rapid expansion of the cities was the disruption of long-established patterns in the countryside. Although attention tended to focus on exploding growth and prosperity in the cities, equally significant changes were taking place in the rural and small-town areas. The sharecroppers' cabins among the cotton fields that had so long been the hallmark of Georgia agriculture became increasingly rare during the post–World War II period. Farm tenancy declined in the 1930s, partly as a result of New Deal farm programs that limited cotton production and paid farmers not to farm, thereby making it profitable for landowners to cast their tenants adrift. The rapid mechanization of Georgia agriculture during the late 1940s and the 1950s further doomed the farm tenancy system. In 1940 there were less than ten thousand farm tractors in the entire state; by the mid-1950s there were some eighty-five thousand, approximately one tractor to every two farms. Governmental restrictions, mechanization of agriculture, and changing marketing conditions made tenant farmers superfluous.

The old and new in mid-twentieth-century Atlanta

Air view of the waterfront in Savannah during the 1950s
Chamber of Commerce, Savannah

In 1940 six of every ten Georgia farms were tenant-operated; by the mid-1950s only a third were and by the mid-1960s less than one in six. The collapse of tenancy meant a sharp decrease in the number of farms and a substantial increase in their size. In 1945 Georgia's approximately 226,000 farms averaged 105 acres; in 1969 there were somewhat more than 67,000 farms containing an average of 234 acres.

Less and less of this acreage was devoted to cotton. In 1940 almost two million acres of Georgia farmland produced more than one million bales of cotton, which was a substantial decline from levels attained during earlier years but still left cotton the dominant cash crop in the state. By the late 1950s cotton produced only 10 percent of cash farm income, and by the mid-1960s the once-proud monarch had fallen behind the lowly peanut in market value. The decline of cotton was a part of the general decline of row-crop agriculture as increasing amounts of land went into trees and pasture and an increasing percentage of farmers devoted their efforts to livestock and poultry. By the early 1970s poultry accounted for almost one-third of farm cash receipts; the major row crops, including peanuts, tobacco, cotton, corn, and soybeans, produced a third; and cattle, calves, and dairy products were the source of about half the remaining third.

In one sense, these developments marked the culmination of long-evolving trends in both Georgia and southern agriculture. But the rapidity with which changes occurred produced formidable consequences. On the positive side, Georgia agriculture became more diversified and more productive. The state produced greater farm income than any other in the Southeast except Florida. Appropriately, the term "Peach State" disappeared from Georgia automobile license plates in 1971, since by that time the state had dropped to third in peach production. Georgia led the nation in production of poultry and peanuts, although neither of these replaced the peach as a state slogan. Actually "Pine State" might be more appropriate for a state with almost 70 percent of its land area in forest. Crop yields per acre increased enormously, as did the value of farm land and output per farm worker. The growing number of acres devoted to forest and pasture, in addition to more enlightened farming methods, salvaged vast amounts of eroded land and made the Georgia countryside more attractive and more productive.

But on the negative side, agriculture had receded to a distinctly secondary position in the economy; the approximately $1.2 billion market value of farm products at the beginning of the 1970s was only a fifth the value of manufacturing production. Georgia farms remained smaller and less productive than the national average. Less than a third reported sales of more than $10,000 in 1969, which was slightly fewer than those reporting sales of less than $5,000. Greater farm efficiency also meant greater investments in machinery, fertilizer, and other things that had become virtual necessities. Thus, while Georgia farms became more productive on a gross basis, net profits going to farmers increased at a considerably slower rate, lagging far behind income levels in urban areas. Federal government payments to farmers, which in the mid-1950s meant more than $670 million per year, went heavily to large farmers and provided very limited assistance to struggling smaller farmers and none at all to farm laborers.

Once the backbone of the economy, farmers often found that a modernizing state no longer needed nor rewarded their services. In 1949 farm families enjoyed little more than half the income of the typical Georgia family. In part, this was the result of the miserable economic situation of black farmers and tenants, who made less than $500 a year. White farm families were better off, but only relatively, as they too struggled to raise families with far less than an average income. The economic situation on the farms improved considerably during the postwar years partly because of better farming methods and even more because most people abandoned the farms for the cities. In 1949 Georgia had 222,000 farm families; in 1969 it had 47,000. The exodus was particularly heavy for blacks. In 1930 a majority of blacks lived on the farms; in 1970 almost none did. White farm families declined from 156,000 households in 1949 to 41,000 twenty years later. It was these hard-working black and white folks who had grown up on the farms in an agricultural era who made the greatest adjustments to urbanization. Those remaining on the farms watched their children move away to the cities in search of economic opportunity; those joining the outmigration, better than others, understood the changes demanded by urban life.

Massive numbers of Georgians moved into the cities or left the state entirely. The 1950 census revealed 1.2 million Georgia-born citizens residing in other areas of the nation. While both blacks and whites sought their fortunes elsewhere, white outmigration was largely offset by other whites moving into the state. In 1950 there were 475,000 people born outside Georgia living in it, and during the 1960s Georgia had a net gain in migration. But as large numbers of blacks left the state few moved into it. The result was a continuing decline in the ratio of blacks to whites. In 1940 more than one-third of Georgia's citizens were blacks; in 1970 just over 25 percent were. Departing

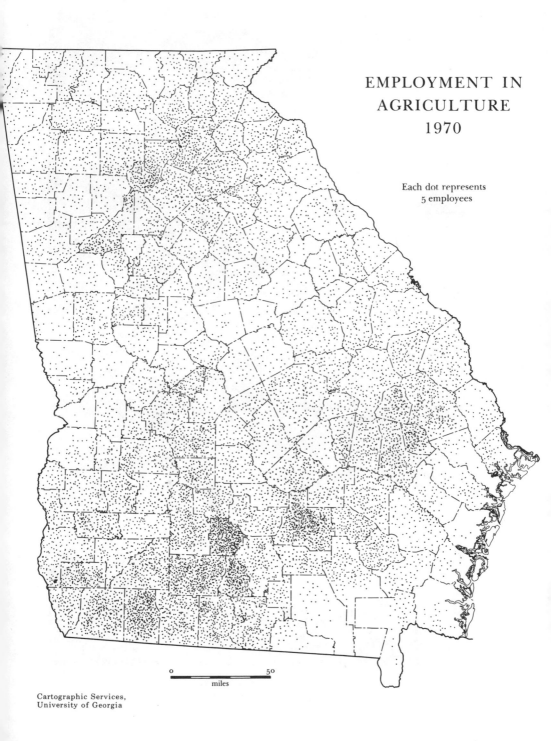

EMPLOYMENT IN
AGRICULTURE
1970

Each dot represents
5 employees

0   50
miles

Cartographic Services,
University of Georgia

Picking cotton the modern way
Agricultural Experiment Station, University of Georgia

Georgians tended to be young adults entering the productive period of their lives; migrants entering the state were often somewhat older and more highly skilled people moving into professional, managerial, and craft positions in the expanding economy. Most of the incoming migrants settled in the cities, where they were joined by the flow of native Georgians from the towns and rural areas. A 1961 study of Atlanta's population found that only 28 percent of the city's people were native-born, while 56 percent were migrants from other areas of Georgia and the remaining 16 percent from outside the state.

The great migration of the postwar years contained the elements of both triumph and tragedy. Certainly the cities offered far more economic opportunity than did rural and small-town areas; the distance from a sharecropper's shack to a factory job was vast indeed. Especially for blacks, the cities were also avenues to a greater degree of social freedom and political influence than was customary in the countryside. But the move also meant a disruption of the closely knit family ties and the status security that had been a part of home. Few of the migrants possessed the skills, the education, even the sophistication to make easily the transition from farm to city. For many blacks the move was to a ghetto where jobs were few and crime and social disorganization frequent. White migrants, simply because of the color of their skin, had much greater access to decent housing and to employment, but for many a country boy, the complexity of the city was difficult to fathom. When a country musician lamented in a popular 1960s ballad about life in "De-troit City" and said "I wanna go home," he was no doubt expressing an emotion experienced by a great many newly urban Georgians.

The blacks and whites flocking from the farms to the cities created major social problems, straining social services and crowding the schools and welfare rolls. The difficulties were particularly acute in black neighborhoods, where segregated housing patterns concentrated a mushrooming population in limited though expanding ghettos. Harried city officials searched for solutions and increasingly turned to the federal government for succor. Many affluent whites left the problems of the cities to others and fled to the suburbs, where housing developments and shopping centers leaped up in what had once been cotton fields. In Atlanta retail sales increased by 78 percent between 1963 and 1972; in the Atlanta metropolitan area outside the city, they grew by 286 percent. In 1963 Atlanta had 4,276 retail firms, compared to 3,870 in the remainder of the metropolitan area. In 1972 Atlanta had 4,605 retail firms, while the number outside the city had increased to 7,948.

Sociologists frequently referred to the proliferating suburbs as urban sprawl and lamented the departure of those most able to pay taxes from the political units desperately needing financial support. To many residents, however, the suburbs were citadels of comfortable homes, relatively good schools, and low crime rates, while the vexing quandaries of poverty and race relations remained in the cities. Public problems and private abundance thus grew concurrently in the booming metropolitan areas.

Urbanization and industrialization contributed to the improving economic climate in Georgia, as, indeed, did the departure of unskilled citizens out of the state and the influx of higher status people into it. But despite the upward trends of the economic indicators, Georgia still housed far more than its share of poverty and deprivation. While some fourteen thousand Georgia families and unrelated individuals got by nicely in 1949 on incomes of $10,000 or above, more than 330 thousand households existed on less than $1,000 per year. This situation improved considerably in the years that followed. By 1959 almost as many families had incomes above $10,000 as had incomes below $1,000, about ninety thousand households in each group, although inflation was partially responsible for these statistics.

Black citizens particularly faced formidable obstacles, since the great transition from a rural-farm economy to an urban-industrial one took place before desegregation and therefore within a Jim Crow social order. Many blacks found themselves in the same position in which their parents had been—the last to be hired and the first to be fired. During the 1940s and 1950s black family income was less than half that of white families. In 1949 a solid majority of black families and unrelated individuals made less than $1,000 per year, while only slightly more than one-quarter of whites did so. In 1959 almost half of black families made less than $2,000 per year, although only 15 percent of white families were in the same circumstance. Despite significant gains during the 1960s, the 1970 census reported black family income to be $4,743 and white family income $9,179. Approximately 40 percent of black families failed to surmount the federally established economic level for poverty, while only 10.5 percent of white families lived at or below the poverty level. Thus, a majority of Georgia's poor were black, even though blacks made up only about a quarter of the state's population.

With increasing numbers of blacks concentrating in the cities, the gap between the $10,316 median income for urban white households in 1970 and the $5,159 for urban black households was particularly

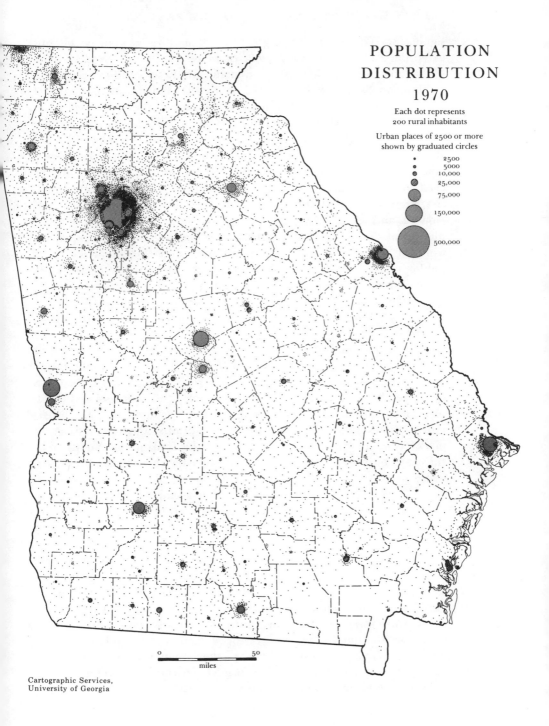

POPULATION
DISTRIBUTION
1970

Each dot represents
200 rural inhabitants

Urban places of 2500 or more
shown by graduated circles

2500
5000
10,000
25,000
75,000
150,000

500,000

0   50
miles

Cartographic Services,
University of Georgia

significant. To be sure, these gross figures smother extremely relevant exceptions. In Atlanta 25 percent of black families enjoyed incomes of $10,000 or more in 1970, and many of these families resided in neighborhoods in the western and southwestern parts of the city that one seasoned journalist described as "doubtless the most expensive, poshest Negro settlement in the United States." This black middle class, much of its recent expansion a direct result of the 1964 Civil Rights Law, was by no means confined to Atlanta, though it was predominantly urban. Yet the majority of black families were not middle class, and increasing numbers of these families were piling into inner-city ghettoes. During the 1960s, sixty thousand whites moved out of Atlanta, and seventy thousand blacks moved into it. Although the population of the Atlanta metropolitan area was well over three-quarters white, a majority of the city's population and three-quarters of its public school enrollment was black by the early 1970s. Other cities evidenced similar population trends. Population estimates indicated that Augusta during the early 1970s became a majority black city ringed by white suburbs and that Savannah was on the verge of becoming the same.

The occupational structure rewarded white males to a greater degree than other Georgians. A majority of black men worked as laborers or operators in 1970, while less than a quarter of white men did so. On the other hand, 26.7 percent of white males held professional, technical, managerial, or administrative positions, compared to the 6 percent of black males who held similar positions. Further hampering black economic progress in Georgia was the continuing exodus from the state of young black adults just entering their most productive years.

An increasing number of women found employment outside the home, and they, like other disadvantaged groups, learned firsthand the perils of the work-a-day world. In 1950 almost a third of Georgia women were in the labor force. The largest number of black women, almost half of those employed, were in domestic household service, tending the children and the kitchens of white people, usually for pitifully low wages. The largest number of white women labored in the mills, where the work was demanding and the income low. In the cities, substantial numbers of white women also performed clerical tasks. Occupational opportunities for women changed relatively little during the 1950s and 1960s. By 1970 the largest number of white females, well over one in three, performed clerical and secretarial tasks, although substantial numbers also continued to work as operatives, mainly in the mills. Together clerical workers and operatives accounted for 57 percent of employed white women in 1970. A majority of black female workers remained in service occupations, both in private households and increasingly in such public accommodations as motels and restaurants; however, by 1970 a rapidly growing number of black women were joining their white sisters in the mills and at the typewriters. The chief professional outlets for women throughout the period were public school teaching and nursing. The approximately 700,000 employed women in 1970 made up 40 percent of Georgia's total work force. National surveys conducted during the 1970s indicated that both blacks and females drew paychecks that averaged between 55 and 60 percent of those earned by white males.

While being on the factory payroll was considerably more lucrative on the average than farm employment, factory wages in Georgia lagged well behind the national average. In part this fact testified to the continuing role played by agriculture in the state's economy. Although sharply declining numbers of people earned their livelihood from the soil, much of the manufacturing growth was concentrated in industries that processed products grown on the farms. Throughout the postwar period, textiles remained Georgia's largest industry. Other leading industries included food processing, apparel, and lumber products, which, like textiles, were low-paying, labor-intensive industries. These four factory groups accounted for three-fourths of all manufacturing employment in 1947, two-thirds in the late 1950s, and just over 57 percent in 1970. Additionally, few of the workers in these and other plants belonged to labor unions. During the late 1940s national unions attempted large-scale organizational activities in Georgia as well as in other southern states, but the drive was largely a failure. Approximately 251,000 Georgians, which was just over 16 percent of the nonagricultural work force, carried union cards in the early 1970s. A good portion of this limited membership worked in branch plants of large northern-based corporations where northern unions could protect the southern branches. Right-to-work legislation enacted in the late 1940s has undoubtedly been one of the several factors hampering union growth in the state. In 1958 the typical Georgia factory worker made $60.45 per week, compared to the $82.71 national average. Even though Georgia industry has gradually become more diversified during recent years and the work force has become more skilled, wage scales in the 1970s remained about 20 percent below national norms.

During the late 1960s and the early 1970s Georgia led other southeastern states in attracting new industries and in expanding older

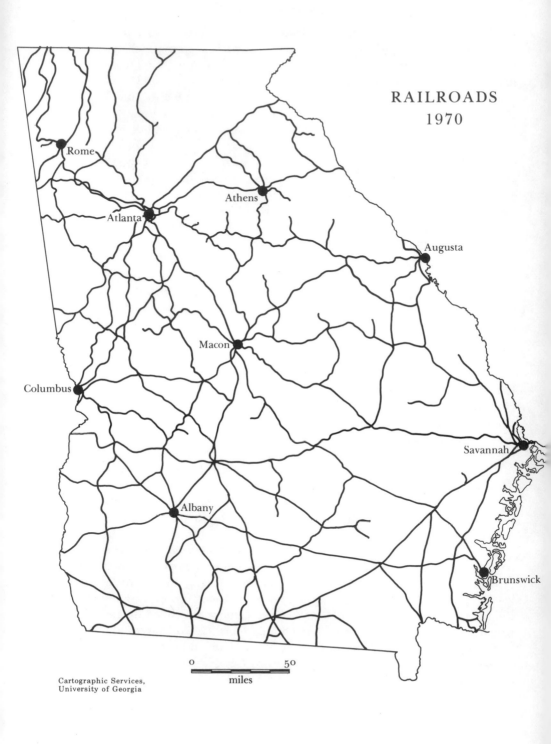

RAILROADS
1970

Rome

Athens

Atlanta

Augusta

Macon

Columbus

Savannah

Albany

Brunswick

0   50
miles

Cartographic Services,
University of Georgia

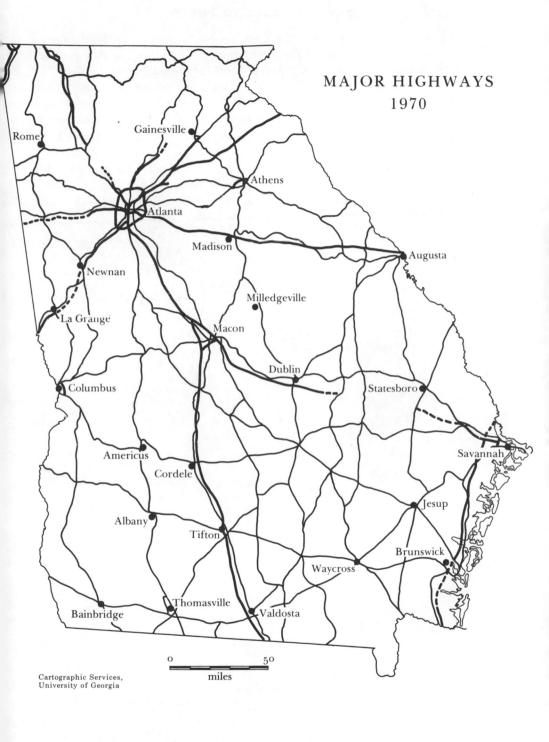

MAJOR HIGHWAYS
1970

Rome

Gainesville

Athens

Atlanta

Madison

Augusta

Newnan

Milledgeville

La Grange

Macon

Columbus

Dublin

Statesboro

Americus

Savannah

Cordele

Albany

Jesup

Tifton

Brunswick

Waycross

Thomasville

Bainbridge

Valdosta

0   50

miles

Cartographic Services,
University of Georgia

ones. The resulting factories, jobs, people, and housing developments placed heavy strains on the environment. The emerging concern over environmental matters received a significant boost in Georgia with the publication in 1971 of *The Water Lords,* the report of a study group associated with consumer advocate Ralph Nader. The report documented the devastating effect of industrial pollution on the Savannah River. So massive was industrial contamination that it dwarfed the environmental impact of the approximately sixteen million gallons of untreated sewage that the city of Savannah daily dumped into the river. Georgians sometimes seemed torn between their desire for economic growth and their concern for ecological balance. The state

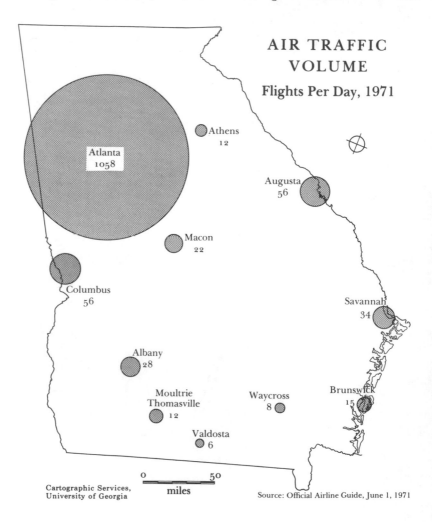

AIR TRAFFIC VOLUME

Flights Per Day, 1971

Atlanta
1058

Athens
12

Augusta
56

Macon
22

Columbus
56

Savannah
34

Albany
28

Moultrie
Thomasville
12

Waycross
8

Brunswick
15

Valdosta
6

0   50
miles

Cartographic Services,
University of Georgia

Source: Official Airline Guide, June 1, 1971

Community Development Department, joined by several private industry hunting groups, promoted rapid industrial expansion, while the Environmental Protection Division evidenced a willingness to discourage new industries that threatened the environment from locating in Georgia.

Overall, Georgia's conservation record has been decidedly mixed. In 1964 the state legislature created the Water Quality Control Board, which was incorporated into the Environmental Protection Division in 1972. Increasingly, the state agency has enjoyed substantial success in protecting waterways, including the Savannah River, from industrial pollution. It has been less successful in curbing the millions of gallons of inadequately treated sewage dumped into streams and rivers by local governments. In the late 1960s an estimated 58 percent of Georgia's citizens lived in governmental districts lacking adequate sewage treatment facilities, and in 1974 Governor James E. Carter estimated that more than a billion dollars would be required to correct this situation.

The state also owed a significant part of its prosperity to military spending. During the late 1960s the military and civilian payrolls at Georgia's fifteen major military installations totaled approximately one billion dollars yearly, and another billion entered the state in defense-contract work, together making Georgia the recipient of more Department of Defense dollars than all but five other states. Some 105,000 military personnel were stationed in Georgia in 1967, approximately 45,000 civilians worked at military installations, and more than 40,000 workers filled jobs created by defense related contracts. These and other defense expenditures, one study reported in the late 1960s, generated about 10 percent of the state's total personal income.

Between 1950 and 1970 the Georgia gross state product (in 1972 dollars) increased from approximately eight billion dollars to approximately twenty-one billion. Because of such vigorous economic growth, shared in varying degrees by other southern states, by the mid-1970s the southern portion of the nation was popularly designated the "sunbelt South." In 1938 President Franklin D. Roosevelt, in the covering letter of a report by a New Deal committee regarding the stringent depression-era conditions in the southern region, labeled the South "the nation's number one economic problem." By 1976 journalists throughout the country were heralding the emergence of the burgeoning sunbelt South, marked by rapid economic expansion and a congenial life style. The economic and urban growth that elevated Georgia from being part of the nation's leading economic problem to being part of the American sunbelt generated environmental and other problems, but the state's changing image accurately reflected Georgia's material progress.

Economic expansion fueled the growing public commitment to further economic growth. In 1963 Governor Carl E. Sanders observed: "I am for progress. I am determined that during my administration this state will move ahead—fast." Much of Georgia's recent political and economic leadership would surely have agreed. The desire for further material progress was a central theme in the state's public philosophy. The maintenance of a "good business climate" in Georgia's part of the American sunbelt appeared to be a leading public concern.

The modernizing Georgia economy benefited some and exploited others, as had been true of northern states that passed through the same process in an earlier period. But this should not obscure the real gains made in the standard of living in the state. By the 1970s economic opportunity was greater for the masses of people than it had ever been before. During World War II and the postwar years, Georgians experienced perhaps more basic change than they had at any time since the creation of an economy based on cotton and slavery a century and a half before. Already faced with dismaying problems of adjustment, they were promptly called upon to make another—one that was to shake the very foundations of the social system.

XXIV

Race Relations and the Quest for Equality

By the World War II years, Georgia's segregated social system had hardened into a rigid caste structure accepted by virtually all whites and substantial numbers of blacks as the ordained and proper way of doing things. The ubiquitous words "white" and "colored" that adorned virtually every public facility from drinking fountains and restrooms to the Bibles used in Georgia courtrooms for administering oaths were an accepted part of the Georgia scene, like red clay and kudzu. To many whites segregation was an element of social stability in a rapidly changing world; it was both an identification with the past and an opportunistic method to limit economic and social opportunities to themselves and their children. But for black Georgians uprooted from the countryside, the system was an increasingly tortuous cul-de-sac. The breakdown of farm tenancy and the escalation of urbanization forced blacks either to drop out of the emerging urban economic system into crime or welfare or, more commonly, the basest poverty-level occupations that whites found undesirable or, alternatively, to break into the broader economic system and compete for jobs that traditionally not only went to whites but that segregaion explicitly reserved for whites.

Some blacks, schooled in the system, accepted it; whites often condemned them for being welfare loafers, resorting to crime or lacking ambition. Others, at first mainly younger, urban, better-educated blacks, demanded equal opportunity and ultimately launched a civil rights movement to attain it; many whites accused them of being outside agitators or communists and called the movement a disruption of law and order. This is not to suggest that white Georgians were ungenerous nor that they were innately more bigoted or more authoritarian than other Americans. Growing up in a segregated society, young white Georgians, like other white southerners, were taught antiblack prejudices, which were simply a part of the socialization of the child; the system placed blacks in inferior positions and social adjustment required the normalization of these patterns. Just as many blacks did not realize the social and psychological importance that large numbers of whites assigned to segregation, many whites failed to comprehend the enormous burdens segregation placed on the aspirations of blacks.

The problems of race relations were, of course, by no means confined to Georgia, and nationally a changing intellectual climate gave impetus to deep-seated historical trends and motivated a redefinition of human rights. Professor Gunnar Myrdal, in an epic study of race relations published in 1944 entitled *An American Dilemma*, referred to the growing conflict within the hearts and minds of white Americans between their belief in the American Creed of liberty, justice, and democracy and their acceptance of segregation with its accoutrements of white supremacy, injustice, and disfranchisement. The paradox between the United States fighting World War II in the name of liberty and democracy and using segregated armies to fight it and the emergence of the United States as the self-proclaimed champion of freedom and democracy in the Cold War while practicing racism at home brought this dilemma to a head, if perhaps in a less direct and immediate fashion than Myrdal had described.

Already the decisions of the United States Supreme Court had begun to reflect a reevaluation of the rights of man, and during the late 1940s President Harry S. Truman undertook the desegregation of the federal establishment, including the armed forces. Since Georgia was heavily endowed with military bases, the integration of the services affected the social climate of the state. Southern influence in Congress prevented significant civil rights legislation until the 1960s, but, nevertheless, both the Supreme Court and the national Democratic party clearly evidenced a willingness to support a color-blind constitution.

White Georgians, for the most part, found no immediate dilemma in their desire to preserve sanctioned social institutions. Governor Eugene Talmadge could on one occasion observe that "no religious or social prejudice has a place in a Christian heart" and on another occasion say, "I like the nigger, but I like him in his place, and his place is at the back door with his hat in his hand," all with no apparent dishonesty or awareness of inconsistency. Black Georgians, however, increasingly found glaring inconsistencies between national ideals and practices. During World War II black soldiers, often northerners unaccustomed to segregated seating arrangements, sometimes refused to sit in the back of public buses, actions that in a number of cases led to arrest of the soldiers or to violence by the bus driver. Young blacks also evidenced impatience with the system. In 1944 some fifty Savannah State College students occupied all the seats on a city bus and refused to give them up when white passengers purchased tickets, which resulted in the arrest of two of the students on charges of attempting to incite a riot. Just after the war black veterans in Atlanta marched on the city hall demanding fairer law enforcement and the hiring of blacks on the police force. Such scattered incidents were important indicators of the changing temper of black Georgians, as was the rapid growth of the National Association for the Advancement of Colored People (NAACP), which by 1946 counted forty Georgia branches with a total membership of more than thirteen thousand people. The NAACP, along with black political clubs, successfully sponsored court cases seeking blacks' right to vote in Democratic primary elections and equal pay for black school teachers.

A series of court decisions during the early 1950s made clear that the United States Supreme Court could no longer accept the "separate but equal" doctrine when facilities were not, in fact, equal. These decisions, which stemmed from cases involving other southern states, focused on the field of public education. Georgia's political leaders responded with an equalization program designed to make separate schools more equal and thereby to buttress segregation laws in the federal courts. Attentive observers in Georgia and elsewhere soon recognized, however, that the trend in federal court decisions was distinctly away from the logic of white supremacy. Georgia's elected officials, reiterating ad infinitum that the state would never accept desegregated schools, took steps to evade a school integration decision. The 1951 legislature wrote into the general appropriation bill a provision prohibiting the expenditure of public funds on desegregated educational facilities and debated a constitutional amendment permitting the state to abolish the public school system in favor of private schools. Two years later the 1953 General Assembly approved the "private school" amendment, which relieved the state of the obligation to provide for public education and authorized the payment of tuition grants directly to the parents of pupils to spend in private schools of their choice. The theory that underlay this action rested on rather dubious constitutional grounds. The United States Constitution required that no state "deny equal protection of the law." Georgia political leaders, fearing the federal courts would find that enforced segregation did deny equal protection, sought to remove the schools from state control. Thus, even if no state could deny equal protection, private schools could, so the reasoning went, discriminate as they saw fit. The problem with this logic, of course, was that should the state provide financial aid through tuition grants to private schools, the schools then would no longer be private. But such constitutional niceties lay in the future. The legislature passed the amendment, and in November 1954 Georgia voters approved it by a relatively narrow margin. The irony of a state's striving to improve its public schools while ratifying a proposal to abolish them testified to Georgia's paradoxical commitment to both the past and the future.

On one point, however, Governor Herman E. Talmadge and the legislature were prophetically accurate. Between passage of the "private school" amendment by the legislature and the voters' ratification of it in November 1954, the United States Supreme Court declared the separate-but-equal doctrine unconstitutional in the momentous case of *Brown* v. *Board of Education*. The court ruled in 1955 that public schools in the southern and border states must desegregate "with all deliberate speed," a rather ambiguous timetable at best, and one that Georgia political leaders apparently interpreted as never.

The Georgia legislature reacted to the *Brown* decision with an awesome array of legislation to prohibit its implementation. A series of laws codified the private school plan, including provisions that terminated state and local funding for desegregated schools, authorized the governor to close such schools, provided for the payment of tuition grants, permitted closed schools and facilities to be leased for private school use, extended teacher retirement benefits to instructors in private schools, and allowed the governor to suspend compulsory attendance laws. Apparently fearful that Georgia law enforcement officers might become confused about the "law of the land," the General Assembly provided specific punishment for any peace officer "who knowingly refuses or fails to attempt to enforce any law of this state requiring segregation or separation of the white and colored races in any manner or activity. . . . " Another law decreed that any state official permitting mixed school attendance could be prosecuted for a felony. Warming to their task, the legislators enacted sweeping legislation designed to prevent the NAACP from supporting desegregation suits. Resolutions censuring the president of the United States and demanding impeachment of the justices of the Supreme Court passed the legislature by large majorities. Other statutes created the Georgia Education Commission and allotted to it vast powers to plot segregationist strategy, publicize the virtues of "the Georgia way of life," and investigate subversives. In keeping with the latter mandate, the commission hired secret investigators who operated not only in Georgia but also in two neighboring states.

These and other laws aligned the power of the state government in direct opposition to the federal courts and gave substance to the concept of interposition. If the states at the time of the formation of the Union surrendered only part of their powers to the federal government, then the states remained sovereign in those areas not allocated to national authority. Therefore, a state could interpose its sovereignty between its own citizens and the federal government. The concept of interposition—the mobilization of state power to block federal action —was the basic constitutional theme that served to justify opposition to desegregation. Most of the other southern states took similar stands, and Georgia was a leader in the regional effort to prevent enforcement of the *Brown* decision, a program termed by its proponents "massive resistance." By massively resisting desegregation, the states could force federal authorities to abandon the principle of equality before the law. The Georgia legislature, like those in other southern states, made its position explicit by adopting an interposition resolution. The *Brown* decision, trumpeted the General Assembly by a virtually unanimous vote, was in the state of Georgia "null, void and of no force or effect. . . ."

Most of the anti-integration legislation that poured forth from the state capitol was unconstitutional; much of it represented a potential threat to the public schools or an overt and immediate danger to civil liberties or both; some of it was simply a nuisance to blacks and often to whites as well. For example, in order to prevent a threatened desegregation suit on the college level, the legislature required that the University System accept applications for admission only from undergraduates who were less than twenty-one years old and graduate students who were under twenty-five, and the Board of Regents established an entrance requirement that all students present letters of reference from two graduates of the college to which they were applying. These obstructions did indeed present formidable barriers for several blacks who were seeking entrance to the night school at the Georgia State College of Business Administration, but they also disrupted the plans of white adults who simply wanted to go to college in Georgia. The resulting outcry ultimately led the Board of Regents to modify these admission standards, and on a few other occasions Georgia public authorities became a bit too enthusiastic in their defense of segregation and sparked white protest. In 1955 Governor S. Marvin Griffin demanded that the Board of Regents prohibit the Georgia Tech football team from playing a Sugar Bowl engagement with the University of Pittsburgh, since Pittsburgh had a black player on its team. The Tech student body hanged the governor in effigy, and the Board of Regents announced that Tech would honor its contract to play in the bowl game. Similarly, when the state Board of Education adopted a policy revoking "forever" the salary and license of any teacher who "supports, encourages, condones, offers to teach or teaches" integrated classes, a sufficient number of newspapers and organizations spoke out against such a massive invasion of freedom of speech that the board beat a hasty retreat and rescinded the measure.

The intolerance sanctioned by massive resistance spilled over into many areas of Georgia life. The Ku Klux Klan enjoyed a revival, once again demonstrating its appeal to whites who felt themselves threatened by social change. The Georgia-centered U.S. Klans, Knights of the Ku Klux Klan received a charter in 1955 and in the fall of 1956 attracted some thirty-five hundred Klansmen to a cross-burning ceremony at Stone Mountain. Although plagued by limited membership and internal bickering, the Klan remained active through the 1960s, and its members lived up to the fraternal order's tradition of mayhem and violence. The shotgun slaying of Lieutenant Colonel Lemuel Penn, an educator and military reservist whose offense was to be black and to be driving a late model car with Washington, D.C., license plates through a rural county near Athens in 1964, was a notable example. Another highly publicized expression of the new mood of white reaction in the state was the virtual siege of Koinonia Farm, an interracial Christian community in Sumter County. Founded in 1942, Koinonia prospered and by the early 1950s housed some thirty adult residents, about a quarter of whom were black. The commitment of Koinonia's members to racial equality and pacifism led to occasional shows of animosity by local residents, but not until the *Brown* decision and massive resistance did Sumter County whites turn solidly against the farm. Beginning in 1956 merchants, bankers, and suppliers refused to do business with Koinonia's residents; unidentified persons whiled away the long evening hours by driving along a nearby road firing rifle bullets into the farm's living quarters; when a local townsman without apparent provocation beat up a Koinonia resident, the local sheriff arrested the battered victim; dynamite twice destroyed Koinonia's roadside produce stand; and an all-white Sumter County grand jury investigated the entire affair and concluded that Koinonia's residents were troublemakers who spent their time bombing and sniping at themselves.

Most white Georgians were not Ku Kluxers, of course, and through all of this they generally continued to live their own lives, tolerating but only occasionally being affected by the frantic efforts of their politicians and some of their zealous neighbors to defend white supremacy. But many of them were concerned about the consequences of integration. White parents struggling to adjust to an urban environment that rewarded education fretted about the impact of school desegregation on academic standards and the educational opportunities for their children. White workers raised on the farm and struggling to adjust to the factory worried about competition for jobs and advancement from black workers. And, most of all, whites who grew up in a segregated society tended to view integration as foreign, a betrayal of their heritage and their family traditions.

Blacks viewed it not differently, but from a different viewpoint. White schools, generously financed relative to the black ones, offered their children broader educational opportunities. Better jobs, heretofore largely monopolized by whites, offered access to affluence and the American dream. A growing number of black Georgians became increasingly impatient with the lack of progress that followed the *Brown* decision. During the 1950s the NAACP was the unchallenged leader of the civil rights thrust, and in the courtrooms NAACP lawyers consistently won cases while being opposed by the best legal talent southern state treasuries could retain. Yet half a decade after the *Brown* decision Georgia schools were totally segregated and race relations had worsened. The NAACP successfully prosecuted suits integrating the golf courses and city buses in Atlanta and pushed ahead with desegregation suits against the Atlanta public school system and the University of Georgia, but the organization also was forced to expend a significant share of its efforts defending itself from state harassment. By the late 1950s membership was declining and other groups had emerged to challenge the NAACP's legal, gradualist approach to civil rights. The Southern Christian Leadership Conference, formed by Dr. Martin Luther King, Jr., after he had successfully led the Montgomery, Alabama, bus boycott, held its first nonviolent institute at Spelman College in 1959, and in early 1960 King returned to his home town of Atlanta, accepting co-pastorship with his father at the Ebenezer Baptist Church. Even before the Southern Christian Leadership Conference established its headquarters in Atlanta, a group of the city's younger and more militant blacks seceded from the established leadership and formed the Atlanta Committee for Cooperative Action to encourage a more aggressive approach to civil rights. In varying degrees in other Georgia cities, impatient blacks laid the groundwork for a revolt against conservative policies.

The inspiration that touched off a new phase of race relations came from outside the state. On 1 February 1960 four black college students in Greensboro, North Carolina, sat down at a Woolworth's lunch counter that catered only to whites and asked for a cup of coffee. On the next day a larger number of unwelcome customers appeared at the lunch counter, and soon sit-ins were occurring in other North Carolina cities and then over the South. The movement reached Georgia when a black college student and army veteran in Atlanta asked another student, "Don't you think we ought to do it here?" Within days they had formed an organization, and, with the support of King and the Atlanta Committee for Cooperative Action, the students published in the Atlanta daily papers on 9 March 1960 "An Appeal for Human Rights" announcing their intention "to use every legal and nonviolent means at our disposal to secure full citizenship rights as members of this great democracy of ours." One week later some two hundred black collegians staged the state's first sit-in. They concentrated on public, tax-supported facilities, demonstrating at the restaurants and lunch counters in the State Capitol building, the Fulton County Courthouse, City Hall, and similar sites. The Georgia General Assembly, anticipating the sit-ins, had already passed a strong trespass law that served as grounds for the arrest of seventy seven of the students. Nevertheless, the movement spread rapidly, as students in Savannah, Albany, and Augusta began demonstrations. Sometimes joined by white student allies, increasingly supported by older blacks, and sometimes going it alone, young black people conducted sit-ins at a variety of stores, bus stations, and lunch counters; kneeled-in at white churches; played-in at public parks; organized buying boycotts of individual stores and sometimes entire downtown business districts; picketed segregated hospitals and sports events; conducted protest marches to dramatize issues; and generally utilized direct action to express dissatisfaction, as the Atlanta student declaration stated, "not only with the existing conditions, but with the snail-like speed at which they are being ameliorated."

Dynamic black demands for desegregation clashed blatantly with the state's policy of massive resistance to any lowering of the color barrier. Governor S. Ernest Vandiver denounced the Atlanta student demands as "left-wing" propaganda "calculated to breed dissatisfaction, discontent, discord and evil." Public officials in some of Georgia's cities sought to suppress white violence toward the demonstrators, showed a willingness to negotiate, and even expressed sympathy with the movement's more moderate demands. Such was the case in Atlanta, where the successive administrations of Mayors William B. Hartsfield and Ivan Allen,

Jr., won national acclaim for fair and constructive government; in Augusta, where Mayor Millard Beckum led the shift away from segregated public accommodations; and in Savannah, where the 1960 city elections brought a moderate administration into office. But outside the larger cities, governmental officials were virtually unanimous in opposition. Even in Atlanta, there was significant white resistance. While blacks picketed downtown stores in the fall of 1960, the Ku Klux Klan picketed the pickets, and other extreme segregationists, led by restaurant-owner Lester G. Maddox, organized Georgians Unwilling to Surrender (GUTS) to boycott any store that changed its racial policies because of the black boycott.

The impasse between black insistence on change and white commitment to the status quo came to a climax over the school desegregation issue. Desegregation suits involving the Atlanta public schools and the University of Georgia were nearing decision, while Georgia laws required that public funding be terminated to any desegregating school and empowered the governor to insure that it be closed. The state was rapidly arriving at a crucial point when the choice would not be whether the schools were segregated or desegregated but whether they would be open or closed, and even the dullest lawyers knew the federal courts would not permit closed schools to be reopened on a segregated basis under the state's specious private-school plan. Many responsible white Georgians who had grown up with the Jim Crow system accepted it as the right and proper mode of behavior but not to the extent of destroying public education and endangering the state's economic advancement. Neither blacks nor the federal courts would any longer accept segregation, and the increasingly acute dilemma in the hearts and minds of Georgia public authorities was the conflict between their commitment to both education and segregation.

The massive resistance front began gradually to collapse, with Atlanta leading the shift in state policy. In the late 1950s a group of concerned Atlanta women organized Help Our Public Education (HOPE), the most important predominantly white group to mobilize support for open schools. Taking no stand on the question of segregation or integration, the organization, composed mainly of women, many of whom had school-age children, simply insisted that the schools not be closed. By 1960 HOPE claimed thirty thousand members and in addition to being a powerful force in Atlanta had established chapters in other major Georgia cities. Mayor Hartsfield vigorously championed an open-schools policy and called upon the legislature not to interfere with Atlanta's orderly compliance with whatever decision the federal courts handed down. The board of aldermen, the city chamber of commerce, the daily newspapers, school groups, and other organizations joined the mayor in demanding that Atlanta be permitted to desegregate without state intervention. The Atlanta stand received some support from other Georgia cities and from the Georgia Education Association. Against this onslaught even the state legislature in its 1960 session relented sufficiently to establish a Committee on Schools, headed by Atlanta banker John A. Sibley, to restudy the school issue and make recommendations. The committee held hearings throughout the state, took testimony from some eighteen hundred witnesses and prepared a recommendation that Georgia repeal its massive-resistance laws and adopt a local-option policy that would allow local communities to determine their own course of action.

While the Sibley Committee's report was being digested, a federal court ordered the admission of two black students to the University of Georgia. Observers had assumed that the test would come in Atlanta in the fall of 1960, but the city was permitted a year's delay, and then, unexpectedly, the university was ordered to desegregate at the beginning of the winter quarter that commenced in January 1961, less than a week after the court order. Surprised state officials briefly terminated funds to the university, and a riotous mob attacked the dormitory where a young black woman had just taken up residence. These events forced the state to choose between closing the university and defying the federal judiciary or accepting the decision. The state legislature chose the latter course of action and abandoned its massive resistance stance by enacting the Sibley Committee recommendations. In the fall Atlanta desegregated four high schools without incident, and in 1963 Savannah, Brunswick, and Athens transferred a number of black students into formerly white schools.

While token school desegregation spread gradually over the state, the sit-in movement continued unabated, reaching its highest level of activity during 1963. Demonstrations occurred in virtually every substantial Georgia city and even some of the smaller ones, the chief exception being Brunswick, where a responsive city government headed off disruptions by negotiating a settlement with black leaders. Several civil rights organizations were active in Georgia, coordinating protest activities and providing assistance and advice to local efforts. The Student Non-Violent Coordinating Committee, formed in 1960, was probably the most energetic group, sending field workers to promote voter registration and protest in numerous towns and counties. While the youth-oriented Student Non-Violent Coordinating Committee sought to build strong, self-sustaining organizations in local communities, the Southern Christian Leadership Conference focused its efforts on the creation of massive confrontations such as the Albany demonstrations in 1962 that were designed to dramatize black grievances and bring pressure on the federal government to enact civil rights legislation. By 1963 the NAACP had caught the new mood of protest and created a Task Force that traveled over the state supporting desegregation demonstrations.

The preeminent spokesman for the civil rights movement in Georgia and the nation was Martin Luther King, Jr. The son and grandson of Baptist ministers, King followed the family tradition and studied for a career in the pulpit, receiving a divinity degree at Crozer Theological Seminary and ultimately a Ph.D. from Boston University. Shortly after becoming pastor of a black Baptist church in Montgomery, Alabama, events catapulted the young minister into leadership of the bus boycott, and he seized the opportunity to put into practice the philosophy of nonviolence with which he had become enamored as a student. During the 1960s King led demonstrations in numerous southern cities, landing in jail as a result on several occasions. Even in jail King was a formidable adversary of segregation; while in solitary confinement he penned the classic "Letter from Birmingham Jail," a moving attempt to explain to white moderates that those who sat down in public facilities "were in reality standing up for what is best in the American dream and for the most sacred values of our Judaeo-Christian heritage. . . ." A magnificent speaker, King's great strength was his ability to fuse Biblical Christianity and the rights of man into an inspirational oratory that made him modern America's outstanding spokesman for human liberty. More than any other individual, King was responsible for guiding the civil rights movement into peaceful, nonviolent channels of protest. In 1964 he became the only Georgian ever to be awarded a Nobel Prize for peace.

Demonstrations and court decisions forced some desegregation in Georgia, but the Jim Crow system collapsed only after enactment of the 1964 Civil Rights Law by the United States Congress. This far-reaching measure included provisions requiring desegregation of public accommodations and equal opportunity in employment, and it banned the expenditure of federal monies to any facility that discriminated. This latter provision led to a complex and protracted struggle between the Department of Health, Education, and Welfare (HEW) and local school districts over the question of discrimination in education. Before releasing federal aid-to-education funds, HEW required positive progress toward integration. Local school officials, especially those in rural and small-town areas, generally sought as little departure from segregation as possible. Ultimately, however, federal court rulings and HEW pressure nudged reluctant administrators into compliance, and by the early 1970s southern schools had achieved more complete integration than those outside the region. In 1965 Congress enacted further civil rights legislation designed to open the franchise to blacks, and federal examiners visited three Georgia counties to guarantee democratic registration procedures. This law had less effect in Georgia than in other Deep South states, since many blacks, especially those in the cities, had been voting since the 1940s and further gains resulted from voter registration projects by civil rights groups during the early 1960s.

The extent of urban residential segregation raised vexing questions about the implementation of school integration in the cities. Since, for the most part, blacks lived in black neighborhoods and whites in white ones, neighborhood schools often meant de facto segregated schools. In a series of decisions beginning in the late 1960s and culminating in the early 1970s, federal courts required that school district officials take positive steps to insure a unitary school system, including when necessary the use of buses to complete the desegregation process. These decisions touched off a storm of debate over "forced busing" in Georgia, as elsewhere in the nation. Georgia had, of course, been busing students to segregated schools for decades, and the number of students riding buses increased from 516,000 during the 1967–68 school year to 566,000 as the busing controversy escalated in 1970–71. Interestingly, however, the number of miles traveled by Georgia school buses declined from approximately 54 million miles to just over 51 million during the same period. The reason, of course, was that two buses no longer had to cover the same route, one carrying white children, the other black youngsters. Nevertheless, busing had never been controversial in the state until it became a factor in the desegregation process. Several Georgia communities, including the city of Athens, instituted quite successful programs of integration that included the use of school buses, but the court decisions also provoked doubts, fears, and hostilities on the part of many parents. By the mid-1970s, it appeared that the United States Supreme Court had begun a retreat away from the concept of positive integration, and the popular outcry over busing quieted.

The plight of the economically deprived ghettoes remained a crucial social problem facing leaders in both Georgia and the nation. Martin Luther King grappled with this problem during the last years of his life. At the time of King's assassination in 1968, his Southern Christian Leadership Conference was organizing a "Poor People's Campaign" to

Maynard H. Jackson campaigning in Atlanta

Martin Luther King Center for Social Change; Southern Regional Council

Martin Luther King, Jr., at his birthplace
on Auburn Avenue in Atlanta

bring together representatives of minority groups and the poor generally to press for a massive federal program to alleviate poverty. Rejecting coalition strategy, the Student Nonviolent Coordinating Committee, during the final fitful years of its existence, sought to organize viable and essentially self-sufficient economies within the black ghettoes under the slogan "Black Power." Increasingly, however, black leaders have turned to politics, as other American ethnic minorities had done in the past. In 1969 Maynard Jackson, a young black lawyer, won election to the office of vice mayor in Atlanta, and four years later he became mayor of Georgia's largest city and state capital. The Reverend Andrew J. Young, one of King's top aides, desegregated the Georgia congressional delegation by winning the Atlanta-based Fifth Congressional District seat in the United States House of Representatives in 1972.

White Georgians gradually accepted the results of the Second Reconstruction, responding to these epic changes frequently with ill-will, sometimes with violence, but often, too, with a sigh of relief that suggested Gunnar Myrdal may, after all, have had a point in arguing that whites were torn between their belief in American constitutional principles and lifelong acceptance of segregation. The civil rights movement rapidly disintegrated during the late 1960s, in part because federal legislation had accomplished many of its basic aims. The deeply rooted legacy of slavery, segregation and lack of opportunity clashed with growing black expectations to create the frustrations and despair that sparked rioting in Atlanta and Augusta ghettoes, although Georgia had less of this aimless violence than did numerous other states. The emergence of black power, the rioting in many areas of the nation during the middle and late 1960s, the economic deprivation experienced by many blacks, and the lingering bitterness of some whites clearly indicated that race relations remained the state's most important problem. At the same time Georgia was closer than it had ever been before to attaining the "dream" enunciated by Martin Luther King "that one day on the red hills of Georgia the sons of former slaves and the sons of former slave-owners will be able to sit down together at the table of brotherhood."

XXV

Society and Culture in an Urban Age

The changes that swept over Georgia after 1940 were in many ways breathtaking. The "Bulldozer Revolution" transformed placid fields and meadows into vibrant shopping centers and subdivisions. The "Negro Revolution" altered social mores long set in the hard mold of custom. Television metamorphosed home entertainment and air conditioning tamed the blazing southern summers. The sharp upsurge in the marriage rate following the return of the GIs from World War II produced a "baby boom" that in turn soon placed heavy pressures on the public schools and ultimately the colleges and universities. The state responded with striking advancements in education and other public services, advancements made possible by the revenues generated by economic growth. Increasingly, Georgians lived in cities or suburbs, worked in factories or towering office buildings, drove on modern and often traffic-jammed highways, watched television in homes equipped with central heating and air conditioning, and sent their children to the best—or at least the most expensive—educational system in the state's history.

But beneath this turbulent change ran strong currents of tradition and continuity. The family and the church survived the transition from farm to city with most basic values intact. Since these two social institutions were the most racially segregated in Georgian—and, indeed, American—life, the achievement of the civil rights movement's integrationist goals was necessarily limited. Housing segregation increased during the postwar period, and integrated neighborhoods on any substantial scale seemed an almost lost cause for the foreseeable future. Professor Charles P. Roland, in a recent survey of historical developments in the modern South, observed: "The vast majority of the members of the two races lived as far apart in the 1970s as they had in the 1940s. Possibly they lived further apart." Economic opportunities for black citizens broadened enormously, and many blacks took advantage of them, but the legacy of segregation and discrimination hung on tenaciously, and the poor black ghettoes served as breeding grounds for urban crime. Women also enjoyed a far wider range of opportunity than they had possessed in the past, but, like blacks, they too continued to face formidable hurdles, symbolized perhaps by the Georgia legislature's refusal to ratify the Equal Rights Amendment. For three and a half decades Georgia enjoyed economic prosperity, but only limited amounts of it trickled down to the lower strata of society. Governmental expenditures and services grew vastly in Georgia, but so did they elsewhere; relative to national norms, Georgia retained its traditional commitment to limited government and low taxes.

Public education exemplified the paradoxes inherent in Georgia's quest for both progress and tradition. Molded by a rural and small-town environment, the public school system proved increasingly unable to meet the demands of an urbanizing state where far more youngsters were destined to work in offices than in cotton fields. The baby boom exaggerated Georgia's already high birth rate, while the scarcity of private and parochial schools concentrated the student population in the public schools. Most of all the paucity of public financing anchored education to a rapidly fading past. In 1941 public expenditures per pupil in average daily attendance was $73.19 for white students and $16.55 for black pupils (although the actual discrimination was even greater, since a higher ratio of white youngsters attended school than did blacks). Annual teachers' salaries averaged $926.55 for whites and $427.54 for blacks. Throughout the 1940s the majority of black schools were one-teacher institutions, and the majority of all public schools in the state were wooden structures that lacked flush toilets. In 1950 one-third of all public schools were one-teacher establishments and almost two-thirds had four or fewer teachers, with the bulk of these located in rural areas. Although students attending schools in affluent urban and suburban districts fared relatively well, Georgia ranked among the bottom half-dozen states in the amount of income expended per pupil in average daily attendance. Despite significant reforms during the 1930s and before, Georgia during the 1940s faced an imminent crisis in education.

At the same time Georgia citizens enjoyed one of the least burdensome tax rates in the nation. Although state revenues increased during the 1940s, Georgia's per capita taxes at the end of the decade were the lowest in the South, with the typical Georgian paying approximately thirty-eight dollars in state taxes in 1949. Few political leaders seemed anxious to shoulder the responsibility for changing this situation. Other factors further complicated the public school debate. Educational reform was linked to school consolidation, which meant the elimination of numerous rural, "neighborhood" schools. As separate-but-equal educational facilities came under attack in the federal courts, racial policy

became increasingly entwined with the formulation of educational programs. Ironically, this fusion of issues benefited the proponents of
reform. Georgia political leaders could support segregation and educational improvements, both of which most white Georgians approved.
Consequently, many segregationists, who hoped to preserve separate
facilities by equalizing them, joined with the school forces, many of
whom had long been struggling to improve education, to generate political momentum. The 1949 session of the General Assembly approved by
large majorities a Minimum Foundation Program, which was designed
to equalize educational opportunities by providing state support sufficient to assure all school districts a minimal level of funding per student. There was, however, the question of funding. The legislators were
not willing to enact the taxes necessary to implement the program;
when the issue was referred to the popular electorate, Georgia voters
refused to vote new taxes for education.

Ultimately, the state opted for better schools at the expense of higher
taxes. In 1951 the legislature, at the urging of Governor Herman Talmadge, enacted a 3 percent sales tax to provide the revenue for initiat-
ing the Minimum Foundation Program in the 1951–52 school year. The
result was a dramatically improved public school system, whether the
improvement was measured in attractiveness of the buildings, educational level of the teachers, or per pupil expenditures of public funds.
By 1960 the rural one-teacher schools had virtually disappeared, as
Georgia children rode school buses to fewer but bigger schools. Indeed,
the number of schools in operation declined by more than half during
the 1950s. Students also remained in school longer. In 1947 the state
legislature authorized state support for the addition of a twelfth grade,
and by 1954 the transition from an eleven- to a twelve-grade system was
complete. Salaries for teachers improved significantly, and the gap between white and black teacher pay was substantially eliminated. By the
end of the 1950s the state was paying almost three-quarters of public
school costs, which in practice meant spending tax monies collected in
the cities and suburbs to support rural schools. Although metropolitan
whites still received the most expensive educations, the disparity in expenditures between metropolis and countryside declined, and the chasm
between expenditures for whites and blacks narrowed considerably. In
the 1953–54 school year Georgia spent approximately $190 per white
student and $132 per black in average daily attendance. Overt racial
discrimination finally ended following the passage of federal civil rights
legislation in 1964. Overall, public expenditures per pupil in average
daily attendance increased tenfold between 1941 and 1970. The Mini-

mum Foundation Program and the consumer-oriented taxation system that supported it launched Georgia into a new era of public education.

Developments in higher education broadly paralleled those in the public schools. During the early 1940s a severe crisis over academic freedom shook the University System. Fundamentally, the controversy involved the extent to which traditionalist political leaders could suppress unpopular ideologies on the state campuses. Governor Eugene Talmadge, shortly after assuming office in 1941, apparently came to the conclusion that unsouthern, integrationist ideas were rife within the University System. In the spring of 1941 the governor demanded that the Board of Regents fire Walter D. Cocking, the dean of the University of Georgia College of Education, and Marvin S. Pittman, the president of Georgia Teachers College at Statesboro. Both were talented and able educators, but both also possessed advanced degrees from a New York university, shared an interest in improving educational opportunities for Georgia children whether white or black, and held key positions in Georgia teacher-training institutions. In a series of meetings during 1941, the Regents, with the governor an ex officio member, voted to fire the two administrators; then, after University of Georgia president Harmon Caldwell threatened to resign over the issue, voted not to fire them; then, after Talmadge replaced three members of the Board of Regents, voted to fire both educators. This action, which Talmadge described as an effort to remove "foreign professors trying to destroy the sacred traditions of the South," was followed by the dismissal of eight other University System employees and a search for "subversive" textbooks used in the Georgia education system. A committee found twenty-three "subversive" texts, which the State Board of Education promptly banned from the public schools. The "subversive" books, it turned out, harbored unwelcome assumptions about such things as the humanity of black people and the scientific inadequacy of the Biblical explanation of the creation.

Within a year the Talmadge administration had established domination over the Board of Regents, arbitrarily dismissed ten educators, and purged the school libraries. The Southern Association of College and Secondary Schools investigated these activities and voted in December 1941 to remove accreditation from the ten state-supported colleges for whites in Georgia, and other accreditation agencies, including those dealing with the state law school and the state medical school, took similar actions. The smoldering controversy became a central issue in the 1942 gubernatorial primary election, with Talmadge defending his position and his leading opponent, Attorney General Ellis G. Arnall, denouncing it. Arnall won the election and, after becoming governor, helped to reorganize the Board of Regents, removing the governor from membership and granting the board greater independence from political interference. This action restored the University System to good standing with accreditation organizations. The result was a crucial victory for academic freedom, and one that has thus far proved enduring.

The University System, like the public schools, suffered from limited financial resources during the 1940s, although returning World War II veterans who took advantage of the GI Bill pushed registration up in the latter half of the decade. Both funding and student enrollment grew significantly during the 1950s and then virtually exploded during the 1960s. With the baby-boom children reaching college age in a time of economic prosperity, financial support and enrollment skyrocketed. The University System's student body numbered 15,458 in the 1952–53 academic year, 44,279 in 1964–65, and 102,542 in 1971–72. The University of Georgia mushroomed from an institution of 4,234 students in 1952–53 to 21,480 in 1969–70. Even more dramatic was the rapid expansion of Georgia State University. Originating as the Georgia Tech Evening School, it became the Atlanta Division of the University of Georgia in 1947, the Georgia State College of Business Administration in 1955, George State College in 1961, and finally in 1969 Georgia State University. At that time Georgia State joined the University of Georgia, the Georgia Institute of Technology, and the Medical College of Georgia as the chief state-supported centers of advanced graduate work. By the fall of 1974 Georgia State had almost nineteen thousand students compared to the more than twenty-one thousand at the University of Georgia and above eight thousand at the Georgia Institute of Technology. These figures, however, included students enrolled in the substantial part-time evening school program at Georgia State. In terms of equivalent full-time enrollment, the University of Georgia had approximately twenty thousand students in the fall of 1974, Georgia State University more than half that many, and Georgia Tech approximately eight thousand. Comparable growth occurred in virtually all areas of the University System, which expanded from seven senior institutions and six junior colleges in 1943 to seventeen senior schools and fourteen junior colleges in the mid-1970s. By the mid-1970s Georgia Southern College at Statesboro enrolled more than six thousand students and West Georgia College at Carrollton approximately fifty-five hundred. Graduate programs at the major institutions experienced

similar expansions. At the University of Georgia the graduate enrollment leaped from just over seven hundred in 1960 to almost four
thousand in the mid-1970s.

Georgia's thirty-three private colleges and universities also enjoyed
flush times during the postwar period. Emory University remained the
most prestigious of the private institutions. Particularly noteworthy was
Emory's Woodruff Medical Center, which included the schools of medicine, dentistry, and nursing, the University Clinic, the Yerkes Regional
Primate Center, two hospitals, and the Division of Basic Health Services. The Medical Center, in combination with the nearby federally
operated Center for Disease Control and other facilities, made Atlanta
one of the nation's leading centers of medical research. The Atlanta
University Center, the world's largest predominantly black college complex, grew substantially and offered a broader range of study. The institutions comprising the center, including Atlanta University, Clark,
Morris Brown, Morehouse, and Spelman colleges, the Gammon Theological Seminary, and the Atlanta School of Social Work, further integrated their educational facilities, including the establishment of a joint
library. As in the past, the center continued to produce graduates who
became leaders in a variety of fields.

Such rapid growth generated a variety of pressures. Harried administrators planned for the construction of more classrooms and laboratories
and recruited new faculty members to man them. Policies conceived in
quieter times often seemed outmoded as institutions expanded. On the
complacent campuses of the 1950s, male students rarely participated in
activities more controversial than an occasional panty raid at a female
dormitory, while female students were subject to a range of in loco
parentis regulations, including dormitory curfews and dress codes. The
students of the 1960s, particularly those in the larger institutions and in
predominantly black colleges, were not only more numerous but also
less docile. Influenced by the civil rights movement and the war in Viet
Nam, students were more likely to participate in protest activities and
to raise objections to restrictive campus regulations. Similarly, the pro-
liferation of new faculty members called traditional practices into question and created pressures for internal reforms. Such activities were
rather modest in comparison to events on the campuses in most other
states; nevertheless, the 1960s was a hectic and, on the whole, probably
a healthy period for the University System. By the mid-1970s both
student enrollment and public largess had leveled off and the era of
rapid expansion in higher education seemed to have ended.

Educational programs absorbed a substantial proportion of governmental dollars during the postwar period. In 1970 Georgia allotted almost half the state budget for the support of education, which was a considerably higher percentage than the national norm. Yet, in spite of important gains, Georgia continued to lag well behind national norms in per pupil funding and in academic accomplishment. Georgia's expenditures per pupil in average daily attendance in the early 1970s was less than three-quarters of the national average. The state also had one of the highest drop-out rates in the nation, ranking second highest during the 1972–73 school year. Only 50 percent of the Georgia youngsters who entered the first grade in 1958 actually graduated from high school, and only about half of these continued on to college. The state chairman of Georgians for Quality Public Education recently reported that half of Georgia's eighth-grade students were one or more years behind the national average in reading skills, and that twice as many Georgians as other Americans failed the mental examinations for draftees.

Similarly, Georgia spent far more on public welfare and health than it had in the past while continuing to lag well behind the performance of other states. In 1970 Georgia dispersed almost $150 million, most of

Cheerleaders lead the Georgia Bulldogs onto the field
University of Georgia

which came from the federal government, to the aged, the blind, the permanently disabled, and to families with dependent children, which was a substantial increase over the approximately $62 million distributed in 1955. The number of people receiving public assistance also grew rapidly, so that by 1973 one Georgian in ten was receiving welfare, a figure that would be even higher if food stamp recipients were included. Consequently, public assistance payments remained extremely low in Georgia. By far the largest of the welfare programs was aid to families with dependent children, for which Georgia paid $28.45 per recipient compared to the national monthly average of $49.50. The gap was greatest at the local level, where general assistance aid in Georgia averaged $21.15 monthly, well under half the national average. In health care, Georgia has come far since the days of hookworm and pellagra, including the lowering of the infant mortality rate from 57.8 per thousand in 1940 to 22.4 in 1970. But this was still above the national average, especially for black Georgians. The state had significantly fewer doctors per capita than the nation as a whole, and of these, almost half practiced in the Atlanta area, leaving the rest of the state and especially the rural and small-town areas with an acute shortage of both doctors and dentists. Federal Medicare and Medicaid programs have made medical care more accessible to low-income and older citizens.

Although historically trailing other states in prison reform, Georgia has made significant strides in recent years, especially as a result of the decline of county work camps. Georgia had 125 county-operated chain-gang camps in 1937, when a federal study concluded "that in the interests of decency and humanity they should be abandoned." By 1950, when the leg irons and shackles were abolished, the state had only 84 camps, and by early 1974 this number had declined to 42 and these on the whole were far more humane than those of the past. Since the county camps were filled by state prisoners farmed out to the counties, the decline in county work camps meant a heavier burden and consequent problems for state facilities. Overcrowded conditions and inadequate rehabilitation programs continued to plague the state prison system. Jails maintained by local governmental units were also a persistent problem. The Governor's Commission on Criminal Justice reported in 1974 that "the conditions in many of the over 150 county jails and 220 municipal jails are a disgrace." Nevertheless, the gradual passing of the county road gang was something that few would mourn, least of all the unfortunate people who had served in one.

The profound changes in daily routine demanded by the transition from a rural to an urban way of life were no doubt of considerably greater significance to typical Georgians than were many of the broader but less personal initiatives in state policy. Rising per capita income accelerated the shift away from homemade and homegrown products and spurred an unprecedented demand for consumer goods and services. In 1940 less than half of Georgia's homes had electricity, only a quarter contained a refrigerator, and hardly any housed an electric cooking range. A large majority of rural homes and a substantial minority of urban dwellings had outdoor toilets. By the 1960s the vast majority of homes had electric lights, radios, refrigerators, cooking ranges, telephones, and indoor plumbing; a significant number contained automatic washers and dryers, automatic dishwashers, and other conveniences. Additionally, there was the largely simultaneous introduction of television and air conditioning. Both items became generally available during the late 1940s and within a decade were household commodities throughout the state.

The first Georgia television station was WSB–TV, which began operation in Atlanta in 1948. Thereafter commercial television developed rapidly, with a fluctuating number of twelve or fifteen stations operating during the 1960s. The Georgia Department of Education owned most of the educational television stations with one operated by the Atlanta City School Board and another by the University of Georgia, the latter the best known and most popular in the state. Most of the commercial stations were affiliated with one of the national broadcasting companies (American, Columbia, and National), while the educational stations were affiliated with National Educational Television. It goes without saying that the educational stations' viewer ratings were very small compared with commercial stations. By the late 1960s, approximately 94 percent of Georgia homes contained television sets, a growing number of them providing color pictures.

Television and temperature control were significant factors influencing the design of houses in the proliferating subdivisions. No longer was the front porch the most comfortable place for a family to congregate in the late afternoon and evening; indeed, newer houses rarely had porches. Instead they had family rooms or dens designed for the viewing of television in air conditioned comfort. Architecturally the dreary sameness of so much of the subdivision housing left much to be desired; nevertheless, these housing developments provided ordinary Georgia families with comfortable homes that were far superior to those generally available in the past. The home-loan guarantee programs of the Federal Housing Administration and the Veterans Administration made modest down payment requirements, low interest rates, and long-term mortgage financing the norm in Georgia, as elsewhere in the nation. The result was a vast increase in both the number of houses constructed and the percentage of families owning their own homes. Between 1940 and 1970 the number of dwelling units in Georgia doubled. The bulk of this construction occurred in urban areas, where dwellings numerically tripled from less than 300,000 in 1940 to almost 900,000 in 1970. Equally dramatic was the expansion of home ownership. In 1940 only three in ten Georgia housing units were owner occupied; three decades later six in ten were. Consequently, during the postwar years most Georgia families could afford—or at least could with some confidence look forward to affording—a house in the suburbs. By the early 1970s the spiraling cost of construction material and energy resources along with heightened interest rates had again elevated such housing above the grasp of most families.

Regardless of the amount of time spent viewing television, substantial numbers of Georgians also found opportunities for church activities. Throughout the post–World War II era, somewhat more than 60 percent of the state's population was affiliated with a religious organization. The majority of church members, according to a study conducted during the mid-1950s, were Baptists. The Southern Baptist Convention claimed more than three-quarters of a million members in Georgia, and black Baptists numbered more than a half-million. Methodists remained the second largest denominational group, with more than a half-million white and black members. A survey in the mid-1960s reported that Georgia contained almost sixty-five hundred white Protestant churches, approximately three thousand black Protestant churches, thirty-one Roman Catholic parishes, and thirty Jewish synagogues. Roman Catholics, most of whom were urban and about two-thirds of whom resided in the Atlanta area, were the most numerous of non-Protestants. The evolution from a predominantly rural to a predominantly urban church membership not only left Baptists and Methodists dominant numerically but also had limited observable effect on the essentially fundamentalist theology observed by most Georgia religious bodies. The urban environment demanded changes, of course, and the social role of the church no doubt declined. In Atlanta in the mid-1960s, investigators found that four out of ten church members were not actively involved in any phase of religious activity, which meant that only about four out of ten Atlantans actually participated in church services. Nevertheless, the urban churches were bigger, employed better-trained ministers, and sponsored a wider variety of functions.

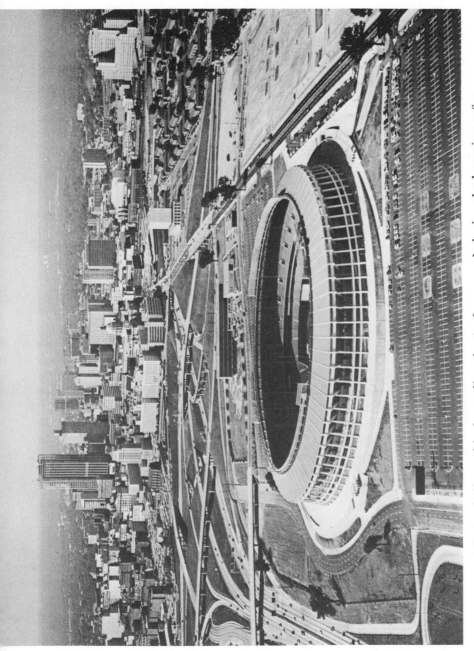

Atlanta skyline, with the stadium in the foreground, during the booming 1960s
Georgia Department of Archives and History

Most of the evidence suggested that organized religion would continue to play a central role in Georgia life.

Atlanta was the social and cultural capital of Georgia to a greater degree than it was the political capital. Only a few years ago, as journalist Neal Pierce phrased it, observers could not "have dreamed that future visitors would discover Yankees on Peachtree Street, Negroes in City Hall, hippies in the parks, and a social scene one reporter called 'the sauciest, swingingest' in America. . . ." During the 1960s Atlanta also became a major-league sports center. The Atlanta Stadium housed the Falcons football team and the Braves baseball team and the Omni coliseum the Hawks basketball team and the Flames hockey team. Culturally Atlanta excelled in architecture, highlighted by Peachtree Center, with its towering Merchandise Mart and the breathtaking Hyatt Regency Hotel. The Arts Festival of Atlanta, held each spring since 1954, brought the best in regional painting and sculpture to a mass audience and included live symphony, ballet, and theater performances. For a more limited audience, Theatre Atlanta, under the direction of Jay Broad, was one of the nation's most vibrant theaters during the 1960s, specializing in both serious drama and iconoclastic political satire, including highly acclaimed productions of the controversial "MacBird" and "Red, White, and Maddox." The demise of Theatre Atlanta coincided with the completion of the Atlanta Memorial Arts Center, which housed the Alliance Theatre Company, the High Museum of Art, the Atlanta School of Art, and the Atlanta Symphony Orchestra, the latter gaining national distinction under the direction of Robert Shaw.

Elsewhere in the state, Savannah enjoyed considerable success in combining change with the Old South charm of Georgia's oldest city. The Historic Savannah Foundation, created in 1954, has conducted a vigorous and thus far successful crusade to restore and preserve the city plan drawn up by James Oglethorpe in the eighteenth century and the city's charming nineteenth-century homes. The tasteful River Street Development, a new civic center, and some of the finest cuisine in the state contributed to Savannah's appeal as a national tourist attraction. The Coastal Empire Arts Festival, held annually since 1959 at Emmet Park, featured a variety of activities in art, music, drama, and crafts. The Savannah Symphony was second only to that of Atlanta, and it has been particularly successful in reaching youthful audiences.

The redefinition of human rights generated by the civil rights movement exerted a strong influence on intellectual life in Georgia. Ralph E. McGill, the state's best-known journalist, won a Pulitzer Prize in

1958 for his editorial opposition to intolerance. Sometimes known as the "Conscience of the South," McGill was editor and later publisher of the *Atlanta Constitution*. Among literary figures, Lillian Smith was one of the first southern authors to deal openly with racial themes. Her first novel, *Strange Fruit,* published in 1944, stirred controversy because of its portrayal of an interracial romance. While writing five other works during the 1950s and early 1960s, Miss Smith was active in the civil rights movement. She was a member of the Congress of Racial Equality until ultimately resigning in protest of the organization's growing militancy. Also active in and influenced by the civil rights movement was Alice Walker, a black author whose work poignantly depicted the trials and sufferings of poorer blacks and especially black women. Interestingly, the leading Georgia-born black novelist Frank G. Yerby specialized in historical romances and popular literature. Viewing the novel primarily as a form of entertainment, he evidenced little concern for social issues. Carson McCullers, another native Georgian who spent most of her life outside the state, dealt in her novels and plays with the paradoxes and tragedies of a deteriorating mill-town, wasteland South peopled with grotesque figures. Also within the southern Gothic school of writers was Flannery O'Connor, whose themes and characters were often grotesque but whose works displayed a concern for the comic and spiritual not found in McCullers's writing. Conrad Aiken, winner of both the Pulitzer Prize and the National Book Award, was the premier Georgia-born poet, and Lamar Dodd, head of the University of Georgia Department of Art, was the state's leading artist.

Georgians found life in an urban age more complex and hectic than it had been in the past. The crowded chain stores in the shopping malls had little in common with the country store of old. Material conditions improved enormously, whether the criteria were the homes in which they lived, the schools to which they sent their children, or the income derived from their employment. The evidence also suggested that the material environment had changed more fundamentally than had Georgians themselves. For the most part, the traditions molded by Georgia history seemed in no immediate danger of disappearance.

XXVI

Politics and Government in the Postwar Era

The epic changes taking place in the patterns of Georgia race relations shaped the political competition of the era. More often than not state-wide campaigns centered on social issues. During much of the period the county-unit system, a malapportioned legislature, and low voter turnout further shackled Georgia politics. While a number of able people served in high offices and the state made important achievements in some fields, Georgia governmental officials devoted much of their attention to resisting the federal government, opposing black gains, and defending the "southern way of life." As a result Georgia politics often appeared out of touch with broader national issues. Not until the break-down of the Jim Crow system and the gradual acceptance of desegregation by white Georgians did the state have an opportunity to reenter the mainstream of national politics.

In the United States Congress the Georgia delegation was with few exceptions during the postwar years united in opposition to domestic reform, especially if it involved civil rights, and in support for military spending and an uncompromising anticommunist stance in foreign affairs. The state's two most influential congressmen—Senator Richard B. Russell and Representative Carl Vinson—served as chairmen of the armed services committees in their respective chambers. Russell was also the acknowledged leader during the 1950s and 1960s of the southern anti–civil rights bloc in Congress. Russell and Vinson as well as Senator Walter F. George, chairman of the Foreign Relations Committee before his retirement in 1957, and Senator Herman E. Talmadge, chairman of the Committee on Agriculture, carved distinguished legislative careers. But as a whole Georgia congressmen remained attuned to the defense of rural and small-town white southern values.

In Georgia the state legislature increasingly reflected acreage more accurately than people. By 1960 legislators representing less than a third of the population commanded clear majorities in both houses. In a care-ful study of the composition of the General Assembly, Hugh M. Thom-ason found that legislators were most likely to be native-born white males who had previously served as local county or municipal officials and who were apt to be lawyers, farmers, or merchants. Not surprisingly, these rural and small-town legislators often showed more interest in local legislation than in broader statewide measures. Legislators were prompt to react to any threat to segregation or the county-unit system, which would have directly affected their own bailiwicks, but otherwise they normally cooperated with the governor in enacting his statewide program. The county-unit system insured, however, that the governor would be heavily indebted to the smaller counties for his election. The 242 unit votes cast by the 121 smallest counties overwhelmed the 168 votes held by the 38 larger counties that contained over two-thirds of the population in 1960.

The county-unit system went hand-in-hand with the domination of state politics by the Talmadge faction of the Democratic party. The 1940s began with Eugene Talmadge once again being elected to the governorship. Shortly after assuming office, Talmadge launched an attack on academic freedom that threatened the accreditation of the ten state-supported colleges for whites in Georgia. College students, struggling to earn degrees that would soon be unrecognized outside the state, hanged the governor—red galluses and all—in effigy, mounted protest demonstrations, and gave strong support to Attorney General Ellis G. Arnall, Talmadge's opponent in the 1942 gubernatorial primary. In the campaign, Arnall labeled Talmadge a "dictator" seeking to control education for "his own selfish ends," a charge that was particularly effective at a time when the nation was at war with fascist powers abroad. Arnall won the election with 57 percent of the popular votes and a solid majority of county-unit votes; he became the first governor under the constitution of 1877 to serve a four-year term as a result of a constitutional amendment ratified in 1941.

The Arnall administration established a national reputation for dignified, honest, and effective government. Arnall successfully sponsored a wide range of significant reforms, including the establishment of a state civil service system, the reorganization of important areas of state government, the extension of the suffrage to eighteen-year-olds and the repeal of the poll tax, the correction of at least the more shocking abuses in the Georgia prison system, and the ratification of a new constitution, which was drafted by a commission with Arnall serving as chairman. The governor also found time during his tenure to lead a successful fight against discriminatory freight rates, personally arguing Georgia's case before the United States Supreme Court. Since Arnall refused to seek a raise in taxes, many of the reforms of his administration suffered from lack of adequate funding and accomplished less than had been hoped. Similarly, the 1945 constitution updated but did not fundamentally change the constitution of 1877. Nevertheless, Georgia's governmental accomplishments were notable.

The 1946 governor's race has often and justly been regarded as a classic county-unit campaign. Eugene Talmadge once again hit the campaign trail, and he was ably assisted by his son Herman Talmadge and by former house speaker Roy Harris, who together organized Ole Gene's last campaign. After analyzing each separate county, they concluded that seventy-five counties could be regarded as safe, fifty-nine counties as hopeless, and twenty-five counties as close. They then concentrated their efforts on those twenty-five counties. Talmadge stressed the racial issue, decrying the political influence of the growing black electorate and promising to restore the white primary. The strongest anti-Talmadge candidate was James V. Carmichael, a Marietta businessman and former legislator. Carmichael avoided race-baiting and promised in his campaign to promote Georgia's economic progress. He also enjoyed the open support of Governor Ellis Arnall, which was undoubtedly an important asset in lining up support in the counties but one that also led to a major problem for the anti-Talmadge faction. Former Governor Eurith D. Rivers had helped Arnall to be elected in 1942, and he expected Arnall to return the favor in 1946. When Arnall instead turned to Carmichael, Rivers ran anyway, thus dividing the anti-Talmadge vote. A heavy turnout gave Carmichael 313,389 votes, Talmadge 297,245, and Rivers 69,489, making Carmichael the popular favorite by a plurality. But Talmadge won the election by securing 242 county unit votes compared to Carmichael's 146 and Rivers's 22.

Talmadge won the Democratic nomination, but by the time of the November 1946 general election it was clear that he was not in good health. Because of this, a group of the family's supporters organized a write-in campaign on behalf of son Herman. Eugene Talmadge won the general election, but he died in December 1946, a few weeks before being inaugurated. The Georgia Constitution charged the General Assembly with tallying the general election ballots and declaring the "person" with a majority the winner. If "no person" had a majority, the legislature was to make the selection from the two candidates with the most votes. The Talmadge forces, with strong support in the legislature, argued that since the elder Talmadge was dead, he was no longer a "person" in the legal sense, and consequently the legislature should choose the governor from the two candidates with the highest number of write-in votes, of whom young Herman Talmadge would be the

Eugene Talmadge on the campaign trail

Georgia Department of Archives and History

logical choice. Governor Arnall, on the other hand, cited that portion of the constitution that required the outgoing governor to remain in office "until his successor shall be chosen and qualified" and insisted he would surrender the office only to incoming Lieutenant Governor Melvin E. Thompson, who Arnall felt was the rightful heir and who was also a member of the anti-Talmadge faction. With the debate well underway, the legislature met and counted the votes. Talmadge leaders were stunned to learn that Carmichael had 669 write-in votes, Republican D. Talmadge Bowers had 637, and Herman Talmadge only 619, thus eliminating him from consideration. Then, fortuitously for the Talmadge forces, an additional 56 votes for Talmadge from his home county of Telfair were surprisingly "discovered," thus raising the Talmadge total to 675 and making him the leader of the write-in candidates. The General Assembly promptly elected him governor. When Arnall refused to surrender the office, the Talmadge forces physically seized both the governor's office and the executive mansion. Finally, Arnall surrendered the governorship in favor of Thompson, who set up a downtown office as governor in exile. In March, just over two months after Talmadge had taken over the executive office, the state supreme court declared Thompson to be acting governor. The affair solidified Herman's position as the new leader of the Talmadge faction.

Upon surrendering the governorship, Talmadge vowed the final decision would be made in "the court of last resort—the people," and in the 1948 special gubernatorial election Talmadge and Thompson were the major opponents. Emulating his father, Talmadge conducted a race-baiting campaign, championing white supremacy and the rights of states and harshly criticizing President Harry S. Truman's civil rights program. Thompson, while also defending segregation, conducted a moderate if somewhat lackluster campaign. In the backwash of the strife-torn national Democratic convention and the formation of the white southern Dixiecrat party, the Talmadge emotional appeal to social conservatism was extremely effective. He won a heavy majority of county-unit votes and a comfortable popular majority.

The 1950 gubernatorial primary presented the anti-Talmadge faction an opportunity for a resurgence but one which its leaders failed to capitalize upon. Important members of the faction had not been enamored with Thompson's uninspiring performance as governor and as a losing candidate two years before, yet he insisted upon running. Since a second anti-Talmadge candidate would simply divide the vote and insure Talmadge's election, a number of prominent anti-Talmadge leaders, including Arnall, remained inactive during the campaign; others who had supported Thompson in 1948, such as E. D. Rivers, backed Talmadge. But despite organizational weaknesses, Thompson made a strong race, almost matching Talmadge in popular votes though trailing considerably in the county-unit tally.

During his six-year tenure, Herman Talmadge proved to be a strong governor and a capable administrator. The most important public policy gains during the Talmadge years were in the field of education. Although knowledgeable observers had regarded as politically dangerous the governor's support for sales tax legislation, the improvements in education and public services won the Talmadge administration high praise. Talmadge's governorship had been free of public scandal, and, indeed, a 1949 voting law establishing a genuine secret ballot in Georgia for the first time largely curtailed the chicanery and graft in the counting and casting of ballots that had plagued the state for almost a century. Additionally, the *Brown* decision requiring desegregation of the schools strengthened the Talmadge faction, which was generally recognized as an unrelenting defender of white supremacy. The governor's prompt and belligerent opposition to the decision, including his sponsorship of the private-school amendment, significantly augmented administration support.

By the time of the next gubernatorial election in 1954, the Talmadge administration enjoyed enormous prestige. Since Talmadge was constitutionally banned from being a candidate for reelection, the 1954 race was a free-for-all, with nine candidates, three of them from the Talmadge faction, declaring for the office. M. E. Thompson was once again the chief anti-Talmadge candidate, although Charles Gowen, a state legislator from Brunswick, also competed for the anti-Talmadge vote. As the campaign progressed, Lieutenant Governor S. Marvin Griffin emerged as the strongest of the Talmadge faction's contenders. A folksy and witty Bainbridge newspaper editor, Griffin had served as adjutant general and had given important support to Talmadge in the three-governors controversy of 1947 before being elected lieutenant governor in 1948. During the campaign Griffin frequently reminded voters that he had served as lieutenant governor during the six years of the Talmadge administration, and he avidly championed "Georgia's two greatest traditions—segregation and the county-unit system." In the backwash of the *Brown* decision, Griffin's folksy defense of old values apparently proved compelling and he won the bulk of the county-unit votes.

Griffin's surprisingly easy victory in the gubernatorial race marked the termination of the heated bifactionalism between Talmadgeites and anti-Talmadgeites that had structured Democratic primary competition. Two years later, in 1956, Talmadge was elected to the United States Senate. The prestigious but aging Walter George chose to retire rather than to defend his seat in what would have been an uphill battle against the popular former governor. With George declining to run, Talmadge faced his customary foe, M. E. Thompson. Talmadge won an overwhelming victory with more than 80 percent of the popular vote. In the 1958 governor's race, S. Ernest Vandiver, a member of the Talmadge faction and a nephew to Senator Russell, won more than eight of every ten votes against weak opposition in the Democratic primary. The racial emotionalism of the massive-resistance era, the county-unit system, and the prestige of the Talmadge leaders effectively destroyed the anti-Talmadge faction, while Talmadge's movement to Washington and the lack of strong opposition undermined the cohesion of the Talmadge faction. Bifactionalism had never been an adequate substitute for a genuine two-party system, but it had succeeded in giving some form to Georgia one-party politics.

During the 1940s and early 1950s the voters responded with considerable consistency to the appeals of the competing factions. Talmadge candidates fared best among white voters residing in rural and small-town areas, especially those in south and central Georgia, and in the working-class districts in the cities. The two Talmadges and Marvin Griffin were all extremely able campaigners adept at projecting a "good ole boy," common man image. As the state's most vociferous proponents of the county-unit system and white supremacy, they appealed to the disoriented whites of the declining rural areas and to lower-status whites who felt threatened by black advancements. Because of its appeal in the rural areas, the Talmadge faction was the chief beneficiary of the county-unit system. Anti-Talmadge candidates ran best in the cities, where they drew their major support from affluent urban-suburban white neighborhoods and from black precincts. Black voters preferred the racially moderate and economically progressive anti-Talmadge faction to its belligerently segregationist rival. The business–professional–white collar whites of the cities and suburbs generally deplored the unfavorable national image projected by the race-baiting antics and rural style of the Talmadge candidates. Committed to economic progress and a good business atmosphere, they looked to the anti-Talmadge faction as the defender of urban interests. This factionalized conflict between the dynamic urban-suburban areas and the static or declining rural and small-town regions decreased in the late 1950s, but during the 1960s it sharply reemerged in a form modified by profound changes in Georgia's political institutions.

The first in a series of seismic shocks to buffet the structure of Georgia politics was the federal district court decision of *Gray* v. *Sanders* in the spring of 1962 declaring the county-unit system unconstitutional. The court ruling, handed down while a special session of the legislature was attempting to modify the system in order to save it, found "invidious discrimination" in the unequal weighing of votes. The United States Supreme Court ultimately upheld and strengthened the district court decision, but in the meantime the state Democratic party executive committee voted to conduct the 1962 Democratic primaries on the basis of popular rather than county-unit votes. For the first time in half a century, the voters were called upon directly to determine the outcome of a primary election, and this novel situation had an immediate impact on Georgia politics. Carl E. Sanders, state senator from Augusta, conducted a media-oriented campaign aimed toward urban voters that differed substantially from electioneering practices customary in county-unit contests. Former Governor Marvin Griffin, generally considered the frontrunner in the campaign prior to the court decision, appeared more vulnerable in a contest based on popular ballots. Griffin conducted a relatively traditional campaign, relying heavily on personal contacts in the counties. With his folksy backcountry speeches and his defense of segregation and the county-unit system, Griffin seemed attuned to the past; whereas Sanders, with his tailored TV style and his support of racial moderation and economic progress, presented a progressive image. On election day, Sanders and Griffin split the votes from the countryside about evenly, with Sanders carrying most of the counties in the northern half of the state and Griffin winning in the south. The election was decided in the metropolitan areas, where Sanders won massive majorities, particularly in black and upper-income white neighborhoods.

The federal court ruled the county-unit system unconstitutional in April 1962; in May the court handed down its decision in *Toombs* v. *Fortson*, which required the General Assembly to reapportion on the basis of population. Just as it had in the county-unit case, the court found "invidious discrimination" in the allotment of legislative seats. The three-judge panel ordered at least one house of the assembly to be reapportioned prior to the 1963 session. Consequently, just after the Democratic primary elections, Governor Vandiver called another special session of the legislature to deal with reapportionment. The legislature revamped senatorial districts and greatly increased urban representation, with Fulton County's senatorial delegation leaping from one member to seven. In 1965 the General Assembly reapportioned the lower house. Although further litigation was required to settle differences between what the court considered fair representation and what the General Assembly found sufficient, Georgia had by the mid-1960s accepted people rather than geography as the determining factor in the allocation of legislative seats. Completing this shift, the legislature complied with the United States Supreme Court decision of *Wesberry* v. *Sanders* and reapportioned the state's ten congressional districts.

These epic events transpired during the same period that the civil rights movement reached its crest and the United States Congress enacted the civil rights laws of 1964 and 1965. If Marvin Griffin was correct when in the mid-1950s he lauded "Georgia's two greatest traditions —segregation and the county unit system," then by the mid-1960s Georgia had undergone changes that were fundamental indeed. A social system based on caste and a political system based on malapportionment had both collapsed under federal governmental pressure. Not surprisingly developments of such magnitude unleashed volatile political currents. Voter turnout increased significantly, and, for the first time since the heyday of populism, an opposition party emerged to challenge Democratic one-party dominance of state politics.

The Republican party had been making gradual progress in Georgia since the early 1950s. General Dwight D. Eisenhower won 30.3 percent of the state's popular vote in 1952, a considerable improvement over the 18 or 19 percent Republican presidential candidates received during the 1940s. Perhaps more importantly, Eisenhower contributed to making Republicanism respectable, at least at the presidential level. Eisenhower in 1952 and again in 1956, and Vice President Richard M. Nixon in 1960, ran extremely well in affluent urban-suburban areas and with somewhat less consistency also fared well in urban black neighborhoods. During these years moderate business-oriented Republicans who had moved into leadership positions in the Eisenhower era dominated the party councils. The emergence of Senator Barry M. Goldwater as a contender for the Republican presidential nomination, however, attracted a vigorous new group of staunchly conservative adherents to the GOP standard, and they won control of the party at the 1964 Republican state convention. The Georgia delegation overwhelmingly supported Goldwater's nomination at the national Republican convention and then organized an impressive campaign in Georgia for his election.

In the 1964 general election Goldwater became the first Republican presidential candidate ever to carry Georgia's electoral votes. Racial issues clearly dominated the campaign. The election followed passage of the 1964 Civil Rights Act, which President Lyndon B. Johnson vigorously supported and Goldwater voted against. White Georgians had traditionally identified the Democratic party as the protector of states' rights in social matters, but by the mid-1960s the national Democrats had become the party of civil rights while the Republicans under Goldwater had assumed the states' rights mantle. Such prominent conservative Democrats as Marvin Griffin and Roy Harris rallied support for Goldwater, while the moderate wing of the state Democratic party headed by Governor Sanders supported Johnson. The voting returns in the election revealed a sharp break with past partisan alignments. The rural and small-town white voters in the south and central parts of the state who had remained steadfastly loyal to the party of their fathers throughout the modern period shifted heavily to Goldwater, joining the affluent white urban-suburban voters as well as the normally Democratic lower-income whites of the cities to give the Republican ticket a solid majority of over 54 percent. Black voters overwhelmingly supported Johnson, as did a majority of the counties in the northern third of the state. The Goldwater coattails were sufficiently long to carry into office a Republican congressman and a number of state legislators. Howard H. Callaway, the wealthy heir to a textile fortune and one of the former Democrats who shifted to the GOP to support the Goldwater candidacy, won in the Third Congressional District to become the first Republican congressman from Georgia in almost a century. Republican candidates also won sixteen seats in the General Assembly, and the party increased this number to thirty-two in the 1965 special house elections. To be sure, Goldwater lost nationally to Johnson by a heavy majority; the Republicans held only one of Georgia's congressional seats; and in a legislature of approximately 260 members the GOP claimed only 32 positions. At the same time the 1964 elections demonstrated the extent to which popular voting loyalties had been disrupted by the hectic events of the 1960s.

The resurgent Republican leadership awaited the 1966 state elections with ill-concealed enthusiasm. Congressman Callaway announced his candidacy for governor, and the early polls showed him holding a commanding lead. To ride the wake of his expected victory the Republicans nominated candidates for ninety-two state legislative and eight congressional seats. The Democrats were in their usual state of disarray. Former Governor Ernest Vandiver was the leading contender for the Democratic nomination until a heart attack forced his withdrawal from the race. That left former Governor Ellis Arnall, who like Rip Van Winkle reemerged after two decades of political retirement, the favorite in the Democratic primary. Distinctly a dark horse in the field of six candidates was Lester G. Maddox, an extreme segregationist who in three attempts had never won an election. Maddox had twice campaigned unsuccessfully for the mayor's office in Atlanta and had run a game but losing race for lieutenant governor in 1962. Formerly the proprietor of a flourishing restaurant in Atlanta, Maddox had made a reputation with his adamant and sometimes almost violent refusal to serve black customers. Ultimately he closed the restaurant rather than comply with the 1964 civil rights law. Lacking both an organization and adequate financing, Maddox traveled about the state, shaking hands and pasting up little signs that read "THIS IS MADDOX COUNTRY." But like Eugene Talmadge before him, Maddox had a genuine appeal to the white common folks, and he did well enough in the primary to finish second behind Arnall and win a spot in the runoff. Although Arnall was the acknowledged favorite in the race, his showing was not impressive. Arnall's last previous campaign had been in 1942, when he defeated Eugene Talmadge for the governorship. Even though he took mildly liberal positions on the issues, his 1966 campaign seemed quaintly dated, whereas Maddox projected a certain charisma with his earnest blend of social segregation and religious fundamentalism. In the runoff Maddox won a substantial victory to become the Democratic nominee for the governorship.

The 1966 gubernatorial election featured the novel spectacle of a hotly contested two-party campaign conducted by candidates who both took ultraconservative positions on the issues. Callaway and Maddox differed primarily in background and style. Callaway had been born to wealth and had earned a West Point degree; Maddox had been born poor and had dropped out of high school to go to work during the Depression. Dismayed Georgia liberals organized a write-in campaign with Arnall as their candidate. The election was extremely close. Maddox piled up enormous majorities in the rural and small-town counties while Callaway swept the metropolitan areas. The overall totals gave Callaway a slight lead, but the write-in campaign siphoned off enough votes to prevent either major candidate from receiving a majority. Once again the state legislature was required to select the winner from the two people receiving the most votes, and the predominantly Democratic assembly promptly chose Maddox as governor. The surprisingly strong Maddox showing doomed Republican hopes of making gains in lesser offices. The GOP lost three seats in the state legislature, although the party did win two congressional seats, both in the Atlanta area.

The political strife of the 1960s drove voter registration and turnout to unprecedented levels, at least by modern Georgia standards. In the presidential election of 1960, approximately 30 percent of the state's voting-age citizenry cast ballots, whereas in the 1964 election, when for the first time in history more than one million Georgians appeared at the polls, 45.2 percent of citizens of voting age exercised the franchise. Voter registration increased from less than half the voting-age population in 1960 to better than two-thirds in 1970. Black voter registration more than doubled during the decade, so that by 1970 Negroes comprised just under 20 percent of Georgia's registered electorate. In 1960 somewhat more than 1 million whites and about 180,000 blacks were registered; in 1970 these figures had increased to more than 1.6 million and 390,000 respectively. With greater numbers of blacks voting, black political candidates became increasingly common. In 1962 Leroy R. Johnson of Atlanta desegregated the General Assembly by winning a seat in the state senate, and by the end of the decade he had been joined by another black senator and twelve black representatives.

The state's expanding electorate turned out in record numbers for the 1968 presidential election, a vigorously contested three-way race that probably delineated the main currents of mass voting behavior more clearly than any modern contest. American Independent party candidate George C. Wallace carried the state with approximately 43 percent of the ballots. His blend of populist economics and social reaction appealed strongly to white voters in rural and small-town counties and in the working-class districts in the cities, the same voting groups that had formed the base of the Talmadge faction's support and had once been the mainstay of national Democratic party support in the state. Republican Richard Nixon's economic conservatism and defense of social stability paralleled the attitudes of the urban bourgeoisie. He finished second in the race with about 30 percent of the vote by carrying affluent urban and suburban white neighborhoods as well as being Wallace's chief competitor among white voters generally. Epitomizing the deteriorating position of the national Democratic party in Georgia, Hubert H. Humphrey ran last with about 27 percent of the vote. His welfare economics and racial liberalism appealed mainly to black voters and to the limited number of liberal whites and loyalist Democrats.

In an earlier time, blacks and upper-income whites tended to support anti-Talmadge candidates, but in recent years the business–professional–

white collar whites have usually voted Republican while blacks have largely remained loyal to the Democrats. The Wallace following of lower-status whites has had seeming difficulty in finding a final resting place. In 1964 many of these voters opted for Goldwater, and in 1972 they overwhelmingly supported President Nixon, joining with the suburbanites to give Nixon a massive 75 percent of the vote. In state politics these voters have usually backed the Democratic candidates, heavily voting for Maddox in 1966 and helping to elect Democrat James E. Carter governor in 1970 and Sam Nunn United States Senator in 1972.

By the 1970s white Georgians, having experienced desegregation, had come to accept it, at least on a token level, and black Georgians had emerged as an important factor in electoral politics. As a result the fiercer defenders of the old order suffered a decline in both electoral support and popular prestige. Lester Maddox, who had been elected governor in 1966 and lieutenant governor in 1970, failed in his attempt to regain the governorship in 1974, when George D. Busbee won an upset victory over Maddox in the gubernatorial primary runoff election. In that contest rural voters divided while urban voters cast heavy majorities for Busbee.

The most dramatic indication of new directions in Georgia politics was the election of Jimmy Carter as president of the United States. The first Georgia governor ever openly to endorse equality before the law, Carter conducted a vigorous campaign to win the Democratic nomination for the presidency. He thereby became the first Georgian to be nominated for the presidency by a major party convention; the first resident of a Deep South state to be so nominated in a century and a half; and only the second resident southerner to head a national major party ticket since before the Civil War. In the 1976 general election Carter carried most of the southern and border states to become the first Georgian to serve as the nation's chief executive. Freed from the obligation to defend the caste system, Georgia and southern political leaders enjoyed greater opportunities in national politics than at any time since the early years of the Republic.

As Carter's presidential victory demonstrated, the events of the 1960s have fundamentally altered Georgia's political institutions. Jim Crow segregation, the county-unit system, one-party politics, disfranchisement, and malapportionment—the institutional pillars of the old order—have all been relegated to the past. When combined with vast economic and demographic changes, these political upheavals tended, understandably enough, to disorient Georgia voters and leave them groping toward either an accommodation with two-party politics or the restoration of a one-party system, perhaps under a different party label. The relatively fluid alignments that have resulted from the tripartite division of the Georgia electorate suggested that the state's politics will remain erratic and interesting for some time to come.

The Georgia government presided over an ever-expanding budget in its efforts to deal with state needs. State expenditures in 1970 totaled more than a billion and a half dollars, an eight-fold increase over the 1950 budget. This figure represented an expenditure of approximately $332 per person residing in the state. Even after taking inflation and increased population into account, governmental appropriations grew substantially, and Georgia public services were considerably better than they had been in the past. Relative to the rest of the nation, however, Georgia's funding for public projects appeared less impressive. Other states also used some of the money derived from postwar prosperity to expand the public sector, and as a result Georgia made little relative improvement and fell further behind in some areas. Georgia tax laws have changed little since the adoption of the sales tax in 1951, and compared to other states, Georgia spent less public money per citizen in 1970 than it did in 1960.

The significant advances in Georgia public programs resulted primarily from the expanding state economy and from federal initiatives that made increasing funds and improved programs available almost in spite of Georgia's political leadership. Although Governor Herman Talmadge's administration in the late 1940s and early 1950s launched a number of innovative programs, the chief executives that followed offered few new departures. Governor Marvin Griffin's administration expended its energies devising new methods to massively resist the Supreme Court's desegregation decree, while lax administration, alleged corruption, and an apparently rampant spoils system undermined governmental effectiveness. Governor Vandiver restored governmental integrity, but his administration was also caught up in the desegregation struggle and his chief accomplishment was that he did not close the schools to avoid desegregation. While Governor Sanders presided over the hectic mid-1960s with a refreshing dignity, his administration found little time or energy to deal with other basic problems. Of modern Georgia governors, Maddox is perhaps the most difficult to evaluate. One respected veteran Georgia journalist observed that "Lester Maddox has successfully demonstrated that Georgia does not need a governor"; another equally respected political reporter in *Newsweek* magazine gave Maddox high marks for a successful administration. As all of this suggests, there is as yet no consensus about the merits or lack thereof of his governorship. Although Maddox was in many ways both good and bad, a more innovative governor than his immediate predecessors, it seems safe to conclude that his administration shifted the course of state policy far less than many Georgians hoped or feared that it would.

It is far too early to offer a meaningful evaluation of the Carter administration, but it may well be that future historians will conclude that the Carter years marked a changed thrust in the course of state government. Most importantly, the Carter administration was the first in Georgia's history openly and affirmatively to espouse human equality. In his inaugural address Carter insisted: "the time for racial discrimination is over. Our people have already made this major and difficult decision. No poor, rural, weak, or black person should ever have to bear the additional burden of being deprived of the opportunity for an education, a job, or simple justice." Whether or not there was validity to the observation made by the state president of the NAACP, that "I haven't found a whole lot Jimmy Carter has done, but he scores 100 per

Jimmy Carter while governor of Georgia
University of Georgia

cent on talk," the fact that a Georgia governor was talking about equality and goodwill was a considerable advance from a few years earlier
when state administrations used their talents and resources struggling
to deny these same ideals. Governor Carter also directed attention to
environmental matters, establishing the Heritage Trust program which,
though operating on a limited budget, made notable gains in the preservation of historical and natural resources. The Carter administration
achieved a reorganization of the state government, reducing the number of bureaus, boards, and agencies to a tenth their former number;
pushed through the legislature a significant campaign financial dis-
closure law; and fought unsuccessfully for consumer protection measures that failed in the legislature. Part of Carter's legislative problems
resulted from his bitter feud with Lieutenant Governor Lester Maddox,
who presided over the senate.

The Georgia legislature has changed considerably since the days of
the county-unit system. A careful study found that the reapportioned
General Assembly was younger, better educated, and more likely to
contain Republicans, blacks, and women, and to be more heterogeneous
generally than it had been in the recent past. Nevertheless, in 1971 the
Citizens Conference on State Legislatures evaluated the legislatures of
all fifty states on the basis of how "functional, accountable, informed,
independent, and representative" they were and ranked the Georgia
assembly a lowly forty-fifth. Despite these findings, the legislature has
certainly become more independent in recent years, a trend observable
since reapportionment and accelerated by the peculiar events of 1967.
In the 1966 gubernatorial election, neither Lester Maddox nor Bo Callaway received an electoral majority, and consequently the legislature
was called upon to make the choice. Traditionally, the governor chose
the speaker of the house, who in turn appointed house members to committees, which gave the governor enormous leverage to insure that his
friends dominated strategic positions in one house of the legislature.
But in 1967 there was no governor-elect, so house members took advantage of the situation to elect their own choice as speaker, and, after that,
chose Maddox as governor. As chief executive, Maddox made little
effort to lead the legislature as had past governors. For the first time in
modern history, Georgia had a governor who was completely devoid of
governmental experience. Not since Herman Talmadge had the state
had a chief executive who had not previously served in a public position, but, unlike Maddox, Talmadge had come from a political family
and was an accomplished practitioner of the political arts. Furthermore,
Maddox did not regard legislation as particularly important. As he ob-

served, "we've got more laws now than we know what to do with." Instead, Maddox took pride in his open-house governorship and the large numbers of people who visited the governor's office and mansion, all of which gave legislators an opportunity to develop independent programs. Governor Carter attempted with limited success to reassert more vigorous executive leadership.

Whatever the relationship between the legislative and executive branches, Georgia remained a low-tax state, and its government continued to encounter difficulties in funding public programs at a level commensurate with national norms. During the early 1970s Georgia collected just over one hundred dollars in state and local taxes from each one thousand dollars in personal income, which was significantly less than the average tax burden in the nation. The Georgia budget in 1970 derived approximately 41 percent of its revenues from general and selective sales taxes, 18 percent from personal and corporate income taxes, and 27 percent from federal governmental aid, with the remainder coming from miscellaneous sources. Thus about two-thirds of state tax collections came from general and selective sales taxes, which in 1972 cost the typical Georgian approximately $170. These levies fell with particular force on low-income groups. A recent study by a congressional committee estimated that the state and local tax burden for a Georgia family of four was approximately 14 percent of family income for a family with an income of $3,000, approximately 11 percent if the family had an income of $5,000, about 9 percent for a family making $10,000, and 5.5 percent for a family with a $50,000 income. Local governments relied heavily on property taxes, as they did elsewhere in the nation, although Georgia's per capita property taxes were only 58 percent of the national norm in the early 1970s. In any case, Georgia's taxes have remained relatively stable for more than two decades; they were lower than the national average, even when controlling for Georgia's lower per capita income; and they were a greater burden for the poor than for the rich.

The unsettling pace of events during the postwar years left many Georgians disoriented and uncertain of the future. The hectic and strife-torn decade of the 1960s brought major changes in social, racial, and political practices, while the cruel dilemma posed by the war in Viet Nam and the divisive impact of President Johnson's Great Society reform program divided Georgians, as they did other Americans. After voting heavily for President Nixon in 1972, Georgians were shocked by the developments that emanated from the Watergate break-in and forced his resignation in 1974. Public opinion polls reflected a growing popular cynicism toward government and suggested a widespread rejection of further adventures in reform at home or involvement abroad. Even the state's impressive economic gains seemed less secure as inflation and other economic difficulties during the 1970s swallowed hard-earned pay raises. Georgia's population spurted upward at the very time that an increasing number of people became aware of the enormous costs that population growth and prosperity inflicted on the environment. The burgeoning cities offered vast opportunities as well as decaying slums, clogged traffic, polluted air, and massive problems. The state government disposed of budgets far greater than those in the past, yet the state still lagged behind national norms in virtually all state services. To contemporary observers, the 1970s seemed to be developing as a paradoxical decade when Georgians struggled to adjust to past changes while attempting to cope with a new generation of problems.

APPENDIXES
AND
BIBLIOGRAPHY

APPENDIX A

Chief Executives of Georgia

The title is governor unless otherwise indicated.
Party affiliation is indicated where it is appropriate or available.

Colonial Period

James Edward Oglethorpe, Resident Trustee	1733–43
William Stephens, President	1743–51
Henry Parker, President	1751–52
Patrick Graham, President	1752–54
John Reynolds	1754–57
Henry Ellis	1757–60
James Wright	1760–76

State Period

William Ewen, President of Council of Safety	1775	Whig[1]
George Walton, President of Council of Safety	1775–76	Whig
William Ewen, President of Council of Safety	1776	Whig
Archibald Bulloch, President	1776–77	Whig
Button Gwinnett, President	1777	Whig
John Adam Treutlen	1777–78	Whig
John Houstoun	1778–79	Whig
William Glascock, President of Executive Council	1779	Whig
Seth John Cuthbert, President of Supreme Executive Council	1779	Whig
John Wereat, President of Supreme Executive Council	1779–80	Whig
George Walton, elected by irregular assembly	1779–80	Whig

1. No attempt is made to differentiate between the different Whig factions in Georgia.

James Mark Prevost, British military governor	1779	
James Wright, restored colonial governor	1779–82	
Richard Howley	1780	Whig
Stephen Heard, President of Executive Council	1780	Whig
Myrick Davies, President of Executive Council	1780–81 (?)	Whig
Nathan Brownson	1781–82	
John Martin	1782–83	
Lyman Hall	1783–84	
John Houstoun	1784–85	
Samuel Elbert	1785–86	
Edward Telfair	1786–87	
George Mathews	1787–88	
George Handley	1788–89	
George Walton	1789–90	
Edward Telfair	1790–93	
George Mathews	1793–96	
Jared Irwin	1796–98[2]	
James Jackson	1798–1801	Jacksonian[3]
David Emanuel, President of Senate	1801	Jacksonian
Josiah Tattnall, Jr.	1801–2	Jacksonian
John Milledge	1802–6	Jacksonian
Jared Irwin	1806–9	Jacksonian
David B. Mitchell	1809–13	Jacksonian
Peter Early	1813–15	Jacksonian
David B. Mitchell	1815–17	Jacksonian
William Rabun	1817–19	Troup
Mathew Talbot, President of Senate	1819	Clark
John Clark	1819–23	Clark
George M. Troup	1823–27	Troup
John Forsyth	1827–29	Troup
George R. Gilmer	1829–31	Troup

2. Beginning by the election of 1796 most Georgians nationally were Jeffersonian-Republicans, and that would be the proper designation of the national party of the governors until about 1828.

3. These Jacksonians were the followers of James Jackson and became the Troup party by 1817.

Wilson Lumpkin	1831–35	Union[4]
William Schley	1835–37	Union
George R. Gilmer	1837–39	State Rights
Charles J. McDonald	1839–43	Union
George W. Crawford	1843–47	Whig
George W. B. Towns	1847–51	Democrat
Howell Cobb	1851–53	Constitutional Union (Democrat)
Herschel V. Johnson	1853–57	Democrat
Joseph E. Brown	1857–65	Democrat
James Johnson, Provisional Governor	1865	Democrat
Charles J. Jenkins	1865–68	Democrat
Brig. Gen. Thomas H. Ruger, Provisional Governor	1868	
Rufus B. Bullock, Provisional Governor	1868	Republican
Rufus B. Bullock	1868–71	Republican
Benjamin Conley, President of Senate	1871–72	Republican
James M. Smith	1872–77	Democrat
Alfred H. Colquitt	1877–82	Democrat
Alexander H. Stephens	1882–83	Democrat
James S. Boynton, President of Senate	1883	Democrat
Henry D. McDaniel	1883–86	Democrat
John B. Gordon	1886–90	Democrat
William J. Northen	1890–94	Democrat
William Y. Atkinson	1894–98	Democrat
Allen D. Candler	1898–1902	Democrat
Joseph M. Terrell	1902–7	Democrat
Hoke Smith	1907–9	Democrat
Joseph M. Brown	1909–11	Democrat
Hoke Smith	1911	Democrat
John M. Slaton, President of Senate	1911–12	Democrat
Joseph M. Brown	1912–13	Democrat

4. When the old Jeffersonian-Republican party began its disintegration after the national election of 1824, the new party designations (Democrat and Whig) were not used in Georgia state politics until about 1843. In Georgia the Union party became the Democratic and the State Rights the Whig when national names began to be used in state elections.

John M. Slaton	1913–15	Democrat
Nathaniel E. Harris	1915–17	Democrat
Hugh M. Dorsey	1917–21	Democrat
Thomas W. Hardwick	1921–23	Democrat
Clifford M. Walker	1923–27	Democrat
Lamartine G. Hardman	1927–31	Democrat
Richard B. Russell, Jr.	1931–33	Democrat
Eugene Talmadge	1933–37	Democrat
Eurith D. Rivers	1937–41	Democrat
Eugene Talmadge	1941–43	Democrat
Ellis G. Arnall	1943–47	Democrat
Melvin E. Thompson	1947–48	Democrat
Herman E. Talmadge	1948–55	Democrat
S. Marvin Griffin	1955–59	Democrat
S. Ernest Vandiver, Jr.	1959–63	Democrat
Carl E. Sanders	1963–67	Democrat
Lester G. Maddox	1967–71	Democrat
James E. Carter	1971–75	Democrat
George Busbee	1975–	Democrat

APPENDIX B

Georgia Population

Before 1790 the best available estimates are given.
Beginning in 1790 United States Census figures are used.

Year	Total Population	Whites	Blacks
1752	3,500	3,000	500
1760	9,578	6,000	3,578
1773	33,000	18,000	15,000
1790	82,548	52,886	29,662
1800	162,686	102,261	60,425
1810	252,433	145,414	107,019
1820	340,989	189,570	151,419
1830	516,823	296,806	220,017
1840	691,392	407,695	283,697
1850	906,185	521,572	384,613
1860	1,057,286	591,550	465,698
1870	1,184,109	638,926	545,142
1880	1,542,180	816,906	725,133
1890	1,837,353	978,357	858,815
1900	2,216,331	1,181,294	1,034,813
1910	2,609,121	1,431,802	1,176,987
1920	2,895,832	1,689,114	1,206,365
1930	2,908,506	1,837,021	1,071,125
1940	3,123,723	2,038,278	1,084,927
1950	3,444,578	2,380,577	1,062,762
1960	3,943,116	2,817,223	1,122,596
1970	4,589,575	3,391,242	1,187,149

Bibliography

This is a working bibliography for students of Georgia history. Readers desiring more complete coverage are referred to the bibliographies below.

Bibliographies

There are three recent bibliographies of Georgia history: John Eddins Simpson, *Georgia History: A Bibliography* (Metuchen, N.J., 1976); Arthur Ray Rowland, *Bibliography of the Writings on Georgia History* (Hamden, Conn., 1966); and John Wyatt Bonner, Jr., *Bibliography of Georgia Authors 1949–1965* (Athens, 1966), with annual compilations 1966–69 found in the *Georgia Review*. Many items, especially for the colonial period, are in the *Catalogue of the Wymberly Jones DeRenne Georgia Library* (3 vols.; Wormsloe, Ga., 1931). Older bibliographies are largely superseded by these recent ones.

General Works

Works that cover all or a major portion of Georgia's history are E. Merton Coulter, *A Short History of Georgia* (Chapel Hill, 1933), revised as *Georgia: A Short History* (Chapel Hill, 1947 and 1960), particularly good for the period through 1865; James C. Bonner, *The Georgia Story* (Oklahoma City, 1958); Kenneth Coleman, *Georgia History in Outline* (Athens, 1960); and Spencer B. King, Jr., *Georgia Voices: A Documentary History to 1872* (Athens, 1966). A volume containing considerable local or specialized history is Works Projects Administration, *Georgia: A Guide to Its Towns and Countryside* (Athens, 1940), revised and extended by George G. Leckie (Atlanta, 1954). The best periodical devoted to Georgia history is the *Georgia Historical Quarterly* published by the Georgia Historical Society since 1917. Some local historical societies also publish journals.

Two good, well-researched, general histories written in the nineteenth century that come no further than 1800 are William Bacon Stevens, *A History of Georgia* (2 vols.; New York, 1847, and Philadelphia, 1859; Savannah, 1972) and Charles C. Jones, Jr., *The History of Georgia* (2 vols.; Boston, 1883). A modern work for the same period, particularly useful for its interpretations, is Albert Berry Saye, *New Viewpoints in Georgia History* (Athens, 1943). Compilations of documents and miscellaneous information are George White, *Statistics of the State of Georgia* (Savannah, 1849) and *Historical Collections of Georgia* (New York, 1854).

Biographical sketches of Georgians are included in William J. Northen, ed., *Men of Mark in Georgia* (6 vols.; Atlanta, 1907–12); Horace Montgomery, ed., *Georgians in Profile* (Athens, 1958); and James F. Cook, *The Governors of Georgia* (Huntsville, Ala., 1977).

Topical Works

Constitutional history is covered by Albert Berry Saye, *A Constitutional History of Georgia* (Athens, 1948, revised 1970); Ethel K. Ware, *A Constitutional History of Georgia* (New York, 1947); Albert Berry Saye and Charles Joseph Hilkey, *The Constitutional History of Georgia: Cases and Comments* (Atlanta, 1952); and Walter McElreath, *A Treatise on the Constitution of Georgia* (Atlanta, 1912). Political history to 1860 is best covered in Ulrich Bonnell Phillips, *Georgia and State Rights* (Washington, D.C., 1902).

Economic history is somewhat slighted, but especially recommended are Milton Sydney Heath, *Constructive Liberalism: The Role of the State in Economic Development in Georgia to 1860* (Cambridge, 1954); James C. Bonner, *A History of Georgia Agriculture, 1732–1860* (Athens, 1964); and Willard Range, *A Century of Georgia Agriculture, 1850–1950* (Athens, 1954).

In education the best works are Dorothy Orr, *A History of Education in Georgia* (Chapel Hill, 1950); E. Merton Coulter, *College Life in the Old South* (New York, 1928; reissued Athens, 1951); and Robert Preston Brooks, *The University of Georgia Under Sixteen Administrations, 1785–1955* (Athens, 1956).

In religion there is Reba Carolyn Strickland, *Religion and the State in Georgia in the Eighteenth Century* (New York, 1939); P. A. Strobel, *The Salzburgers and Their Descendants* (Baltimore, 1855; reissued Athens, 1953); and a number of denominational studies mainly written by clergymen of varying merits as historians. A broad study of race and the southern churches is H. Shelton Smith, *In His Image, But . . . Racism in Southern Religion, 1780–1919* (Durham, N.C., 1972).

Other social items are treated in Louis Turner Griffith and John Erwin Talmadge, *Georgia Journalism, 1763–1950* (Athens, 1951), and Thomas Franklin Abercrombie, *A History of Public Health in Georgia, 1733–1950* (Atlanta, 1953).

Part One: Chapters I–VI, to 1775

A few general works that deal with the entire sweep of colonial Georgia stand out. Stevens, *A History of Georgia*, Jones, *The History of Georgia*, are both sound works. Bonner, *A History of Georgia Agriculture*, contains insights for the entire period, as does Strickland, *Religion and the State in Georgia*. Particularly useful are Saye, *New Viewpoints in Georgia History*, and Heath, *Constructive Liberalism*. Kenneth Coleman's *Colonial Georgia* (New York, 1976) supersedes other works dealing with the British portion of Georgia history. The best documentary collection is Allen D. Candler, et al., eds., *The Colonial Records of the State of Georgia* (26 vols. to date; Atlanta and Athens, 1904–76).

The recognition that Georgia had a long history under Spain came rather late. Full and adequate study of this little-known period was undertaken in the 1920s and 1930s and resulted in several studies. John Tate Lanning, *The Spanish Missions of Georgia* (Chapel Hill, 1935), and Mary Ross and Herbert Bolton, *Arredondo's Historical Proof of Spain's Title to Georgia*, of which "The Debatable Land" is the introduction (Berkeley, 1925), are the most valuable single items. See also E. Merton Coulter, ed., *Georgia's Disputed Ruins* (Chapel Hill, 1937).

Some of the best information concerning the Spanish period is in scholarly articles. Bolton's "The Mission as a Frontier Institution in the Spanish-American Colonies," *The American Historical Review* 23(1917):42–61, is useful reading as are Mary Ross's articles in the *Georgia Historical Quarterly*, of which the most helpful is "The Restoration of the Spanish Missions in Georgia, 1598–1606," 10(1926):171–99. More recently, see Fred Lamar Pearson, Jr., "Early Anglo-Spanish Rivalry in Southeastern North America," *ibid.*, 58(1974):157–71, and the same author's "The Arguelles Inspection of Guale: December 21, 1677–January 10, 1678," *ibid.*, 59(1975):210–22.

On developing tensions between Spanish, French, and English, see Verner W. Crane, *The Southern Frontier, 1670–1732* (Durham, N.C., 1928), and Bolton's "Spanish Resistance to the Carolina Traders in Western Georgia (1680–1704)," *Georgia Historical Quarterly* 9(1925):115–39. M. Eugene Sirmans, *Colonial South Carolina* (Chapel Hill, 1966) is instructive, as is Verne E. Chatelain, *The Defenses of Spanish Florida 1565 to 1763* (Washington, D.C., 1941), and John J. TePaske, *The Governorship of Spanish Florida, 1700–1763* (Durham, N.C., 1964).

An enormous amount has been written on the origins of the Georgia movement. Much of the most valuable information can be found in articles; the following is but a sampling: Crane, "The Philanthropists and the Genesis of Georgia," *American Historical Review* 27(1921):63–69, and "Dr. Thomas Bray and the Charitable Colony Project, 1730," *William and Mary Quarterly*, 3rd ser., 19(1962):49–63; Richard S. Dunn, "The Trustees of Georgia and the House of Commons, 1732–1752," *ibid.* 11(1954):551–65; Albert B. Saye, "Was Georgia a Debtor Colony?" *Georgia Historical Quarterly* 24(1940): 323–52. Crane's "The Origins of Georgia," *ibid.* 14(1939):93–110, and Kenneth Coleman's "The Southern Frontier: Georgia's Founding and the Expansion of South Carolina," *ibid.* 56(1972):163–74, round out some of the best material on the subject. Saye's *New Viewpoints in Georgia History* has stimulated thought on various topics concerning early Georgia.

South Carolina's contribution to the early founding of Georgia can be seen in Phinizy Spalding, "South Carolina and Georgia: The Early Days," *South Carolina Historical Magazine* 59(1968):83–96. Geraldine Meroney's "The London Entrepôt Merchants and the Colony of Georgia," *William and Mary Quarterly*, 3rd ser., 25(1968):230–44, gives a lucid account of the importance of London mercantile interests to Trustee policy.

In spite of his prominence, James Edward Oglethorpe's American career has only recently received full treatment. For such a study see Phinizy Spalding, *Oglethorpe in America* (Chicago, 1977). Amos Aschbach Ettinger's *James Edward Oglethorpe, Imperial Idealist* (Oxford, 1926) is the best biography but is brief on his American years. Leslie F. Church's *Oglethorpe* (London, 1932) gives more Georgia detail but lacks insights. For a biographical resumé see Spalding, "James Edward Oglethorpe: A Biographical Survey," *Georgia Historical Quarterly* 56(1972):332–48. Larry E. Ivers, *British Drums on the Southern Frontier* (Chapel Hill, 1974), is the best account of the strictly military phase of Oglethorpe's American career but is weak on interpretation.

Overall Trustee policy is ably handled in the old but reliable James R. McCain, *Georgia as a Proprietary Province* (Boston, 1917), and the nineteenth-century histories of Charles C. Jones and William B. Stevens. The latter two should be supplemented by recent source materials not available to their authors. Trevor R. Reese, *Colonial Georgia* (Athens, 1963), is reliable but too brief. Jones, *The Dead Towns of Georgia* (Savannah, 1878), still has value but must be used with care. Possibly the most stimulating handling of the Trusteeship period can be found in Milton S. Heath, *Constructive Liberalism.*

For the three acts of the Trustees, Handy B. Fant's articles in *Georgia Historical Quarterly* 15(1931):207–22; 16(1932):1–16; and 17(1933):286–92 are sound. Betty Wood, "Thomas Stephens and the Introduction of Black Slavery in Georgia," *ibid.* 58(1974):24–40, and Milton L. Ready, "Land Tenure in Trusteeship Georgia," *Agricultural History* 48(1974):353–68, are solid achievements, but see also G. Melvin Herndon, "Timber Products of Colonial Georgia," *Georgia Historical Quarterly* 57(1973):56–62. For Indian relations John P. Corry, *Indian Affairs in Georgia, 1732–1756* (Philadelphia, 1936), is essential. See also Charles Hudson, *The Southeastern Indians* (Knoxville, 1976).

The coming of war with Spain is handled in Lanning, *The Diplomatic History of Georgia* (Chapel Hill, 1936). John D. Wade, *John Wesley* (New York, 1930), is adequate, as is Stuart C. Henry, *George Whitefield* (New York, 1957). David T. Morgan, "Judaism in Eighteenth Century Georgia," *Georgia Historical Quarterly* 58(1974):41–54, is the best overview on the subject.

Social and cultural history is amply covered by Sarah B. G. Temple and Kenneth Coleman, *Georgia Journeys* (Athens, 1961), and by Harold C. Davis, *The Fledgling Province: A Social and Cultural History of Colonial Georgia* (Chapel Hill, 1976). See also Mollie C. Davis, "George Whitefield's Attempt to Establish a College in Georgia," *Georgia Historical Quarterly* 55 (1971): 459–70, and Corry, "Education in Colonial Georgia," *ibid.* 16(1932):136–45.

On the question of growth and expansion of Georgia, a sampling would include Marguerite B. Hamer, "Edmund Gray and his Settlement at New Hanover," *ibid.* 13(1929):1–12, and E. R. R. Green, "Queensborough Township: Scotch Irish Emigration and the Expansion of Georgia, 1763–1776," *William and Mary Quarterly*, 3rd ser., 17(1960):183–99. Particularly informative is Louis DeVorsey, Jr., "Indian Boundaries in Colonial Georgia," *Georgia Historical Quarterly* 54(1970):63–78.

The royal period of Georgia history is covered by William W. Abbot, *The Royal Governors of Georgia* (Chapel Hill, 1959) and by Kenneth Coleman, *Colonial Georgia.* The latter's essay on James Wright in *Georgians in Profile*, ed. Horace Montgomery (Athens, 1958), pp. 49–60, provides insights. Kenneth Coleman, *The American Revolution in Georgia, 1763–1789* (Athens, 1958), is a must for any serious student of Revolutionary Georgia. See also C. Ashley Ellefson, "The Stamp Act in Georgia," *Georgia Historical Quarterly* 46(1962):1–19, and Harvey H. Jackson, "Consensus and Conflict: Factional Politics in Revolutionary Georgia, 1774–1777," *ibid.* 59(1975):388–401. Some pertinent documents and items from the period are reprinted in Ronald G. Killion and Charles T. Waller, *Georgia and the Revolution* (Atlanta, 1975), but the narrative introduction contains errors.

Part Two: Chapters VII–X, 1775–1820

More facets of the American Revolution are covered in Coleman, *The American Revolution in Georgia, 1763–1789,* than any other works on that subject. Other books with good coverage are Saye, *New Viewpoints in Georgia History;* Jones, *The History of Georgia;* William Bacon Stevens, *A History of Georgia;* and Alexander A. Lawrence, *Storm Over Savannah: The Story of Count d'Estaing and the Siege of the Town in 1779* (Athens, 1951). Documentary sources are found in Allen D. Candler, ed., *The Revolutionary Records of Georgia* (3 vols.; Atlanta, 1908); White, *Historical Collections of Georgia* (New York, 1854); and Killion and Waller, *Georgia and the Revolution.*

For politics in the postwar years, the best general coverage is Phillips, *Georgia and States Rights.* Other useful works are Albert Berry Saye, *A Constitutional History of Georgia;* Lucien E. Roberts, "Sectional Problems in Georgia during the Formative Period," *Georgia Historical Quarterly* 18 (1934) : 207–27; and several biographies listed below. Georgia's relations with Florida are treated in Richard K. Murdoch, *The Georgia-Florida Frontier 1793–1796* (Berkeley, 1951), and "Elijah Clarke and Anglo-American Designs on East Florida, 1797–1798," *Georgia Historical Quarterly* 35 (1951) :173–90.

The broadest economic treatment is in Heath, *Constructive Liberalism.* More specialized studies which supplement Heath are Bonner, *A History of Georgia Agriculture, 1732–1860;* Ralph Betts Flanders, *Plantation Slavery in Georgia* (Chapel Hill, 1933); E. Merton Coulter, *Thomas Spalding of Sapelo* (Baton Rouge, 1940); Ulrich Bonnell Phillips, *A History of Transportation in the Eastern Cotton Belt to 1860* (New York, 1908); John H. Goff, "The Steamboat Period in Georgia," *Georgia Historical Quarterly* 12(1928):236–54; and Fletcher M. Green, "Georgia's Board of Public Works, 1817–1826," *Georgia Historical Quarterly* 22(1938):117–37.

Religion is best treated in Strickland, *Religion and the State in Georgia.* Various denominational histories are sometimes helpful. Of special interest for individual pioneer churches are James M. Simms, *The First Colored Baptist Church in North America* (Philadelphia, 1888), and James Donovan Mosteller, *A History of the Kiokee Baptist Church in Georgia* (Ann Arbor, 1952). Education is treated in Orr, *A History of Education in Georgia,* and E. Merton Coulter, "The Ante-Bellum Academy Movement in Georgia," *Georgia Historical Quarterly* 5(1921):11–42. For the University of Georgia see E. Merton Coulter, *College Life in the Old South,* and Robert Preston Brooks, *The University of Georgia.* Other social items are covered in Griffith and Talmadge, *Georgia Journalism* (Athens, 1951); E. Merton Coulter, *Old Petersburg and the Broad River Valley in Georgia: Their Rise and Decline* (Athens, 1965); and E. Merton Coulter, "The Great Savannah Fire of 1820," *Georgia Historical Quarterly* 23(1939):1–27.

The Cherokee Indians before removal are best treated in Marion L. Starkey, *The Cherokee Nation* (New York, 1946), and Henry Thompson Malone, *Cherokees of the Old South. A People in Transition* (Athens, 1956). For the Creeks see Angie Debo, *The Road to Disappearance* (Norman, Okla., 1941); Randolph C. Downes, "Creek-American Relations, 1782–1790," *Georgia Historical Quarterly* 21 (1937) :142–84; John Walton Caughey, *McGillivray of the Creeks* (Norman, Okla., 1938); Merritt B. Pound, *Benjamin Hawkins, Indian Agent* (Athens, 1951); and Antonio J. Waring, *Laws of the Creek Nation* (Athens, 1960).

Collective biographies of political leaders include Montgomery, *Georgians in Profile*; E. Merton Coulter, *Wormsloe: Two Centuries of a Georgia Family* (Athens, 1955); Edith Duncan Johnston, *The Houstouns of Georgia* (Athens, 1950); and Charles C. Jones, Jr., *Biographical Sketches of the Delegates from Georgia to the Continental Congress* (Boston and New York, 1891). Individual biographies of political leaders are Charles Francis Jenkins, *Button Gwinnett: Signer of the Declaration of Independence* (New York, 1926); William O. Foster, *James Jackson: Duelist and Militant Statesman, 1757–1806* (Athens, 1960); Henry C. White, *Abraham Baldwin* (Athens, 1926); Patrick J. Furlong, "Abraham Baldwin: A Georgia Yankee as Old Congress-Man," *Georgia Historical Quarterly* 56(1972):51–71; Louise Frederick Hays, *Hero of Hornet's Nest. A Biography of Elijah Clark* (New York, 1946); and Chase C. Mooney, *William H. Crawford* (Lexington, Ky., 1974).

Part Three: Chapters XI–XIX, 1820–1865

Several significant works examine the complexities of antebellum politics. Somewhat outdated but still useful is Ulrich B. Phillips, *Georgia and State Rights*. Paul Murray, *The Whig Party in Georgia, 1825–1853* (Chapel Hill, 1948), is heavily detailed and based mainly on newspaper accounts, and Richard Harrison Shryock, *Georgia and the Union in 1850* (Durham, N.C., 1926), thoroughly and broadly describes a crucial year. The politics of the last fifteen antebellum years are skillfully and minutely examined in Horace Montgomery, *Cracker Parties* (Baton Rouge, 1950), and sophisticated statistical analyses are made in Donald A. Debats, "Elites and Masses: Political Structure, Communication and Behavior in Ante-Bellum Georgia" (Ph.D. dissertation, University of Wisconsin, 1973). Late antebellum Georgia is also scrutinized in sections of two works by Ralph A. Wooster, *The Secession Conventions of the South* (Princeton, 1962), and *The People in Power: Courthouse and Statehouse in the Lower South: 1850–1860* (Knoxville, Tenn., 1969).

Valuable biographies are Alexander A. Lawrence, *James Moore Wayne: Southern Unionist* (Chapel Hill, 1943); Mooney, *William H. Crawford*; Alvin Laroy Duckett, *John Forsyth: Political Tactician* (Athens, 1962); Royce Coggins McCrary, "John MacPherson Berrien of Georgia (1781–1856): A Political Biography" (Ph.D. dissertation, University of Georgia, 1971); Len G. Cleveland, "George W. Crawford of Georgia, 1798–1872" (Ph.D. dissertation, University of Georgia, 1974); Rudolph von Abele, *Alexander H. Stephens, A Biography* (New York, 1946); William Y. Thompson, *Robert Toombs of Georgia* (Baton Rouge, 1966); John Eddins Simpson, *Howell Cobb: The Politics of Ambition* (Chicago, 1973); Percy S. Flippin, *Herschel V. Johnson of Georgia, State Rights Unionist* (Richmond, 1931); and Joseph H. Parks, *Joseph E. Brown of Georgia* (Baton Rouge, 1977).

Important articles analyzing crucial political events are E. Merton Coulter, "The Nullification Movement in Georgia," *Georgia Historical Quarterly* 5 (1921):3–39; Edwin A. Miles, "After John Marshall's Decision: *Worcester v.*

Georgia and the Nullification Crisis," *Journal of Southern History* 39 (1973) : 519–44; and Michael P. Johnson, "A New Look at the Popular Vote for Delegates to the Georgia Secession Convention," *Georgia Historical Quarterly* 56 (1972):259–75.

The plight of the Indians is described in Henry T. Malone, *Cherokees of the Old South*; Grant Foreman, *Indian Removal: The Emigration of the Five Civilized Tribes of Indians* (Norman, Okla., 1953); Starkey, *The Cherokee Nation*; and Debo, *The Road to Disappearance*.

The best economic study is Heath, *Constructive Liberalism*, and useful supplements are Thomas P. Govan, "Banking and the Credit System in Georgia, 1810–1860," *Journal of Southern History* 4(1938):164–84, and Peter Reeve Wallenstein, "From Slave South to New South: Taxes and Spending in Georgia from 1850 Through Reconstruction" (Ph.D. dissertation, Johns Hopkins University, 1973). Phillips, *A History of Transportation in the Eastern Cotton Belt to 1860*, is still valuable.

Chapter 1 of Range, *A Century of Georgia Agriculture: 1850–1950*, is a fine factual introduction to the backbone of the antebellum economy, and Bonner, *A History of Georgia Agriculture: 1732–1860*, is comprehensive and emphasizes increased efficiency. Useful grassroots studies are James C. Bonner, "Profile of a Late Ante-Bellum Community" (Hancock County), *American Historical Review* 49(1944):663–80; John A. Eisterhold, "Savannah: Lumber Center of the South Atlantic," *Georgia Historical Quarterly* 57(1973):526–43; F. N. Boney, "Thomas Stevens, Antebellum Georgian" (Baldwin and DeKalb counties), *South Atlantic Quarterly* 72(1973):226–42; and E. Merton Coulter, *Auraria: The Story of a Georgia Gold-Mining Town* (Athens, 1956).

Prominent antebellum capitalists are closely examined in E. Merton Coulter, *Thomas Spalding of Sapelo* (University, La., 1940); Edward M. Steele, Jr., *T. Butler King of Georgia* (Athens, 1964); Robert Neil Mathis, "Gazaway Bugg Lamar: A Southern Entrepreneur" (Ph.D. dissertation, University of Georgia, 1968) ; and Ralph B. Flanders, "Farish Carter, A Forgotten Man of the Old South," *Georgia Historical Quarterly* 15(1931):142–72. Much economic information is found in Adiel Sherwood's *A Gazetteer of the State of Georgia*, which was first published in 1827 and then updated in 1829, 1837 and 1860, reprint Athens, 1939.

Formal contemporary glimpses of the antebellum way of life are provided in White, *Statistics of the State of Georgia* and *Historical Collections of Georgia*; Stephen F. Miller, *Bench and Bar in Georgia: Memoirs and Sketches* (2 vols.; Philadelphia, 1858); and Sherwood's *Gazetteers*. Lively personal accounts by temporary residents are Frances Anne Kemble, *Journal of a Residence on a Georgian Plantation in 1838–1839* (New York, 1863), and Emily P. Burke, *Reminiscences of Georgia* (Oberlin, Ohio, 1850), and remembrances by native Georgians are found in the early sections of the *Autobiography of Col. Richard Malcolm Johnston* (Washington, D.C., 1900) and Rebecca Latimer Felton, *Country Life In Georgia In the Days of My Youth* (Atlanta, 1919). Basil Hall, James Stuart, Tyrone Power, George W. Featherstonhaugh, Harriet Martineau, James Silk Buckingham, Charles Lyell, Alexander Mackay, James Stirling, and other foreigners visited Georgia and left at least some impressions in subsequent travel books, but probably the best known of such accounts comes from a critical, antislavery New Englander in Frederick Law

Olmstead, *A Journey in the Seaboard Slave States, with Remarks On Their Economy* (New York, 1856). The extensive, revealing correspondence of the elite Charles Colcock Jones family in the 1850s is edited by Robert Manson Myers in *The Children of Pride: A True Story of Georgia and the Civil War* (New Haven, Conn., 1972) and *A Georgian at Princeton* (New York, 1976). William Warren Rogers, *Ante-Bellum Thomas County, 1825–1861* (Tallahassee, Fla., 1963), and Ernest C. Hynds, *Antebellum Athens and Clarke County, Georgia* (Athens, 1974), are thorough local studies.

The shaky school system is examined in Orr, *A History of Education in Georgia*; Elbert W. G. Boogher, *Secondary Education in Georgia: 1732–1858* (Philadelphia, 1933); Forrest David Mathews, "The Politics of Education in the Deep South: Georgia and Alabama, 1830–1860" (Ph.D. dissertation, Columbia University, 1965); and Coulter, *College Life in the Old South*. Other intellectual studies are John Donald Wade, *Augustus Baldwin Longstreet: A Study of the Development of Culture in the South* (New York, 1924), and Bertram H. Flanders, *Early Georgia Magazines: Literary Periodicals to 1865* (Athens, 1944). Two views of the evolving penal system are James C. Bonner, "The Georgia Penitentiary at Milledgeville, 1817–1874," *Georgia Historical Quarterly* 55(1971):303–28, and Lewis W. Paine, *Six Years in a Georgia Prison* (Boston, 1852).

Slavery is described in a somewhat outdated but still useful volume, Ralph Betts Flanders, *Plantation Slavery in Georgia* (Chapel Hill, 1933). The best local study is Clarence L. Mohr, "Slavery in Oglethorpe County, Georgia: 1773–1865," *Phylon: The Atlanta University Review of Race and Culture* 33 (1972):4–21, but William G. Proctor, Jr., "Slavery in Southwest Georgia," *Georgia Historical Quarterly* 49(1965):1–22 and the first chapter of Albert S. Foley, *Bishop Healy: Beloved Outcast; The Story of a Great Man Whose Life Has Become a Legend* (New York, 1954), are also informative. The differing opinions of two New England visitors are shown in Nehemiah Adams, *A South-Side View of Slavery* (1854), and C. G. Parsons, *An Inside View of Slavery* (1855) (boxed together by Beehive Press, Savannah, 1974). Slave smuggling is described in Tom Henderson Wells, *The Slave Ship Wanderer* (Athens, 1967), and the difficulties of emancipation are detailed in James M. Gifford, "Emily Tubman and the African Colonization Movement in Georgia," *Georgia Historical Quarterly* 54 (1975):10–24 and "The African Colonization Movement in Georgia, 1817–1860," (Ph.D. dissertation, University of Georgia, 1977). Ralph Betts Flanders, "The Free Negro in Ante-Bellum Georgia," *North Carolina Historical Review* 9(1932):250–72, and Edward F. Sweat, "The Free Negro in Ante-Bellum Georgia" (Ph.D. dissertation, Indiana University, 1957), describe the plight of the half-free.

Some black testimony about slavery is now readily available. F. N. Boney, ed., *Slave Life in Georgia: A Narrative of the Life, Sufferings, and Escape of John Brown, A Fugitive Slave* (Savannah, 1972), is a memoir originally published in 1855 and reissued with much additional annotation and explanation. William Craft, *Running A Thousand Miles For Freedom: Or the Escape of William and Ellen Craft From Slavery* (London, 1860, and New York, 1969), has a much briefer account of slavery in Georgia. George P. Rawick, ed., *The American Slave: A Composite Autobiography: Georgia Narratives* (vols. 12 and 13, Westport, Conn., 1972), presents elderly former slaves' reminiscences that were collected by the WPA in the 1930s, and similar interviews are recorded in J. Ralph Jones, editor, "Portraits of Georgia Slaves," *Georgia Review* 21(1967):126–32, 268–73, 407–11, 521–25; and 22(1968):125–27, 254–57.

The Civil War period is covered in detail in T. Conn Bryan, *Confederate Georgia* (Athens, 1953). Also useful are Allen D. Candler, ed., *The Confederate Records of the State of Georgia* (5 vols.; Atlanta, 1909–11), and Lillian Henderson, *Roster of the Confederate Soldiers of Georgia: 1861–1865* (6 vols.; Hapeville, 1959–64). Wartime leaders are examined in James Z. Rabun, "Alexander H. Stephens and Jefferson Davis," *American Historical Review* 58 (1953):290–321; Louise B. Hill, *Joseph E. Brown and the Confederacy* (Chapel Hill, 1939); Horace Montgomery, *Howell Cobb's Confederate Career* (Tuscaloosa, Ala., 1959); and Bell I. Wiley, ed., *Letters of Warren Akin, Confederate Congressman* (Athens, 1959).

Valuable homefront studies are Florence Fleming Corley, *Confederate City: Augusta, Georgia, 1860–1865* (Columbia, S.C., 1969); Kenneth Coleman, *Confederate Athens* (Athens, 1967) and, ed., *Athens, 1861–1865; As Seen Through Letters in the University of Georgia Libraries* (Athens, 1969); and William Warren Rogers, *Thomas County during the Civil War* (Tallahassee, Fla., 1964). Also useful are Alexander A. Lawrence, *A Present for Mr. Lincoln: The Story of Savannah from Secession to Sherman* (Macon, Ga., 1961), and Diffie William Standard, *Columbus, Georgia in the Confederacy: The Social and Industrial Life of the Chattahoochee River Port* (New York, 1954), and Book II (pages 619–1269) of *The Children of Pride* contains the interesting wartime letters of the Jones family. The best noncombatant diaries are Richard Barksdale Harwell, ed., *Kate: The Journal of a Confederate Nurse* (first published by Kate Cumming in 1866 and reissued at Baton Rouge, 1959); Eliza Frances Andrews, *The War-Time Journal of a Georgia Girl: 1864–1865* (New York, 1908; Macon, Ga., 1960); Spencer Bidwell King, Jr., ed., *Ebb Tide: As Seen Through the Diary of Josephine Clay Habersham: 1863* (Athens, 1958); James I. Robertson, Jr., ed., *The Diary of Dolly Lunt Burge* (Athens, 1962); James C. Bonner, ed., *The Journal of a Milledgeville Girl: 1861–1867* (Anna Maria Green) (Athens, 1964); and Joseph LeConte, *'Ware Sherman: A Journal of Three Months' Personal Experience in the Last Days of the Confederacy* (Berkeley, Cal., 1937).

Combat in Georgia is described dramatically in Gleen Tucker, *Chickamauga: Bloody Battle in the West* (Indianapolis, 1961), and A. A. Hoehling, *Last Train from Atlanta* (New York, 1958), and the last relentless Union offensives are covered in Mills Lane, ed., *War Is Hell: William T. Sherman's Personal Narrative of His March Through Georgia* (Savannah, 1974); Samuel Carter III, *The Siege of Atlanta, 1864* (New York, 1973); and James P. Jones, *Yankee Blitzkrieg: Wilson's Raid Through Alabama and Georgia* (Athens, 1976). Ovid L. Futch, *History of Andersonville Prison* (Gainesville, Fla., 1968) tells a grim story of Yankee prisoners of war.

Wartime slavery is most fully described in Clarence L. Mohr, "Georgia Blacks During Secession and Civil War, 1859–1865" (Ph.D. dissertation, University of Georgia, 1975). A more conservative local study is E. Merton Coulter, "Slavery and Freedom in Athens, Georgia, 1860–1866," *Georgia Historical Quarterly* 49(1965):264–93. Other useful works are Horace Montgomery,

Johnny Cobb: Confederate Aristocrat (Athens, 1964); Rabun Lee Brantley, *Georgia Journalism of the Civil War Period* (Nashville, Tenn., 1929); and chapter 2 of Willard Range, *A Century of Georgia Agriculture.*

Part Four: Chapters XV–XVII, 1865–1890

Georgia is fortunate that so much that has been written on her Reconstruction experience is of such high quality. One of the oldest studies is still one of the best and by far the most complete—C. Mildred Thompson, *Reconstruction in Georgia: Economic, Social, and Political, 1865–1872* (New York, 1915; Gloucester, Mass., 1964; Covington, Ga., 1971; and Savannah, 1972). A somewhat shorter, but more modern and readable, revisionist account is Alan Conway, *The Reconstruction of Georgia* (Minneapolis, 1966). See also, for the traditional, conservative interpretation, pertinent chapters in E. Merton Coulter, *Georgia, A Short History*, as well as his *The South During Reconstruction, 1865–1877* (Baton Rouge, 1947). For a readable and valuable account of life on a Georgia rice and cotton plantation after the war, see Frances Butler Leigh, *Ten Years on a Georgia Plantation Since the War* (London, 1883).

Unfortunately for the period of Redemption and Bourbonism, that is for the 1870s and 1880s, much less has been written that is readily available to the student, for much of it is in unpublished master's theses and doctoral dissertations. Generally the doctoral dissertations are available in book form from University Microfilms, Ann Arbor, Mich. The most valuable of these studies, however, is not available from University Microfilms, being an older study—Judson C. Ward, "Georgia Under the Bourbon Democrats, 1872–1890," (Ph.D. dissertation, University of North Carolina, 1947). This is the only general yet detailed study of the entire Bourbon period, covering not just politics and elections but the Bourbons' sometimes paternalistic, sometimes realistic, but always cost-conscious response to the social and economic problems of the period. A valuable interpretative article by the same author, drawing largely on the contents of the larger study, is "The New Departure Democrats in Georgia: An Interpretation," *Georgia Historical Quarterly* 41 (1957):227–36. Especially valuable for the role of the Negro in politics for the period is Horace Calvin Wingo, "Race Relations in Georgia, 1872–1908," (Ph.D. dissertation, University of Georgia, 1969). For a study of the nearest thing Georgia had to an opposition political party in the period, see George L. Jones, "William H. Felton and the Independent Democratic Movement in Georgia, 1870–1890" (Ph.D. dissertation, University of Georgia, 1971). On the Republican party throughout this period (1865–1890), see Olive Hall Shadgett, *The Republican Party in Georgia from Reconstruction Through 1900* (Athens, Ga., 1964). And to place the Georgia Bourbons in regional context, see C. Vann Woodward, *Origins of the New South, 1877–1913* (Baton Rouge, 1951).

Economics, "the dismal science," has attracted far less scholarly interest than has Georgia politics, but fortunately some of the better political studies also treat of economics, among them Thompson, *Reconstruction in Georgia*, and Ward, "Georgia Under the Bourbon Democrats." Containing much valuable information on Georgia agriculture for the period is Range, *A Century of Georgia Agriculture, 1850–1950.* By far the most detailed and clearest account of the emergence of Georgia farm tenantry is Enoch M. Banks, *The Economics of Land Tenure in Georgia* (New York, 1905). A somewhat similar but broader study is Robert Preston Brooks, *The Agrarian Revolution in Georgia, 1865–1912* (Madison, Wis., 1914). Placing both Georgia agriculture and Georgia industrialization in the broader context is Woodward, *Origins of the New South.*

The best study of education is Orr, *A History of Education in Georgia.* On the history of Georgia's Negro colleges, see Willard Range, *Rise and Progress of Negro Colleges in Georgia, 1865–1949* (Athens, 1959). A short, interesting article on Georgia's G.I. education bill for ex-Confederates is Darrell Roberts, "The University of Georgia and Georgia's Civil War G.I. Bill," *Georgia Historical Quarterly* 49(1965):418–23.

Information on religion and Georgia's churches is scattered, institutional, and denominational, but some generalizations are to be found in Thompson, *Reconstruction in Georgia,* Coulter, *The South During Reconstruction,* Woodward, *Origins of the New South,* and Smith, *In His Image, But.*

On the Negro and race relationships in Georgia, see James L. Owens, "The Negro in the Reconstruction of Georgia" (Ph.D. dissertation, University of Georgia, 1974), and Wingo, "Race Relations in Georgia" (Ph.D. dissertation, cited above).

For a general study of the origins and development of the convict lease system, in which Georgia's system is placed in regional context, see Fletcher M. Green, "Some Aspects of the Convict Lease System in the Southern States," *The James Sprunt Studies in History and Political Science* 31 (Chapel Hill, 1958). On the Georgia system alone, see A. Elizabeth Taylor, "The Origin and Development of the Convict Lease System in Georgia," *Georgia Historical Quarterly* 26 (1942) :113–28.

Information on Georgia's literati is diffuse and relatively plentiful but calls for much winnowing, to separate the chaff from the wheat and true literary assessment from mere state-pride posturing. This is best done in Coulter, *The South During Reconstruction,* Woodward, *Origins of the New South,* both cited above, and in R. C. Beatty, F. C. Watkins, T. D. Young, and Randall Stewart, *The Literature of the South* (New York, 1952). On Georgia newspapers, see Griffith and Talmadge, *Georgia Journalism.*

Among the better biographies of men's lives who touch at least a part of this period (1865–1890) , see Haywood J. Pearce, *Benjamin H. Hill, Secession and Reconstruction* (Chicago, 1928); Raymond B. Nixon, *Henry W. Grady, Spokesman of the New South* (New York, 1943); Allen P. Tankersley, *John B. Gordon: A Study in Gallantry* (Atlanta, 1955); William Y. Thompson, *Robert Toombs of Georgia;* Rudolph R. Von Abele, *Alexander H. Stephens, A Biography;* C. Vann Woodward, *Tom Watson: Agrarian Rebel* (New York, 1938); and Joseph H. Parks, *Joseph E. Brown of Georgia.*

Part Five: Chapters XVIII–XXII, 1890–1940

Two broad studies on southern history afford insight into economic conditions in Georgia: C. Vann Woodward, *Origins of the New South, 1877–1913;* George Brown Tindall, *The Emergence of the New South, 1913–1945* (Baton

Rouge, 1967). The best account of agricultural developments in the state is Willard Range, *A Century of Georgia Agriculture, 1850–1950*. For information on the development of textile mills see Clare de Graffenried, "The Georgia Cracker in the Cotton Mills," *Century* 19(1891):483–498; Herbert J. Lahne, *The Cotton Mill Worker* (New York, 1944); Harriet L. Herring, *Passing of the Mill Village* (Chapel Hill, 1949). Georgia's most successful business is described in E. J. Kahn, Jr., *The Big Drink: The Story of Coca-Cola* (New York, 1960). The effects of the New Deal on economic developments in Georgia are explored in Michael S. Holmes, *The New Deal in Georgia: An Administrative History* (Westport, Conn., 1975). Two sociological studies written by Arthur F. Raper contain much important material on the economic consequences of the New Deal: *Preface to Peasantry: A Tale of Two Black Belt Counties* (Chapel Hill, 1936) and *Tenants of the Almighty* (New York, 1943). For information on the New Deal community program see Paul K. Conkin, "It All Happened at Pine Mountain Valley," *Georgia Historical Quarterly* 48(1963):1–42. The development of organized labor prior to 1930 is examined by Mercer Griffin Evans, "The History of the Organized Labor Movement in Georgia" (Ph.D. dissertation, University of Chicago, 1929). Elizabeth Mack Lyon studied the influence of high-rise office buildings and hotels on Atlanta's economy: "Business Buildings in Atlanta: A Study in Urban Growth and Form" (Ph.D. dissertation, Emory University, 1971).

For an account of election practices in Georgia and the county-unit system see Lynwood M. Holland, *The Direct Primary in Georgia* (Urbana, Ill., 1949). Also helpful is James C. Bonner, "Legislative Apportionment and County Unit Voting in Georgia since 1877," *Georgia Historical Quarterly* 47 (1963):252–74.

Alex M. Arnett, *The Populist Movement in Georgia* (New York, 1922) provides a starting point for the study of Populism. The most important book on Georgia Populism is C. Vann Woodward, *Tom Watson: Agrarian Rebel*. Two articles offer a different interpretation of Watson's role as a Populist leader: Charles Crowe, "Tom Watson, Populists, and Blacks Reconsidered," *Journal of Negro History* 55(1970):99–116; Robert Saunders, "The Transformation of Tom Watson, 1894–1895," *Georgia Historical Quarterly* 54(1970):339–56. Among the other works that offer insight into Georgia Populism are James C. Bonner, "The Alliance Legislature in 1890," in James C. Bonner and Lucien E. Roberts, eds., *Studies in Georgia History and Government* (Athens, 1940); Lewis Nicholas Wynne, "The Alliance Legislature of 1890" (M.A. thesis, University of Georgia, 1970); Olin B. Adams, "The Negro and the Agrarian Movement in Georgia, 1874–1908" (Ph.D. dissertation, Florida State University, 1973).

There is one general survey of the Progressive Era for the state: Alton D. Jones, "Progressivism in Georgia, 1898–1918" (Ph.D. dissertation, Emory University, 1963). Some biographies are particularly helpful for this period: Dewey W. Grantham, *Hoke Smith and the Politics of the New South* (Baton Rouge, 1958); William M. Gabard, "Joseph Mackey Brown: A Study in Conservatism" (Ph.D. dissertation, Tulane University, 1963). Two studies have concentrated on Georgia cities: Thomas M. Deaton, "Atlanta During the Progressive Era" (Ph.D. dissertation, University of Georgia, 1969);

Richard Henry Lee German, "The Queen City of the Savannah: Augusta, Georgia During the Progressive Era, 1890–1917" (Ph.D. dissertation, University of Florida, 1971). A valuable study that examines the experiences of black Georgians during this time is John Avery Dittmer, *Black Georgia, 1900–1920* (Urbana, Ill., 1977).

A. Elizabeth Taylor has written a series of articles in the *Georgia Historical Quarterly* on the convict lease system and the woman suffrage movement: "The Origin and Development of the Convict Lease System in Georgia," 26 (1942):113–28; "The Abolition of the Convict Lease System in Georgia," 26 (1942):273–87; "The Origin of the Woman Suffrage Movement in Georgia," 27(1944):63–79; "The Revival and Development of the Woman Suffrage Movement in Georgia," 42(1958):339–54; "The Last Phase of the Woman Suffrage Movement in Georgia," 43(1959):11–28.

Historians have devoted little attention to political developments in Georgia during the 1920s, and consequently it is a rich field for future investigation. Fortunately, the 1930s has been the subject of a number of solid studies. A well-written book that captures the personality of Eugene Talmadge is William Anderson's *The Wild Man From Sugar Creek: The Political Career of Eugene Talmadge* (Baton Rouge, 1975). Important material on Talmadge is also contained in Sarah McCulloch Lemmon, "The Public Career of Eugene Talmadge, 1926–1936" (Ph.D. dissertation, University of North Carolina, 1952); William Anderson Sutton, Jr., "The Talmadge Campaigns: A Sociological Analysis of Political Power" (Ph.D. dissertation, University of North Carolina, 1952). For a sympathetic study written by a close personal friend of Talmadge see Allen L. Henson, *Red Galluses: A Story of Georgia Politics* (Boston, 1945). An able survey of political developments in the 1930s is presented in R. E. Fossett, "Impact of the New Deal on Georgia Politics, 1933–1941" (Ph.D. dissertation, University of Florida, 1969). The most thorough study of Governor Rivers's administration is Jane Walker Herndon, "Eurith Dickinson Rivers: A Political Biography" (Ph.D. dissertation, University of Georgia, 1974). A well-written account of the senatorial campaign of 1938 is presented by James C. Cobb, "Not Gone, But Forgotten: Eugene Talmadge and the 1938 Purge Campaign," *Georgia Historical Quarterly* 59 (1975) :197–209.

Clarence A. Bacote, "The Negro in Georgia Politics, 1880–1908" (Ph.D. dissertation, University of Chicago, 1955), provides an excellent starting point for learning about the experiences of black Georgians. An especially valuable work that contains an abundance of information on many aspects of Negro life is John M. Matthews, "Studies in Race Relations in Georgia, 1890–1930" (Ph.D. dissertation, Duke University, 1970). Several works offer insight into the enactment of Jim Crow laws: Horace C. Wingo, "Race Relations in Georgia, 1870–1908" (Ph.D. dissertation, University of Georgia, 1969); John H. Moore, "Jim Crow in Georgia," *South Atlantic Quarterly* 66(1967):554–65. The experiences of Andrew Sledd are analyzed in H. Y. Warnock, "Andrew Sledd, Southern Methodists, and the Negro: A Case History," *Journal of Southern History* 31(1965):251–71.

For accounts of black protests against Jim Crow laws and the disfranchisement amendments see: August Meier, "Boycotts of Segregated Street Cars, 1894–1906: A Research Note," *Phylon* 18(1957):296–97; Clarence A. Bacote,

"Negro Proscriptions, Protests and Proposed Solutions in Georgia, 1880–1908," *Journal of Southern History* 25(1959):471–98; Edgar A. Toppin, "Walter White and the Atlanta NAACP's Fight for Equal Schools, 1916–1917," *History of Education Quarterly* 7(1967):3–27; August Meier and Elliott Rudwick, "The Boycott Movement Against Jim Crow Streetcars in the South, 1900–1906," *Journal of American History* 55(1969):765–75.

Charles Crowe wrote two articles on the Atlanta race riot of 1906 in *Journal of Negro History*: "Racial Violence and Social Reform—Origins of the Atlanta Race Riot of 1906," 53(1968):234–56; "Racial Massacre in Atlanta, September 22, 1906," 54 (1969) :150–73.

The most valuable study of the economic condition of Negroes for this period is Edward A. Gaston, Jr., "A History of the Negro Wage Earner in Georgia, 1890–1940" (Ph.D. dissertation, Emory University, 1957). Michael S. Holmes has examined the economic impact of some New Deal agencies upon blacks: "Blue Eagle as Jim Crow Bird: The NRA and Georgia's Black Workers," *Journal of Negro History* 57(1972):276–83; "New Deal and Georgia's Black Youth," *Journal of Southern History* 38(1972):443–60. Important insight into economic competition between blacks and whites is contained in John M. Matthews, "The Georgia 'Race Strike' of 1909," *Journal of Southern History* 40(1974):613–30.

Anti-Catholicism is explored in Edward Cashin, "Thomas E. Watson and the Catholic Laymen's Association of Georgia" (Ph.D. dissertation, Fordham University, 1962). Leonard Dinnerstein, *The Leo Frank Case* (New York, 1968), provides a thorough study of that subject. The Ku Klux Klan is treated in Clement C. Mosely, "Invisible Empire: A History of the Ku Klux Klan in Twentieth Century Georgia, 1915–1965" (Ph.D. dissertation, University of Georgia, 1968). For an account of the Klan's operation at the local level see Roger Kent Hux, "The Ku Klux Klan in Macon, 1922–1925" (M.A. thesis, University of Georgia, 1972). The Klan's attempts to bar Catholics from teaching in Atlanta public schools is explored in Philip N. Racine, "The Ku Klux Klan, Anti-Catholicism, and Atlanta's Board of Education, 1916–1927," *Georgia Historical Quarterly* 57(1973):63–75. William F. Mugleston, "Fruitful and Disastrous Years: The Life of Julian Larose Harris" (Ph.D. dissertation, University of Georgia, 1972), tells the story of one of the Klan's strongest opponents. For an account of the Atlanta Black Shirts see John H. Moore, "Communists and Fascists in a Southern City: Atlanta, 1930," *South Atlantic Quarterly* 67(1968):437–54. Charles Henry Martin, *The Angelo Herndon Case and Southern Justice* (Baton Rouge, 1976), provides a sound study of that subject. Ann Wells Ellis, "The Commission on Interracial Cooperation, 1919–1944: Its Activities and Results" (Ph.D. dissertation, Georgia State University, 1975), presents a detailed account of an organization that worked to alleviate the harsher aspects of racism.

Although the best way to become familiar with Georgia writers is by reading their works, some secondary sources are helpful. Robert Bush, "Will N. Harben's Northern Georgia Fiction," *Mississippi Quarterly* 20 (1967) :103–17, presents an assessment of Harben's works. Corra Harris is the subject of a sound, critical biography: John E. Talmadge, *Corra Harris, Lady of Purpose* (Athens, 1968). A number of works proved helpful in understanding Erskine Caldwell: Robert Canwell, *The Humorous Side of Erskine Caldwell* (New

York, 1951); Robert Hazel, "Notes on Erskine Caldwell," in Louis D. Rubin and Robert D. Jacobs, eds., *Southern Renascence: The Literature of the Modern South* (Baltimore, 1953); Malcolm Cowley, "The Two Erskine Caldwells" *New Republic* 111(1944):599–600. Two articles deal with the writing of poetry: Katharine H. Strong, "The Poetry Society of Georgia," *Georgia Review* 8(1954):29–40; Monroe F. Swilley, "Ernest Hartsock and His Bozart Magazine," *Georgia Historical Quarterly* 53(1969):57–67. Griffith and Talmadge, *Georgia Journalism*, presents a survey on that subject. For an anthology containing some of the articles that appeared in the journal edited by Lillian Smith and Paula Snelling see Helen White and Redding S. Sugg, Jr., *From the Mountain* (Memphis, 1972).

Gladys Schultz, *Lady From Savannah: The Life of Juliette Low* (Philadelphia, 1958), tells the story of the founder of the Girl Scouts.

The starting point for information on educational developments is Orr, *A History of Education in Georgia*. Louis Harlan, *Separate and Unequal: Public School Campaigns and Racism in the Southern Seaboard States, 1901–1915* (Chapel Hill, 1958), contains a valuable chapter on Georgia. Philip Noel Racine, "Atlanta's Schools: A History of the Public School System, 1869–1955" (Ph.D. dissertation, Emory University, 1969), is a well-written account of educational developments in that city.

A number of studies proved helpful in tracing developments in higher education for whites: G. R. Mathis, "Walter B. Hill, Chancellor, The University of Georgia, 1899–1905" (Ph.D. dissertation, University of Georgia, 1967); Brooks, *The University of Georgia*; Thomas H. English, *Emory University, 1915–1965: A Semicentennial History* (Atlanta, 1966); M. L. Brittain, *The Story of Georgia Tech* (Chapel Hill, 1948). The best study to date of Martha Berry and her schools is Harnett T. Kane, *Miracle in the Mountains* (Garden City, N.Y., 1956).

For a survey of higher education for blacks see Range, *The Rise and Progress of Negro Colleges in Georgia*. Also helpful are Clarence A. Bacote, *The Story of Atlanta University* (Atlanta, 1969), and Florence M. Read, *The Story of Spelman College* (Atlanta, 1961).

A social history of Georgia for the late nineteenth and early twentieth centuries has not yet been written. An entertaining account of life in the north Georgia hills is contained in Floyd C. and Charles H. Watkins, *Yesterday in the Hills* (Chicago, 1963). An important county study is James C. Bonner, *Georgia's Last Frontier: The Development of Carroll County* (Athens, 1971). For the role of music in rural life see Karen L. Jackson, "The Royal Singing Convention, 1893–1931: Shape Note Singing Tradition in Irwin County, Georgia," *Georgia Historical Quarterly* 56(1972):495–509.

Part Six: Chapters XXIII–XXVI, 1940–1975

No adequate history of Georgia during the 1940 to 1970 period exists, though several helpful works have sought to evaluate the Georgia "scene" at various times during the postwar period. The best book dealing with the 1950s in Georgia is John C. Belcher and Imogene Dean, eds., *Georgia Today: Facts and Trends* (Athens, 1960), which contains a collection of fourteen generally well-conceived and in some cases outstanding essays evaluating trends and developments in the state. Also valuable on the early postwar years is John C. Meadows, *Modern Georgia* (rev. ed.; Athens, 1954). The best analysis of contemporary Georgia is the "Georgia" chapter in Neal R. Peirce, *The Deep South States of America: People, Politics, and Power in the Seven Deep South States* (New York, 1974). Peirce's emphasis on the role of Atlanta in shaping the course of recent Georgia history has influenced the four chapters of this section. Less successful but well worth cautious examination is William H. Schabacker, Russell S. Clark, and Homer C. Cooper, eds., *Focus on the Future of Georgia, 1970–1985* (Atlanta, 1970), an uneven collection of essays ranging from extremely provocative to terrible. A careful study of Georgia developments during the World War II years is a major void in the literature, although George B. Tindall, *The Emergence of the New South, 1913–1945* (Baton Rouge, 1967), includes an excellent summary of the southern region during this period. The best survey of the postwar South is Charles P. Roland, *The Improbable Era: The South Since World War II* (Lexington, Ky., 1975).

The massive economic and demographic changes that have swept over Georgia in recent decades have crucially affected all other aspects of the state's modern history. The best study of postwar economic developments is Charles F. Floyd, *The Georgia Regional Economies: The Challenge of Growth* (Athens, 1974). Other valuable studies of economic developments have emanated from the Industrial Development Branch of the Engineering Experiment Station at the Georgia Institute of Technology. Among the most helpful of these are Kenneth C. Wagner and M. Dale Henson, *Industrial Development in Georgia Since 1947: Progress, Problems and Goals* (1961) and Amy Collins, *Industrial Development in Georgia, 1958–1965* (1967), both published by the Engineering Experiment Station. The Georgia Department of Labor has also sponsored helpful works such as John L. Fulmer, *Georgia Employment Trends: 1947–1960, 1965, 1970* (Atlanta, 1961). Good studies of demographic change are John C. Belcher, *The Dynamics of Georgia's Population* (Athens, 1964), and John C. Belcher and Carolyn N. Allman, *The Non-White Population of Georgia* (Athens, 1967). Gretchen Maclachlan, *The Other Twenty Percent: A Statistical Analysis of Poverty in the South* (Atlanta, 1974), documents the persistence of poverty in Georgia and the region. James M. Fallows, *The Water Lords* (New York, 1971), is a powerful study of the impact of rapid urban and industrial growth on the environment in Savannah. Most of the statistics used in the four chapters of this section, however, came from the periodic reports of Bureau of Business and Economic Research, Graduate School of Business Administration, University of Georgia, *Georgia: Statistical Abstract* (Athens, 1951–1972), and U.S. Bureau of the Census, *U.S. Census of Population, Characteristics of the Population* (Washington, D.C., 1940–70).

The best study of race relations in Georgia during the recent period is Paul D. Bolster, "Civil Rights Movement in Twentieth Century Georgia" (Ph.D. dissertation, University of Georgia, 1972). Bolster writes from the perspective of black citizens seeking changes in racial patterns. A number of studies have focused on the pivotal role played by blacks in Atlanta, among the most valuable of which are Jack L. Walker, "Protest and Negotiations: A Study of Negro Political Leaders in a Southern City" (Ph.D. dissertation, State University of Iowa, 1963), and Jack L. Walker, *Sit-ins in Atlanta* (New

York, 1964). Probably the best of numerous biographies of Martin Luther King, Jr., is David L. Lewis, *King: A Critical Biography* (New York, 1970), although the six books penned by King himself between 1958 and 1968 are even more valuable. Benjamin Muse, *The American Negro Revolution: From Nonviolence to Black Power, 1963–1967* (Bloomington, Ind., 1968), is good on the national civil rights movement, and Numan V. Bartley, *The Rise of Massive Resistance: Race and Politics in the South during the 1950s* (Baton Rouge, 1969), is a discussion of conservative white defenders of the social status quo. Desegregation of the University of Georgia is insightfully reported in Calvin Trillin, *An Education in Georgia: The Integration of Charlayne Hunter and Hamilton Holmes* (New York, 1964). Clement C. Moseley, "Invisible Empire: A History of the Ku Klux Klan in Twentieth Century Georgia, 1915–1965" (Ph.D. dissertation, University of Georgia, 1968), is helpful, as is Dallas Lee, *The Cotton Patch Evidence* (New York, 1971), a study of Koinonia Farm. The busing controversy is treated in United States Commission on Civil Rights, *Your Child and Busing* (Washington, D.C., 1972), which was written by former Atlanta journalist Marvin Wall. The "Georgia" section in the state-by-state summary in *Southern School News*, the monthly publication of the Southern Education Reporting Service during the 1954–65 period, is the most reliable chronological summary of events affecting race relations. Also invaluable are the numerous publications of the Atlanta-based Southern Regional Council, including *New South* (1946–73), *South Today* (1969–74), *Southern Voices* (1974–76), and special reports on a variety of subjects relating to race relations. Gunnar Myrdal, *An American Dilemma: The Negro Problem and Modern Democracy* (2 vols.; New York, 1944), a monumental and enormously influential work, remains the best summary of race relations at the time of World War II.

The mandatory starting point for any examination of modern political developments in Georgia as elsewhere in the South is the classic study by V. O. Key, Jr., *Southern Politics in State and Nation* (New York, 1949), written with the assistance of Alexander Heard. The best studies of Georgia politics during the recent period are Joseph L. Bernd, *Grass Roots Politics in Georgia; The County Unit System and the Importance of the Individual Voting Community in Bifactional Elections, 1942–1954* (Atlanta, 1960); Bernd, "Georgia: Static and Dynamic," in William C. Havard, ed., *The Changing Politics of the South* (Baton Rouge, 1972); and Numan V. Bartley, *From Thurmond to Wallace: Political Tendencies in Georgia, 1948–1968* (Baltimore, 1970). The most recent comprehensive examination of Georgia and southern politics is Numan V. Bartley and Hugh D. Graham, *Southern Politics and the Second Reconstruction* (Baltimore, 1975). The best work dealing with a modern Georgia governor is Bruce Galphin, *The Riddle of Lester Maddox* (Atlanta, 1968). Also valuable are James F. Cook, Jr., "Politics and Education in the Talmadge Era: The Controversy over the University System of Georgia, 1941–1942" (Ph.D. dissertation, University of Georgia, 1972); Thomas E. Taylor, "A Political Biography of Ellis Arnall" (M.A. thesis, Emory University, 1959); and Val B. Mixon, "The Growth of the Legislative Powers of the Governor of Georgia: A Survey of the Legislative Program of Governor Herman Talmadge, 1949–1954" (M.A. thesis, Emory University, 1959). Among the rapidly growing literature on Jimmy Carter, the best book thus far published is Carter's memoirs: *Why Not the Best?* (New York, 1975). Hugh M. Thomason, "The Legislative Process in Georgia" (Ph.D. dissertation, Emory University, 1961), and Jane W. Gurganus, "A Study of the Composition of the General Assembly of Georgia, 1959–1966" (M.A. thesis, Emory University, 1966), are good on the General Assembly. Albert B. Saye, *A Constitutional History of Georgia*, the standard source for constitutional developments, devotes adequate attention to the recent period, as does Ida M. Chiaraviglio, "The Supreme Court, the National Government, and States Rights: An Analysis of Georgia Cases" (Ph.D. dissertation, Emory University, 1962). Louis T. Rigdon, *Georgia's County Unit System* (Decatur, Ga., 1961), is a good analysis of that subject, and Matt W. Williamson, "Contemporary Tendencies toward a Two-Party System in Georgia" (Ph.D. dissertation, University of Virginia, 1969), details the emergence of a contemporary Republican party in Georgia. The standard source for voter registration statistics and black political participation in Georgia as elsewhere in the South is the monthly publication of the Voter Education project, *V.E.P. News* (1967–): Portions of the chapter on politics during the recent period appeared previously in Numan V. Bartley, "Moderation in Maddox Country?" *Georgia Historical Quarterly* 58 (1974):340–48.

Excellent studies of taxation policies in Georgia are Robert P. Brooks, *Georgia in 1950: A Survey of Financial and Economic Conditions* (Athens, 1950), and Eva Galambos, *State and Local Taxes in the South, 1973* (Atlanta, 1973). Statistics on governmental expenditures used in the preceding four chapters came primarily from *Georgia Statistical Abstracts* (cited previously); Georgia Department of Public Welfare, *Official Report for the Fiscal Year* (1940–70), and Georgia Department of Public Health, *Annual Statistical Report* (1955–70).

Other sources that proved helpful include Carlyn Fisher, *The Arts in Georgia: A Report to the Georgia Art Commission* (Atlanta, 1967), Edward D. Mobley, "An Inventory of Cultural Activities in Selected Georgia Cities" (Ph.D. dissertation, Florida State University, 1967); *Report of the Governor's Commission on Criminal Justice Standards and Goals* (Atlanta, 1974); and the special March 1972 edition of *Atlanta Magazine*, published by the city Chamber of Commerce, that marked Atlanta's 125th anniversary.

INDEX

Index